HARVARD THEOLOGICAL STUDIES
X

RUSSIAN DISSENTERS

BY

FREDERICK C. CONYBEARE

HONORARY FELLOW
UNIVERSITY COLLEGE, OXFORD

NEW YORK
RUSSELL & RUSSELL · INC
1962

PREFACE

THIS work was begun in 1914 and completed nearly as it stands early in 1917, about the time when the Russian Revolution began. It is too early yet to trace the fortunes of the Russian sects during this latest period, for the contradictory news of the struggle is not to be trusted; and few, if any, know what is really happening or has happened in unhappy Russia. Since, however, the future is largely moulded by the past, I trust that my work may be of some use to those who sincerely desire to understand and trace out the springs of the Revolution.

It is not a work of original research. I have only read a number of Russian authorities and freely exploited them. I have especially used the History of the Russian Raskol by Ivanovski (two volumes, Kazan, 1895 and 1897). He was professor of the subject in the Kazan Seminary between 1880 and 1895. He tries to be fair, and in the main succeeds in being so. Subbotin, indeed, in a letter to Pobedonostzev, Procurator of the Holy Synod, who had consulted him about the best manuals on the subject, wrote slightingly of the work; but I think unfairly, for the only concrete faults he finds with it are, first, that the author allowed himself to use the phrase; 'the historical Christ,' which had to his ears a rationalist ring; and secondly, that he devoted too little space to the Moscow Synods of 1654 to 1667.

Another Russian work I have transferred almost bodily to my pages. This is the extremely rare brochure of I. Uzov or Yusov, *Russkie Dissidenty*, St. Petersburg, 1881. This is a work of impartial and independent criticism, and valuable for its numerous and well chosen citations from earlier works on the subject. In many cases where I have identified these citations I have found them accurate.

After these two authors, I am most indebted to the works of J. V. Liprandi, of H. I. Kostomarov, of Meliukov, of Macarius, archbishop of Moscow, author of a History of the Raskol, published in 1889, of Kelsiev, of whose *collectanea* about the sects several volumes were printed in London between 1860 and 1870, of Th. Livanov, of our own William Palmer, the Historian of the Patriarch Nikon, of Paul Miliukov, of Father Palmieri, author of an Italian History of the Russian Church, of O. Novitski, and of a few other authors whose names I have given in my pages.

It remains for me to express my gratitude to those who have helped me in my work; first and foremost to the Harvard Faculty of Divinity for their adoption of it; to the Librarian of the Widener Library for the generous way he granted me every facility for study; to Dr. R. P. Blake for reading the final proof-sheets, and giving my readers the benefit of his great knowledge of the Russian language; and to Professors George Foot Moore and Kirsopp Lake for reading my work in advance. If there is any good order in my presentation of the subject, it is chiefly due to the latter of my two friends.

F. C. CONYBEARE.

OXFORD, 1921.

LIST OF RUSSIAN PERIODICALS CITED

Библіотека для Чтенія; С. Петербургъ.	Library for reading; St. Petersburg.
Братское Слово	The Brotherly Word.
Время	Time.
Вѣстникъ Европы; С. Петербургъ	Messenger of Europe; St. Petersburg.
Вѣстникъ Московской Эпархіи	Messenger of the See of Moscow.
Голосъ Старообрядца	The Voice of the Old believer.
Другъ Истины	The Friend of Truth.
Душеполезное Чтеніе	Edifying Reading.
Дѣло	The Affair.
Журналъ Кавказской Эпархіи	Journal of the Caucasian See.
Знаніе	Knowledge.
Извѣстія Императорскаго Общества Исторіи и Древностей при Московскомъ Университетѣ	The Proceedings of the Imperial Society of History and Antiquities at the University of Moscow.
Исборникъ	The Elect One.
Истина	Truth.
Миссіонерское Обозрѣніе	Missionary Review.
Невскій Сборникъ	Neva Collection.
Обзоръ	Review.
Пермская Эпархіальная Газета	Gazette of the Perus See.
Православныя Бесѣды	Orthodox Conversations.
Православное Обозрѣніе	Orthodox Review.
Православный Собесѣдникъ	Orthodox Conversationalist.
Православный { Путеводитель Спутникъ	Orthodox Traveller.
Приложеніе къ Журналу Калужской Эпархіи	Supplement to the Journal of the See of Kaluga.
Русскій Архивъ	Russian Archive.
Русскія Вѣсти	Russian News.
Русскій Міръ	Russian World.
Русская Старина	Russian Antiquity.
Слово	The Word.
Слово Правды	The Word of Truth.
Современныя Лѣтописи	Contemporary Chronicles.
Старообрядецъ	The Old-believer.
Старообрядческій Вѣстникъ	The Old-believer Messenger.
Страна	The Country.
Странникъ	The Wanderer.
Труды Кіевской Духовной Академіи	Works of the Kiev Ecclesiastical Academy.
Христіанскія Чтенія	Christian Readings.

CONTENTS

PART I

THE OLD BELIEVERS OF GREAT RUSSIA

Introduction. The Struggle against Centralization. Russia and
Tartar Influence. Russian Ritualism and Liturgical Controversy.
Nikon. Nikon's Reforms. The Council of Stoglav. The position
of affairs in 1655. The Fall of Nikon. From the Fall of Nikon to
1666. The Council of 1666.

P. Aurelio Palmieri's Account of the Russian Clergy.

The Rebellion at the Solovetski Monastery. The Revolt of 1682.
The Ukaze of 1685 and its Results. Tsardom and Antichrist.

The Settlements of the Popovtsy. The Search for Priests. Epiphanius, the First Raskol Bishop. The Uniat Movement. The Concessions of Paul I. The Persecution of the Raskol by Nicholas I. The
Austrian Hierarchy. The General Character of the Popovtsy.

The Various Settlements of the Bezpopovtsy. The Stranniki. The
Netovtsi and the Self-Baptizers. The Prayerless and the Sighers.
The Intellectual Development of the Bezpopovtsy. Opinion on
Priesthood and Sacraments.

Marriage among the Stranniki. Varieties of Opinion among the
Bezpoptovtsy. Theodosius Vasilev. Ivan Alexiev. I. A. Kovylin.
The Present Situation.

PART II

THE RATIONALIST SECTS OF SOUTH RUSSIA

PART III

THE MYSTIC SECTS

RUSSIAN DISSENTERS

INTRODUCTION

ONE cannot better approach the study of the Russian
Dissenters or *Raskol* (i. e. division, schism) than by repeating
the words with which I. Uzov begins his work upon them.
They are these: "Haxthausen need not have warned Russia
how serious a peril to her security her dissenters formed,
nor have warned her to have regard thereto;[1] as if in order to
compass their destruction she had not all along resorted to
the auto-da-fé, the knout, gallows and every sort of slow and
painful death. Mindful of the proverb: 'Beat a man not
with a stick, but with roubles,' the Government has imposed
on them double taxes and curtailed their civil rights. Every
petty official has been at liberty to help himself out of their
pockets, and yet dissent has not weakened or diminished;
on the contrary it has struck roots ever deeper and stronger
into the life of the people." When at last the Government
realized that the old system of frank and fearless extermina-
tion could not stand criticism, it was pretended that the best
way of getting rid of them was to encourage among them
reading and writing and general enlightenment. It may be
that if the Tsar's Government had given all its citizens at the
least a middle class education, Dissent in the form in which
it now exists might be weakened. But this was never done.
Such instruction as was usually reckoned to be good enough
for peasants was not of a kind to induce them to give up
dissent, as is shewn by the fact that most dissenters had already received it. We have the testimony of an official,
Liprandi, commissioned by the Government of Nicholas I
to hold an inquisition into them, that "the range of their

[1] Aug. Haxthausen. *Researches into Inner Life of the People of Russia.* Han-
nover, 1847, i, 415. A. H. aims his remark at the Dukhobortsy only.

1

activity is not lessened but extended by education." [1]   Count
Stenbok, another official set to study them by the Government, affirms that "Dissent perpetually spreads and becomes
stronger," that, "notwithstanding a weakening of religious
interest, their adherents are no weaker as a body," and that
"all measures taken against them, by the government are up to
the present unavailing." [2]   An anonymous authority, S. M. V.,
states as a fact fully known, that "as of old dissent flourished
upon persecution in secret, so now with freedom (?) it flourishes
in the open." [3]   We could produce many more attestations
of the kind, but rest content with the above in order to avoid
reiteration.

Uzov infers that Dissent flourished just the same, no matter
whether the Government was strict or lenient; and that it did
so proved that it is not engendered by temporary or transient
causes, but is founded on deep cravings and satisfies daily
spiritual needs of individuals.

Yet "neither Russian administration, nor Russian polite
society understands thoroughly what sort of thing Dissent
is";[4] and this not from want of facts accumulated by students,
but from their onesidedness. By preference they have directed their attention to the ceremonial peculiarities which
distinguish dissent from orthodoxy, without remarking, nay
rather, without wishing to remark, that the dissenters' outlook is framed on quite other principles than those which
underlie our present social structure.

"We believe," says Uzov, "that the period of social experi-
ments made on the inarticulate masses is drawing to a close,
and that we are being driven to the conclusion that ameliora-
tions of a community must be based on a profound study of
the nature of the individuals who compose it, because in no
other case can reforms reap any success.

"The intellectual and moral characteristics of our people
are peculiarly prominent in the Raskol; and that is why a

---

[1] Lectures at Imperial Historical Society in Moscow University for 1870, Bk.
2, by Liprandi, p. 83.

[2] Kelsiev, IV. 325.   Stenbok had in view in particular the Stranniki.

[3] Strannik, 1871, 2nd Art. S. M. V. p. 93.

[4] P. Melnikov, *Treatise (Pismo) on the Raskol*.

study of it is indispensable for any statesman who desires to pursue with even tenour and without groping or guesswork, the pathways of his activities and enterprises."

I have begun my study of Russian dissent with the above words of Uzov, because they rightly insist on the importance of understanding the social, moral and religious characteristics of a great people in order to obtain a general comprehension of its origin and character.

Dissent, by which I render the word *Raskol*, implies, like our own word 'nonconformist,' the existence of a dominant and established Church against whose doctrines, rites, and oppressive tendencies (inherent in every such Church) the dissenters are permanently in revolt. In Russia this Church knows itself under the title of Orthodox, and has been from its earliest age, when the first metropolitan, Leontius was dispatched from Byzantium with a cortège of Greek bishops by the patriarch Nicholas Chrysoverghes (983–996), a purely exotic, imported and foreign product in all that regards beliefs, discipline and ceremonies.

In this respect it is in strong contrast with the old Armenian Church, in which, in spite of the fact that its doctrine and rites were of Greek or Syriac origin, there nevertheless remained much that was racy of the soil, in particular the institution of animal sacrifice for the sins of the living, for the repose of the souls of the dead, and for the support (by the assignment to them of the Levitical portions of the victims) of the priesthood. The Christian priest of Armenia was the direct heir of the pagan priest who preceded him; the Armenian patriarch was for long generations a scion of the Arsacid house which occupied the throne, and when that throne finally disappeared in the fifth century the Patriarch, or Catholicos, as he was styled, retained a large portion of the loyalty which had upheld it against the combined assaults of Roman Emperor and Sassanid oppressor. Even as late as the crusading epoch the patriarchs of the Armenian Kingdom of Cilicia boasted themselves to be of the old Arsacid lineage. Ecclesiastical office in Armenia was based on heredity rather than on charismatic gifts, and none that did not belong to the old priestly families could be ordained.

In Russia, on the other hand, though the old pagan superstitions long survived, and survive to-day in popular magic and song, the orthodox Church never possessed such an odour of pagan antiquity as the Armenian. It was in no sense a native product; and if the priesthood has tended to become hereditary, this is because the village popes began to own their manses, and the difficulty of providing an incoming parish priest with a residence was most easily met by choosing his son to succeed him. It was not because sacerdotal gifts ran in the blood of certain old families. Of the twenty-four successors of Leontius, the first Russian metropolitan (who died in 1004 or 1008), there are barely two or three during the two hundred and thirty years that preceded the Mongol conquest of Russia that do not bear Greek names, and they were all nominees of a patriarch of Byzantium who regarded Kiev and Moscow as mere provinces of his own church, or of a Greek emperor who regarded the rulers of Moscow as his vassals.

In one respect, however, the Russian Church resembled the Armenian, as it did other early Christian Churches, namely in the predominance of the monasteries. Greek asceticism took firm root among the Slavs. The convent, richly endowed with fields, villages and serfs, was the teaching church; and until Peter the Great forbade its inmates the use of pens and ink, it was the home of all the intellectual work, and of all the writers of the land. The parish priests, who must be married men, have never counted. They are an inferior order of beings, in spite of their white habiliments. The higher clergy and episcopate have been recruited among the cowled and black-coated monks. Peter the Great made a fierce attack on the monasteries, raised the age of the noviciate to thirty, reduced the number of monks by half, made most of them work with their hands, denied them paper and ink in order to prevent them from describing him as Antichrist, filled their houses with his discharged soldiers, subjected them to a thousand indignities; but even he did not venture to break with the rule that every bishop must be a monk. This exclusion of the "white" clergy from all positions of emolument and authority has created for centuries a chasm in the ranks of the clergy; and under the rule of the Tsars the Russian bishop was a mere courtier and functionary of the state; he stood for absolutism, for oppression in every form and of every grade of society; he was a spaniel fawning on the Government which distributed the sweets of office. He detested above all things light, liberty, free growth and living development of institutions; he was a parasite, but, alas, he was the Russian Church, an incarnation of Byzantinism. It is important to grasp this distinction between the parish clergy and the monks. Possibly under the Mongol régime in Russia which began in 1237 the monasteries were hearths of Slav patriotism, but even in 1294 under the patriarch John XII the secular clergy were already loud in their complaints of the exactions of the bishops. Certain it is that the great schism of which the Raskol is the permanent fruit was largely due to friction between the parish clergy and the monkish agents of the absolutist and centralising government of Moscow.

Historians of Russian dissent, no matter to what school they belong, whether, like Uzov, sympathetic, or, like Prof. N. Ivanovski,[1] partisans of the Holy Synod, agree in dividing it into three classes, or categories, of Old ritualists or Old believers, Rationalists and Mystics.

Ivanovski seeks to load upon the dissenters and lift off the Church, of which he is a modern spokesman, the onus of blame for the great Russian schism of two hundred and fifty years ago. He sets undue store by the old appellation of the Raskol of *Staroobryadets*, "Old ritualist." He would have us believe that the schism was created by ignorant people who could not distinguish between what was "of faith," and what was unessential, such as matters of discipline and posture and vestment.

The Old ritualists took their rise in the XVIIth Century by way of protest against the correction of church books and

---

[1] History of the Raskol, 1897, Introduction, pp. 3 ff.

rites under the patriarch Nikon. Their essential characteristic lay in their confusion of rite or ceremony with dogma, and in the attribution to ritual and to the letter of the prayer books of the Russian Church of a fixt invariability. Old ritualism therefore consists in the upholding of the rites in vogue before the time of Nikon, and rests on the false assumption that no other rites but these went back to the age of Prince Vladimir under whom Christianity was adopted as the national religion. In fact, argued the dissenters, the rites introduced by Nikon were *new* rites. They acted in separating themselves from the Church as if orthodoxy was bound up with the preservation of certain rites, and precluded all change in matters unessential. For example, worshippers are to prostrate themselves exactly as of old, to keep exactly the same fasts and in the same way; even old customs in daily life are to be maintained as if a religious interest was subserved in doing so. In church, for example, the same garb is to be worn as was anciently in vogue. In all such ways, Ivanovski concludes, these sectaries cling to life as it was in the XVIIth Century.

It is probably true that the Raskol regarded such unessentials with what to-day would be considered superstitious veneration. But did the Patriarch Nikon and the innovating section of the Russian Church, which, having the Tsar and his army on their side, were able to enforce their will upon the conservatives, attach less weight to them? If the Raskol confused mere rites with dogma, did their antagonists not do the same? If the points at issue were so insignificant, why could not the party of Nikon allow these simple folk to keep the religious customs and forms of words which from time immemorial had been in vogue, and be content themselves in their own superior enlightenment to adopt the new and, as they — in most cases falsely — imagined, correcter ones in their own churches? Instead of saving the position by a little well-timed tolerance, the Patriarch Nikon resorted to the knout, the sword, the stake; and getting together a council of his partisans, excommunicated and anathematized his opponents as heretics *en masse*. Now it is, as Ivanovski admits, quite uncanonical for orthodox churchmen to have recourse to these extreme methods of argument, unless the unchangeable dogmas of the Christian religion be at stake and directly impugned. It is evident then that the Russian Authorities made the changes as much a matter of faith as did the Raskol, who at least had on their side that prescription of antiquity to which Christian Fathers like Tertullian and Augustine regularly appealed as decisive against innovators and heretics. The Fathers of Nicea in 325 professed to base their decision on the rule: "Let what is ancient prevail." The Raskol have never appealed to any other canon. They are accused of 'blind adherence to antique details.' Was the adherence of Nikon to modern details any less blind?

Quite other is the basis of the antagonism to the Church of what Ivanovski labels the Rationalist sects, viz. the Dukhobortsy—whose name is a translation of the Greek πνευματομάχοι or battlers with the Spirit, but which is usually rendered in English Spirit-wrestlers, in the sense of men in whom the Holy Spirit wrestles for utterance; the Molokanye or milk-drinking sect; the recent sect of Stundists and some others. These sects, in his opinion,— an opinion which, as we shall see later on, is erroneous — reflect an intrusion about the year 1700 of the ideas of Western Europe. He terms them rationalist because they reject the authority of the Church and claim a liberty to interpret Scripture as they like. The Old ritualists attach importance to ceremonies; the 'Rationalists' repudiate them and reject all the externals of worship, sacraments, ikons or holy pictures and relics. None of these aids to devotion appeal to them. Of fasting in the sense of a rejection of this or that diet they will not hear; and their worship consists wholly of prayer and singing of hymns. They call themselves 'Spiritual Christians' in token that they set no value on the outer husks of worship, but only on the kernel of religious faith.

The third group is the Khlysty or flagellants, of which the Skoptsy or self-emasculators are an offshoot, dated by Ivanovski at the middle of the XVIIth Century, though he admits their origin to be obscure and that some features of their teaching go back to remote antiquity, to paganism and old Christian heresies. They were never, like the Old ritualists, champions of externals, of the letter, nor like the Molokanye, of the human reason; but are mystics, that is creatures of irresponsible feeling, believing in the immediate relationship of man to God to the extent of accounting themselves Gods, Christs, Prophets, divinely born, soothsayers. These sects enshroud themselves in almost impenetrable secrecy, but in presence of strangers call themselves orthodox Christians.

Uzov's own preliminary account of the first two divisions is as follows, and he claims to adopt the terminology of the sectaries themselves: "The first division comprises the Old believers; the second the Spiritual Christians. The Old believers have split up into two chief groups, the Popovtsy, or priest-sect, and the priestless, or Bezpopovtsy (*Pope* in Russian = priest). The latter are divided into minor sects, the Pomorskiye, Spasovo, Thedosyevo, Philippovo or Lipovany, Wanderers (Stranniki or Beguny), and finally the Prayerless Ones. And in this list we only enumerate the stronger and typical sects omitting the minor ones. The most extreme and typical of these is that of the Wanderers (*Stranniki*) and particularly the Prayerless, who closely resemble the Spiritual Christians and even so call themselves. Many writers, indeed, who are ill acquainted with the Prayerless doctrine refer them to that group; nevertheless their derivation from the Old believers is so indelibly stamped upon them, that those familiar with their teaching have no difficulty in recognizing in them all the characteristic marks of the 'Old belief.'"

"The 'Spiritual Christians' are divided into Dukhobortsy, Molokanye, Communists, and Evangelicals or Stundists.

"Over and above these main groups there remains," says Uzov, "a diminutive residuum, the Khlysty and Skoptsy." This group is very small and looked askance at by the common people who have given it the appellation of the 'dark' sect (cf. Liprandi, p. 104),— a sect which we may better define as being of a mystico-religious character. The sects forming this group have no future; their propaganda amounts to nothing, notwithstanding their age (for they were derived from Byzantium along with Orthodoxy), and notwithstanding that they are the only group of Raskol which can be called universal.

In it courtiers are found side by side with peasants, Finns with
Great and Little Russians. The common people have various names for them according to the places where they are
found, for example, Liads, Vertuns, Medoviks, Khanzhas,
Kladentsy, Kupidons, Shaloputs, etc. The chief danger of
this group, according to Ministers of the Interior, is that it
venerates "some of the Emperors, that have already passed
away into another life, as being still alive"; in other words
"assumes the existence of a second lawful ruler." This ruler
was Peter III (Liprandi pp. 93 and 95). The only intelligible
basis of such a belief is to be found in an *express* ukase of Peter
III of Jan. 20, 1762, to the effect that the Raskolniks (dissenters) are not to be persecuted, because there "exist in the
Empire not only men of other faiths, such as Mahomedans and
idolaters, but also dissenting Christians whose superstition and
obstinacy are such, that it is hopeless to convert them by
duress and ill-treatment, from which they would only flee
across the frontiers." [1]

It is moreover clear that the Old believers of both groups
belong to Great Russia, and that Moscow is their centre of
origin, while the Spiritual Christians belong to the South, to
Little Russia — the Ukraine,— and to Kiev rather than
Moscow. It has therefore seemed best to divide the discussion into three parts, dealing with (1) the Old believers of
Great Russia, (2) the Spiritual Christians of South Russia,
(3) the Mystics.

[1] Cf. *Collection of Statutes regarding the Raskol*, Bk. 1, p. 586."

PART I

THE OLD BELIEVERS

OF GREAT RUSSIA

CHAPTER I

THE CONDITIONS LEADING TO THE SCHISM

No Church historian believes that great schisms are wholly due to the insignificant and unmeaning dogmatic problems and differences to which ecclesiastical writers attribute them. Who, for example, will believe that it was the question whether the Spirit proceeded from both Father and Son or from Father alone which caused the great schism of East and West? It is obvious to a student of Mommsen or Gibbon that the real cause was a difference of national temperament which divided the Roman Empire into two halves, Greek and Latin. Long before the advent of the new religion, there had arisen a fundamental antagonism between the Greek and Romans in matters political, moral, and intellectual. Similarly the schism between Byzantium and the Armenians was the expression of a desire for independence, an instinct of home-rule on the part of the latter. They wanted an excuse for quarreling with the Greeks and found it in religion, and in the Armenian Fathers it is not uncommon to find the boast that they adopted such and such a fashion in religion in order to "raise a hedge" between themselves and the Greeks. The German and Anglican reformations, so-called, were not motived by dogmatic, nor even by ritual quarrels. Both nations wanted to eliminate Italian clergy and to say their prayers in the vernacular, above all to keep their spare cash at home instead of sending it abroad as Peter's pence.

Such considerations suggest that in the genesis of the Old believers, social and political causes must have co-operated with those on which Russian churchmen insist, and several Russian historians have given due weight to these. Kostomarov [1] for example wrote as follows:

"As we survey the history, phenomena and structure of the religious life of the Russian people in the past, and try to seize its characteristics, enduring even up to our own age, we are

[1] *Messenger of Europe*, 1871. No. 4, April, p. 471 and p. 480.

13

struck by the fact that there hardly ever was, in all Christendom, a land less inclined to religious movements, less prepared for them than Russia, especially Great Russia. That such movements were not in keeping with the coldness of their temper in such matters, is often revealed in our history. We hear nothing but complaints of the alienation of the people from the Church, of its indifference thereto, of its failure to live a Christian life. . . .

"It is the last thing one would have expected, that, among people whose leading trait had for so long been religious indifference, heresy and raskol (dissent) should manifest itself, much more that it should spread among the masses."

And Shchapov says:

"Popular indifference in respect of religious ceremonial was so strong in the age which witnessed the emergence and spread of the Raskol, that not only in the XVIIth Century the Tsars Michael Theodorovich and Alexis Michaelovich, but also at the beginning of the XVIIIth Peter the Great, had to drive the people by means of ukases to go to church, to confess and communicate."[1]

"The Russian people," says Palmieri, p. 402 (following Golubinski, ii, 871) "had a singular understanding of what constitutes piety. Many took no pains to observe the essential rules of Christian life, only attended Church two or three times a year, very seldom went to confession or communion, and waited for the deathbed before they could be induced to receive the Sacraments." Golubinski also dwells on the coldness of religious sentiment and supine ignorance of the lower classes in Nikon's age, and in the century which preceded. Further back in the age anterior to Maximus the Greek we have no data on which to base a judgment.

Nevertheless, writes Uzov, we are suddenly confronted in Nikon's age with a vigorous propaganda and an obstinate struggle. How shall we explain it? He believes the true explanation to be that in the Raskol the true driving force was not religion, but other factors, which may be summarised as the struggle against centralisation and the growth of Tartar

---

[1] A. Shchapov, *Russian Raskol*, p. 163.

influence. The reforming zeal of Nikon, the liturgical controversy of the sixteenth and seventeenth centuries, and the
councils of 1551 and 1667 were only the more spectacular
symptoms of these deeper causes.

The Struggle against Centralisation

"In the XVIIth Century, before the time of the Raskol, it
often happened that the inferior clergy in an entire province
or in special districts refused to obey the orders of its archpriest and endeavoured to free itself not only from the payment
of legal dues, but from the jurisdiction of the Metropolitan.
Already prior to the Raskol, priests were occasionally found
imbued with a manifestly Raskol-like temper of insubordination despising the hierarchical piety." More than once the
clergy had aspired to independence of the spiritual authority,
and laymen presumed to follow their example.

"Indifference towards the Church naturally led on to dis-
obedience, opposition to Church authorities and in general to
suspicion of and want of respect for the clergy. Attempts
were already visible to achieve complete freedom from their
jurisdiction or at least to get control thereof."[1] "In some
places and especially in Pskov and Novgorod there had occurred open revolts against Church jurisdiction and administration. In Novgorod the movement in favour of independence
from Moscow was so strong that on one occasion they sent to
the Patriarch of Constantinople to urge their case: ' We do not
want to be judged by the Metropolitan,' they said, 'but we ask
for your blessing; and if you will not give it, then we will take
sides with the Latins.'"[2] "The ills of the Russian Clergy,"
writes Palmieri (p. 253), reproducing the words of Golubinski's
History, "were due to the infiltration into Russia of Byzantine
ideals. The priesthood lacked from the beginning the characteristics of an apostolic ministry. The priests were looked
upon as artisans for whom it was enough to be able to read and
celebrate the rites. Their spiritual labours were miserably

[1] Shchapov, op. cit., pp. 77, pp. 168, 169.
[2] D. D. Sontsov, *Hist. of Russ. People up to XVIIth Century*, p. 60.

recompensed, and as a class they made no pretence of educating and guiding the people. The difference of moral conditions dug an abyss between the episcopate and the lower clergy. The bishops needed vast sums to keep up their retinues which often numbered a hundred persons. In their palaces, courtiers, stewards, major-domos, chamberlains, exactors of dues, secretaries, sacristans, hieromonachi (i. e. monks ordained as priests) and so forth elbowed one another. Episcopal revenues were beyond doubt large; thus early in the XVIth Century the Metropolitan of Moscow possessed 100,000 desiatines (1 des. = 2.70 acres), and he of Novgorod had still ampler estates. Nevertheless such resources did not suffice them, and they took to robbing in order to satiate the voracity of their satellites. Priests had to toil like slaves in order that their bishops might live like princes. Nobles, pages and dignitaries had no scruples in the petty episcopal courts against plundering the country clergy who flocked in vain to the Tsar, the patriarch, and the bishops, to protest against the injuries inflicted on them. Their protests fell on deaf ears, and to losses were added jeers and insults. It is no wonder if now and then the unhappy popes, reduced to desperation, refused to pay the episcopal dues and resisted violence with violence. The populace flew to help them, and hunted away or roughly handled the episcopal tax gatherers, as happened at Pskov in 1435 and later at Vyshgorod, whose inhabitants after duly cudgelling the agents of the Metropolitan Iona, expelled them from the vicinity."

"There is no age," he writes again (p. 256), "in which we do not feel the deepest pity for the much ridiculed popes. It is on them that the fatal consequences of the Byzantine system of the Russian Church fell, and episcopate and State vied with each other to sink them to the level of brutes and turn them into civil and ecclesiastical pariahs. Thus the latent schism of that Church to-day has historical roots. The *presbyterian* movement of the present time, to use the expression of certain Russian bishops, is the fruit of a policy of oppression which has rendered the hierarchy hateful to the lower clergy, which has drawn the latter closer to the people who share their misery with them, and actually drives many of the rural popes into the ranks of socialism and of those who are in revolt against Church and State." . . . .

"Over against the bishops we behold the insurrection of a down-trodden clergy, upheld in their demands by an oppressed people. The popes cannot see why the highest posts of the hierarchy should be kept for monkery alone. No canon of councils, ecumenical or particular, sanctions such a custom." (p. 689).

The truth is, writes Uzov, that in the times prior to the Raskol the relations of the clergy to the people were utterly different from what they are now. The clergy were "the toy outright, the servant of what was then the all-powerful factor in Great Russia, the *mir* or village commune, whose members selected them and exacted of them a written pledge to obey the *mir*, which formed the parish, in all sorts of ways. Without permission of the *mir* they could not quit the parish nor meddle with the economy of the church, still less of the *mir*; the priest even had in celebrating the rites to consult the likes and dislikes of his parishioners. In their court the members of the *mir* tried priest and layman alike for violations even of church regulations. The priest was like any other official chosen by the community."[1]

Such was the status of the clergy when a man of severe and despotic temper, Nikon Mordvinov[2] was made patriarch; and he lost no time in rousing against himself all the inferior clergy, towards whom he conducted himself with such excess of strictness and oppression that he was dubbed a second Pope.[3] For Nikon a priest was a mere nobody. "For any negligence in the discharge of his duties Nikon put him in irons, tortured him in prison and dispatched him whither he chose to beg his bread." [4]

I. Ya. Goremykin in his *Sketches of Peasant History in Poland*, p. 13, has a passage which goes some way to explain the antipathy of Russian peasants towards the Latin Pope that is

---

[1] Quoted by Uzov from *Nevskii Sbornik* 1867, art. by Vishnyakov, p. 80.
[2] See further, pp. 41 ff.
[3] i. e. of Rome. A. Shchapov, *Russian Raskol*, p. 78.
[4] N. Kostomarov, *Russian History in Biographies*, Ed. iv. pp. 178–9.

implied in the above comparison with him of Nikon. "The preaching," he says, "of the Byzantine missionaries of the IXth Century met with success and encountered no opposition on the part of the tribes, among whom it spread; the preachers from the west did not achieve the same success. The reason was that the former chose as a means for their propaganda the diffusion of Slav writing, and taking their stand on a popular platform introduced together with the light of Christianity the light of a native learning that could be understood. It would not appear either, that they meddled with the Government, or tried in their own interests to influence the social order of the countries they were missionizing. For this reason people listened to them without misgivings and accepted their teaching of their own free will and readily. The Apostles of the Roman Church on the other hand were for the most part Germans, and, besides conducting their preachings in a tongue the Slavs did not understand, they brought with them principles of overlordship in society that were German and to Slavdom repugnant. The Slavs resisted and defended their popular rights with all their might."

The above extracts help to explain the popular fury which Nikon's so-called reforms aroused. He imported State despotism; introduced or rather enforced the German principles of overlordship in every village; anticipated that harsh and brutal officialdom, that despotism of bureaucrats and multiplied ministries which we to-day associate with Prussia, but which was really more rampant, and infinitely less plastic and intelligent in Czarist Russia. One cannot but be reminded of the words of the strange thinker Nietzsche, — so often invoked, so seldom read and so little understood — which better than all else explain the genesis of the Raskol:—

"Somewhere there are still people and herds, but not with us, my brethren: with us there are States.

"The State? What is that? Well, now open your ears, for now I deliver my sentence on the death of peoples.

"The State is the coldest of all cold monsters. And coldly it lieth; and this lie creepeth out of its mouth: 'I, the State, am the people.'

"It is a lie. Creators they were who created the peoples and hung one belief and one love over them; thus they served life.

"Destroyers they are who lay traps for many, calling them the State: they hung a sword and a hundred desires over them.

"Whatever a people is left, it understandeth not the State, but hateth it as the evil eye, and a sin against customs and rights."

Nikon, writes Uzov, encroached on the local life of Russia. He overwhelmed every town and village with taxation. Not a priest or deacon but had to pay tithes on every truss of hay, every bushel of corn. Even the beggars were made to pay. But in particular his reforms were aimed to strengthen the grip of the higher grades of the hierarchy on the people, and to make himself Pope on the Roman model. But while striving to subject the clergy to the despotic power of the Patriarch, Nikon at the same time devoted all his energies to releasing them from subjection to the *mirs*. In his time the parish was turned "as it were into a clerico-political circumscription." [1]

The reforms of Nikon drew on him the hatred of every class of the people, to whom they seemed violations of their customs and rights. The principle of authority which he invoked as between the clergy and the people offended the customs of both and was reckoned to be a form of Latinizing and of Popery. "Nothing," wrote the protopope Avvakum in a petition to the Tsar Alexis Michailovich, "so much engenders schism in the churches as overbearing love of domination on the part of the authorities." [2]

Nikon's reforms encountered from the lower clergy in particular a stubborn resistance, because they tended to strengthen the powers of the archpriests. His despotic freaks aroused the indignation of the upper classes as well. The Pious Tsar Alexis in his letter to Nikon remarked that he had to find fault with him, because "he drove men to fast by force, but could not drive anyone by force to believe in God." [3]

[1] V. Andreev: *The Raskol and its significance in Russian popular history,* Petersb. 1870, p. 96.

[2] Ibid. p. 58.

[3] Ignatius, *History of the Raskol,* pp. 188–9.

One of the malcontents, the Boyarin Simeon Streshnev,
"having taught his big dog to sit up on his hind-quarters and
to bless with his front paws in the manner of an archpriest,
gave him the name of Nikon. The mockery was carried on
in public without shame or fear." [1] Nikon's comment reveals a
lack of humour: "If a mouse eats the host, it does not communicate. So neither is a dog's blessing really a blessing."

After rendering himself odious to the lower clergy and the
people, Nikon embarked on the correction of church books
and of sundry rites, and carried out his plan with his accustomed masterfulness. It was less that the plan was destestable
than that its executor was; for, to begin with, the so-called
reforms, no less than the opposition to them, appealed to the
clergy alone, and outside its ranks textual emendations neither
interested, nor were understood by anyone. The majority of
the Russian people, as might be expected, regarded the matter
with ancestral indifference and phlegm.[2] Andrew Denisov,
an early leader of the Raskol, admits that there was at first no
popular opposition to the new editions promulgated by Nikon.
The masses had no idea what it was all about. How should
they when the services were in old Cyrillic, a dead language
which they could understand no more then than now? For a
long time "they failed to discern that anything new was
happening and were wrapt in their usual pall of ignorance." [2]
Ecclesiastical dignitaries whose chief characteristic it was "to
be easy-going and indolent in their own affairs and occupations
were obviously not going to resist." [2] And this was just what
Nikon counted on,— all the more so, because the changes had
already begun under his predecessors, and "the innovations
had already appeared outright in the newly printed books
under the four patriarchs who preceded Joseph." [3] "In
particular the books issued under Joseph were full of variants
from the earlier printed editions, as is evidenced by the very
ones to-day in use among the old-ritualists." [3]

"In order to bring about everywhere the suspension of the

[1] Ignatius, *History of the Raskol*, pp. 188–9.

[2] Kostomarov, in *Messenger of Europe*, 1871, No. 4, pp. 481–2.

[3] Ignatius, *History of the Raskol*, pp. 140, 151.

old style of Church-service, Nikon ordered the old books to be taken away in every parish, both in towns and villages. In so acting he was merely following the example of the patriarch Philaret, who not only everywhere removed, but even burned the order for prayer and ministration printed in Moscow in 1610." [1]

But Nikon, continues Uzov, by his rasping severity had already inflamed the clergy against himself. They hated him because he had done all he could to substitute for the old and more or less fraternal ties which bound the common clergy and ecclesiastical superiors together, a new relationship of harsh subordination. In this connection we must not forget that in the Eastern Churches the parish clergy must be married men like their parishioners, whereas the higher clergy have taken monastic vows. A family man and a monk easily lose touch with each other. The lower clergy were thus all of them ready to oppose Nikon's textual innovations, so soon as they were pointed out to them; and the tactless way he went to work only hardened them in their opposition. It was at his instance, as we have seen, that in the Council of 1656, the higher clergy solemnly anathematized those who crossed themselves with two fingers.[2] This resort to anathemas gave to Nikon's work the stamp of an abomination, for his opponents could, and did, at once accuse him of levelling a curse against all former generations of saints that had crossed themselves in that manner. It gave them a good excuse for pronouncing in their turn an equally solemn curse on Nikon and all his works.

More than all else this one innovation provided all who were discontented with the administration of Church matters with a battle-cry and a standard round which to rally. "As in Moscow the capital, so in the provinces, the revolt of the lower clergy and their leaning to dissent was due to a clerico-democratic instinct to free themselves from the restraints imposed by the higher hierarchy, and in particular from its jurisdiction, its crushing imposts and dimes." [3] We must bear in

---

[1] P. Melnikov: *Historical Sketch of Popovshchina*, Moscow, 1864, p. 14.

[2] *op. cit.* Melnikov, p. 14.

[3] A. Shchapov, *Russian Raskol*, p. 204.

mind that in the good old times the parish priest was amenable
to the jurisdiction of the village elders among whom he lived and
who knew him personally and intimately. Nikon withdrew
him from their jurisdiction and placed him under the surveillance of monks who lived far away and were foreign to him.
Nor is there any reason to suppose that fees for ordination
payable to the bishop were reduced by transferring to the
latter so much of the authority which by ancient usage belonged
to the *Mir*. The undivided Church, as is well known, recognized but a single charismatic dignity alike in bishop and
priest, and accordingly one of the earliest Raskol teachers,
the protopope Neronov, wrote to the Tsar that "the priestly
grade is one and the same in all. You cannot, he argued,
speak of one man's holy orders as being perfect, of another's
as imperfect, for all priests are on a level. If archpriests are
successors of the highest Twelve Apostles, yet the priests and
deacons are successors of the Seventy Apostles; and among
themselves they are all brethren, servants of one Lord." For
the settlement therefore of ecclesiastical disputes, he proposed
the convening of a council at which should be present not only
archpriests, but archimandrites, hegumens, protopopes, divines,
priests and deacons, and "also those who inhabit the village
communes (*mirs*) and who, no matter what their rank, lead
good lives..." [1]

The Old believers, in fact, were intent on defending the rights
of the locality and of the individual; accordingly when the
patriarch reproached them in public debate for not obeying
their archpriests, they pointed out that "respect is not due to
persons, when the faith is being tampered with or even when
the truth is at stake, and it must be proclaimed not only in the
presence of the priestly caste, but of Tsars, inasmuch as to
apostatize from true religion is to apostatize from God." [2]

At the beginning of their struggle with the Church authorities the Old believers imagined they would meet with the support of the civil ones; thus it is that the Raskol began its

---

[1] I. Kharlamov in *Strana*, 1880, No. 57.

[2] *Three Petitions*, pp. 1 and 96. The one I cite is given by Will. Palmer, *The Tsar and the Patriarch*, Vol. II, p. 449. It was presented to the Tsar Oct. 6, 1667.

history with petitions to the civil rulers.[1] "Gracious Tsar,"
wrote the monks of Solovets, "we beseech you with tears and
lamentations, suffer not this new doctor and ecumenic patriarch to change our true Christian faith delivered to us by our
Lord Jesus Christ and his holy apostles, and by the seven
general Councils upheld. Let us abide in the piety and traditions in which our wonder workers Zosimus and Sabbatius and
Germanus and Philip, metropolitan of Moscow, and all the
saints found favour with God." Here there is no accent of
disloyalty and revolt. But they were soon disillusioned, for,
in what was really a struggle between the democratic elements
and the authorities of the Church, the Tsar's Government
speedily took the side of the latter and proceeded to punish
the opposition with all severity. The Old believers promptly
made up their minds that Tsar Alexis Michailovich "was no
Tsar but a tyrant."[1]

The Church Council of 1666 decided to punish the dissidents
"not only with ecclesiastical but with imperial penalties, i.e.
by civil statute and execution."[2] Persecutions and atrocities
began, and a talented Old believer, the protopope Avvakum,
wrote in view of what was occurring: "'Tis a marvel how little
they think of argument. It is by fire, nay by knout, by the
gallows, they want to affirm the faith. What Apostles ever
taught such courses? I know not. My Christ never bade our
Apostles to teach that fire, knout and halter are educators
in faith. . . . The Tatar God Mahomet wrote in his book:
Our behest is to strike off with the glaive the heads of those
who will not submit to our tradition and statute."[3] But such
protests did not avail against the enemies of the Raskol, and
persecution waxed all the fiercer.

The intervention of the Tsar's Government in a dispute
between the people and Church Authorities could only result
in "the rebel movement, which the teachers of the Raskol had
begun on strictly ecclesiastical ground, being suddenly transferred to the sphere of civilian and popular life; and at the head

[1] *Imperial Society of History and Antiquities*, 1863, bk. 1, p. 57.
[2] *Some Words on the Raskol*, by I. Nilski, p. 63.
[3] *Life of the Protopope Avvakum, written by himself*, pp. 93–4.

of it popular leaders made their appearance and took command, partisans opposed to the imperial Government, such as Khovanski, Stenka Razin, the Denisovs and others."[1] But this doubling, says Uzov, of ecclesiastical protest by civil did not come at once, but only gradually, and ill-success attended the first essays of the Raskolniks to link their own fortunes with revolution against the civil powers. Thus, for example, in the time of the revolt of the Streltsy guards, the dregs of the populace rose along with them against the princes and boyars and massacred many...[2] They tore up judicial writs and ordinances affecting the serfs, burned the stores in the fortresses, made havoc of legal decisions, declared the serfs to be free, rescued from prisons the interned.[3] When they began to pillage boyars and princes, the Streltsy did not spare even the Tsar's treasury. The Sovereign's enemies were joined by the foes of the ecclesiastical authorities, and these Old believers, though a small group to begin with, formed a welcome accession of strength to the rebel soldiers, who regarded them as men of learning; not that they had the least idea of how the party of Old believers differed from Nikon's, indeed the majority of them had not the least desire to know; they were only minded to end the old régime, and so were led incidentally to demonstrate in favour of freedom of conscience. Meanwhile the Government was well aware that the Streltsy took no interest in the struggle of the Raskol as such and presently succeeded in detaching them. "Why," asked the heads of State and Church of them, "why sacrifice us and the whole Russian realm for half-a-dozen monks?" The soldiers gave ear and answered: "With that (viz: the quarrel of the Old believers with the heads of the State) we have nothing to do."

The Old believers, however, were not disheartened by this first repulse of fortune, but pursued their aims unswervingly and with superhuman fortitude. The party of opposition among the clergy was in itself weak, but allied itself with any sort of popular agitation, however much the result of motives

---

[1] A. Shchapov, *Russian Raskol*, p. 218.
[2] *Three Petitions*, pp. 72, 60, 89, 137, 142.
[3] *Three Petitions*, pp. 137, 142.

and convictions other than its own; among the people there
were great numbers who were ready to adhere to anything
which magnified, much more sanctified, their old grudge against
authority in general; and the Raskolniks ranged themselves
in opposition to the Government under the banner of holy writ
and of theology. Their protest against social abuses was
formulated in phrases culled from theological texts. Theology
of course was the only "science" known to the Russian of that
age, and it does not surprise us that he threw his feelings and
aspirations into the mould of its terms and conceptions.[1]
It really signified little in what form his feelings and ideas were
moulded,— his chief concern was to arrange them in a system
of teaching intelligible to others, and here theology stood him
in good stead. Yet, asks Uzov, how explain the fact that discontent with social institutions in thus moulding itself in
religious form, to wit in that of the Raskol, announced that it
could only be satisfied by a return to the ancient order? Why
did it not aspire to something newer, as is usually the case?
To answer this query we need to consider wherein consisted
this old order and who it was that was intent on its abrogation.

Russia and Tartar Influence

"In old Russia every province enjoyed a certain autonomy
of its own, freely evolved an independent life, conditioned only
by locality, by tribal character, by the special nature of its
occupations and activities. As the forces of centralization
waxed stronger, this independent life was levelled out and
conformed to a general current and plane. Localities, however,
that had enjoyed such independence and freedom gave it up
reluctantly; for they were loth to forfeit their privileges and
aspirations, and continued for long to oppose a centralizing
administration and policy that was new and alien to them.
In the turbulent age of the impostors the forced and artificial
unification of the provinces was temporarily relaxed, and every
local centre endeavoured to strengthen itself and recover its
old independent life, to regain its ancient rights. But when

---

[1] Today (1919) the Political Economy of Karl Marx has taken the place of the
'Science' of theology of the 17th century.

with Michael Theodorovich and Alexis Michailovich Russia was once more 'collected,' i.e. unified, the bonds were forged anew.[1]

And why, asks Uzov, was the transition, when it came, one from old and more liberal and humane institutions to those of Moscow? Was this the natural course of development for the Russian social organism? Here is a question which admits of no other answer than this: the new institutions which now developed in Russia were a consequence of the external pressure of the Tartar invasion. A savage people by dint of brute force had wiped off the face of the land a genuine Russian civilization that was already maturing; and it was relatively easy to do so, because it was not a warlike but a peaceful civilization. All the dark forces latent in the Russian people leaned to the side of the Tartars, accepted their civilization and by flattering and shuffling before them fettered — thanks to Tartar aid — the Russian people and riveted their yoke upon it.

"Thus Moscow fraternized with the Tartars, and under the shadow of their anti-nationalist system managed to gather round herself the provinces of Novgorod, Pskov, Tver, Ryazan, Perm and Kiev. In a Moscow torn from Southern Russia a *Moscovite* world emerged and entrenched itself. In the XVth Century when the rest of the Slav nationalities were reviving, when among Poles, Croats, Slovenes, Serbs, Bulgarians, and in South Russia a popular literature was beginning to appear, there opened in Moscow an era of final decadence. The art of writing, enlightenment, literature, art, wholesome international relationships, which had all aforetime culminated in Kiev in the XIIth Century — these perished in Moscow. Russian equity took flight and fled to heaven, and in Moscow quibbling chicanery and Moscovite intrigue took its place."[2]

To the Tartars Russia owes the introduction of iron rule with all its attractions, and the institution of draconian statutes. The code of Alexis Michailovich was a product of Tartar character rather than of Slav. To the Tartars is due the substitution of despotism and autocratic bureaucracy for the

---

[1] N. Aristov, in *Vremya (Time)*, 1862, No. 1, p. 76.

[2] *History of Cabarets in Russia*, by Iv. Pryzhov, Moscow, 1868, p. 45–6.

ordinances of common councils and provincial autonomy. Tartar civilization having forcibly cankered Russian society, took Tartars into its service, for the insufficiency of its own powers was realized, and it resorted to such means in order to safeguard its own existence.

"In the XVIth Century a fresh flood of violence and barbarity inundated Russia along with the irruptions of Kazan, Astrakhan and Siberian Tsars, Tsaritsas, Tsareviches, princes, petty princes, who offered their services to the Tsar's government in Moscow and married into the Russian noblesse, so constituting themselves defenders of Russian territory and acquiring control of the cities of Kasimov, Zvenigorod, Kashir, Serpukhov, Khotun, Iouriev, along with many villages and hamlets." [1] And thus in this period the proverb was coined: "Live, live, until Moscow gets hold of you." Andreev states that the forefathers of the majority of Russian nobles in the realm of Moscow, were emigrants from Tartary or settlers from Western Europe.[2] We may thus unhesitatingly conclude, writes Uzov, that in the age which gave birth to the Raskol, Russian society under stress of violence on the part of these Tartars had entered on a retrograde path. The latter were installed in the highest administrative positions in the society of the time, and were sustained in them by our own Russian home-bred Tartars. Christian standards of morals were overwhelmed by Tartar ones, national peculiarities were wholly lost sight of, all the more so because the governing caste, being principally composed of elements alien to the Russian genius, altogether lacked any idea of the character and aspirations of the people they ruled.

Russian Ritualism and Liturgical Controversy

Though great movements have always great causes, nevertheless relatively petty circumstances seem always to provide their starting point. The great Russian schism was no exception. It began not with any articulate protest against Tartar customs, or Byzantine polity in general, but with opposition

---

[1] *ib.* p. 48.
[2] Andreev, *The Raskol and its Significance,* p. 14.

to small details of ritual and the corrupt text of service books. Ivanovski gives a full account of these details, and the criticism to which he is justly subject is not that he is wrong in what he states, but that he neglects the greater though less spectacular points.

George Bourdon in his graphic history of the revolutionary convulsions, which in Russia followed the ill-starred campaign of 1904 against Japan, describes the religion of the Russian peasant as consisting mainly in the kissing of dirty greasy boards dignified with the name of ikon or holy picture, but often anikonic, in the sense that the images they once portrayed are no longer decipherable. This superstitious respect for representations of the human face and person was well exemplified in the invasion of East Prussia with which the war of 1914 began. Then, as Mr. Stephen Graham attests in his work *Russia and the World* (London, 1915), the only objects in German houses which escaped the destructive zeal of the Russian infantry were the pictures on the walls. Pianos, violins, books, furniture of all sorts were smashed to atoms, torn up and cast into the gutters, or burned, but never a picture was touched. These poor barbarians, of whom, according to the French statistics of 1911, nearly three out of four could neither read nor write, had never set foot in a civilized dwelling before; and they assumed that the pictures and paintings which adorned the walls harboured spirits or were holy ikons. Even the busts of the Kaiser, so Mr. Graham assures us, were spared, no doubt because he was mistaken for a saint.

It is then to such a respect for the external trappings of religion that Prof. Ivanovski traces the origin of the Raskol. It was from the first, he thinks, the essential character of popular religion among his countrymen, the expression of their soul. They were, he says, in their infancy when they were converted, and his argument requires us to believe that they were still 'in their infancy' in the second half of the XVIIth Century when the Patriarch Nikon introduced his 'reforms'; and, to judge from the hold which Dissent still has upon them, they have not yet emerged from childhood. Their political development had been arrested by the Mongol yoke, and religion supplied the only channel along which their inner life could flow; but, like children, they could not embrace a religion which was abstract and meditative; they needed rather one of external aids and outside shows, in the absence of which they could not be stirred to faith and prayer. Temple rites and adornments, vestments, shrines, pilgrimages, miraculous pictures, divine volumes, houses adorned in the style of churches, life in strict accordance with ecclesiastical rule, all these, he argues, were of the essence of religion in the age which gave birth to the Raskol. At that time few minds rose to the level of distinguishing between these unessentials and the essential dogmas that embody eternal truth and are therefore unalterable. How low the general level of intelligence really was is proved by the frequent complaints to that effect on the part of the higher clergy; thus in the year 1500 Gennadius, Archbishop of Novgorod, attests the general ignorance in his epistle to the Metropolitan Simon, and in the middle of the XVIth Century it had reached its nadir. He complains that candidates for ordination could not read the Apostle or chant the Psalms or recite an *ektenia*.

As an example of lamentable confusion of ritual with dogma, Ivanovski instances the dispute which arose in the XVth Century as to whether the Alleluia should be recited twice or thrice before the *Gloria* in the psalmody. The antecedents of the dispute are wrapt in obscurity; but it is clear that early in that century (1419) the clergy of Pskov began the triple recitation by the advice of the Metropolitan Photius; nevertheless in 1450, thirty years later, the abbot Euphrosyn of Pskov still entertained misgivings about it. In the hope of laying to rest his doubts, about which he consulted the Elders of his own Church, but in vain, Euphrosyn paid a visit to the Patriarch Joseph of the 'Royal City' Tsargrad (Constantinople), where in the churches of Sancta Sophia he observed that the Greeks only recited it twice. This led him on his return to Russia to insist on the Greek usage in his monastery, thereby making enemies of the clergy of Pskov, where a certain Job, respected by laity and clergy as 'a philosopher, a sound teacher and a pillar of the Church' headed the opposition. Euphrosyn was

now accused of violating the canons of the Church, of denying
the Trinity, of being a heretic and so forth. He retorted that
he was following the usage of Tsargrad and of the ecumenic
Church, while Job was a pillar, not of the Church, but of dung.
This invited similar amenities from Job who persuaded his
followers at Pskov, whenever they passed by the Monastery
of Euphrosyn, not to bow, but to call out: 'There lives a
heretic, ripe for anathema.' Both parties appealed to the archbishop Euthymius of Novgorod, who saw no way to reconcile
them, and the quarrel went on after the protagonists departed
this life in spite of the efforts of a learned Greek, Demetrius
Gerasimus (Tolmach), to make peace between them. He
wrote in 1493 from Rome a letter to Gennadius, Archbishop
of Novgorod, to prove that one usage was as legitimate as the
other, seeing that the one manifested the trine hypostasis of the
consubstantial Godhead, the other the two natures in Christ.
Such impartiality was not good enough for Russians, and
finally the Council of the Hundred Heads[1] (Stoglav) in 1551
decided in its 42nd canon in favour of the double Alleluia,
stigmatizing the triple one as a Latin heresy and as tantamount
to the inclusion of four persons in the Trinity!

Nor was this the only dispute which ruffled the calm of the
Orthodox Church in the XVth Century, for in its last years
princes and bishops were divided on the question whether in
solemn processions the priests and people should move ' withershins' or no. Over this point the Prince, Ivan Vassilevich III,
and the Metropolitan Gerontius shewed little of the love which
Christians should bear one another. The bishop Gerontius,
consecrating the Uspenski church in 1479, ventured to walk
with his cross withershins round the new fabric, so offending
against the Sun of Righteousness and outraging the feelings
of Ivan who had on his side not a few bishops and monks,
especially the lively archimandrite Gennadius, afterwards
Archbishop of Novgorod. The withershins party pleaded in

---

[1] So called because their debates were resumed in 100 chapters. At this
council there were no representatives of Kiev. Orthodox Russians seek to impugn
the authority and even authenticity of the 100 chapters. For the description
of this important council see pp. 51 ff.

vain that they advanced not to affront and insult the Sun, but to greet him; but as no canons existed to settle so vital an issue, the parties remained irreconcilable. The Metropolitan would not yield, retired in dudgeon to the Simonov Monastery, and for several years refused to consecrate any more churches, until the Prince gave way.

Another such dispute arose on the point whether documents should be dated according to the era which began with Creation or that which began with Christ; for a monk Philotheus of the Eleazar Monastery revealed the fact to the world about 1500 that in old Russian MSS. both eras were met with. The Armenians solved the riddle by setting down both in their colophons, but then they were monophysite heretics. It did much harm to Peter the Great that he banished the old era for good. He was generally regarded as Antichrist because of the innovation.

But the most formidable and fertile source of dispute was the importance attached to the correct use of liturgical formulae, and — notwithstanding this — the almost infinite extent of textual variation in manuscripts and books.

In that age in Russia prayer was barely differentiated from magic spells; as is manifest from a fourth quarrel that raged in 1476 over the issue whether in a certain passage of the liturgy the clergy should cry 'Lord, pardon us,' or 'O Lord, pardon us.' Ivanovski complains that in such cases the Old-ritualist temper betrayed itself in those who demanded the continuance of the usage to which people were accustomed merely because it was the old one. It does not occur to him that it was at least as reasonable to demand its continuance as its discontinuance, and that if it mattered nothing one way or the other, the old usage might as well have been tolerated and not penalised with knout and rack.

If we open any collection of liturgical texts taken from ancient MSS., for example the Greek Euchologion of Goar, or that of Prof. Dimitrievski of Kiev, or my own *Rituale Armenorum*, we are at once struck by the infinite variety of text and rite in one and the same church. In the Church Books of the Orthodox Faith variety was all the greater because

the Monks of Athos and other centres who translated them
from the Greek made so many blunders. Moreover some of
the books passed into Russian not direct, but through Moravian, Serb and Bulgar versions.[1] Already in the XIIIth
Century the Metropolitan Cyril complained of the errors
which from these and other causes had crept into the service
books of his church. In the XVIth and XVIIth Centuries
such errors, duly multiplied by transcribers, passed at length
into the printed texts. One common source of error was the
intrusion into the text of glosses which should have been left
in the margin, and Ivanovski gives one curious example of the
sort in a MS. of the XIth Century. The passage is Matt.
XXVII. 65, where Pilate says to the high priests and Pharisees:
"Ye have got a guard." Here the Slav translator, puzzled by
the Latin word *Custodia*, assumed it to be the name of Pilate's
maiden chatelaine! Ivanovski informs us that there is much
discrepancy between one text and another of the Baptismal
rite; and one would like to know if it was not in the Epiphany
rite celebrating the Benediction of Rivers in memory of the
Baptism of Jesus, that the variants occur — to his mind so
deplorable — which imply that Jesus was merely human until
the Spirit descended upon him in his thirtieth year. For this
was the old Ebionite or Adoptionist belief, which is prominent
in old Armenian Epiphany homilies and not wholly absent
from their hymns sung at the Blessing of the Rivers. We
need pay no attention to Ivanovski's conjecture that Jews had
tampered with these rites; for this very belief characterizes
the Dukhobortsy and Khlysty sects and is therefore very ancient on Russian soil.

Slav divines already recognized in the XIVth Century how
imperfect were their versions, and the Metropolitan Theo-
gnostos (1328–1353) tried to correct the *Trebnik*, a book which
answers to the Roman missal. The Metropolitan Alessios
(1354–1378) compared the Slav N. T. with the Greek text,
and another Metropolitan, Cyprian, a Serb or Bulgarian — it
is not known which — devoted much attention to the correct-

---

[1] The Moravian Versions were the most ancient, and of them Serb or Bulgar
translations seem to have passed into Russia.

ing of his liturgical books, as Mansvetov has pointed out in his appendix (*Pribavleniya*) to the great series of Russian versions of the Fathers, Moscow 1882, vol. 29, pp. 152–305; 412–480.[1]

As an example of the dangers which beset a scholar, Ivanovski relates the career of a Greek monk, Maximus, invited to Moscow in 1518 by Prince Basil Ivanovich to take charge of the royal library and make a fresh translation of certain books. He was an Albanian by origin, had studied in Italy, and was a member of the Vatopedi convent on Mt. Athos. A man learned in Greek and Latin, he won the favour of the Prince and the friendship of the Metropolitan Barlaam, and was commissioned by them to revise the service books, though he deplored the recent severance from Constantinople of the Russian Christians and their new claim to constitute an independent national church, to be in fact the only orthodox body in the entire world. He did not possess Russian, and was therefore supplied with two interpreters, named Demetrius Gerasimov and Vlasius who also knew Latin, and with their aid he corrected the *Triodion*, the *Hours*, the *Menaion*, and the *Apostolos*. He rendered the psalter from Greek into Latin and the Latin was turned by his coadjutors into Slav. He is said, as we saw above, to have noticed gross errors in these books, intentionally introduced by Judaizers, for Jesus Christ was denominated in them a mere created man and declared to have died an eternal death.[2]

But neither the detection of these heretical opinions nor his polemics against the Latin and Armenian Churches and against Jews and Mohammedans saved his own reputation for orthodoxy, and he was soon accused of having insulted the Russian saints and workers of miracles of old and of deflowering the old and sacred books of Cyril and Methodius. On Barlaam's death, the new Metropolitan Daniel, formerly prior of the Volokolam Monastery, openly charged him with arbitrarily altering the texts, and, like Henry VIII, the Tsar withdrew

[1] Palmieri, *Chiesa Russa*, p. 400. I have not been able to gain access to this publication of Mansvetov.

[2] See Plotnikov, *Istoriia russkago Raskola*, Petersb. 1905, p. 13.

his patronage for the excellent reason that he would not join Daniel in sanctioning his divorce of the childless Empress Salomona.

In 1525 Daniel convened a council of doctors and condemned Maximus as a heretic, it is said because he had tripped in Russian grammar. He was deported to the Volokolam Monastery where, illtreated by the monks, he nearly died of smoke, cold and hunger. In 1531 another council, at the instigation of Daniel, accused him of altering the creed by eliminating the epithet *true* used of the Holy Spirit. He was banished to the Otroch Uspenski Monastery in Tver, and forbidden to receive the Sacraments,— for him a great privation. In vain the Greek patriarchs interceded in his behalf and the bishop of Tver befriended him. The utmost concession made was to permit him to communicate, and he died, almost friendless, imprisoned in the Laura of S. Sergius in 1556.[1]

Yet he left behind him rules, simple and sagacious, for the guidance of future revisers, and described the corrector's art as a gift of the Holy Ghost. Above all he prescribed a knowledge of tongues, which must be studied under good teachers. His rules were expressed in the form of Greek *stichoi* or stanzas. A century later under Nikon his principles triumphed and the intimacy of the Russian with the Greek Churches was revived and encouraged.

We noticed above that Maximus gave offence by expurging the one word *true* in the Creed. It comes in the eighth clause: *And (we believe) in the Holy Spirit Lord true and giver of life.* The older Slav MSS. are said to omit the word, and prior to Nikon some Service-books contained it, others not. The Stoglav[2] (or hundred-headed) Council in 1551 decided in favour of omitting either *Lord* or *true*, but did not say which. A glance at the original Greek explains the difficulty. It runs: Καὶ εἰς τὸ πνεῦμα τὸ ἅγιον τὸ κύριον τὸ ζωοποιοῦν. Now the word κύριον may be rendered either as *true* or as *Lord*, and an early Russian translator had set one rendering in his text, the other no doubt in his margin, whence it had crept into

[1] Ivanovski has 1566.
[2] See p. 51.

the text, so that many MSS. had the conflate reading: *Gospoda, istinnogo*, i. e. 'Lord, True.'

Somewhat later than the accession to the throne of Tsar Michael Theodorovich a tragic dispute arose over a variant in the Epiphany rite of the Benediction of the Waters, a variant that must itself have had a long history behind it. In old copies it was asked that the water might be sanctified "by the Holy Spirit and by Fire," a reminiscence perhaps of a variant found in some ancient sources which add after Matt. 3, 15, the words: "And when he was baptised, a mighty light shone around from the water, in such wise that all who had come thither were struck with fear." This addition, if not suggested by, at least accords with John the Baptist's prophecy contained in a preceding verse (3, 11) that the Messiah "shall baptise you with the Holy Spirit and with Fire." However this may be, the words 'and with fire' were expunged from a revision of the Russian Euchologion or *Potrebnik*, made chiefly from Slav MSS. by a certain archimandrite Dionysius of the Trinity-Sergius Monastery, who found the phrase in only two copies of the old Slav version, and in no Greek copy at all. He had two collaborators in his work of revision, which occupied a year and a half, the Elder Arsenius and a priest of the village of Klementev attached to the Monastery, named Ivan Nasedkin. Another important change they made was to exclude the two prayers before the liturgy in which the priest seeks remission of his sins.

The excision of the words 'and with fire' drew down on these correctors the wrath of a member of the Laura of St. Sergius, Longinus, who is said to have regarded the arts of reading and writing as almost heretical. He had himself passed these supposed errors in his edition of the year 1610 and prided himself on his learning. He now accused them of denying the Spirit to be composed of fire — a very ancient opinion. Philaret, his abbot, encouraged him and by the joint efforts of the two Dionysius and his fellow-students were in 1618 haled before the Patriarch Iona's court, and subjected to torture in the cells of the Ascension with the approval of Martha Ivanovna, mother of the Tsar. The mob raged against them, being told that they were guilty of the unparalleled heresy of banishing fire from the universe, and they were accused of heresy in front of the Kremlin and pelted with mud. Dionysius and Ivan Nasedkin were excommunicated by a council over which Iona presided, and imprisoned in the Novospasski Monastery, to be dragged in fetters on festivals to the feet of Iona the Patriarch. Arsenius who was deaf was imprisoned in the convent of S. Cyril. In the end however the new patriarch Philaret (1618) who had been ordained by Theophanes, Patriarch of Jerusalem, entertained Ivan Nasedkin's plea for mercy, and in 1619 they were pardoned. Ivan even received marks of the Tsar's favour, and was made priest of the court church. Dionysius also came into favour. Philaret at first did not venture to eliminate the words 'and with fire' from the printed editions of the rite. In 1625 however, the patriarchs of Alexandria and Jerusalem decided against them, and Philaret had them struck out in all editions, although the immersion of lighted tapers in the water remained part of the Epiphany rite commemorating the Baptism of our Lord. Thus an ancient and respectable rite was mutilated of one of its most characteristic traits. It could hardly be otherwise in that ignorant age. A corrector was more likely to deprave a text than better it, for a little knowledge is a dangerous thing.

In short, as Ivanovski himself recognizes, such corrections as scholars of that age could make, were as likely to be for the worse as not, for how could they distinguish good from bad? Any attempts of the kind were sure to bear the impress of arbitrariness and ignorance; and it was futile for the Stoglav Council of 1551 to complain of church books being faulty. Their canon prescribing to copyists the use of correct versions and warning the higher clergy to supervise their industry was as difficult to observe as it was well meant.

The first printing press was set up in Moscow in 1552, in the reign of Ivan, Vassilevich; it had been brought from Denmark by a printer named Hansa, who was assisted by the deacon Ivan Thedorov or Feodorov and Peter Timothy Mstislavets. Only church books were issued from it, and the *Apostolos*[1]

---

[1] Rambaud, *History of Russia*, more correctly, says: Acts of the Apostles.

was the first book printed. It was followed by a *Description of Moscow* and the *Book of Hours*. It was hoped that the texts issued would be more correct, but the printers confessed their ignorance of what was or was not correct, and the press could but stereotype the errors of the particular MS. used. No better success greeted the laudable efforts of the Patriarch Hermogenes (1606) to obtain more correct texts by attaching to his press at Moscow a corps of scholars charged to compare the books already printed with the MSS. and to collate these with each other. It would seem that they confined themselves to Slav MSS., and those recent ones, sparing themselves the trouble of following the precept of the wise Maximus to study the Greek originals. As an example of the inefficiency of Russian scholars of that time, Ivanovski instances the Canon or Rule of divine service (*Ustav* = τυπικόν) printed in 1610, of which the Patriarch Philaret was obliged subsequently to collect and burn all copies, because its contents were of so startling and unauthorized a character. I should conjecture that they were merely archaic and original, and not in accord with then current standards of orthodoxy. I once saw the copies of old Nestorian codices upon which was based Bedjan's great repertoire of the liturgies of that ancient church, so beautifully printed at the Propaganda press in Rome. The copies were plentifully scored and underlined with red and blue chalk; the red signifying, so I was informed, passages to be entirely removed, the blue those to be amended in the interests of Roman orthodoxy; and I regretted greatly that these original readings were not given in an appendix or otherwise recorded for the use of scholars. In mentioning this case, I convey no censure of the Roman Propaganda, for I am sure that the only intelligible procedure is that on which Rome insists, namely, on the one hand to print for modern church use officially authorized texts agreeable to current standards of orthodoxy, and on the other to allow scholars and liturgiologists to edit for the learned world the more ancient texts exactly as they stand in the most ancient codices. This procedure the Roman Church follows in the case of Latin texts, and it encourages the Uniat Churches to do the same.

No objection, for example, is placed in the way of the Armenian Mekhitarists of Vienna and Venice, if they like to print for liturgical scholars an Euchologion containing the ancient rites for the sacrifice of birds and fourfooted animals; but they would not be allowed to print these interesting but out of date rites and disseminate them for popular use.

A number of grammarians and rhetoricians were employed by the patriarch Philaret (1612) to assist in editing the Church books, among them the Elder Arsenius the Deaf, Antony Krylov, the priest Ivan Nasedkin already mentioned, Elias the hegumen of the Theophany convent and even a layman Gregory Onisimov. One or two of these could read Greek, but made no use of their gift. But it marked a real advance when the Patriarch ordered a search to be made for older MSS. in other cities besides Moscow. Even texts written by the western Slavs were collected, though sparingly consulted from fear of their having been contaminated by Latin influences. Philaret's efforts were of course doomed to disappointment, and Ivanovski remarks that between later and earlier editions of the same service book wide discrepancies were discovered as soon as they were compared, especially in the rites of Epiphany and of Baptism; again, the Euchologia printed in 1625 and 1633 included the rites for the adoption of children and of brethren (ἀδελφοποιία) given in Greek prayerbooks; that of 1623 omitted them. It is clear that what the Russian Church dignitaries were intent upon was uniformity, and it was bound to be a mere accident if, in arriving at it, they did not exclude much that was old and had better have been retained, and include much modern rubbish which it was better to omit.

The Patriarch Joasaph who succeeded Philaret in 1634, and died Nov. 28, 1640, issued edition after edition of Psalter, Euchologion, Menaea, Hours, Gospels, Triodion, Nomocanon, etc. Though he too insisted on old MSS. being consulted, he only made confusion worse confounded; and some of the books printed by his authority were in startling disaccord with his predecessor's editions, especially the Euchologion of 1639, which stigmatized Philaret's rite for the Burial of Priests as having been drawn up by the heretical pope Jeremia of Bulgaria. Among the new books issued by him were a spelling book, an anthologion, a Triodion in four volumes, and a life of Nicholas the Wonder-worker.

The activity of the Moscow Press was great under the next Patriarch, Joseph, who acceded in March, 1642.[1] He appointed Ivan, sacristan of the Uspenski Church; Joseph Nasedkin, the controverter of the Lutheran propagandist Prince Valdemar of Denmark, Protopope Michael Stephen Rogov; Silvester, archimandrite of the Androniev Monastery, Joannes, Protopope of the Alexandronevski Church along with certain presbyters and laymen as a college of "correctors." But they did not go beyond Slav books in their quest for correcter texts, and the press under the direct management of the Tsar's favourite divine, Stephan Boniface, and of John Neronov, Protopope of the Kazan Church, for the most part merely issued reprints of the earlier editions of the Patriarchs Job, Philaret, and Joasaph. Some slight changes, however, were now made to suit the prescriptions of the Stoglav Council of ninety years before. Thus the passage where in earlier editions the *Alleluia* was thrice repeated, was now printed: "Alleluia, Alleluia, glory to thee, O God." At the same time a Cyrillic rubric appeared in the Psalter, enjoining the faithful to cross themselves with two fingers instead of three conjoined. Editors and controllers of the new presses generally adopted the two fingers, though within a few years the question of two or three fingers was to become a burning one. The Stoglav Council had enjoined the use of the two fingers only. A Russian grammar was printed in 1648, a Lives of Saints in 1646, Homilies of Ephrem Syrus in 1643, a catena on the gospels by Theophylact the Bulgarian, Anastasius Sinaita, and others in 1649.

It speaks well for the Tsar Alexis Michailovich, that he undertook in May 1649 an edition of the Russian Bible revised from the Greek original, and wrote to the half Polish Metropolitan of Kiev, Silvester Kossov, to send to him scholars competent for the task.[2] Two monks arrived, Epiphan Slave-

---

[1] Macarius *Hist.* t. 11, pp. 94–97.

[2] Macarius *Hist.* t. 12, p. 112 foll. *Christian Readings* 1883, Nov.–Dec. Art. *Materials for Russian History.*

netski and Arsenius Satanovski, an ill-sounding, but really local name. A young seigneur, Theodor Michailovich Rtishchev (1625–1673), shared his prince's enthusiasm, and at his own expense erected outside Moscow, on the Kiev road, two versts away, a monastery in which the newly arrived teachers of Greek, of grammar, and of rhetoric, were to find a home. He himself was their first pupil, and the learned men assembled there began at once the work of collating Slav texts with the Greek, and presently gave their results to the world in a new edition of the Church book called the *Shestodnev* (Hexahemeron); first printed in Cracow in the year 1491. This was the first work to be revised from 'good' Slav MSS. and at the same time from a Greek text, and Nikon put it forward as an example for future editors of sacred texts. At the instance of this Tsar sundry Greek divines now began to visit Moscow, where alone in the Orthodox world they could collect alms for themselves. One of the best-known was Paisius, Patriarch of Jerusalem, who stayed there four months during which he consecrated Nikon archbishop of Novgorod, and had time, according to Nikon, to notice not a few ritual discrepancies between his own and the Russian Church. The result was that a Russian Presbyter, who knew Greek, Arsen Sukhanov, was commissioned in 1649 to accompany Paisius, Patriarch of Jerusalem, on his return in order to report upon Greek rites. Arsen was a cultivated man for his age and architect of the Theophany convent in the Kremlin, a dependency of the Trinity-Serge Laura, and a partisan in religion of the old national tradition. On their way they halted at Jassy, in Roumania. In the sequel he twice went to Greece and back, and in the course of one of his journeys brought back some hundreds of Greek codices which are among the treasures of the Synodal library of Moscow. For this alone his name deserves to be remembered. He also published the results of his investigations in four "*Dialogues upon Faith with the Greeks*," [1] in which he somewhat

---

[1] *Prenia o Viérié*. It is doubtful if they were written as early as 1650; the *Proskinitari* (i. e. Worshipper), on which see below p. 44, was written after his return from the East in 1653. In the first dialogue held April 24, 1650, the Patriarch Meletius, Metropolitan of Braila, challenges the Russian use of two fingers only in blessing, and Arsenius defends it as the usage of St. Andrew, the

wavered over the use of the three fingers in blessing, though he observed it among the monks of Athos. We shall see later on that members of the Raskol appealed to Arsen's work in evidence of the fatal decadence and even apostasy of the Greeks; judged from an old Russian standpoint, with no little reason. About the same time Gabriel, metropolitan of Nazareth visited Moscow, and while there took no less exception to the use of two fingers than his colleague of Jerusalem.

Nikon

In 1652 the patriarch Joseph died, to be followed by one whose fanaticism was to break the orthodox church in two over utterly insignificant issues, and originate a schism which lasts until to-day with results to Russian society and polity of which the importance can hardly be overestimated.

This was Nikon,[1] named Nicetas in the world before he donned the monastic garb. Born in 1605 of peasant and possibly Finnish stock in Veldemanov, a village in the province of Nizhegorod, he learned to read and write at the village school, bringing to his task the rugged strength and superstitious temperament of a common peasant. At twelve years of age he entered the monastery of St. Macarius of Zheltovody on the Volga in the same Government, where he soon distinguished himself above other novices by his application to learning and his asceticism. When he was twenty his parents persuaded him to marry, and, ordained one of the white clergy, he took a cure of souls in Moscow; before he was thirty his three children died, and, persuading his wife to take the veil, he himself took monkish vows and retired to the Skete or hermitage of Anzer on the White Sea. His was an imperious nature, and within five years, in consequence of a quarrel with his colleagues over the building of a church, he departed thence to become the hegumen or prior of the Kozheozerski [2] Monastery

illuminator of Russia. Arsenius equally maintains the Russian baptism by triple immerson to have been introduced in Russia by the Apostle and condemns the Greek usage of baptising sick infants by sprinkling only.

[1] Strannik 1863, t. 3: Macarius *Hist.* t. 11: Solovev. *Hist. Russ.* t. 11.

[2] Perhaps Kusheryetskoe, close to Onega, in the railway map of A. Ilin of 1908. Waliszewski, however, locates it in the district of Kargopol in the eparchy of Novgorod, so also the Russian Encyclopedia, xxi, 139.

on Lake Kozhe on the western shore of the White Sea. In that capacity he had occasion to visit Moscow to attend a council held there in 1645-6. There he attracted the notice of the Tsar Alexis who preferred him to the position of archimandrite in the Novospasski convent in the Capital. The Tsar entrusted him with the fulfilment of many public duties and invited him every week to the Kremlin in order to converse with him, and it is a good trait in the ecclesiastic that he availed himself of his intimacy with the Prince to intercede in behalf of widows and orphans denied their rights by venal courts of justice.

Two years later he was made Metropolitan of Novgorod where he helped to put down the revolt of 1650, sheltering in his own house the Voivoda Khilkov, when his own life also was threatened by the populace. In July 1652, at the age of forty-seven, he was chosen patriarch at the Tsar's instance, though on his own terms, and with the approval of Synod, clergy and people, who had to go down on their knees to him before he would accept the Patriarchate. He was already, as we saw, a favourite with the Tsar, who presently (1654) conferred on him the title and authority of grand vizier, Gosudar or Regent, never till then conferred on anyone except Philaret, Patriarch in 1618, and the father of Michael Theodorovitch the first of the Romanov's. When the Tsar was away conducting his wars, it now devolved on Nikon to look after his family, govern the State and control the Boyars or great nobles who had to make to him the reports which they ordinarily made to the sovereign, and render to him an account of all their doings.

Historians give no unfavourable picture of his activity at the beginning of his patriarchate. He was severe indeed with his clergy and so rigid a disciplinarian that some charged him with being a tyrant, but in so disorderly an age it was necessary to be strict. One step he took at once which commends itself to all Church reformers. Instead of the ready-made homilies for all sorts of occasions he tried to revive the art of preaching, and encouraged his clergy to use their natural gifts of eloquence. This was to innovate on old custom, and contrasts with the system which was in vogue in the Russian Church a few years ago, if it is not still,[1] of obliging the clergy to submit their sermons to censors before they are delivered from the pulpit. Another of his aims was to introduce uniformity, a measure which needed much tact in view of the discrepancies which existed between the rites of one place and another, for editions of church-books differed and still more widely the manuscript copies still in vogue; and in different localities the clergy and monks were likely to be jealous of interference with rites already in use. But there was also much disorder in Church Services that called for instant correction; for example it was only decent that prayers and canticles should be recited or sung in one tone *unisono*, and not in several at once, and it was a scandal that in order to get through the liturgy as quickly as possible it was customary for one priest to be reading, another singing, and the deacon crying his *ecteni*, all three at once. In the church singing it was also usual to interpolate vowels and prolong the voice upon them to the detriment of the sense. This was, it appears, an offence in Nikon's eyes, though it is not unknown in other Churches, and as it is the rule in the Armenian Church, it may have been ancient in the Slav Churches. Most of these irregularities had already been reproved by the Stoglav Council, as well as by the Patriarchs Hermogenes and Joseph, but in vain. Nikon now set about to correct them by sterner methods, and he also lost no time in chastising the fashionable artists who were beginning to paint ikons for rich men's houses in the gaudy style of the Latins. He collected their masterpieces, burned them, and on pain of anathema forbade painters for the future to prostitute in such a manner their sacred craft. In spite, however, of such conservatism in the matter of art, Nikon threw the weight of his authority on the side of those who favoured the correcting of the old rites and service books, and even headed the new movement, choosing Greek and Slav of western origin as his models. "Though I am Russian,' he said at the Council

---

[1] Pobedonostseff, Procurator of the holy Synod, in his *Reflections of a Russian Statesman* (London 1898), after insisting on the want of simplicity, unnatural intonation, conventional phrases of Protestant preachers, adds: "We feel here how faithfully our Church has been adapted to human nature in excluding sermons from its services. By itself our whole service is the best of sermons," p. 214.

of 1656, 'I am in faith and convictions a Greek." Accordingly
he introduced Greek ambons, Greek pastoral staffs, Greek
cowls, cloaks, hymns, painters, silversmiths, Greek architec-
ture. He invited Greeks to Moscow and followed their advice
in everything.

We have already mentioned the trips to Greek centres undertaken by Arsen Sukhanov at the instance of the Tsar Michael.
When he returned to Moscow in June 1653 he dedicated a volume entitled *Proskinitari* to his prince and to the new Patriarch
Nikon; to this book, although it barely influenced the latter's
reforms, as it had been intended to do, a certain importance
attaches, because upon it, as upon his four discussions with the
Greeks, alluded to above (p. 40), the Raskol teachers later
on based their charge of apostasy against the Greeks, a charge
sufficiently absurd in view of the fact that the author expresses
no sort of doubt about the orthodoxy of the Greek Churches
and even regards them, especially that of Alexandria, as a
court of appeal for the resolution of doubts which had arisen
in Russia with regard to particular points of ritual. It contained a pilgrim's guide to the Holy Places, of the kind familiar
in the early literature of every church, along with the answers
of the Alexandrine Patriarch to certain questions propounded
by Arsen. One of these regarded the *Alleluia*, as to which
the Patriarch decided that it ought to be repeated thrice with
the addition of the words: "Glory to thee, O God!" Arsen
notes sundry liturgical variations in the Greek Churches from
Russian usage, e. g. the use in the Eucharistic office of only
five *prosphorai* instead of seven, withershins processions, etc.
But it was especially the concessions to Western or Latin
usages that shocked him; for example, they admitted baptism
by sprinkling, they had adopted Frankish vestments; they as-
sociated with the Franks even in church, ate in their society
and intermarried with them. In Jerusalem the orthodox and
Armenian patriarchs visited one another and went to church
together. The Armenian even delivered the Benediction in
church, and afterwards entertained the Greek patriarch, the
Turkish pasha being among the guests.[1]

---

[1] From time immemorial the monophysite Armenians have shared the Church

Arsen also criticised the slovenliness with which the Greeks conducted their services. Their priests, no less than their laity, wore turbans in church, and the monks attended without their cloaks. Their Patriarch ate sweetmeats in Lent and on fast days; at Bethlehem on the feast of the Nativity a mass of pilgrims slept in the church and defiled it. The reference here is hardly to the usage of incubation in a church, which still lasted on in the Caucasian Churches, especially on the night of the Feast of St. John. Probably the pilgrims used the Church of Bethlehem as a caravanserai. Is it possible, however, that Arsen merely witnessed the all-night service which we find in old Eastern prayerbooks, e. g. in the Armenian? It is noteworthy that he says nothing in the book either for or against the use of the two fingers in blessing.

This wholesale canonization was both cause and effect of the growing belief that Moscow was the third Rome. Russia was no longer beholden to a Constantinople that was become a centre of Mahommedan heresy. The Sun of righteousness there eclipsed shone afresh on the Moskva.

Three men above others had worked for this triumph of nationalism in the ecclesiastical sphere, Joseph Sanin, prior and founder of the Volokolam monastery and his disciples Daniel and Macarius, both metropolitans of Moscow. They represented three generations from 1500 to 1550. Their monastery was a fashionable training school for the higher clergy and a focus of nationalist propaganda. They had not however Nikon's idea of asserting the rights of the Church as such; and consolidation of the spiritual ran for them hand in hand with aggrandisement of the Moscovite despotic state. The Church consecrated the State which in return protected it and guaranteed its privileges. The way was marked out for the Church in Russia to become what it was in old Byzantium, the humble servant of secular despotism. Nikon a century later essayed to free the Church of which he was the head from

of the Sepulchre with the Latins and Greeks and great pictures of their saints adorn its walls. If ever the Holy Synod of Moscow acquires jurisdiction over the Holy places, the Armenian heretics certainly, and the Latin schismatics probably, will be served with notices to quit.

Erastian control. He met the fate of St. Thomas of Canter-
bury. He championed the Patriarchal against the Imperial
prerogatives, and failed. His failure signified the erection in
Russia of a lay Papacy of the Tsar which lasted until yesterday.

Nikon's Reforms

Shchapov fifty years ago compared the Raskol to Lot's
wife who looked back, and in the act of doing so was turned into
a pillar of salt. The comparison is unfair; for the schism was
for those who engaged in it the beginning of religious emancipation, of inward liberty and comparative enlightenment.
It is the dominant orthodox Church which may rather be
accused of petrifaction and putrifaction. It remains true
however that the Raskol leaders in the 17th century stood for
the exclusive nationalism in spiritual matters that had triumphed a hundred years earlier under Ivan in the Stoglav
council. They could not rid themselves of the old suspicion
of the Levantine Greek. Nikon conquered it, and even headed
a reaction against a nationalism which prejudiced the ecumenicity of his country's Church, and was an implicit negation of
its claim to be a worldwide and ancient faith. In his ignorant
zeal for ecumenicity he was ready to adopt from the fawning
Greek ecclesiastics, whom he invited to Moscow and who were
ready to deceive him, much that was merely modern, much that
was trivial. The partisans of antiquity were shocked to note
how whimsical were his alterations of the old service books.
Why substitute *temple* for *church* and *vice versa*? Why change
children into *scions*, *cross* into *tree*, and so on? Why was a
new fangled phrase better than an old one? How did the old
reading violate divine writ? They discerned accordingly little
in his corrections but wilful hatred of the old, and parodied his
instructions to Arsenius thus: "Print the books as you like,
provided only you discard the old way."

Their disgust with the correctors was complete, when it was
found — what modern scholarship confirms — that they did
not in practice adhere to their own canon of comparing the
Cyrillic texts with *old* Greek books. Recent liturgical scholars
in Russia have shewn that of the 500 Greek MSS. brought to

Moscow by Sukhanov for Nikon's use from the East only seven were consulted in editing the service books afresh. The Greek euchologion printed by the Latins at Venice in 1602 was almost the only text which they regularly employed. Nikon's intentions no doubt were good, but he and his band lacked the scholarship necessary to carry them out. Well might Avvakum, the Raskol leader, write to the Tsar as follows: "Thou, Michailovich, art a Russian, not a Greek. Then use your own native tongue, and forbear to depreciate it in Church, in home and elsewhere. Does God love us less than the Greeks? Has he not given us our books in our own tongue by the hand of Cyril and Methodius? What do we want better than that? The tongue of angels? Alas, that we may not hear until the general resurrection comes!" It was Nikon's substitution, probably suggested by Latin texts in which it survives, of *Kyrie eleison* for the old Russian equivalent *Gospodi pomilui* which motived this outburst. Avvakum and his partisans, notably Ivan Neronov and Stephan Boniface, were not in principle opposed to the use of Greek texts in editing the Russian ones. Under the patriarch Joseph (died 1652) they had even participated in the work of revision led by the learned monks whom Rtishchev brought from Kiev; and the old believers still use today the editions printed under Joseph. Their revolt was due to three causes: the violence of Nikon, the capricious manner in which under his auspices their Church was being Grecized, and the insolence with which the monks of Athos condemned their earlier essays in correction and made a bonfire of the service books printed in Moscow.

Having equipped himself, as he imagined, with the authority of the Sister Churches, Nikon took the first step in 1653 of imposing the use of three fingers in blessing. This at once evoked a protest from Paul, bishop of Kolomna, from Ivan Neronov, Protopope of the Kazanski church and from another Protopope Avvakum, or as we say, Habakkuk, of the ancient Yurievets convent on the Volga who was staying in Moscow. "It looks like winter coming," the latter is said to have remarked; and with the aid of another Protopope, Daniel of Kostroma, he proceeded to draw up a catena of authorities in

support of the use of two fingers — no less Greek in origin
than the rival use —and of the old fashion in the matter of
prostrations.   They presented their catena to the Tsar, thereby
embittering not a little their relations with Nikon, to whom the
Tsar passed it on and whose election as patriarch they had
opposed.   They pretended that any books corrected before
Nikon were orthodox, any after him Latin and heretical.
There was nothing he could do or suggest that was right.
But Nikon was too strong for them and Neronov quickly
found himself relegated to the Kamenski Monastery on the
Kubenski lake near Vologda.   Avvakum also found himself
excluded by his fellow clergy from the Kazanski Church when
he went thither prepared to celebrate as usual and read his
sermon to the congregation; thereupon he retired to Neronov's
house, where he read vespers in the bath-house and succeeded
in getting some of his old parishioners to attend his ministrations.   He did not, however, despair of the Tsar, and, in conjunction with other Protopopes, Daniel of Kostroma and
Longinus of Murom, who had been correctors of Service books
for the press under the Patriarch Joseph, drew up a petition
and despatched it to his prince.   The only result was that
Daniel was unfrocked and exiled to Astrakhan where he died;
Longinus was also unfrocked, and banished to Murom.   Avvakum, still a young man (he was born near Novgorod in 1620)
was spared at the Tsar's instance and banished with all his
family to the depths of Siberia, to the region called Daura.
On his way thither he sowed the seeds of religious revolt.
Such was the result of trying to preserve a mode of blessing
himself which every Russian had learned on his mother's knee,
Nikon himself among others.

From his place of exile Neronov wrote to the Tsar, accusing
Nikon of heresy, and the latter, aware of the fact that his prince
was not yet won over to the use of two fingers,— as according
to Ivanovski, Nikon himself was not at this stage, having only
taken action to please his Greek colleagues,— resolved to lay
matters before a Council, which was accordingly convened in
1654 in the royal palace.   Before it Nikon, no doubt ignorantly,
condemned the secret recitation at the beginning of the liturgy

of the priest's prayer for remission of his sins,— a topic I have discussed above; and he also urged the practice of depositing relics under the altar when a church was first consecrated. He thus reserved the issue of the two fingers, but in other respects aspired to change old customs in accordance with the Greek books. The plan of issuing corrected service books was not opposed, though it was found impossible to come to an agreement about prostrations and genuflexions. In support of the old rule on such points observed in Moscow, Paul of Kolomna, appealed to an old parchment, and recorded his opinion in the acts of the Council. By doing so he drew down on his head the wrath of Nikon who objected to learning when it did not accord with his views. No sooner was the Council at an end, than Paul was expelled from his see, subjected to corporal punishment and locked up in prison where he lost his reason and died in a manner unrecorded. The Raskolniki of the time, however, testify that he was burned alive near Novgorod.

Nikon had already despatched afresh Arsenius Sukhanov, on his return to Moscow, to Athos and other centres of the East in quest of Greek originals on which to base the revision he had in mind of the old Russian service books; for the proceedings of 1653–4 seem to have inspired even him with misgivings, not to be silenced by any knouting and exiling of his opponents. Accordingly he had resolved in 1654 to send a fresh mission of enquiry to Constantinople, and this time he selected a Greek named Manuel, who had lived for a time in Moscow, to lay his queries before the Patriarch Paisius and the doctors of New Rome. A year later about May 1655, Manuel returned with the answers which Paisius [1] of Constantinople had penned Dec. 1654 to the twenty-eight queries put to him by Nikon, and being on his own ground Paisius, after dealing with them, ventured to address to Nikon some very sound advice as to the necessity of compromise in such trumpery disputes: "You complain," he wrote, "of discrepancies on certain points of ritual which exist in local churches, and you apprehend harm to our faith from these differences. For that much I commend

[1] *Christ. Readings*, 1881, No. 3–4.

you, since one who so keenly fears to slip in small things is
likely to safeguard himself in great; nevertheless we would
correct your timidity.... If it should happen that certain
churches vary from others in usages of no importance and
unessential for the faith, for example with regard to the time [1]
when the liturgy is performed or over the question with what
fingers a priest ought to bless,[2] and such like, these issues should
provoke no dissensions... Nor ought we to imagine it to be
prejudicial to our orthodoxy, that somebody or other enter-
tains other modes of ritual observance than ourselves in matters
that are not essential to the Faith." He appeals to Epiphanius and other Fathers in proof that rites had grown up
little by little and were never uniform.

As to Nikon's queries with regard to the Sacraments he
writes: "As touching the polemics which you raise over the
rite of the divine Sacrament, we implore you to put a stop to
them; for a servant of the Lord it is unbecoming to embroil
himself over trifles which do not belong to the articles of
faith." This good advice Paisius tendered in the name of the
Council he had convoked at Constantinople to discuss the
Russian business. It was attended by 24 metropolitans.

None the less Paisius tempers these mild rebukes with stern
reproaches against Nikon's opponents, Paul of Kolomna and
Ivan Neronov, who had denied their signatures to the decrees
of the Moscow synod of 1654. They are corrupt and stiff-
necked schismatics whom Nikon will do well to excommunicate,
because they have impugned the validity of the prayers that
Paisius and other Greek Patriarchs have approved. As to
the number of fingers, although, as we have seen, Paisius
regarded it as a matter of little importance, he recognizes
that ancient Greek custom in making the sign of the cross was
in favor of joining the first three fingers, for the three joined
together symbolized the Trinity better than two. The epistle
of Paisius was accepted later on as authoritative by the Russian
Council of 1667.

---

[1] The Greeks celebrated at the third hour, except on Holy Thursday and Saturday, when the service was held in the evening, as in Armenia.

[2] Palmer in his work "The Patriarch and the Tsar," vol. II, p. 408 inexplicably
omits the words: "with what fingers to bless."

To return to Nikon. Duly installed as patriarch, he proceeded to search the library of his residence, and in it he found a chrysobulla or patriarchal document relating to the establishment of the Russian Patriarchate in 1589. It was dated May 8, 1590 and bore the subscriptions of the Eastern patriarchs, who assisted, Jeremiah of Constantinople, ecumenical patriarch, and others. In it, it was stipulated that the said patriarch must in all matters agree with them, and it contained the symbol of faith in Greek, with the single epithet τὸ κύριον (Lord or chief) in the eighth clause. He found the same symbol inscribed in Greek letters upon a cope brought to Moscow two hundred and fifty years before by the Metropolitan Photius. He also noted sundry omissions and additions in the service books of his Church.

A visit was paid to Moscow in April, 1653, by the deposed Athanasius Patellarius, formerly Patriarch of Constantinople, nine months after Nikon's elevation to his new dignity. Athanasius died in April, 1654, on his return journey, at the monastery of Lubni in the Government of Poltava, but during his stay in Russia in receipt of royal alms, he had urged Nikon not to insist on the use of the two fingers in blessing, and also to promulgate the rest of the so-called 'reforms' which he was minded to introduce, regardless of the circumstance that they directly violated the decisions of the Council of Stoglav or a hundred heads.

The Council of Stoglav

This Council had been held in 1551 expressly to decide many of the issues now to be decided by Nikon according to his newer lights. The first of these regarded the number of fingers to be extended in blessing or exorcising oneself or others (it is all the same thing) with the sign of the cross. The Council was motived in its decision by various reasons: because Christ had so blessed his apostles at his ascension; because the ikon of Tikhvin at Novgorod, of the Mother and Child, painted, like so many holy pictures, by St. Luke, represented the Messiah extending two fingers, and not one, as the Monophysites, or three, as the Latins were supposed to do. Ivanovski irreverently suggests that the said ikon was never painted by St. Luke at all. Thirdly, the Council appealed to a passage of the Father Theodoret, which Ivanovski, who is monstrously critical when by being so he can upset Old believers, declares to be supposititious. He deals similarly with a certain legend about S. Meletius, bishop of Sebaste and later on patriarch of Alexandria, and shews that the Stoglav misinterpreted their Theodoret and Sozomen.

The same Council had insisted on a double *Alleluia* as opposed to a triple one, and had argued, with more subtility than we might expect from such an assembly, that as the word *Alleluia* already signified the same thing as *Glory to thee God*, therefore, if you repeated it thrice and added that formula, you really repeated it four times, at the risk of implying four persons in the Trinity instead of three,— a shocking impiety of which in the fifth and succeeding centuries the Armenians and other monophysites commonly accused the adherents of the Council of Chalcedon. In favour of the double *Alleluia* the Stoglav Fathers also adduced an old 'Life' of S. Euphrosyn of Pskov according to which the Virgin herself stood sponsor, in a dream she vouchsafed to the saint, for this particular usage. But the Council of 1667, which could be critical at the expense of a theological antagonist, unkindly voted this 'Life' to be an apocryph. We have already noticed that the Stoglav decided in favour of reciting in clause 8 of the symbol not both, but only one, no matter which, of the rival epithets which in many MSS. dignified the Spirit. Another of their canons, No. 95, is of peculiar interest, because it prescribes the keeping of the Sabbath, no less than of the Sunday, as a holy day or feast, in accordance with the so-called canons of the Apostles, already abrogated by canon 29 of the Council of Laodicea of A. D. 343–381. In Russia it seems that the former set of canons were ascribed to Saints Peter and Paul, and Joasaph, a Patriarch who preceded Nikon, had anathematised those who sabbatised[1] and blasphemously invoked in favour of doing so the authority of St. Peter. This Sabbatarian precept

[1] The Sabbatarians still exist in Russia as a separate sect.

of the Stoglav Council the Raskol themselves set aside, so exposing themselves to a charge of inconsistency.

Nikon's adherents in 1667 imputed no malice to the Bishops who formed the Stoglav Council in 1551, nothing worse than simplicity and ignorance, as if Moscow had made a great stride in the matter of enlightenment during the hundred years. What had really happened in the interim was that the Rulers of Moscow had got into touch with the leading Greek sees in the epoch of their deepest decadence and darkest ignorance, with the result that a certain revival of Greek learning was observable in the higher ranks of the Russian clergy. Any revision of Slav rites and texts could under such conditions only lead to elimination of much that was ancient and sincere. But the chief significance of the Stoglav council lay in this:— it marked the triumph of a tendency, which had long been at work, to elevate the Russian Church from being a mere see under the jurisdiction of Constantinople to the dignity of an independent national Church. It was a grave shock to Russian Christians when the Patriarch of Constantinople insisted that the metropolitan Isidore, lately consecrated by him, must attend the Council of Florence. He did so, but on returning to Moscow was deposed. The fall of Constantinople was regarded in Moscow as a punishment of the Greeks for their apostasy, and the conviction gained ground that, old and new Rome having both of them apostatised, Moscow was the third Rome and the Tsar the only orthodox prince. Russian divines now began to cast about for an apostolic origin of their Church, and the legend grew up that St. Andrew had founded it. Nikon accepted this myth.[1]

A legend was also started that the rulers of Moscow derived their secular authority direct from Prus, a brother of the Emperor Augustus. With the triumph of the centralized state at Moscow over the appanages, or more or less autonomous

[1] Similarly the Armenians, when they began to quarrel with the Greeks and wanted their Church to be something better than a dependency of Caesarea of Cappadocia, invented the fable that Christ had descended in person at Valarshapat before the eyes of a Catholicos — who was really a Greek missionary. Simultaneously they appropriated to themselves the Syriac legend of King Abgar and Addai.

local Slavonic provinces, it was also felt to be necessary to assemble in the capital the local cults of saints dispersed all over Russia in almost every town and village. It was like the ancient Roman adoption of the gods of Veii, which were dragged with due pomp from their own city to Rome. The famous ikon of the Saviour reverenced at Novgorod was now removed to Moscow, as were countless relics and miraculous pictures from other places. By order of Ivan the terrible, a search for local saints and legends began in 1547; and 40 were promptly discovered, whose miracles entitled them to a place in the new national pantheon. Macarius the metropolitan was charged to compile an all-Russian hagiology, and thenceforth the Russian Church could not be accused of lacking saints and miracle-workers.

The position of affairs in 1655

We are now at the year 1655, and twelve years are to pass before the Council of 1667 consummates the schism already begun in the bosom of Russian Christianity. During those years no effort was spared to bring Moscow into closer association with Greek centres of piety, to assimilate old Slav rites to such Greek models as were obtainable. Russian prelates could not but reverence the Greek Church as the parent of their own religion, and their first patriarch Job had been consecrated by Jeremiah of Constantinople, as Philaret by Theophanes of Jerusalem. It was after all a slender minority that raised among themselves doubts as to the orthodoxy of the Greeks, and Stefan Bonifatsi, Nikon's rival for the patriarchate, expressly bore witness thereto in his *Book on the Faith*, printed in Moscow in 1649,— a work much appealed to at a later date by the Raskol on account of the chronology it afforded them of Antichrist's reign on earth. Nevertheless, as Ivanovski candidly recognizes, there was always a school of thinkers in his country that distrusted the Greeks. The early chronicler of Kiev, Nestor, wrote that they were ever deceivers, and the natural antipathy of a virile race for the debased Levantine was intensified by the open apostasy to Rome of the Greek Emperor, John Palaeologus and his higher clergy at the Council of Florence in 1439, when under the guidance of the Patriarch Ignatius even Isidore, the Greek Metropolitan of Moscow, became a backslider, to the horror of Prince Vasili and his subjects. The result was that Russian Christians then formed the conviction that no orthodoxy survived in the entire world outside their own pale, and the fall of Constantinople was regarded as a judgment upon backsliders. As for the Western Church the Russians consistently regarded it as the vilest of heresies, and have never ceased to empty the vials of their wrath and scorn upon the Poles, because, being Slavs, they are filled with the spirit of apostasy. The recent war, as regards Russia and Austria, was, from one point of view, an episode in the age-long struggle of Byzantium and Rome. It reproduced once more the quarrel of the Patriarch Photius and the Pope of Rome for jurisdiction over Bulgaria just over a thousand years ago.

Abominating the West and suspicious of the East, it is not wonderful that the Orthodox Church has ever suffered from intellectual anaemia and chosen for its motto: "no learning, no heresy." Nikon's patronage therefore of Greek learning only served to rouse distrust of his new methods and placed a fresh weapon in the hands of those whom his autocratic violence had already alienated. His associations with Kiev and the doctors of South Western Russia did not in any way weaken these prejudices, for Kiev during the XVIth and XVIIth Centuries was little more than a centre of Latin culture; amid the Little Russians there had been a movement in the XVIth Century for union with Rome; and not only in Eastern Galicia, but also in the Polish province of Cholm (or Holm), there are still found millions of Ruthenes or Little Russians, who were educated by those greatest of teachers, the Jesuits, three centuries ago, still retaining the Cyrillic Slav rites, but recognizing the jurisdiction of the Bishop of Rome.

It deepened popular suspicions against the "Correctors," that they allowed to be printed in Moscow various books of doubtful orthodoxy written by divines of these outlying and more or less Latinized Slav churches. Such was the "Catechism" of Laurence Zizania (an ominous name) of Korets,

now in the Volynski or Volhynia Government. Zizania wrote
in Lithuanian about 1600 and was a teacher at Lvov, or Lemberg, in doctrine opposed to the Uniats. Nevertheless, as we
might expect in a book written in a city so deeply influenced by
Jesuit learning, his Catechism was tainted with Latin heresies
and even inculcated the doctrine of Purgatory. The Boyar
Rtishchev incurred censure because in his school near Moscow
he admitted teachers from Kiev; and in 1650 three conservative Russian divines, Ivan Vasilev Zasetski, Luke Timothy
Golosov, and Constantine Ivanov, clerk of the Blagoveshchenski or Annunciation church met at the monk Saul's lodg-
ings in order to formulate their indictment against an institution in which Greek and Western Slav learning was held in
esteem.

In the Spring of 1655 Nikon [1] availed himself of the presence
in Moscow of two foreign prelates, Macarius of Antioch and
Gabriel of Servia, to convene a synod, which he hoped would
support him in his emendations of the Russian Service books,
and in the use of three fingers instead of two. There was also a
dispute as to the right ceremony of reconciling Latins, which
meant Poles, to the Orthodox Communion; some holding that
they should be rebaptized; others, merely anointed. Nikon
here shewed better sense than the Greek Church did, by rang-
ing himself with the latter party, who had on their side the
weight of the ancient and undivided Church. The synod met
in March and confirmed the decisions arrived at by the Council
of the year before. It also gave its formal approval to a new
edition of the *Sluzhebnik* or missal which was printed and distributed towards the close of the year to all the churches in
Russia; it was the first of the corrected books to be thus distributed "by authority."

Nikon, in spite of his dictatorial instincts, was consistently
anxious to present his reforms as an expression of the mind of
the entire Orthodox Church and not of the Russian hierarchy
alone. For this reason in 1655–56 he had printed and distributed a collection of writings, called *Skrizhal*, relative to the crisis,
penned in 1653 by Paisius of Jerusalem, which Arsenius had

[1] Macarius *Hist.* vol. 11.

rendered into Russian. The Synod of April 1656 ratified its contents. *Skrizhal* was the Russian equivalent for the tables of the Mosaic commandments or a bishop's pectoral. The book contained a commentary on the liturgy and other priestly rites, with the Byzantine prelate's letter on the use of the two fingers and the *credo*. In a later edition were included Nikon's address to the Synod of 1656 and other controversial tracts. In that year Nikon thought the time was at last come for putting an end to the differences which prevailed in the rites and books used in the churches all over Russia, and he resolved to call in *en masse*, in order to bring about their destruction, all the discordant texts, and to issue instead to all parishes his authorized versions. He was willing to brave the chorus of disapproval sure to be roused by the wholesale condemnation of books printed by his predecessors as well as of MSS. which had been for centuries the object of almost superstitious reverence and had been from the beginning in the hands of Russian saints and workers of miracles; for he had secured in advance the approval of Macarius, Patriarch of Antioch, of Gabriel of Serbia, of Gregory of Nicea and of Gedeon of Moldavia, who were all staying in Moscow and present at his Synod in 1656. The Synod met on February 12, the day of St. Meletius, and began with the perusal of an apocryphal life of the Saint, in which it was related how, when engaged in a controversy with the Arians, he had drawn sparks of fire from heaven by joining two fingers together and then adding a third in crossing himself.[1] Next Macarius was formally asked to interpret the legend, and answered that it signified the usage on which Nikon had set his heart; whereupon the Synod ratified it as an act symbolic of the Holy Trinity. The members of the Council then proceeded to the Uspenski church to hear mass which was performed by the prelate Macarius, Gabriel

---

[1] The usage condemned was that of extending the index and middle finger, while crouching the fourth and fifth over the thumb in the palm of the hand. The extended middle finger was slightly bent. The explanation now given of this usage by Greek monks is that the first two fingers represent IC, the other two and the thumb XC, i.e. the customary Greek abbreviations for 'Jesus Christ.' Nikon substituted the rule to make the sign on the forehead with the first three fingers of the right hand.

and Gregory, Metropolitan of Nicea; and solemnly standing
before the Tsar who was present, these three anathematized
the use of two fingers as an Armenian heresy approved by
Theodoret, the Nestorian, all present joining in their anathema.
But this somewhat mechanical unanimity did not yet satisfy
Nikon, so he summoned yet another Council in the following
April (25th), at which he adduced the authority of Athanasius
and Paisius, the Patriarchs of Constantinople and Jerusalem
for the change; once more the use of two fingers was anathematized, this time as an innovation (!) and as savouring of the
Arian and Nestorian heresies.

The rebaptism of Latins was also condemned, and more
wisely, and six Poles were marched in *ad hoc* and reconciled
to the Church merely by unction with the *Muron* or holy chrism
mixed by Nikon on the Great Thursday.   Some of the Russian
clergy present were nevertheless scandalized at such facility
of conversion being granted to Latin heretics; but in the end
they yielded to the arguments of Macarius who adduced precepts in favour thereof from the nomocanons or books of ecclesiastical law and discipline, and the Tsar clinched the matter by
lending the weight of his authority to a recognition of the orders
and baptism of the Catholic and Southern Russian Churches.
The decision, we may remark, was nevertheless in direct contra-
vention of the earlier rituals (*potrebnik*) issued under the
Patriarchs Joasaph and Joseph and of the rule made by the
great Patriarch Philaret; for these authorities laid it down that
not only Latins, but orthodox White Russians as well, who had
received baptism by sprinkling only, were to be rebaptized.

Orthodox historians naively remark that these "reforms"
roused the opposition of many who by reason of the excessive
belief in mere ritual were unable to distinguish it from dogma,
as if the older practices had not been anathematized by the
subservient Greek patriarchs mustered in Moscow *as heretical,*
e. g. as Armenian, as Arian, as Nestorian.   If Paul of Kolomna
could not distinguish ceremony from belief, neither could
Nikon and the Tsar.   You do not excommunicate and hurl
anathemas except at heretics, still less whip and burn alive
men who are perfectly orthodox, and only err by being simple-

minded and conservative. The "reforms" outraged not a few of the higher clergy; some openly murmured, others kept silence from fear of sharing the fate of Paul; and their stiff-necked obstinacy and restlessness, as Ivanovski styles their feelings of dissatisfaction, rapidly spread beyond the clergy and took hold of the masses of the people, who could not believe that men whom they so deeply venerated were misguided heretics.

The Fall of Nikon

And now a reaction set in against Nikon and all his works, provoked by his headstrong courses, cruelty and violence. For a time the stars seemed to fight in their courses against him. As is usual in times of popular excitement, portents were seen, the heavens were darkened and comets sped across the void. Dreams and visions were of the order of the day. The Almighty himself appeared demanding that the printing presses should be suspended from their impious work and destroyed. The Virgin and St. Paraskeve joined in his expostulations. Not only the inferior clergy were outraged; their indignation spread to the Boyars or great proprietors above and to the peasants below; it even penetrated the Palace of the Tsar. Plague and war were endemic then as now in the land, and served to enhance the general discontent. In August 1656 the mob broke into the Uspenski Church and assailed Nikon with the accusation of having set a heretic, Arsenius Sukhanov, to tamper with the holy books. Overwhelmed by their menaces Nikon hastily quitted Moscow, and retired to the Voskresenski monastery of New Jerusalem built by himself in 1656 in imitation of the Church of the *Anastasis*.

The very forwardness of Nikon in exiling his antagonists served indirectly to diffuse over Russia the rumour of his own impiety and apostasy. He had had Avvakum (Habbakuk) deported to Siberia, but he had forgotten to cut out his tongue beforehand,— a precaution he took with many of his antagonists. The result was that the exile spread the tidings, as he travelled, of the profanation of the old religion. In scores of villages they listened to his seductive preaching, and at Tobolsk

he even converted to his views the Archbishop Simeon. Neronov, we saw, had been incarcerated at Vologda in the Simonov
Spasso-kamenski monastery, but the conditions of seclusion
in that day were not so rigorous as a modern State knows how
to impose. Villagers anxious to know what was passing in
Moscow flocked round him and eagerly imbibed his teaching,
for men are everywhere more prone to believe evil than good
about the men in authority, especially in Russia. For a time
it looked as if Nikon might share the fate of Maximus, the over-
bold Greek corrector of a generation earlier. Even in modern
England it is easy to get up a heresy hunt. How easy then
must it not have been in XVIIth Century Russia. Western
Europe was in those far-off days, as in our own, envisaged by
all "true" Russians as a contaminated region, the home of
Satan and of every Satanic innovation. Even to-day there
are innumerable Old believers in Russia who eschew tobacco
and potatoes on the ground that they were brought in from the
West by the accursed *nemtsy*, i. e. Germans and Scandinavians.
When the first Duma was instituted in 1905, and certain liberals
therein ventured to ask questions about how the money of
taxpayers was being spent, Russian conservatives denounced
them as infected with the "Western Poison." It was worse in
the XVIIth Century to be accused of Latinizing than of Judaizing. Nikon accused some of his opponents of using tobacco,
but that was barely so grave as the charge of Latin heresy now
spread abroad against himself, and the grand Seigneur or
Boyar Pleshcheev reminded Neronov of the prophecy contained in the *Book of Faith* (see above p. 54) of schisms and
dissensions in the Church; that book, he said, was full of warn-
ings concerning the backsliding of the West and the apostasy
of the Uniats to the Western Church. Let Nikon beware lest
thereby they also should suffer. Most of Nikon's little
improvements in ritual were set down to his Latin heresy, in
particular the use of three fingers in blessing, the impressing on
the eucharistic wafer of a four-cornered cross, the triple Alleluia, and the substitution in the phrase "offering the thrice
holy hymn" (trisagion) of the word *chanting* or *intoning* for
offering. For the word substituted among the Latinized

Slavs signified accompaniment by the organ of the voice, and of the organ the Eastern Christians had the same horror as John Knox of the "box o' whistles." Nikon was freely likened to the Greek apostates Isidore and Ignatius, and accused of truckling to the Pope of Rome.

Ivanovski and Macarius set before us a graphic account of the events which ensued and culminated in the emergence of the Raskol as a counter-Church after the Councils of 1666–7. In 1658 the opposition to Nikon, confined five years before to a few of the higher ecclesiastics, began to swell into a popular movement of such dimensions as to engender misgivings in the Tsar. It was in vain that Nikon at the eleventh hour was cowed into making a few concessions; for example, to the clergy of the Uspenski Church in Moscow permission was given to use as they liked either the old or the new Service books. This was because Neronov, who had now been shorn as a monk and taken the name of Gregory in religion, had from fear of schism relaxed his opposition to Nikon's revision of the church books. Nikon had many enemies in the hierarchy itself, in especial Pitirim of Krutits. Not a few ladies of the court and relatives of the Tsar were inflamed against Nikon by Avvacum's denunciations. Boyars or nobles whom he had treated with such rigour, when in the Tsar's absence he was entrusted with the administration of the realm, now saw their opportunity to retaliate. They cast all their influence with the Tsar against Nikon, who in 1658 suddenly found himself fallen from the royal favour.

On July 6th of that year Teimuraz, the prince of the neighbouring little kingdom of Georgia, whose capital was at Tiflis, visited Moscow. He was a Christian and orthodox, for early in the VIIth Century his ancestors had abandoned their communion with the monophysite church of Armenia and gone over to the Byzantines. In an age when few independent Christian states survived in the East, the warriors of Georgia retained their freedom; it was natural therefore that this prince, who bore the ancient name of Teimuraz, should be accorded a splendid reception in the Tsar's capital. On such an occasion the Patriarch would naturally have taken, after the Tsar, the most prominent part in the ceremonies, but it was noticed that he was absent. He had not been invited, and his emissary on his way to the reception was assaulted by the Tsar's attendants and told to get out of the way. On July 8th, the feast of the Kazan ikon of the Theotokos, the Tsar in turn absented himself because Nikon was celebrating. On the 10th he also took no notice of Nikon's invitation to him to attend the Hours, and he sent a noble to inform the prelate that he was offended and would not come to hear him repeat the liturgy.

Nikon was not the man to admit himself in the wrong or to take the first step in reconciliation with his prince. He quitted the church on foot leaning on a common crutch, and turned his steps to Ilinka, where lay the hostel of the Resurrection Monastery. There he halted three days and then quitted Moscow for good, declining any more to occupy himself with the business of the patriarchate. His quarrel with the Tsar, according to Ivanovski, was due to nothing in particular. They no longer sympathized; the nobles had stirred the Tsar's distrust, and the latter looked askance on Nikon as one who had pressed him to undertake the unsuccessful war with Sweden from which he had lately returned. The chief reason was that Nikon interfered in the administration. There was no room for two heads of the State.

From the Fall of Nikon to the Council of 1666

A time of chaos followed the departure of Nikon. The affairs of the Church were entrusted to his enemy Pitirim, the Metropolitan of Krutits, the nobles had succeeded in thoroughly poisoning the mind of their Sovereign against him, and even incited the people to protest openly against his reforms. The Raskolniki now began to shew themselves in public, and Avvakum after many years exile in Siberia was recalled and given a position in the Kremlin. The Tsar patronized him afresh and went out of his way to ask his blessing. There was even talk of his being made the Tsar's chaplain. The renewal of Court favour, however, did not abate Avvakum's Raskol enthusiasm. He undertook to debate with Theodore Rtishchev the subject of Nikon's reforms, and these discussions degenerated into noisy scenes.

About the same time the monk Gregory Neronov returned from his place of confinement. Haunted with the fear of a schism between the Russian and the Eastern Churches, he had, as remarked above, left the ranks of the Raskol; but he continued to agitate against the correction of the Service books, and addressed petitions to the Tsar stigmatizing Nikon as a son of perdition and demanding his condemnation by a Council. In this agitation he was joined by several notables who till now had maintained a guarded silence. Among these were Spiridion Potemkin of the Pokrovsky Monastery, an uncle of Theodor Rtishtchev, and Theodor Trofimov, deacon of the Church of the Annunciation, Dositheus and Cornelius. Dositheus later on headed the Raskol among the Don Cossacks of Olonets. Nicetas, a pope in Suzdal, and Lazarus of Romanova also repudiated Nikon's reforms.

The populace of Moscow was by now infected with enthusiasm for Avvakum; his adherents ran along the streets and stood in the public places proclaiming "the grace of the old piety." Street fanatics pursued the Tsar's equipage, appealing to him to restore the ancient religion. In the provinces equally agitation raged against Nikon and petitions from the clergy and bishops poured in to the Tsar, denouncing the book *Skrizhal* which Nikon had disseminated in defence of his policy. Raskol and Boyars joined in demanding the expulsion of Nikon from the patriarchate. Even members of the royal family joined in the outcry, for example Theodosia Morozov, one of Avvakum's penitents and widow of Glieb Ivan Morozov, with her sister the Boyarina Eudokia Urusov. They even went to the length of repudiating Nikon's baptism. They died in 1675 after being scourged, racked and imprisoned in underground cells at Borovsk in the Kaluga Government, their martyrdom aiding the spread of the Raskol.

It is not wonderful if the clergy in many places resumed the old books and modes of singing; and if the authorities had been capable of good sense and moderation, they would have accepted the warning. The spiritual temperature was indeed rising, and as has happened again and again in times of stress, fanatics began to read the signs of the time in that fertile storehouse of religious dementia, the Apocalypse.

When the year 1000 of the Christian epoch arrived it was generally supposed that the reign of Antichrist was at hand and preluded the end of the world. It had passed away however, without much harm, and now the year 1666 was at hand, a date which the Raskol teachers connected with the number of the Beast, which, as everyone knows, was 666. *The Book of Faith*, widely current, as we have seen, in Russian religious circles, prophesied that this mystical date would witness a grand apostasy from the faith and the advent of the precursor of the Man of Sin or Antichrist, if not of that personage himself. Men's minds were stuffed with such speculations, and a seer from the Volga, a compatriot of Nikon, appeared on the scene with stories of his visions. He had passed a night in the company of Nikon and had witnessed a number of demons install him on a throne, crown him as if he were a king, prostrate themselves before him and cry: "Of a truth thou art our beloved brother," and so forth. Another fanatical monk, named Simeon, had his vision also of a huge serpent coiling his scaly folds around the palace of the Tsar and whispering into the latter's ear the blasphemies of the contaminated service books. Needless to say, the serpent was Nikon. The Tsar himself wrote despairingly to Nectarius, the patriarch of Jerusalem: "In our entire Church rites there lacks all uniformity, everyone in the churches follows what order he chooses." A Tsar of that age could not perhaps be expected to realize what is even among ourselves on the threshold of the XXth Century so little understood or desired that in religion the important thing is not conformity but communion.

And now the pendulum began to swing once more the other way,[1] for those who had brought back Avvakum and their partisans from the obscurity of their places of exile or of hiding, began to tremble at the wild success of their propaganda, which seemed to strike at the roots of all authority in ecclesiastical

---

[1] *Acts of the Moscow Councils of 1666-7*, Moscow, 1881, with introduction by Prof. Subbotin: Macarius *Hist.*, t. 12, p. 640 foll.

and even in political matters. Hatred of Nikon had temporarily won for the Raskol teachers the support of the Boyars, but this alliance now began to crumble. The Tsar was persuaded in 1664 once more to relegate Avvakum to exile, and sent him this time to Mezen near Archangel. In those days travel was slow, and prisoners less circumscribed in their activities than to-day. It amounted in effect to a missionary tour; the following year Avvakum started back to attend the Council of 1666. On his way to and from Archangel he had spread his tenets right and left.

The Council of 1666

The Council of 1666 was ostensibly summoned by Imperial decree to pass sentence on the fallen Nikon, still the victim of the Tsar's displeasure and doubtless unpopular with many powerful people. In the first session, after the *credo* had been duly recited by all the members, three leading questions were put to each and all: "Do you accept the four Greek Patriarchs as orthodox? Do you accept as such their printed books and MSS.? Do you accept the findings of the Council of 1654?" These questions only bore indirectly on Nikon and removed the question of his personal actions from purview. The Council could condemn him, yet accept his handiwork, the corrected books, the three fingers and the rest. They did both. The result of the manoeuvre was what might be expected. All present answered the questions in the affirmative and gave their signatures in that sense. The next session was held under the presidency of the Tsar himself, in his *Stolovaya* or banqueting hall, his privy council assisting. The Tsar took up his parable against the Raskol propaganda, declaring it to be directed against the Church and its sacraments. He recited the symbol from the Chrysobull of 1593, in the eighth clause of which, as we saw, the one epithet *Kyrion* was used of the Holy Ghost. As he was certainly unacquainted with Greek, this was for a Tsar of that age a very impressive feat. Pitirim, formerly Metropolitan of Novgorod, who had taken charge of the affairs of the Church when Nikon was disgraced, tendered in the name thereof its thanks to the Monarch for his defence of orthodoxy, which the Raskol had never in any way assailed. All who were present, Pitirim affirmed, unfeignedly accepted the said symbol.

In the third session the Raskol teachers were called up for judgment singly or in batches. They were invited to accept the corrected books and to repent, the charge preferred against them being, not that they adhered to the pre-Nikonian texts and rites, but that they condemned the new ones, that they decried the authority of the Eastern patriarchs, calumniated Nikon and falsely accused the Muscovite clergy of denying the dogmas of the Incarnation and Resurrection. Some of the accused remained impenitent, led by Avvakum and Lazar; some sincerely abjured the supposed errors, as Alexander, Bishop of Vyatka, who in 1663 had protested to the Tsar against Nikon's correction of the creed and service books. An abjuration of his errors was also forced from the monk Gregory Neronov; others abjured, but, as the event proved, insincerely, such as Nicetas and the Deacon Thedor or Theodore, who eventually had his tongue cut out. The obstinate were excommunicated and sent to prison; the rest were hurried off to monasteries to undergo discipline and be subjected to further examination. The synod closed its deliberations by unanimously condemning the new sect and ordaining that all incumbents should use the new books.

The Raskol leaders were confirmed in their opposition by the knowledge that the Greek Ecclesiastics brought to Moscow were ignorant of the issues at stake. The latter could not speak Russian and were tools in the hands of Nikon and of the court party who alternately cajoled and overawed, bribed and menaced them. They countersigned Nikon's edicts, but did not in the least understand them. The Raskol leaders had on their side a learned Greek, named Dionysius, a monk from Athos, who had lived in Moscow for ten years before the patriarchs arrived and was familiar with the ins and outs of the quarrel, for he knew the Russian language and liturgies thoroughly well. A letter of his survives, written in 1667, in which he accuses them of being deceived, of knowing nothing of what was going on, of believing whatever they were told. ' If," he writes, "you would exercise your own judgment, avoid honours and gifts from princes and ecclesiastical authorities. But if you do, I warn you that you will share the fate of Maximus. They will intern you in a monastery, and you will never see your homes again."

Never was a great schism forced on a great Church upon a flimsier pretext, and the feverish anxiety of the triumphant faction to obtain the approval of foreign prelates for their innovations shewed plainly that in their hearts they felt many misgivings. This was why a few months later, in November 1667, the return to Moscow of Paisius of Alexandria and of Macarius of Antioch after a lapse of eleven years was made the occasion of a fresh meeting, this time to deal expressly with Nikon. The other Eastern prelates who had attended the last council were present along with sundry of the Greek clergy. Nikon was condemned — Ivanovski does not seem to know what for, but really of course because in an autocracy there is no room for two supreme authorities — and exiled to the Therapontov cloister; none the less the Synod approved of his revision of the Church books, as also of the book *Skrizhal* which as we saw above, was a stumbling-block in the path of old-fashioned Churchmen. The condemnations of 1666 were reaffirmed and those who resisted were anathematized, on the ground that, in adhering to the old order, they thwarted ecclesiastical authority and calumniated the orthodox eastern church as an heretical body. The excommunications pronounced against the dissidents were superfluous, for most of them had already withdrawn from communion with the Church. Three Patriarchs, fourteen metropolitans and eight archbishops, and others, in all 76 ecclesiastics signed the acts of this Synod which were then laid up for a perpetual record in the cathedral of Moscow.

But the decisions of the Stoglav council a century before had also to be got out of the way. It had solemnly anathematized the practices now declared to be orthodox. Accordingly its anathemas were as solemnly revoked as they had been pronounced, and the doctors who had attended it declared to have been the dupes of dreams and forgeries. Thus began that famous Raskol movement which still divides Russians, yet has undoubtedly contributed much to the social, moral and intellectual progress of the people and is destined, we may hope, to contribute yet more in the future.

K. Waliszewski, the historian of the first Romanovs, in his work (Paris 1909) entitled *Le Berceau d'une dynastie*, insists hardly less than Kostomarov and Miliukov on the fact that the events of 1667 laid the foundations of liberty and revolution in Russia. In respect of its originating causes and conceptions the schism, he freely admits (p. 416), "wore the air of a petrified fragment of old Moscovy. And yet its heart beat with an intense life, and it shewed itself capable of such a power of resistance and propaganda, of such a capacity for independent development, as two centuries of persecution could not master or subdue. It was to endure and grow, and in doing so itself to unfold new phases in spite of the immobility which its initial principle seemed to impose on it. It was to diversify itself in an infinity of ways; robust organisms were to spring up in its bosom and seek to bring about manifold phases of existence in harmony with all sorts of creeds. A day was also to come when revolutionaries, freed from all confessional interests, and also reactionaries, no less indifferent to dogmatic controversies, will contend for this problematic ally, the one party hailing him as an instrument of their socialistic and even anti-religious agitation, the other as an element of political and social regeneration... The Lazars and Avvakums vowed the society of their time to eternal fixity, and yet none the less and all unconsciously implanted therein principles that utterly contradicted their postulate. Stationary or retrograde in regard to the intellectual movement of their country along the paths of civilization, they nevertheless were sharers in that progress and added to the awakening of thought the awakening of conscience. The subjection of the Church to the State was only rendered possible by the general indifference of those concerned. By attracting to itself such believers as were more jealous than the rest of the liberties thus set at nought, the Raskol facilitated that policy; but at the same time it furnished the spirit of independence with an asylum of refuge of a kind to keep it alive and develop its energy."

APPENDIX TO CHAPTER I

P. AURELIO PALMIERI'S ACCOUNT OF THE RUSSIAN CLERGY

It is opportune, in illustration of Uzov's contentions, to add here the strictures on the status of the Russian country clergy in *La Chiesa Russa* by P. Aurelio Palmieri, O. S. A. (Firenze, 1908). He writes, p. 164, as follows: —

"Dobroklonsky, an esteemed historian of the Russian Church, thus speaks (t. ii, p. 147) of the defects which the inferior clergy contracted from the very beginning of Russian Christianity, and which still paralyze its mission: The chief defects of the clergy (in the 17th century) were the multiplicity of its members, the dependence of parish priests, their want of means, their intellectual ignorance and moral shortcomings. Against these drawbacks provisions were indeed made, but they did not avail to eradicate the evils and neutralized them only for a short time. The result was that they became inveterate."

"This author," continues Palmieri, "does not touch upon one of the principal defects, the absence of abnegation and of apostolic spirit in the clergy, a direct result of the servility to which it was habituated by the social conditions of Russia and the draconian laws of the Government.

"The inferior clergy live in parishes which in Russia have undergone the strangest vicissitudes, and have been reduced step by step from an unlimited autonomy to the level of mere succursals, branch offices, of the police or bureaus of the State. The Russian inferior clergy, from the first dawn of Russian Christianity, appear to us to have been already predestined to servitude. In the pre-Mongol epoch the material and moral conditions of the priesthood were so low that it was not the sons of boyars or of merchants or of well-to-do families that aspired to it, but only persons belonging to the lowest social strata, who regarded it as a rise morally or an employment for the sake of making both ends meet. This resulted,

as Golubinsky, the historian of the Russian Church, expresses
it (i. p. 448), in a priesthood of cossacks and proletarians....

"The ancient Russian Church was not organized, and the
choice of priests belonged more to the faithful than to the
bishops. In the Byzantine Empire, owing to the large number of dioceses, there was more familiarity between the hierarchy and lower clergy. Christian Russia in contrast possessed
to begin with a very limited number of sees, which were of
great territorial extent. There were no schools for the education of the clergy, and the bishop was not in a position to grasp
the needs of the new forms of Christianity growing up among
the Russian pagans who were embracing it. At first the
monasteries supplied the deficiency of pastors. The churches
of the cloister were transformed into parish churches, and
certain monks also devoted themselves to the task of sacerdotal ministry in the cities.

"The Parish churches were, to begin with, founded by
Russian princes or by private individuals or by the communities themselves. The first were kept up at the expense of the
princes, the second belonged exclusively to those who had
built them; they could be alienated or let, and formed part
of the hereditary patrimony. This gave rise to abuses, and
Russian councils, especially that of the Hundred Capita (or
Heads, *Stoglav*), sanctioned measures intended to put an end
to this traffic in edifices of worship. The other churches were
the property of the *mirs* or communities which erected them
in cities and villages. To the right of ownership the *mir*
added that of supervision, particularly in respect of the goods
belonging to the Church. The *mir* chose delegates whom it
charged to look after the economical interests of the parish,
one only at first, later on two. There were no laws relative
to the parochial clergy, and the faithful could increase or
diminish it at their pleasure. This right was a corollary of
the material conditions of the clergy in that age, for they
derived their livelihood from the community or *mir* which
sought their services.

"The priests of parishes were chosen by popular suffrage.
The choice made, a candidate presented himself before the

bishop, who laid hands on him, and ordained him, if he was not a priest: or, in case he were such already, he blessed him.[1] The bishop had no right to refuse a candidate so proposed, and, moreover, the ample gratuity which he received for the ordination of any priest whatever effectually silenced conscientious scruples, if he felt any. As years rolled by, the ease with which the priesthood was acquired and the lightness of the work required by the ministry produced a plethora of popes... It was enough for a candidate to secure a few votes or to adduce two witnesses to affirm that a certain parish needed a priest, and the bishop ignorant of the real facts, ordained the postulant. So the caste of popes assumed the aspect of a set of sweated operatives. The priests remained under the thumb of the laity, which could deny them the means of livelihood and expel them from their offices. Among the many competitors who presented themselves for the posts vacant in parishes, the *mir* chose those who most lowered the scale of their salary and of their tariff for ecclesiastical functions. This led, as a Russian bishop deplored, to lazy or drunken priests being chosen in preference to priests that were lettered or led good lives.[2] The nobility contributed to the decadence of clerical prestige. In fact many nobles scrupled not to present to the bishops, as candidates, their own serfs in order to secure for themselves part of what they earned as priests....
He continues on p. 168:—

"Notwithstanding, the progressive decadence of the autonomous régime of parishes and of the free choice of priests, though it led to so many evils, is deplored nowadays by reformers of the Russian Church, as an element in the dissolution of orthodoxy. The ancient parish was considered a juridical unit, legally organized and in political and religious aspects enjoying autonomy. The bishops had not the right to make what rules they liked in parishes, and if occasionally they attempted to, conflicts arose which dragged on for years. The *mir* had its *starosta* or head who together with the parishioners and clergy

---

[1] *Dobroklonsky*, iii, p. 53.
[2] Znamensky *Uchebnoe Rukovodstvo po Istorii russkoi Tserkvi*, 144–5, "School Handbook on the History of the Russian Church."

conducted the affairs of the Church. The constitution of parishes was in consequence lay rather than ecclesiastic, and it is exactly this lay character which so much recommends it to apostles of a laicization of the church of such a kind as would assimilate priests to municipal counsellors and the bishops to parliamentary deputies, the one group like the other subject to the jurisdiction of their electors.

"In the 18th Century the autonomy of parishes, opposed by the hierarchy and looked askance at by the Government, gradually declined, and its diminution contributed to the enslavement of the peasants, the spread of the Raskol and anaemia of religious sentiment.[1] In the *Ecclesiastical Code* of Peter the Great the parish is still regarded as a juridical personality, a legal association invested with the right to elect its own priests and those who served in the Church, and to agree with the clergy on terms that were legitimate. The parishioners also retain the right to nominate the *starosty*, who were allowed out of the collections made in church to raise hospices for beggars and hospitals or asylums for foundlings... Peter the Great limited the parochial right of choice by requiring that only men should be chosen as ministers who had completed their studies in diocesan schools. In the reign of Paul I, in order to render the parish clergy more docile instruments of Government, the Synod, in accordance with an imperial ukase, decided that the worthiest and best instructed candidates should be given preference over those who enjoyed the confidence and goodwill of the people; in this way Government candidates won a preference over parochial ones. At last an ukase of July 24, 1797, decreed the abolition for good of the custom of electing the parish clergy, and also annulled the permission given in the 18th century to the parish to present to the bishop for acceptance and confirmation a list of candidates enjoying the people's confidence. Later on the statute of ecclesiastical consistories, promulgated March 27, 1841, cancelled the last traces of parochial autonomy, and laid it down that sacerdotal ordination is a right which belongs immediately and exclusively to the eparchial or episcopal authority. Thus the political slavery

---

[1] Papkov, in *Revue Internationale de Théologie*, 1900, t. 8, p. 554.

of the Church entered the last phase of its evolution. The lower clergy, withdrawn from the free choice of the people, became a laughing-stock in the hands of the hierarchy, and the latter in its turn, transformed into one of the many cog-wheels of the State, ceased to feel any solicitude for the liberty of the Church, and took its orders blindly from the lay bureaucracy of the Synod. In addition the parish clergy were condemned to truckle to a hierarchy they cordially hated just because, being enrolled in the monasteries, it was dominated by ascetic ideals, and could not understand the wants of married priests." He continues on p. 174: —

"The movement of reform now (1908) afoot in Russia aims at the resurrection of the parish as the chief factor in a renovation of the Church. The memorandum of Count Serge Witte on the present situation of the Orthodox Church published in the *Slovo* of March 28, 1905, insists before all things on the reorganization of the primitive Russian ecclesiastical communities. The ancient parish, so his memorandum runs, was as it were the channel in which religious life flowed. The pernicious revolution in ecclesiastical administration, thought out and effected by Peter the Great, paralyzed its energies. In the parishes religious and social life before his time excelled in intensity. They formed juridical entities, autonomous units. The community built its own church, chose its own pastor and parochial ministrants. The parochial budget was regarded as of considerable importance, and out of the resources of the members of the community were maintained the church, the manse, the school and works of charity. The parochial balance also took the place of an agrarian bank, and could be used to aid the necessitous. The community judged its members and scrupled not even to penetrate the sanctuary of the home in order to restrain it from moral ruin. And yet an institution so useful for the development of religious sentiment and social harmony crumbled to nothing after the reforms of Peter the Great were adopted, and of it nothing remained but the name.

"What causes produced the fall of the parish? Witte shows it with a sincerity rare in a statesman, and therefore, if we quote his words, we run no risk of deserving the epithet of systematic detractors of the Russian Church. The aggrandisement in the 18th century of the rights of the nobility over the bondmen of the glebe suffocated ever more and more the initiative of the communities which had lost their religious autonomy. The Government policy of concentration, pursued with such obstinate ferocity that any union of people which took the name of a *fraternal association* was looked upon as a revolutionary or secret society, dealt pitiless blows at the autonomous organization of the parishes. More than that, the reformer of Russia looked upon the Church as part of the complex mechanism of the State, and linked with its holy duties a policeman's and inquisitor's tasks, utterly out of keeping with the dignity of its character. The priest was charged to draw up an exact list of those who paid the imposts and was obliged, in violation of the secret of the confessional, to draw up a report of political plots or offences. With the change of their character from that of shepherds of souls to inspectors of police, the clergy forfeited the confidence of the people, and the ties which united them with it were snapt for good.

"The decadence of the parish brought with it another inconvenience. The community ceased to take an interest in the material conditions of its pastors, and the latter had to provide for the support of their families out of the scanty glebe the State allotted to the parochial clergy and out of the legal contributions of the villagers. The result was that they fell into extreme indigence, and often the Government was obliged to assign to their orphans lands intended for the maintenance of the churches; by consequence the clergy little by little took on the aspect of an hereditary caste and alienated still more completely the sympathies of the people.

"For the resurrection of the parish it is needful to reëstablish the participation of the parishioners in the economic management of the goods of the parish and in the choice of the clergyman.

"In the first centuries of Christianity not only priests, but bishops as well were chosen by the people, with the result that the one and the other came before their flocks as true pastors, and not in the character of intruders sent to govern a church by way of an act of grace or of rigour on the part of the political authority. In the case of the bishops the day seems still to be far off when their nomination will be made with the assistance of the people."

With these views of Palmieri may be compared those of Miliukov in his *Russian Civilization*, 1905, pt. 1, p. 149. He allows that the Raskol, though more attached to the letter and form of rites, yet were more penetrated than the masses around them by their inward spirit, and anyhow *lived* their religion. But he doubts whether it was so much a protest, as the above writers contend, against new restrictions imposed by the authorities of the Church on the free spiritual life of parishes and on their choice of parish priests. It is true that the priest as the elect of the mir little by little had his place taken by the *nominee* of the bishop, in such wise that the parish became a half administrative, half religious unit. But the change was less due to systematic crushing out of the interest taken by the laity in church matters than to the fact that most who were so interested went over to the raskol. Indifferentism was not forced on them, but was a natural growth. That is also, as we saw above, the view of Waliszewski.

Indeed the free election of the pope, even when it was a reality, formed no spiritual tie between pastor and flock, just because they exacted of him no gifts of teaching or knowledge. They wanted mass to be sung regularly and the Sacraments administered, especially to the dying, and no more; consequently they used their right of election to procure a pope as cheaply as possible, and they wanted in their deacon just one gifted with a big voice for the responses. His function was that of a deep tongued bell. He also served them as a clerk to keep accounts etc., but was in any case a luxury, and was usually the gift of a rich elder, like the chorister of today. The government never overruled the choice of the parishioners, and it was their indifference which turned the ministry into a sort of trade. "What made you turn priest?" asked Dimitri of Rostov of one early in the 17th century. "Was it to save yourself and others?" "No," was the answer, "but to support my wife and children."

The mere fact that parochial election was conducted on such grounds did not in itself cause episcopal nomination to take its place. The bishop did not grasp a privilege the parishioners resigned. They were not his rivals, but merely let things take their course; and the result was that parishes, like other offices, became hereditary, and particular families, son succeeding sire, held particular benefices generation after generation, very much as is the case in England, where 'family livings' are equally an institution. In some parishes one family owned the office of priest, another that of lector, and every clerical grade was hereditary. There was in fact a tendency for the clergy to become a close guild, not through legislation to that effect, but as the result of social tendencies working equally in other spheres of administration, to which free access was as difficult for all and sundry as to the clerical office. Officially the priest was supposed to feel a vocation; in practice he became a wheel in the bureaucratic machine, and in this he occupied no exalted position, but was humiliated to the lowest rung of the ladder. It was only in 1796 under Tsar Paul that proprietors lost the right of knouting the village priests; their wives were only exempted under Alexander I in 1808, their children under Nicholas I in 1839. Moreover the Government, while closing all other careers to the sons of popes, set itself to cut down the number of parish clergy to the lowest possible limit, and so forced the younger sons into the army. These disabilities lasted from the reign of Peter I until 1869, when at last other services and professions were thrown open by Alexander II to clergymen's sons. In earlier days, when the office of pope was still open to others than sons of the clergy, those who assumed it usually did so not from religious impulse, but in order to avoid the taxation which pressed so hard on the individual in other walks of life.

The Raskol were sensible of this regress and naturally preferred the old institutions to the innovations. They set to work to defend national peculiarities on the plea that the innovations were borrowed from the Latins, which was partly true, inasmuch as the outward veneer of the Government set up in Moscow was borrowed from the West. They were the champions of personal liberty and maintained that the new and harsh system of law was an anti-Christian institution. The *Code* of Alexis Michailovich was and still is regarded as a violation of Christian faith.[1] Accordingly in constituting themselves the champions of the old, they really took their stand not on the side of what was old as being old, but as being better.

[1] A. Shchapov, *Russian Raskol*, pp. 468, 477.

CHAPTER II

THE EARLY DAYS OF THE SCHISM

With the council of 1666 the Old believers began their history as a body separate from the official church. The principal events of the next few years were the Rebellion at the Solovetski Monastery, and — even more important — the Revolt of the Streltsy in Moscow, which led up to the great dispersion of the Old believers far and wide in Russia and even beyond its borders.

The Rebellion at the Solovetski Monastery

Ivanovski gives a graphic account of the rebellion which took place in the Solovetski Monastery, on the White Sea; and as it was typical of the age, it is worthy to be narrated.[1]

Already before the final rupture took place the inmates of this convent had shewn themselves hostile to Nikon's ecclesiastical improvements. It is true their abbot Elias attended the Council of 1654 and even subscribed to the resolution passed by it in favour of more correct Service-books. But he could not get a hearing for such a project among his brethren, who formally declined in June 1658 to accept the new editions and adhered to the old texts. Even before that date their archimandrite during the Great Fast had induced them to sign an abjuration of such impious novelties, and fortified by the assent of his monks had administered a sort of anti-modernist oath to the clergy of the villages grouped round the Monastery. Elias' leading supporters were the Cellarius Serge, Sabbatius Obryutin, Gerasimus Thirsov and some other Elders. Three of the brethren, however, dissented and sent a petition to Nikon, which never reached him, for he had already fallen into disgrace with the Tsar before it arrived.

---

[1] Simeon Denison's homeric account of the Siege is accessible to English readers in Will. Palmer's *the Patriarch and the Tsar*, vol. II, p. 439. He also gives the petition sent from the convent to the Tsar in Oct. 1667.

In 1659 Elias died, and his successor Bartholomew of Vologda was irresolute. He had indeed been consecrated Archimandrite at Moscow according to the new rites, and he went thither in 1660 and 1664 to take part in Nikon's Synods. Nevertheless he took no steps to impose Nikon's decrees in his monastery, and for eight years the brethren continued in the old ways without the clerical bureaucrats of Moscow taking any notice of them. It was quite in keeping with Bartholomew's toleration of the old rites that in other respects he was a martinet, maintaining an iron discipline among his monks. He even went to the length of imprisoning and scourging such of them as offended by rioting in church or complaining of his rigour. The Monastery, however, remained a centre of Old believers; and the Government did not mend matters by sending thither for confinement numbers of rebellious clerks and elders, as well as sundry of the laity, exiled from their homes as criminals or notorious Raskolniks. A militant complexion was lent to the monastic society gathered there by various fugitive Cossacks who had belonged to the band of Stenka Razin.[1] The ringleaders of the place were Gerasimus Thirsov, Gennadius the Elder, Jona Bryzgalov, a runaway deacon of Tula who had taken monkish orders, John Stukalov and the deacon Ignatius. Among the exiles sent to the convent by way of punishment was Prince Lvov, who had directed the Moscow printing press. The name is familiar as that of a leader of the first revolutionary government in Petersburg; another exile, who presently led the revolt, was the archimandrite Nicanor, who was in villeggiatura there after being prior of the Monastery of St. Sabba at Zvenigorod, the Tsar's summer residence. He was a friend of Nikon's two arch-enemies, the Elder Theoktistus and the Protopope Avvakum.

In 1666 the monks addressed a petition to their archimandrite, then attending the Council at Moscow, to be laid before the Tsar. It contained a request that they should be permitted to continue with the old rites; but instead of presenting it, Bartholomew did penance for observing them so

---

[1] A Don Cossack who revolted and after ravaging all the cities of the Volga was caught and executed in Moscow in June 1671.

long and rejecting the new. In this he set the example to the other members of the Council on July 13. Nicanor was not present at the Council, and had pleaded old age as an excuse for keeping away from it. Offended by the subserviency of Bartholomew, the monks at the instigation of Gerasimus Thirsov, petitioned to have him replaced by Nicanor, and in this demand Prince Lvov supported them. But Gerasimus in turn was now summoned to Moscow, required to do penance and despatched to the Volokolamski Monastery, where according to Denisov he was strangled. The rebels at Solovets were thus obliged to choose new ringleaders and they selected Alexander Stukalov, Gennadius and Ephrem.

The authorities in Moscow now began to feel concern, and sent Sergius, archimandrite of Yaroslav, to reduce the mutinous monks to order. He was to communicate to them the decision of the Council in favour of the new rites and to hear their complaints against Bartholomew. To support him, there were sent with him members of the Tsar's bodyguard. But before he arrived Stukalov and Nicanor had overcome the hesitancy of the brethren, deposed the Cellarius Sabbatius and appointed in his stead an illiterate monk Azariah, whose function was to awaken the brethren of a morning. At the same time a fresh remonstrance was despatched to Moscow. Sergius when he arrived was treated with contumely, confined with his suite in dark cells, and guarded by men armed with clubs. No monk was allowed to communicate with him except in a general audience, and the population of the neighbourhood made as if they would stone him as an emissary of Antichrist. Ultimately he managed to escape, and warn the authorities at Moscow. He was no sooner departed than the treasurer, who bore the Coptic name of Barsanuphius, no doubt in honour of the monophysite monk of Gaza of that name, was deprived of his office, and Gerontius, a hieromonachus, entrusted with his functions. Stukalov at the same time was sent with an elder and a couple of attendants to Moscow to lay a fresh petition before the Tsar who by now was thoroughly incensed at the spirit of insubordination evinced by the brethren. It seems, however, to have been a principle with this Tsar, in cases of ecclesiastical squabbles, to punish the ringleaders on both sides; and accordingly, while he sent the petitioners to monasteries under ecclesiastical censure and restraint, he also sent Bartholomew about his business. Nicanor too was doomed to disappointment; for though he was in Moscow at the time, he was not preferred to the vacant priorate, which was assigned instead to the Elder Joseph, architect of the Hostelry in Moscow. The comparative benignity, remarks Ivanovski, with which the Tsar treated the recalcitrant monks only served to excite their fanaticism and tempt them to commit further excesses. There speaks the orthodox historian.

The three, Joseph, Nicanor and Bartholomew, all quitted Moscow for the Monastery at one and the same time. The first two were intended to stay there for good, the last no longer than he would need to do in order to make over the conduct and goods of the convent to Joseph. Nicanor, however, gave his companions of the road the slip in Archangel, and sent the brethren a letter by his valet warning them not to admit Joseph or receive his benedictions, and this advice they carried out. Ten days later, Sept. 23, Nicanor and his partisans sent the Tsar another petition by the hand of an Elder, Cyril Chaplin, whose English name recalls the discovery of Russia by the Merchant Adventurers more than a century before; he also bore a missive from the archimandrite Joseph, whom, along with Bartholomew, the monks were treating with disrespect, confining both of them to cells from within which they could hear abuse lavished on them by all without. They were boycotted and threatened and forbidden to approach the altar, to kiss cross, gospel or ikons. Finally they were bundled out in mid-winter on to the bank of the river. Simultaneously the monks sent the Tsar a fifth petition, drawn up by Gerontius the treasurer, more stringent than any of the former ones. It is not known if it ever reached the hands of the Tsar; but in any case it was printed later on and scattered broadcast among the Raskolniks.

Joseph's letter denouncing the mutinous conduct of the brethren reached the Tsar, who promptly ordered the goods of the convent to be sequestrated; while the council of Moscow which had not yet broken up, excommunicated them. But confiscation and anathema had lost their terrors for the ringleaders, who merely set about to strengthen their defences against the Tsar's officer Volokhov who in the autumn of 1668 was sent with a troop of soldiers to reduce them to obedience. They began by allowing such of the inmates as were unwilling to face a siege to depart, and of this privilege, eleven of the monkish and nine of the white clergy availed themselves, and crossed over to the Sumski bank of the river which the convent over-looked,— a circumstance that alone enabled its defenders to stand a siege.

Volokhov unsuccessfully beleaguered the place for four years, at the expiration of which Clement Iovlev, captain of the Moscow imperial guard, took his place; a year later he in turn gave way to Meshcherinov the voevoda or general. Nicanor meanwhile was life and soul of the defence, ably seconded by his valet or body servant Thaddeus. The garrison sustained a heavy blow, however, in the loss of Azariah the Cellarius, who, before Volokhov took his departure, was caught out fishing by the enemy along with a few other monks and sundry laymen, assisting in so necessary a sport. Their boats armed with small guns also fell into the possession of the enemy. Early in 1670, against the better judgment of several of the monks, the ringleaders had determined to use the Dutch artillery, with which the convent was armed, against the imperial troops, and Nicanor having mounted the tower and sprinkled the guns with holy water, had apostrophised them in the words: 'Little Dutch mothers, our hopes are centred in you, protect us!"

Eventually internal quarrels led to the downfall of this old-believing fortress. Several monks who wanted to surrender are said to have been starved to death, and it is possible that the more resolute in their determination to hold out kept the dwindling stocks of provisions for themselves; the victims are said to have courted their fate by insisting on continuing to pray for the Tsar in the liturgy. After they had been got rid of in this cruel manner, certain unordained monks, says

Ivanovski, ventured to celebrate the rites and to hear confessions and grant absolution, while some even were left, if indeed they had any choice, to die without the Sacraments.

Among the few brethren who, escaping from the fortress on the arrival of Meshcherinov, went over to the enemy, was an Elder named Theoktistus, and he revealed to the Voevoda a secret entrance by way of a conduit under the White Tower, so, Denisov quaintly adds, betraying the convent as Aeneas and Antenor betrayed the Trojans. Through it the troops gained access to the interior, and in a moment, the siege, which had lasted eight years, was at an end, Jan. 22, 1676. All the monks were pitilessly executed, and a fresh company of celibates, more amenable to the new discipline of Moscow, was sent to take their place.

The importance of this episode, rightly remarks our historian, was not to be measured so much by its military aspects as by its effect on the imagination of a religiously-minded peasantry. For ages the convent had been a centre of popular pilgrimage, and continued to be so all through the siege. It was the shrine of the great Christian athletes Zosimus and Sabbatius. The pious arrived beneath its walls and, finding it beleaguered, so that they could not gain admission, returned to their homes with indignant tales of the oppression and violence exercised by the ecclesiastical authorities of Moscow. Not only the pilgrims, but inmates of the convent who escaped before and during the siege, carried far and wide over The Pomorye, as the drear coastlands of the White Sea are called, the legend of the brilliant exploits and ultimate martyrdom of its gallant defenders. Forty years later Semen Denisov, a poet of the Raskol, celebrated the siege in an epic which has enjoyed an enormous success for two centuries. The poem of course teems with visions and miracles; the rebels are extolled as martyrs, the Tsar is an emissary of Satan, who perishes on the very day the convent fell. He really died a week later; but the religious, like the patriotic propagandist, prefers poetical justice to that of dates, and the sacrifice of truth in this case was slight. Ivanovski plaintively remarks that Denisov and his readers should have borne in mind that Christian martyrs never either rioted or rebelled against an emperor's authority, and argues that the defenders of the Solovets convent had no title to be called martyrs, for they were only mutineers. He is strangely ignorant of the *Acta Sanctorum*.

The Revolt of 1682.

On May 15, 1682, a revolution [1] broke out in Moscow which continued until it was repressed with ruthless energy by Peter the Great in 1698. In essential respects this resembled that of 1917. For it, too, was a joint revolt of the Streltsy, the Praetorian guard of the day, and of the populace. After rioting for three days, and murdering many who were obnoxious to them, the soldiers proclaimed the two striplings John and Peter Alexeevichi to be both Tsars under the regency of their elder sister Sophia. A certain Prince Ivan Khovanski who possessed a mansion in Moscow was a partisan of the Raskol, and had long incurred suspicion by harbouring fugitive priests and using the old books in his private chapel. He was captain of the Streltsy and had little difficulty in investing what was in origin a mutiny of soldiers with the character of an Old believer rising. To him as officer of the guard was presented a petition for the restoration of the old piety drawn up by a monk Sergius. He professed his readiness to champion the cause and promised to allow the Raskolniks to discuss publicly their faith in the square where executions took place. It sounds a grim project, but we must not forget that the finest open spaces in Europe were but a few generations ago consecrated to such uses. The petition was naturally approved by the mutinous soldiery who can have had no idea of what it was about. Nicetas Dobrynin, also named Pustosviat, who had been pope or parish priest of Suzdal and had hypocritically given his adherence at the council of 1666 to the new church regulations, was chosen to conduct the debate in the presence of the young princes and the regent.

The project failed however for the moment, and the petition alone was presented to the royalties. On June 25 took place

---

[1] Macarius, *Hist. of Raskol:* Solovyev, *Hist. of Russ.* t. 12: *Bratskoe Slovo*, 1875, bk. 4.

the coronation of the two little Tsars, the rite being performed from the new books, and in the liturgy instead of seven, only five *prosphorae* [1] were offered, a number displeasing to the Raskolniks. Nevertheless Nicetas held a service in honour of the occasion in the Uspenski Church along the old lines as a sort of counter-demonstration with the permission of Khovanski; and this modest success inspired the partisans of the 'old piety' to conduct a procession through Moscow with ikons and books. Street preachers denounced the profanation of the churches and service-books, and appealed to the multitude to defend the old faith. Adherents of the new order were roughly handled by the crowd.

On July 3 the Raskolniks began a public discussion with Joakim the patriarch in his palace of the Cross, of which Sabba Romanov, one of those who took part in it, has left us a description. It was renewed two days later in the square of the royal palace. The Old believers came with their books and their cross, their pulpit and their lighted tapers, and Nicetas standing on a dais began to read his diatribe before the people. He wanted a public discussion of his thesis, but the authorities declined this as unseemly and invited him into the palace, where the lady regent Sophia was present with several other princesses, her aunt Tatyana Mikhailovna, her sister Maria Alexeevna and the Tsaritsa Natalia Kirileovna. There were present also the patriarch and sundry archpriests. Asked what he wanted, Nicetas returned: "To supplicate humbly concerning the correction of the books. A new faith has been introduced among us." Athanasius, bishop of Kholmogory, replied for his patriarch, whereupon Nicetas, according to the official report of the case, struck Athanasius and abused the Patriarch. Sabba however who was present states that he merely led him slightly aside with his hand. The Princess Sophia then began to reproach Nicetas with having recanted in 1666, and Nicetas replied, no doubt truly, that he had only done so out of fear. The Princess thereupon irritated by the way her father Cyril and brother Ivan were

---

[1] i.e., the loaves from which bread for consecration was taken. These loaves were offered in the deacon's chamber and not at the altar on the bema.

spoken of in the petition (both of them had been murdered by the mutinous soldiers) threatened to withdraw from Moscow with the rest of the Royal Family. At the same time, Joakim, gospel in hand, proceeded to address a reprimand to the Old believers, who received his remarks with derision, signing themselves with two fingers — their most effective method no doubt of exorcism,— and shouting 'Thus, thus!' The interview then broke up, and the Raskolniks proceeded to promenade about the city, entered the churches and said prayers in their own fashion, and beat the bells.

Sophia, a capable and determined woman, like most of the women who have from time to time controlled the fortunes of Russia, now took prompt steps to separate the cause of the revolted soldiery from that of the populace. She succeeded by means of her donatives, and so far regained their loyalty that they made themselves the agents of the arrest of Nicetas, who was instantly beheaded for rebellion. This was July 21, 1682. His followers were banished to monasteries for correction. The revolt of the Streltsy, it is true, was not quelled and went on simmering; but henceforth it had little or no connection with the grievances of the Old believers.

The Ukaze of 1685 and Its Results

There followed the Tsaritsa Sophia's ukase of 1685, one of the most draconian statutes on the page of history. It utterly proscribed the dissidents and forbade their very existence. If detected, they were to be subjected to three-fold torture, after which, if they did not recant, they were to be burned alive. If they repented they were to be sent for correction to an ecclesiastical prison. Those who had rebaptized a convert were to be put to death, no matter whether they repented or not; those they baptized to be knouted in case of repentance, but, in the opposite case, slain. Anyone who harboured them, even unwittingly, was liable to a fine of 5 to 50 roubles, in those days a great sum of money.

As might be expected, the dissidents did not wait to be caught, and a great flight of them followed into the farthest forests and deserts of Russia and even across the frontiers, for it was impossible to draw such a cordon that they could not escape from the Empire.

"In order the more freely to wander from city to city and from village to village, the itinerant preachers and missionaries cleverly assumed all sorts of disguises. Sometimes they made their way in the garb of beggars, with wallet on back. This was supposed to hold the alms of the charitable, but more often it concealed Raskol books and tracts; at other times they assumed the garb of pilgrims; often they travelled as peddlers and colporteurs, with bags on their backs in which equally they hid the literature of their teachers." [1]

For all that, remarks Uzov, they were caught often enough, and it was not for nothing that the teaching grew up among them of the expediency of suicide en masse. P. Miliukov (Outlines of Russian civilization, 4th ed. pt. 1, p. 71) estimates that from the beginning of the Raskol to end of 1689 as many as 20,000 burned themselves alive, and most of these in the last nine years when Sophia's ukase was being executed against them.

"The self-immolation of the Raskolniks was in their time as heroic an exploit as we should to-day account a similar action on the part of the defenders of a fortress." [2] "Let us baffle Antichrist," [3] was the cry with which the Raskolniks rallied one another's courage and declared it preferable to burn themselves alive than give themselves up into the hands of a Government they detested. For the rest, it must be admitted that "it was perfectly logical reasoning on their part; it was better once for all to settle accounts with this life than be deprived of it by inhuman tortures; moreover, they argued, you may fail in the trial and against your will deny your convictions after all." [4] "Many have affirmed that self-immolation was a peculiar dogma of the Raskolniks. Had this been so, we should meet with cases of voluntary self-immolation, provoked by this teaching, without any other incentives. But in fact in all the

---

[1] Shchapov, *Russ. Rask.*, p. 313.
[2] *Vestnik, Evrop.* 1871, No. 4, Kostomarov's art., p. 494.
[3] *The Raskol revealed in their own Hist.* p. 228.
[4] *Vremya*, 1862, No. 1, art. by Aristov, p. 95.

known cases this form of death was chosen as an alternative to forcible capture by army commandos, and for the most part it was only adopted when their homes were being attacked. What was there to induce a few fanatics, who had won over ignorant peasants, to resort to so horrible a measure? They furnish themselves an answer to the question in the historical and trustworthy pictures they penned of contemporary persecution: "Everywhere blows resound; everywhere thrashings and subjugation to his yoke follow in the train of Nikon's teaching; everywhere whips and rods soaked daily in the blood of confessors. The preachers of Nikon's new ideas breathe, not the spirit of gentleness, but that of fury, wrath, tyranny. Beatings and wounds, such are the methods of their instruction, and not the grace of Christ; guile and evil deceit, and not apostolic humility; with these they would spread their faith, and the outcome of their cruel violence and tyranny is a rain of blood. Village and field are bathed in tears, wilderness and forest are loud with weeping and moaning and groaning... Some suffered for the faith, others hid themselves wherever they could, others when the invaders, the persecutors, shewed themselves with guns and weapons, assured of martyrdom, burned themselves alive." [1] Now and then, when they saw the forces sent against them to be weak, they tried to escape, and for a time were successful. Thus, for example, they one day forced a commando to retire, having slain the captain, Portnovski; but on that occasion they only fired with the wads, out of terror; but irritation against the authorities took the shape of cutting the dead body of Portnovski to bits. [2]

We may thus affirm without injustice to the facts "that self-immolation was their last mode of escape. In no other sense was it ever adopted as a dogma than as a way of avoiding persecution and of escape from the rack, which was always in store for such Old believers as fell into the hands of the Government." [3]

---

[1] *Hist. of the Vygovski Old bel. hermitage*, By Ivan Philippov, V and VI.
[2] *ibid.* ch. 7.
[3] *Nation. Memorials*, 1863, No. 2, art. by Esipov, p. 607.

Peter the Great

In the year 1689 another political revolution took place;
Sophia was driven from power and sent into a convent; and
her brother, Peter the Great, mounted the throne. He was
for some time too occupied with more pressing matters to
turn his attention to the Raskol, and they made use of the
precious respite accorded them to establish their various
settlements, which were at first formed, if not along strict
monastic lines, at any rate with a show of monastic terminology.

One of his first actions was to suppress the lingering revolt
of the Streltsy. "Rumours of their awful punishment were
carried all over Russia and struck terror into the hearts of
the people," [1] who regarded their Emperor with horror, and the
word *Antichrist*, whispered by the Raskolniks, was now
bruited far and wide. "But Peter annihilated the Streltsy,
and the popular risings came to nothing. The power was in
the end in his hands... After his terrible vengeance was wreaked
on the Streltsy, he could do exactly as he pleased." [2] So-called
"European reforms" were forthwith sprung upon the people,
tax-gatherers and press-gangs were everywhere, the peasant
labourers were lowered to the condition of serfs. A hundred
thousand of the people perished on public works, i.e. in the
building of Petersburg, of fortresses, canals; for the Sovereign
in his reforms had at heart the strengthening of his own prerogatives and not the happiness of the people.

"The system of administration he raised was mechanical
and arbitrary, centralization was carried in dry hard style into
ridiculous details. Multiplication of provincial bureaucrats,
division of his subjects into castes, contempt for Russian popular life with all its traditions and leanings to local peculiarities,
— all this served to rouse the hostility of the people for the
amelioration of whose fate he did nothing at all." [3] Under
Peter the Government steadily pursued its work of centraliza-

---

[1] *Raskol Happenings in 18th Century*, by H. (G) Esipov, t. 1, p. 8, and t. 2,
p. 162.

[2] *Ibid.*

[3] Aristov in *Vremya* (Time) 1862, No. 1, p. 77.

tion, yet the masses "impelled by mediaeval tendencies to separation and setting at naught the new ideas of administration, refused to submit to a scheme of unification, and with considerable resilience strove to maintain the ancient system or, as the documents characteristically put it, to break off." [1]

The administrators "did everything they could to bind the people with eternal bonds, spared no effort to reconstruct society according to an arbitrary plan which lacked all basis in life and reason nor had any roots in popular ideas, feelings or aspirations." [2]   A fresh swarm of about 10,000 foreigners from the West, mostly Germans, descended upon Russia, and were concentrated by Peter in Moscow, "illuminated instructors who made no effort to grasp the deeper popular tendencies and needs of the national spirit, but held the people tight by the bearing-rein of their methods and regarded them as so many country bumpkins." [2]   But "in the soul of the people was engrained a deep and powerful bias against royal prerogatives, and a profound distaste for a flat governmental rule the same for all, an instinct to be free from the strict régime of a single absolute authority, to assert their own will and manage their own affairs.   The very idea of a supreme authority, of autocracy, which attained full development in the rule of an Emperor had never yet penetrated the entire people." [3]   "Seditious" tracts were published, penned, by the admission of the authors, "because of their sympathy with the people," or "for their advantage and in order to alleviate the weight of taxation."   In these it was contended that God made man "in his own image and likeness, and that it was God's own ordinance that man should be absolute master of himself." [4]   The Russian steam-roller invented by Tartar tyranny and perfected by Peter the Great was never much admired by the Russians themselves.

The Old believers led the opposition to the reforms of Peter I, alleging that he "was an agent of all wickedness and of Satan's will, and had raised himself on high above all false gods."

---

[1] Shchapov, *Russian Raskol*, p. 465.

[2] *Vremya*, 1862, No. 1, art. by Aristov, p. 78.

[3] Shchapov, *op. cit.*, p. 471.

[4] Esipov, *op. cit.* t. 1, pp. 165, 182.

He was, they declared, a false Messiah who magnified himself and surrounded himself with glory before all. In 1721 Peter assumed the title of Patriarch, took the name of Father of his country, as the pamphlet 'Kingdom of the Dead' attests against him (p. 115), made himself head of the Russian Church and autocrat; he now had no one on an equality with himself, and appropriated not only the authority of Tsar, but of priesthood and Godhead. He became absolute shepherd of a headless church, the adversary of Christ, in a word Antichrist." [1] As Shchapov remarks, the Old believers ominously complained that Peter the Great "called himself Emperor and Monarch, that is to say sole ruler and sole authority, thereby assuming the title of God of Russia, as is testified in the pamphlet 'Peter's Cabinet' in which it was said: "Behold thy God, behold thy God, O Russia!" [2]

Accordingly the Raskolniks rose against all the statutes and edicts by which Peter set himself to uphold his autocratic rule. They declared the census list to be Antichrist's list, and taught the people not to inscribe their names in it. "We," they wrote, "have been instructed by Christ in his law, and we keep his commandment and preserve the holy faith; and therefore we refuse to submit ourselves to such a false Christ and to obey him; never will we inscribe ourselves in his books and share the transgressions of the impious, nay, we will not counsel anyone to do so who desires to be saved." "Verily we see fulfilled the mystery of the Apocalypse; the reign of the primal beast is established among us, and the earth and all that live thereon are made to bow the knee to Satan and say: 'Settle our account, we beg you humbly to grant us passports.' He will answer: 'Out with your poll-tax for the new year, and are there no other arrears to pay up, for you live on my earth?' There you have a deep pit for the destruction of the human race." [3]

From the time of Peter the Great the Russian Government

---

[1] Proceedings of the Imperial Society of History and Antiquities, 1863, bk. 1, pp. 53 and 63.

[2] Shchapov, *Russ. Rask.*, p. 478.

[3] Imperial Society of History and Antiquities, 1863, vol. 1, pp. 55, 58, 59.

spent time and trouble on the compilation of statistics, of which, however, it never made much use. If we bear in mind that the project of a methodical census of the inhabitants of the United Kingdom when it was first mooted late in the XVIIIth Century, provoked angry protests from religious people, and was actually rejected in the House of Lords on the ground that, like the similar experiment of King David, it might call down upon the land the wrath of God, we shall not be surprised at the acute displeasure of the Raskol when Peter the Great imposed a census and a poll-tax on them nearly a century earlier. In 1890 it was still one of the chief griev-ances of the Armenians under Russia's rule, that the Govern-ment obliged them to register their births, deaths and mar-riages. They had suffered no such indignity under Turkish and Persian rule, and it partly explained the saying, then and now common among them, that whereas the Turk only slew their bodies, the Russian slew their souls. We shall have occa-sion, however, to point out later on that the religious census prepared under the auspices of the Russian State and Church has no statistical value whatever and was only contrived to deceive and conceal facts. It is noteworthy that the Raskol also, in combating a census under Peter, adduced the warning example of King David's reign.

"The Raskol rebelled against the very structure and organi-zation of the imperial government, beginning with the Senate and the provincial administration. Everywhere the dissidents found fault with aspects of the administration which conflicted with the welfare of the people, and exploited the disorders which broke out in the provinces for strengthening their influence and extending it." [1]

Pitirim, bishop of Krutits, Nikon's successor, in his report to Peter I, said of them: "Wherever you find them, instead of being pleased with the good fortune of the Sovereign, they delight in his misfortunes." [2]

Such was the attitude of the Old believers to the policy of Peter the Great, and they continued their hatred of his govern-

[1] Shchapov, *Russ. Rask.* p. 515.
[2] Imperial Society History and Antiquities, 1860, bk. 4, p. 281.

ment to that of his successors: "We behold," they said, "what a spirit of impiety works and shall work to the end of the world in all holders of power." [1] They remained obstinate, and to this day, says Uzov, the Old believers retain this conviction; only a fraction of them under the influence of the reforms of the present régime (1881), have begun to relax the severity with which they judge the Government. Their spokesman, Macarius Ivanovich Stukachev, an adherent of the Theodosian sect, in his address to the Tsar Liberator in the Sixties, intimated as much: "In the innovations," he wrote, "of your régime we seem to behold our good old time." [2] In such words we detect the point of view of the Old believers in their opposition to the Government and seize the meaning of the 'good old times' for which they stood.

Tsardom and Antichrist

Almost from the dawn of Christianity the teaching about an Antichrist or counter-Messiah, if not Satan himself, at any rate his lieutenant, has furnished enthusiasts with a theme for prophecy and dreary dissertations; and it has been cynically observed that no student can long preoccupy his mind with that most characteristic work of mixed Jewish and Christian piety, the so-called Book of Revelation, without jeopardizing his reason. Never have the Kings of the Gentiles raged furiously and devoted themselves to the ever congenial task of violating the essential spirit and precepts of Jesus of Nazareth by setting their subjects to cut one another's throats, without an appeal being made by each side to this bizarre monument. During the recent war French divines found in it a prophecy of German barbarism, and their German counterparts read in it a record of French, Russian and English impiety. We are not therefore surprised to find that such vaticinations filled a large space in the mind of the Russian dissidents. Their attitude towards Nikon and the Tsar of the time was summed up in the belief that the two men were the instruments, if not the impersonation, of Antichrist.

[1] *Ibid.*, 1863, Bk. 1, p. 59.
[2] Istina (Truth) 1867, bk. 2.

The Messiah himself, according to an early tradition, had disclaimed knowledge of his second advent on earth, but was sure that it would on the one hand usher in the end of the world, on the other be preceded by the appearance of Antichrist; and accordingly in the 24th and 25th chapters of the first Gospel we find enumerated from some contemporary apocalyptic document the signs that are to herald the last days. But in every age Christian teachers have claimed a knowledge which was denied to the Founder; and the author or redactor of the Book of Revelation which closes the canon of the New Testament was already acquainted with the exact chronology of Antichrist and knew that Satan was to be bound for a thousand years, whence it was argued that the world would end in A. D. 1000.

But alongside of this belief was current another, equally ancient, that this great event was timed 7000 years from Creation, because one day in the Scriptures symbolizes a thousand years, and as the world took seven days to complete, so it will run for an equal period. Rome, the imperial city, was to endure to the end. When old Rome fell in the fifth century the religious imagination found no difficulty in readjusting itself to events, and it was agreed that the prophecy regarded not old but new Rome or Byzance. Presently new Rome fell also into the power of the Turks in 1453, and then it looked as if the visions of the seer were really to be fulfilled, for 5508, the tale of years which according to Christian chronologists had preceded the birth of Jesus added to 1453 made a total of 6961 which was not far from 7000. The full period would mature in 1492.

That year also came and went without any cataclysm; and then in Russia arose a new interpretation of the prophecy, of which few echoes ever reached Western Europe. This was the remarkable theory that in default of old and new Rome, Moscow was the imperial city, was the third Rome of which, as was thought to be foretold by St. Paul in II. Thess. ii, 7, the mission is to be the last refuge of orthodoxy and to hold down the Antichrist. The Russians shared the Hussite belief that by A. D. 1000, if not earlier, the Pope of Rome had become the precursor of Antichrist, and this view is enunciated in the so-called *Book of Cyril* compiled by Zizania. The author of another work, which circulated in XVIIth Century Russia, the *Book of Faith*, shewed that in 1439 at the Council of Florence the Western Slavs had apostatized to Rome and therefore to Antichrist, and hinted that the turn of the Great Russians and of Moscow was coming. Chance arranged the year 1666 as that of the final triumph of Nikon's 'reforms.' Now 1000, the date of old Rome's final apostasy, added to 666, the apocalyptic number of the Beast, just made that date. It was inevitable that the Raskol teachers should put two and two together and teach that the prophecy of the *Book of Faith* was being fulfilled before their eyes. About that they were all agreed.

The only point left doubtful was this: in whom was the Antichrist to be recognized? Who was the Man of Sin? Was it Nikon or the Tsar? or both? It was not difficult to find, among the martyrs of the Raskol, incarnations of Elias and Enoch who according to ancient prophecy were to confute Satan and his emissaries; but neither Nikon nor the Tsar bore the distinguishing marks of the Antichrist, beyond the fact that they were real men of flesh and blood. That much the Antichrist was to be, but then he was also to reign for three and a half years; his mother, like Christ's, was to be a virgin, and even the traits of his personal appearance were prescribed in old prophecies. In some ancient documents, for example, the picture of St. Paul in the Acts of Thekla was adopted unchanged as that of Antichrist — an indication of a Judaizing source hostile to the Apostle of the Gentiles. An Elder of the Raskol, Abraham, set about to prove that Nikon was Antichrist, with the aid of passages from St. Cyril of Jerusalem and from Hippolytus' tract on the subject; but his arguments did not please everybody, and Avvakum more modestly pretended that Nikon was only the Precursor of Antichrist, for as Christ had a precursor in John the Baptist, so it was necessary for his antitype to have one.

Theodore the deacon broached a third view to the effect that Antichrist was no other than Satan himself, an invisible spirit who issues from the abyss at the end of a thousand years to corrupt Rome with heresy and Lithuania with apostasy. In 1666 this serpent entered into his two chosen vessels, the Tsar and Nikon. Thus there came into being a counter Trinity of serpent, beast and lying prophet. This theory of the incarnation of Antichrist in these two men was a step in the development of a doctrine which the Bezpopovtsy adopted later on; they broached the view that the entire series of Tsars from 1666 onwards were and are incarnations of the Evil One. Antichrist to their imagination is rather an ideal of evil, a tendency that makes for Hell rather than Heaven, than a real person. The excellent Ivanovski sets out arduously to overthrow these old world opinions and argues seriously that Antichrist when he appears will be a circumcized Jew of the tribe of Dan, of miraculous birth, etc. in the same spirit as is found in pseudo-Hippolytus, in John of Damascus, and in Andrew of Caesarea's Commentary on the Apocalypse.

The mediaeval Cathars were on rather safer ground when under stress of Papal persecution they argued that this world is already Hell, so that we need not wait for another existence in order to experience its tortures. For them as for the Raskol the government of Kings and princes was a manifestation of the power of Satan. The régime of persecution under which they groaned was hardly worse than that which until yesterday existed in Russia. It would be interesting to know what the Raskol thought of the Russian Revolution. Did they see in the deposition of the Tsar an end put to the reign of Antichrist? Will they be grievously disappointed if the end of the world and the last great assize fails to ensue? Intellectual progress had undermined for many of them these grotesque beliefs, but the war may have revived them. If there were any Cathars left to-day they might justly hail it as a confirmation of their beliefs.

Excommunicated by the Council of 1667 the Raskolniks [1] resolved to hold no more relations with the dominant church. "It behoves us," they said, "as orthodox Christians not to accept from the adherents of Nikon either benediction, or ceremonies, or baptism, or prayers, not to pray with them

---

[1] *Material for the History of Raskol*, t. 5, pp. 217 foll. and 231 foll.

either in Church or in private, not to read their heretical books
nor follow their heretical chantings." The Cathars of Europe
pronounced the prayers of the Roman Church to be *magis
execrabilis quam impetrabilis*, "worthy rather of execration
than of being asked for"; the Raskolniks regarded the devotions
of the Holy Russian Church in exactly the same way.

But in an age of fierce and searching persecution it was
difficult to carry out a program of complete and unconditional
abstention; Avvakum therefore drew up rules by observing
which the dissidents might as far as possible keep themselves
uncontaminated by Nikonian rites. "If they drag you into
Church, then," so he wrote, "whisper your prayer to Isus";
They objected, it may be remembered, to the substitution in
the Service-books of the correcter spelling *Iesus* for *Isus*. "On
no account," continues Avvakum, "join in the singing; nor
salute the Saviour's image along with the rest, but so soon as
the Nikonians cease to pray, then make your own prostration.
Whenever on a feast day the Pope comes to your house with
cross and holy water and wants to sprinkle your home, follow
him round and sweep it out with a broom." One recalls the
way in which on certain holy days the Greek islanders sweep
the evil spirits out of their houses crying ἔξω κάρες, 'out with
the unclean ghosts.' "Tell your children," he continues, "to
hide away from him behind the stove, but go forward yourself
and your wife and give him a drink and say: 'We don't deserve
to be blessed.' He begins to sprinkle about, but get him into
a corner, give him another drink, and tip him a coin or two.
Your wife can go about her household affairs and say: 'I have
no time. You've a wife of your own, father, and can understand how busy I am.' If they haul you off to make your
confession to one of Nikon's priests, talk rubbish to him. But
any one who takes the Sacrament in an orthodox church, even
involuntarily, must do six months' penance, must not communicate with the faithful, but weep for his sins." Avvakum likewise imposed penance on anyone who even in mockery crossed
himself with three fingers. By such devices he trusted to
keep alive the spirit of the Raskol, and at the same time ward
off persecution. In the churches the ikons of ancient saints

might be venerated, but only after the congregation had left the church.

It is pathetic to observe that the dissidents cherished as long as they could the belief that the Tsar was the victim of fraud and had been deceived by Nikon. They continued for long to think that he had only to be undeceived, and continued to address petitions to him [1] pleading their cause. The dismissal of Nikon and the favour shewn to Avvakum [2] by members of the Royal Family, like Fedosia Prokopievna Morozova and Eudokia Urusova, encouraged them to beseech their Sovereign to restore the old piety, to abolish the use of the three fingers which was the sign of Antichrist, to let them retain the old books. It was only gradually that the fire of persecution burned into their souls the conviction that the Tsar was himself the Antichrist. At first, accordingly, the tone of their petitions was loyal and humble. They approached their liegelord in tears, praised his piety, termed him a child of light, a son of the resurrection. But presently they began to hint at impending calamities,— a menace to which then as now the Russian despot was singularly susceptible; they even invoked against him the judgment of Christ. Nikon, so Avvakum warned him, had slain his soul and he would answer for it in the great assize. He had given ear to the flatterers of this world, the Nikonian doctors to wit, wrote Abraham, and the consequences would be war and discord. Terrible dreams, as always in such times, were in fashion. Avvakum at last wrote to the Tsar that he had in a vision beheld a gaping wound in his back and belly; and after the Tsar's death he wrote in 1681 and informed his son Theodor or Fedor that he had been vouchsafed a vision of his father in the torments of Hell. The Tsar's answer was to condemn the writer to the stake along with his three companions, Lazar, Epiphan and Nikiphor. Avvakum died crossing himself with two fingers and consoling his friends as the flames rose and encircled them.

[1] *Mat. for Hist. of Raskol*, vols. 3–7.
[2] *Russk. Viestnik*, 1865, Sept., p. 33.

CHAPTER III

THE DISPERSION

THE death in 1656 of Paul of Kolomna, the only bishop who had joined the movement, had left the seceders without priests and split the movement into two wings, called Popovtsy or Bezpopovtsy according as they fell back on the use of priests who came over to them from Nikon's heresy or made up their mind to dispense with priests altogether. The Popovtsy can be taken first.

The Settlements of the Popovtsy

The Popovtsy were a more united body than the priestless, and as with the aid of runaway orthodox popes they merely continued the old orthodoxy, there was nothing except the need of hiding from the Government to cause scissions among them, but they were widely dispersed.

In Nizhegorod their earliest leaders were contemporaries of Nikon, the hieromonachus Abraam, the monk Ephrem Potemkin, the Elder Sergius. They built the Kerzhen settlements among the forests of the Balakhnovski district, which were called after the Elder Onuphrius, who was their prior in 1690. Onuphrius inherited the writings of Avvakum and these became for the Popovtsy what the writings of Luther are or were for the Lutheran church. This however, did not prevent microscopic dogmatic errors being detected in them about Christ's descent into Hell, which almost led to schisms. Onuphrius' followers were numerous early in the 18th century among the forests of Bryn in the Kaluga government and in the see of Rostov. Avvakum at first had insisted on the rebaptism of Nikonian converts, but his followers, when they found themselves dependent on fugitive priests of the dominant confession relaxed their severity. In Nizhegorod and the surrounding district 3000 followers of Avvakum burned themselves alive early in the movement, and many more starved themselves to death to avoid the rack and the glaive.

Other Popovetsy settlements were organized on the Don and

101

the Kuban rivers, by the Elders Job and Dositheus, who also founded the monasteries of Rakov and Nikolski in the district of Tver. A third monastery, the Lygovski, was founded as early as 1669 in the Rylsk district in the Kursk government by Job, who was a Lithuanian monk. He built a fourth on the River Chir in the Don region to which he had to flee. There Dositheus, hegumen of Tikhvin, consecrated the first Raskol church after Job's death about 1683. In 1688 the flight extended to Astrakhan where Dositheus with the help of two priests Pafnutius and Theodosius organized settlements on the River Kum on the Cherkess steppes. Others followed near Tambov, in the Crimea, and on the Terek. In 1708, a rebel against the Tsar's government named Ignatius Nekrasov after raiding Saratov, Tsaritsyn and Dmitrevsk, fled with his clan to the River Kuban, where he made his submission to the Khan of the Crimea and founded the Raskol community known under his name which subsequently was settled in Turkish territory. The famous rebel Pugachev was also a Raskolnik of the Don, and was assisted in his exploits by Nekrasov and his followers.

These active Raskolniki of the Don and Kuban were in regular communication with communities of Popovtzi established at Vetka in Poland and at Starodub in the Tchernigov Government. The latter was founded by Kosmas, once priest of All Saints in Moscow. Condemned in 1667, he had fled with 22 of his parishioners. He was befriended by the military officer of Starodub, Gabriel Ivanov, who got permission in 1669 from the Ataman Lamak of Kurkub for Kosmas to settle on the River Revna at Ponurov. In the surrounding forests of Starodub the fugitives multiplied and organized four villages, where one Stephanus, who had been ordained before 1666, aided by his son Dmitri, celebrated Mass and other rites for the inhabitants. In 1682, at the death of Tsar Theodor Alexiev the regent Sophia ordered the Starodub fugitives to be driven back to their homes. Thereupon Kosmas and Stephanus with their followers fled into Poland and settled at Vetka, which soon became a leading focus of propaganda.

A dispute over the use and making of the holy chrism led to the formation of a group called the Diakonovo by a deacon

Alexander. Its members continued to live in Kirzhen, Starodub and other Popovets centres.

When the Vetka settlement was wrecked by Col. Sytin and
his five regiments by order of the Empress Anna Ioannovna in
1733–4, the survivors asked permission to transport their
church called Pokrovski or of the Intercession to Starodub.
They took it down, made a raft of the beams and planks and
floated it down the river Sozh as far as the village Svyatki,
where a storm wrecked it and they only saved the Royal door
and the two side doors and four ikons. They also had the
ikonostasis in bits, for they took that by road. Sytin wanted
to leave them the relics of their four founders and patron
saints, Joasaph, Theodosius, Alexander and Antony. But
near Novgorod Sieberski the Tzar's agents violated the reli-
quaries, opened them and cast the remains into the river.
Then, relates Macarius, the modern orthodox prelate and
historian, "the victims of superstition saw in the coffins not
incorruptible relics, but just a few old bones. They smelled
their stench, and left off boasting about their pretended saints.
The coffins were burned"!

The Starodub colony inherited something of the old glory
of Vetka when the latter after being again and again raided
was finally destroyed in 1762–4. It had been founded, as
we saw, in 1682, under John and Peter Alexeievich, the young
Tsars. As many as 17 hamlets in time grew up amidst the
impenetrable forests of the region. In 1708 when Charles
XII of Sweden, by reason of the treason of Mazeppa, invaded
little Russia and reached Starodub, the sectaries attacked him
with much vigour. As a reward of their loyalty Tsar Peter I
granted them lands and certain immunities.

In 1775 two laymen, originally of Vetka, who had settled
in Starodub, broke off because of some small dogmatic dispute
and settled in Chernobol in Poland on the estates of the Pan
Khatkyevich. Their names were Nikephorus Larion and
Pavel Grigorev. The Suslovo sect of Popovtsy was founded
from Starodub by one Theodor Suslov who disapproved of
runaway popes being accepted from Little Russia where in
certain places they accepted baptism by sprinkling only.

But the two chief fresh settlements to which the final destruction of Vetka gave rise were on the River Irgiz in Saratov and in Moscow itself. As many as 120 families settled on the Irgiz where now is situated the city of Nikolaevsk. They built shrines and sketes after the Raskol custom in the surrounding forests, and in 1770 obtained a regular priesthood. In the next year 1771, the sect managed at last to establish itself in some force in Moscow itself, a century after the first flight thence. The Priestless sect had set an example which the Popovtsy now followed. This was the establishment of a hospital for the sick called the Kladbich in the village of Rogozh, just outside the capital. Two shrines were dedicated to the intercession of the Virgin Mary, and adherents all over Russia sent liberal gifts for its endowment. By 1800 it had several hundred inmates, and 20,000 parishioners in Moscow.

As to the early history of Popovtsys in Siberia few data are preserved, but entire villages fled thither at an early date with their priests, and took refuge in the regions where iron and gold were mined. In 1722 ukases were issued against further flights thither, and enacting penalties against priests of the orthodox church who should join them. Nevertheless their colonies were numerous, and Ekaterinburg became their centre. Many rich merchants and citizens there belonged to the sect, which obtained popes from Irgiz. As early as 1800, there were more than 150,000 Popovtsys in the governments of Orenburg, Perm and Tobolsk, and in Ekaterinburg they had a church built of stone.

Ivanovski, dwelling on the above facts, strives to shew that the dissidents were not punished on account of their religious opinions, but for opposing the Tsar's Government, as if such opposition itself needed no explanation. A modern historian is astonished rather than the reverse, that so slight resistance was shewn throughout to the centralizing policy of Moscow. Had the Raskolniks been Quakers they could hardly have shown less. In contrast with the Huguenots of France, the Protestants of the Netherlands, the Roundheads of England, even with the Anabaptists of the continent, they were emi-

nently peaceful people, inspired with the spirit of a Tolstoy
rather than of a John of Leiden. In the few cases Ivanovski
enumerates of their offering resistance, one discerns,— what
Macarius equally admits,— that they were the assailed and
not the assailants. Thus he describes their "attack" upon
the Paleostrovski Monastery in Pomorye, where they seized
the treasury, bound the hegumen or abbot, and fortified
themselves in it. They only did so because here, as in the
Solovets Convent, they had the sympathy and approval of the
monks; so also at Pudozh, where two hundred of them took
possession of the church and held services in it of the ancient
style. In the case of the Paleostrovski Convent and of
Pudozh, Ivanovski's further narrative confirms this interpretation of the facts, for he relates that in both places the Raskolniks committed themselves to the funeral pyre rather than be
taken, and that in the first-mentioned of them they burnt
the hegumen and the monkish inmates along with themselves.
It is obvious that the brethren were in sympathy with the
Raskol, for they could easily have escaped, if they had wanted
to. In general the dissidents fled into the forests, just as did
the Latin Uniats of the Ruthene province of Kholm during the
last thirty years; there, they fasted, prayed, confessed to one
another and then perished of hunger, fully persuaded that the
end of the world was at hand. They even dug their own
graves and lay down in ditches, momentarily expecting the
last trump to strike their ears, now that Antichrist was come.

The Search for Priests

The Russian Orthodox Church, from which the Raskolniks
of 1667 were driven, possessed, like the other great churches
of the East and West, a threefold hierarchy of bishop, priest
and deacon; and the chief external difference which has for
centuries separated the Eastern Churches, not only those
which arrogate to themselves the title of orthodox, but the
Monophysite Christianity of Armenia, Egypt and Abyssinia,
and still older Nestorianism, is one of discipline. In the East
the Parish Priest, the Papa or Pope, must be a married man,
though, if his wife dies, he cannot take a second. In the West

ever since the age of Hildebrand, if not earlier, the parish clergy are celibate, and have taken in effect not only the ordinary vows of ordination, but monkish vows as well, though they are known as secular clergy in opposition to the Regulars who live under a monastic rule. In the East, in strong contrast to the parish clergy, the bishops or 'higher clergy' are monks, usually of St. Basil's rule, and have all at one time or another been inmates of a monastery.

In both East and West, the priest alone can administer the Sacraments, and to that effect can only be ordained by the laying on him of a bishop's hands.

In 1667 the Russian seceders were faced with the difficulty that the entire body of Russian bishops submitted to the Government, very much as early in the English Reformation the entire bench of bishops, with one or two honourable exceptions, submitted with indecent haste to the decrees of Henry VIII. The difficulty was even greater in the Russian Church than in the English, because the *myron* or holy chrism, used for various sacramental acts of unction, can only be consecrated on Thursday in Easter Week by a Patriarch. Then again as the pope or priest could only be ordained by a bishop, and as no pope is immortal, the time was bound to come when the seceding clergy would be as extinct as the dodo and none left to administer the sacraments. As early as 1681 the Raskol teacher Avvakum wrote to the Tsar Theodore that "their patriarchate was in ruins, their priesthood decayed, and their entire clergy moribund." Of dire need he had to counsel his followers to follow the precept of the Apostle James, and dispensing with the services of a priest, confess to one another and repent before God. They might communicate in the reserved host, without a priest being present, and for the purpose might carry it about with them — a practice for which they might, had they known of it, have found a precedent in the Church of Africa in the days of Tertullian. Until the death of the Tsar Alexis they procured reserved hosts in Pomor from the Solovets Convent. The hegumen Dositheus built a church in 1686 at Chir with pre-Nikonian Antiminsia and accumulated a quantity of reserved hosts for distribution among Old believers. But how could they hope to obtain on all occasions even a reserved host? [1]

In the presence of this difficulty Avvakum sanctioned recourse to the ministration even of priests whose ordination dated from after the year 1667, and was therefore heretical. But another Raskol teacher, Theodor the deacon, altogether rejected the ministration of heretically ordained priests and would hear of none ordained later than 1666. On those who took up this attitude the situation was bound to press with ever increasing weight, and in the course of a generation to become irremediable; at first it was in some degree masked by the belief that Antichrist was come and the end of the world was at hand, but this belief began to fade or replace itself with the milder theory that Antichrist was a tendency that makes for evil.

As might be expected, the need of a hierarchy would be met in different ways according to circumstances, and Ivanovski points out that the North of Russia, which was densely wooded, sparsely populated, and contained few churches and fewer roads, was more favourable than other regions to the growth of Bezpopovets usage, i. e. of those who, making a virtue of necessity, resigned themselves to dispensing altogether with a hierarchy and to getting along with no rites and sacraments at all, or at most with those which according to ancient ecclesiastical usage laymen can in cases of dire need themselves discharge, for example baptism, confession, burial (which a monk can canonically perform), the Hours, *Te Deums* and *Pannychidia* or all night long vigils. In such rites the parts reserved to priests could be omitted. Such was the solution adopted by the settlers on the Vyg, and their example was soon copied far and wide.

In all this the Raskol leaders had no thought of depreciating the Sacraments of the Church or of minimising the importance

---

[1] Miliukov (Outlines, pt. 2, p. 56) states that the last of the pre-Nikonian popes Theodosius, having escaped from persecution, led a group of Old believers from the forests of Kirzhen to Vetka in the Polish marches, and on the way prepared in a ruined church at Kaluga a number of reserved hosts, which later on made the reputation for a time of Vetka, where in 1695 he consecrated a church, the only one after the destruction in 1688 of that at Chir.

of a hierarchy. They had nothing in common with Protestants who understand that Sacraments whether pagan or Christian are *magis opinione quam re*, and so have learned the secret of each believer being his own priest. It was indeed all the other way with the Raskol; through no fault of their own they found themselves marooned without a priesthood, yet thoroughly convinced of its need and efficacy for salvation.

The so-called *Pomorian Responses* of the year 1720 were the first official recognition of the Bezpopovski or *No Priesthood* position. It rested on the distinction between sacraments universally necessary to salvation, and sacraments not so necessary; to the former class belong baptism, repentance and communion; to the latter all the rest. It was decided that in case of need a Church could do without the sacraments of unction with holy Chrism, of marriage, of holy orders. There were, as remarked above, precedents for the celebration of the sacraments of baptism and penitence by laymen, the applicability of which to the case of the Raskol Ivanovski somewhat ineptly disputes; but how dispense with a priest in the Communion? It was decided in the Responses that it was enough to use a reserved host and substitute for the presence of the priest an ardent desire for Communion; they might even content themselves altogether with a "spiritual Communion."[1] Thus was laid by urgent need and force of circumstances the basis among these poor people for a worship of God in spirit and truth alone.

In their *Responses* of 1720 the Raskol teachers furthermore urged that the advent of Antichrist had exterminated both the priesthood and the divine sacrifice, that under the circumstances the individual Christian becomes his own priest. In such an exceptional era it is legitimate, they argued, for laymen to conduct the sacraments of baptism and confession and to celebrate sundry rites. They also claimed the right to rebaptize converts from the orthodox church, a pretension somewhat galling to the latter.

The Old believers of Starodub, a portion of which later on removed to Vetka, had, when they first fled from Moscow,

[1] Subbotin, *Materials* Vol. V, p. 224, 230; VI, p. 60–79, 310–312.

priests among them who had been ordained before the schism;
thus first Cosmas and after him Stephan ministered to them.
These two were followed by Joasaph, a black or monkish pope,
whose baptism was anterior to 1667, but as to whose ordination there were doubts whether it was not posterior. After
him Theodosius, who was ordained by Joasaph's predecessor,
supplied their needs, and under his guidance they built a
church, and so were able for the first time to conduct the divine
liturgy. As long as they had at their disposal priests of the
old ordination, such communities were inclined to reject those
of the new; but in time, as the stock of old priests more and
more exhausted itself, they had to face the same problem which
the Bezpopovtsy settled in the negative; and they settled it
in the counter-sense. They felt they must have priests at
any cost, and decided to adopt those of the new order in
case they could be persuaded to join them and were willing
to use the rites they considered ancient. The settlers on the
Don, at Kerzhen and in general those of middle and Southern
Russia, adopted the same solution. From the circumstance
of their adopting fugitive or runaway priests the sect came to
be known as *Begstvuiushchiye*, sometimes as *Oratorians* or
Tchasovennyie, the latter term implying that (except in Vetka
or Starodub, and later on in Irgiz and the cemetery of Rogozh)
they had no churches, but only chapels or oratories, *proseuchai*
as the Greek Jews called of old their synagogues.

By accepting the ministration of runaway popes the Popovtsy
sect exposed themselves to a crossfire of criticism both from
the orthodox and from the priestless sect; for both these parties
urged against such a compromise that it mined the position
the Popovtsy had in 1666 taken up, when they abandoned the
Nikonian Church as an heretical body. If it was heretical,
how could its baptisms and ordinations also not be heretical?
How again, urged Ivan Alexev, a doctor of the priestless
sect, can you retain an order of priests, if you have no bishops?
It was in vain that the Popovtsy tried to justify their position
from early Church history, pointing out that the see of Chalcedon at one time got on without a bishop for thirty years,
that the see of Hippo had done likewise. The Orthodox

replied that no Church claiming ecumenical authority can permanently exist without a head, and that, the triple ordination being indispensable in a real Church and the three orders indissolubly bound up in one another, you cannot logically have a clergy without a bishop. They are a trunk without a head.

The Popovtsy were then reduced to analogy and prophecy; and argued that, as the temple fire of the Jews lay hidden during their Babylonian captivity in a dry well, so it was possible for the true charismatic gift of priesthood to lurk in an heretical medium. There would have been something in this contention, if the Popovtsy had not repudiated the baptism of the Orthodox Church; but baptism is the portal of all the Sacraments, and they scrupled not to rebaptize converts who came over to them, so contravening a canon of procedure established in the undivided Church as early as the third Century.

How heavily the difficulty weighed upon the Popovtsy is shewn by the many attempts they made in the next 150 years to secure an episcopate for themselves, attempts which Ivanovski relates with sardonic humour. From the first the sect cherished the belief that a genuine church still existed somewhere in the world, and their aim was to discover it and link up with it. One is reminded of the similar endeavours of the English non-jurors. Oddly enough the latter entered into long-drawn-out negotiations with the Orthodox Russian Church, which the curious will read in Monsignor Louis Petit's Appendix to the new edition of Mansi's *concilia*. If the non-jurors had been better informed they might, when the Russian Government abruptly and in an Erastian spirit repudiated them on discovering that they were ranged in opposition to the English monarchy, have opened negotiations with the Popovtsy whose case strikingly resembled their own, with the exception, however, that the non-jurors, had bishops of their own. They could have supplied the Raskolniks with bishops.

One of the earliest doctors of the Russian sect, the deacon Theodor, was convinced that a real Christian community survived in Jerusalem, preserving the use of two fingers in blessing, the double Alleluia and other peculiarities dear to the

Raskol. Others among their teachers held that a genuine
piety survived in Antioch, and that the Patriarch Macarius
of that see did not really represent the faithful there when
he came to Moscow and prostrated himself before Nikon and
the Tsar. It will be remembered that he died on his way
back, and in this the Raskol discerned the finger of God.

In the XVIIIth century a doctor of the rival and priestless
sect came to their aid. This was Mark, an inmate of the
Topozer Skete in the Kemski district of the Archangel Government. He adduced the evidence of a traveller to Japan to
the effect that in Belovod in that land there existed a church
subject to Antioch and endued with all charismatic gifts, with a
patriarch of its own, 179 places of worship and four metropolitans. This tale was an echo of the Latin Christianity implanted in Japan in 1549 by St. Francis Xavier. It enjoyed
a vigorous life, and by the end of the century numbered 250
churches, and nearly half a million adherents; but the Japanese had extinguished it with horrible cruelty a hundred years
before its echoes reached the ears of Mark, and when he wrote
its martyrs were already being enrolled in the Roman calendar.
There is a strange irony in the Russian Raskol teacher imagin-
ing that ancient piety was to be restored from such a quarter.

Still more romantic was another legend which in the early
years of the XVIIIth Century floated before the eyes of these
desolate sectaries in quest of a bishop. There was a sub-
terranean Church in the city of Kitezh on the bank of Lake
Svetloyar. Kitezh was a town in Suzdal which disappeared
from human ken on the approach of the conqueror Batus.[1]
It was to abide invisible until the end of the world, and it
contained churches and monasteries and a large population.
Of a summer's evening the dwellers on the lake could hear
beneath its waters the sound of the Kitezh bells; and a letter
was circulated addressed to his father by a son who lived below.
It told how happy he was in a holy monastery, hidden from
human eye, and besought the habitants of this dull skyward

[1] Grandson of Chingis Khan of the Golden horde and hero of many Russian
legends. The Russian Encyclopedia locates the legendary site of Kitezh near
Semenov in the Nizhigorod Government.

earth not to repine nor say mass for his soul; for he was not
dead, but alive in a realm, terrestrial indeed, but blest with all
the joys of happy repose, replete with delights, not gross and
carnal, but spiritual and refined.

Japan, however, was far away, and Kitezh was a dream, and
it was hopeless to try to win over to themselves a bishop of the
orthodox church, for as we saw Russian bishops were not of the
stuff of which martyrs are made. The only hope was to secure
one across the frontiers, and as early as 1730 they besought the
bishop of Jassy, the metropolitan Antony, to ordain as their
bishop a certain monk of Vetka named Pavel or Paul; but the
latter could not conscientiously subscribe to the twelve tenets
imposed by the Metropolitan, says the Bezpopovets writer
Ivan Alexev. Jona Kurnos, a Popovets author, relates that
the same community made fresh overtures to Jassy the next
year, when the Pope Basil of Kazan, who in religion bore the
name Barlaam, was dispatched thither for ordination. But
this scheme bore no more fruit than the former.

Epiphanius, the First Raskol Bishop

Epiphanius was a monk of the Kozelski monastery in the
see of Kiev, where he had relations, to whom he ever shewed
kindness and consideration. At Kiev he was in good repute
with the Archbishop Varlaam Vanatovich, who according to
one account took him as his lay-brother and afterwards made
him hegumen of the Kozelski monastery; according to another
he was steward of the archbishop's household. From the
Kozel treasury, however, he was accused of having stolen 240
roubles, and to escape the consequences forged himself a passport. Armed also with a forged seal of the Archbishop of Kiev
as well as with another genuine one of the metropolitan of
Lvov or Lemberg which he found in the church archives of
Kiev, he now crossed the frontier and passed himself off
as an archpriest *in partibus*,— an easy thing to do, as there
were many such nomads in Podolia and Galicia, men who
without belonging to any particular see undertook the task of
ministering to the Uniats of Poland. He also bore with him

an apocryphal letter purporting to be from the hand of the archbishop of Kiev and to represent the clergy of the Ukraine. This complained of a recent act of the Moscow Synod which deprived the metropolitan of Kiev of his old grade and dignity, and besought the metropolitan of Jassy to confer on Epiphanius episcopal orders. To this letter was attached the supposititious seal he had cut out. As it was necessary by canon law for a candidate for episcopal ordination to bear a letter from the faithful of the see he was to occupy, Epiphanius had forged one from the inhabitants of the city of Chigirin in the Ukraine. The metropolitan of Jassy fell into the trap and ordained him July 22, 1724. Instead, however, of repairing to his see Epiphanius betook himself to other parts of the Ukraine, where at the request of the Raskolniks he ordained for them fourteen priests and several deacons. But he did not long enjoy episcopal freedom, for the Russian Government pounced on him, and the Senate sentenced him May 6, 1727, at the end of Catharine's reign to seclusion for life in the Solovets Convent. Thence he escaped after nearly three years (in 1729) in the disguise of a pilgrim, but was twice rearrested and was sent to Moscow in November 1731. There he foregathered with the Old believers who offered to smuggle him across the frontier to their settlement at Vetka in Poland. This was in 1733. He had been previously condemned first to seclusion in Solovets as a monk, and then later on to be unfrocked and sent to Siberia.

Ivanovski contends that he had scant regard for the sect, and knew that he was betraying the orthodox church, yet yielded to their importunities because he yearned for rest and freedom in Poland. The doubts, however, which he casts all through on the genuineness of Epiphanius' transactions contradict one another no less than they do the general situation, as he depicts it. Why, if Epiphanius was a convinced adherent of the Orthodox Church, should he have wanted to put himself out of reach of the Russian Government? Ivanovski's *arrière pensée* is evident. He can not admit that any genuinely ordained bishop ever sided with the Raskol. Why again should the sectaries have rescued him from the Government

convoy charged to transport him to Yaroslav and Vologda?
Yet they did so, and got him safely to Vetka.

There it was established to the satisfaction of the Popovets
community that his orders were genuine, though some reserves
were made as to his baptism, which was reported to have
been performed, not by immersion which alone they regarded
as canonical, but by aspersion. Ivanovski relates that they
were reassured when they learned that as a small boy he had
been ducked in play by his companions. The apocryphal
character of this part of Ivanovski's narrative is evidenced by
the fact that this incident is derived from the life of St. Athanasius.

In August 1734 Epiphanius was accordingly installed as their
bishop by the Old believers of Vetka, though he was not recognized by all the Russian congregations; for example that of
Kerzhen repudiated him, and accused that of Vetka with being
victims of a phantasy offensive to heaven and little conducive
to salvation.

The new bishop did not enjoy at Vetka the peace and calm
he longed for. He so openly displayed his contempt for the
Raskol, was so little disposed to comply with their rules and
grew so weary of their long-drawn-out ceremonies and strict
fasts as to make himself unpopular; and their distaste for him,
already excited by the doubt about his baptism, was changed
to dismay by the discovery of a letter written by him to his
relatives in Kiev, in which he accused his new congregation of
having deceived and kidnapped him into their 'cave of heresy.'

Epiphanius then discharged his episcopal functions for no
more than eight months, until April, 1735, when the Tsarina
Anna Ioannovna, profiting by the weakness of Poland and the
disturbances that arose over the election of a new king to succeed Augustus II, ordered her general Sytin to make a descent
on Vetka and drive the Old believers who had fled thither,
back to their homes. Epiphanius was hunted back along with
the rest and jailed in Kiev; but shortly afterwards fell ill and
died, in communion, according to Macarius and Ivanovski,
with the Orthodox Church. The Old believers, however, who
were surely in a position to know the facts, had another story

and declared that he died a martyr by the violence of the Government, and in communion with themselves. That is the more probable account. His tomb in the fortress church of S. Theodosius at Kiev became a resort of Old-believing pilgrims, and many were called after his name. The clergy ordained by him never entertained any doubts as to the validity of their orders. The last pope consecrated by him died in 1790, when there was still at Starodub a church dedicated to him. Such was the history of the first Raskol bishop; and in spite of the jaundiced character of Macarius' and Ivanovski's narrative, we discern the fact that he was a success.

The Uniat Movement

Ivanovski relates with the same *parti pris* the fortunes of four other bishops obtained from one quarter or another by the Popovtsy during the XVIIIth Century. These need not delay us, and we come to the effort made by one Nicodemus, a monk of Starodub, to make good the want by summoning a council of Old believers at Moscow in 1765. It was chiefly remarkable because both sects were represented at it, a proof that they had not then drifted so far apart, as they have to-day. It was resolved to discuss whether they could, compatibly with the ancient canons of the Church, appoint a bishop *de suo*, in other words by presbyteral appointment only. It is still a burning question to-day whether in sundry ancient churches the episcopate had any other origin, but of these deeper problems of church history the Raskol knew little, and no one apparently questioned the doctrine of apostolical succession. One of them, according to Ivanovski, had found a story in an old chronicle to the effect that Clement, a metropolitan of Kiev, had been created such behind the back of the Greek patriarch by use of a holy relic, to wit the head of St. Clement of Rome,— a mode of ordination to which apparently the orthodox historian has no objection provided it is a chapter of bishops who make such use of a relic. His only criticism of the Old believer's project is that laymen, not bishops, were to work the miracle. As they had no head of St. Clement, it was proposed to use the hand of St. Jona, a much venerated

relic in the Uspenski Church. The idea of laying the dead
hand of a saint on the head of a living man for purposes of
ordination was a familiar one in the Middle Ages, and the
Armenians were accused of making similar use of the dead
hand of Gregory the Illuminator which is among the relics
of the patriarchal church at Valarshapat. In 1765, however,
the project fell through for the excellent reason that in order
to have true ordination there must be an intention to ordain
on the part of the priest who lays on his hand. Of every sacramental act such intention forms a part. Now who was to
guarantee such an intention on the part of the defunct saint?
Who moreover was to recite the pontifical prayers? Should
it be a Popovets or a Bezpopovets? A fugitive pope out of the
Orthodox Church or a Pomorski elder? Surely too the dogmatic complexion of the new bishop would alter according as
one or the other officiated? We learn from Ivanovski, perhaps rightly, that the two parties in the Council parted on
terms less friendly than those on which they met, and he
unkindly suggests that the project was a sacrilegious one.

But Nicodemus was not discouraged, and began to cast
about for a patriarch who would appoint him a bishop. He
seemed for a little time to have discovered one in the patriarch
of Georgia, Athanasius, who was staying in Moscow at the
time. By his advice Nicodemus set out for Tiflis, but by
reason of a war that was raging failed to reach his goal. Better
luck attended an application to the patriarch of Antioch,
Daniel, who no doubt was not disinclined to receive ordination
fees even from Russian Old believers. Anyhow he turned
Joasaph, one of the monks of Starodub, into a archimandrite,
and another of them, Raphael, into a bishop; but, as bad luck
would have it, the latter died on his way home, so that both
the Russian Government and the Raskol were cheated out of
him. Joasaph on reaching Starodub had the mortification of
finding that Nicodemus was intent on asking the Orthodox
Russian Synod to appoint a bishop for his adherents, and this
movement ultimately led to the formation of a body of Uniat
Old believers.

An Uniat is one who conditionally enters into communion

with a Church which he esteems to be orthodox, retaining his own rites and traditions. The Uniat Ruthenes for example used the Cyrillic rites which are those of the Russian and South Slav Churches, but recognized the Bishop of Rome's jurisdiction in matters of faith and dogma. The Uniats we are now to consider were Old believers, and were allowed the continued use of the old service-books, of the two-fingered blessing and other peculiarities they set store by, on condition they went back into communion with the Orthodox Church. Macarius and Ivanovski, as is natural, relate the fortunes of this movement at greater length than its results warrant, because from their standpoint it was an act of resipiscence on the part of the Raskol.

In 1781 Nicodemus, who had sent Raphael and Joasaph to Antioch, found himself on the estate of a Count or Graf Rumyantsev, then viceroy or, as we should say, lord-lieutenant of Little Russia. The latter, aware of the scruples he entertained respecting the ministry of runaway popes and his anxiety to obtain a bishop for his communion, advised him to apply for one to the Russian Government and promised to interest the Empress in his behalf. Nicodemus mooted the project in his own sect of the Diakonovski (p. 102) which admitted orthodox priests to minister for them without insisting on their being anointed afresh as did other Popovets groups. Just then a certain monk Gerasim Knyazev, who was in his confidence, was starting for Petersburg, and he undertook to sound the Holy Synod there about the matter. On his way, being still in Moscow, Gerasim called on the venerable bishop Plato, and, when he reached Petersburg, on Gabriel the metropolitan and Innocent archbishop of Pskov, and on Prince Potemkin-Tavricheski, who all three favoured the scheme. Not so however Nicodemus' co-religionists at Starodub, for when he returned thither a considerable party of them were inclined to stone him. But Nicodemus persevered, and wrote to Gabriel and to Prince Potemkin, and Graf Rumyantzev-Zadunaiski, whom he had come to know, for their advice. They answered him sympathetically, and Nicodemus in 1782 went to the Capital where Potemkin presented him to the broadminded Empress Catharine II, who, touched by his appeal, promised her aid. The result was that in 1783 as many as three thousand [1] Old believers drew up a petition for reunion and sent it with Potemkin's and Rumyantsev's recommendations to the Synod, while Nicodemus was advised to return to Petersburg to plead his case in person.

The conditions proposed by him were three: that the Orthodox Church should withdraw the anathemas pronounced in 1666–7 against Old believers, that the latter should be allowed to conduct their services from the old books, and that the Holy Synod should appoint a bishop or a chorepiscopus and send him to Nicodemus' monastery, the Uspenski at Starodub, to regulate their clergy all over Russia, to consecrate churches, and ordain pastors; the said bishop was to be under the control of the Synod, but the Raskolniki were everywhere to retain their ancient service books and rites.

Nicodemus' expectations were not destined to be realized in their entirety. It was objected that the canons of the Russian as of any other Church, forbade the presence of more than one bishop in a diocese; it was also argued that the institution of Chorepiscopi had died out, and that a bishop presiding over the Raskol all over Russia would be equivalent to a patriarch. Peter the great had done away with Patriarchs. Potemkin himself after encouraging Nicodemus to make the demand, no longer urged it when the latter reached Petersburg at the end of 1783; and finally an ukase of March 11, 1784, addressed to Gabriel, merely contained a license for the archbishop of Mohilev to allow the Old believers the priests they desired, but was silent about the grant of a bishop. Nicodemus however professed himself satisfied, and went back to Starodub, where he died on May 12, 1784, in communion, according to Ivanovski, with the Orthodox church.

Four of his adherents now journeyed to Petersburg to ask Gabriel to consecrate Joasaph, one of themselves, and, as we have seen an archimandrite, abbot of the Uspenski convent at Starodub; but a year elapsed before so moderate a demand was granted, and the favour was coupled with a requirement that

---

[1] Acc. to Palmieri, *Chiesa Russa*, p. 452, only one thousand.

the villages of Old believers round Starodub should be transferred to Potemkin's property in Novorossia. The truth
was, this grand seigneur was trying to exploit the Old believers
in his own interest, and, though they would not fall in with his
schemes, he did induce Joasaph to become prior of a monastery
he had built in the new locality, so leaving the Uniats of
Starodub without a clergy. If one bears in mind the fact that
Russian proprietors reckoned their wealth not by the number
of their acres, but of their serfs, one understands the anxiety
of Potemkin to acquire such valuable colonists for his new
estates.

The Starodub uniats made a despairing appeal to Gabriel
to influence Ambrose to ordain them a priest, but he was
afraid of Potemkin and presently sent them one named Andrew
Ioannov Zhuravlev, a missionary appointed by the Orthodox
Authorities to convert the Raskol and a frank enemy of everything connected with them. A renegade himself, "he knew
from experience how most successfully to influence the hearts
of Raskolniki."

Nevertheless he was well received when he first arrived in
1788; but he immediately set himself with the help of the armed
forces of the Government to oust the majority of the Old believers of Starodub, who had not fallen in with Nicodemus' Uniat
movement, from their churches and other buildings, in particular from their Pokrovski Church and monastery. The Old
believers, in a work entitled the *Synaxary*, i.e. the Church
hagiography embellished with records of their own saints who
had suffered for the truth as they understood it and answering
to Foxe's Book of Martyrs, described the violence, robbery
and martyrdom to which they were subjected by this "uniat"
apostle. In the end, it is pleasing to relate, he was worsted,
though he is said to have converted some of Nicodemus'
adherents to the ministration of orthodox popes.

Nor was it in Starodub alone that a handful of the Raskolniks entered into the Uniat movement, merely to find that the
Government took advantage of it to fix a noose round their
necks to be drawn tight on the first occasion. In Irgiz also
the monk Serge, Abbot of the upper Preobrazhenski monastery,

took up the idea, influenced it is said by the scandalous life of
the renegade clergy on whom his sect depended for the administration of the Sacraments, though it is difficult to conceive,
in view of what one knows of Russia in that age, how they could
differ for the worse from the orthodox clergy. He took council
with Nicephorus Theotoki, bishop of Astrakhan, who at his
instance addressed in 1786 an epistle to the Raskol, conceived
in a spirit of charity. Serge thereupon drew up fifteen questions relating to the differences which kept the sect separate
from the Orthodox Church, and embodying the conditions upon
which they would make their peace with it. He then proceeded to call together a number of the heads of Irgiz, and
Raskol monasteries in Moscow and Petersburg and read his
document to them. They approved and in 1790 it was for-
warded to Nicephorus for him to lay it before the Governor of
Saratov whose rule extended over Astrakhan. Serge received
an answer in due time and, having converted a rich merchant of
Volsk of the name of Zlobin to his point of view, set about to
realize his scheme. But the merchant had not consulted his
own wife Pelagia who was a stubborn Raskolnik, and who,
having acquainted herself with what was afoot, set herself
to frustrate what she regarded as an act of treachery with the
aid of Serge's own sister Alexandra, prioress of a Raskol nunnery and as resolute as herself. The plan was to arrest Serge
and hold him prisoner or even slay him, but he made good his
escape to Petersburg before the two ladies could execute it.
Zlobin also reached the Capital, and the two having gained the
ear of Gabriel, by his advice petitioned the Holy Synod to send
priests of their own to Irgiz; and Serge was himself allowed
to select two from the Tikhvin monastery. But the two
encountered no friendly reception; Serge, who on his return
to Irgiz took up his quarters in the Uspenski monastery in the
room assigned to the Abbot, was all but suffocated by the
Cellarius and two other monks. They set upon him by night
and locked him up in the larder, whence he was only rescued by
the local police of Volsk, warned by his nephew of his grave
plight. The brethren appointed another Abbot, Prokhorus,
in his place, and Serge despairing of Irgiz retired with his

nephew and some of his kindred to a Starodub village where Nicodemus had a monastery at his disposal. Of this he was made hieromonachus, and having frankly joined the Orthodox Church avenged himself on his former co-religionists in a book entitled "A Mirror for Old Believers." His confederate Zlobin, after a feeble attempt to convert the village of Volsk, where he lived, to the Uniat faith, died, according to Ivanovski, a sincere believer in the same, though he had wavered much in his opinions. Orthodox historians, it will be noticed, rope in on their death-beds all Old believers who ever made even the least rapprochement towards orthodoxy. In the Nizhegorod the Bishop Paul in 1797 represented to the Synod that they ought to send priests to the Raskolniks of his see, of whom according to him there were a thousand in favour of reunion; the Tsar Paul I accordingly issued an Ukase allowing priests to be sent in such cases without an appeal being on every occasion addressed to him. We realize from the necessity of such an ukase how thoroughly the Orthodox Church was subordinated to the State. It was a mere department of it.

About the same time a number of the Old believers of Kazan asked for orthodox priests; and the archbishop, Ambrose, prevailed on the Synod to allow him to place at their disposal the church of the Four Evangelists on lake Kaban along with a priest named Andreev.

In Petersburg in 1799 an Old believer Ivan Mylov found it expedient on being ennobled to desert so plebeian a cult as that of the Raskol; he had a private chapel, which he enlarged and had it consecrated to St. Nicholas. Whereupon the Tsar Paul I paid him the compliment of hearing mass said in it.

The Concessions of Paul I

About this time the Tsar sanctioned a code of rules for such Popovtsi as could be persuaded by force, fraud or personal and spiritual advantages to join the Orthodox Church. The occasion was a request made in 1799 by the Old believers of Moscow that the Church would supply them with Priests and Holy Chrism. It was addressed to Plato the Metropolitan, who refused on the suspicion that they were not sincere.

They then applied to Ambrose, archbishop of Kazan, whereupon the Tsar put an end to these negotiations. The would-be
Uniats however did not acquiesce in the refusal, and formulated sixteen conditions under which they would renew communion, which after examination by Plato were sanctioned by
the Tsar Paul I, Oct. 27, 1800. Of these conditions, some old,
some new, the chief were the remission of the anathemas of
1666–7 and permission to use the old books. The priests to
be accorded to the Raskol were to be of the Orthodox rite or
expressly ordained for the purpose; but in no case were they
to be fugitives from the Church. Such of the Raskol as had
taken monkish orders were to be accepted as monks, and chrism
was to be provided by the bishop of each see in which it was
required.

Under these conditions the Uniats were to retain their own
ecclesiastical establishments, but for the consecration of new
churches Uniat priests were to be employed. In case an orthodox pope officiated in an Uniat church he was to use the old
books; nay even prelates were to do likewise. They were
also to cross with the two fingers. On the other hand Uniat
clergy were forbidden to take part in public services or processions, and were only to officiate inside their own churches.
If an Old believer desired it, an orthodox priest was free to
confess and communicate him, but not *vice versa*. Plato was
willing that an Uniat priest should administer the last Sacraments to members of the Orthodox Church, but only if no
orthodox pope was at hand. So much anxiety was felt on the
point that every precaution was taken to prevent any leakage
from the orthodox into the Uniat camp. All these privileges
however, were of narrow range, for they were confined either
to the registered Raskol, who as we have seen tended to be a
small majority, or if to others than them, only to those who
possessed the warranty of an orthodox prelate that they had
never tried to pass themselves off as orthodox. A mixed marriage might be held in whichever church the parties could
agree upon, and children of the marriage baptized in accordance with a similar agreement. The demand of the Raskolniks that the Uniats should receive the Sacraments of the

orthodox and *vice versa* with complete reciprocity was rejected *sans phrase*.

The above provisions were liberal if we consider the age and time in which they were drawn up; and if Nikon had been less intransigent and had granted them 140 years earlier, schism would have been avoided. All the same, as Ivanovski allows, many Uniats were not satisfied with such concessions, for they wanted permission for the orthodox to join themselves and they also wanted a bishop of their own. These concessions the Church would not make, although it was ready to facilitate in any way the transference to the Uniat body of unregistered Raskolniks; and at the instance of the Bishop of Perm it was arranged that Raskolniks of ten years' standing might join the Uniats. In 1881 the Holy Synod reduced this term to five years, and at the same time it was conceded that an Uniat priest might hear confessions from orthodox laymen and administer the Sacraments to them on condition the orthodox priest of the parish was informed of the same in writing. In the same year the Greek Patriarch of Constantinople gave a faculty to the clergy under his jurisdiction to use pre-Nikonian rites. This concession was made chiefly in view of a colony of Old believers who had long before settled at Maenos on the Bosphorus. At the same time a priest was ordained in Moscow for this congregation.

The Persecution of the Raskol by Nicholas I

The Uniat concessions made by Paul I might conceivably have borne fruit in the XIXth Century except for the incomprehensible ferocity of the attempts made under Nicholas I to force orthodoxy upon the Raskol at large.[1] These attempts began in 1827 with a threat on the part of Prince Golitsyn, Governor of Saratov, to break up the monastery of Nizhni-Voskresenski, unless they became Uniats. He went in person among the monks and read them an imperial ukase to the effect that all the monasteries of Irgiz should be destroyed in the event of their non-compliance. The next day the prior Adrian and a dozen of the brethren submitted to the bishop

[1] Sokolov, *Raskol in Saratov*, p. 297.

of Saratov, Moses; by their craven action they so incensed the
rest of the settlement that the police had to be called in to
protect them, and the recalcitrants having been either pressed
for the army or sent to Siberia, the fabric was handed over to
the servile minority. Such was the fate of this one convent.
The others remained defiant, and enjoyed a certain respite
from Nicholas' fury, for the two successors of Golitsyn in the
Governments of Saratov, Roslavlev and Pereverzev, to their
credit, did their best to protect them.

But the calm did not last long. In 1836 a certain Stepanov,
was made Governor of Saratov; and in appointing him the
Tsar remarked [1] on the abundance of sectaries in that region
and especially in the monasteries of Irgiz. Stepanov promised he would reduce them to a single denomination. The Tsar
assented, but deprecated violence. "Proceed warily," he said,
"and do not exasperate them." Stepanov determined to
begin with the Middle-Nikolski convent which was at the village of Mechetnoe within the pale of the newly constituted
town of Nikolaev; and advised the Minister of the Interior
that the task was a feasible one. The monks, if they would
become Uniats, were to retain the premises, but their house
was to pass under the control of the archimandrite Zosimus,
prior of the Kostroma Vysokovski Uniat Monastery; and it
was resolved by the Governor with the connivance of Jacob,
bishop of Saratov, to execute the measure by surprise and by
way of a *coup de main*. Accordingly, the provost of Nikolaev
and the Commissioner of Saratov suddenly presented themselves on February 8 before Cornelius the Abbot, shewed him
the imperial edict and demanded the keys and property of the
house. Cornelius refused, unless the surrounding population
assented, and, as the secret had been badly kept, some three
hundred of the latter had gathered round and shouted: "We
will not give up the Monastery, no matter how much you shed
our blood." [2]

[1] Russkaya Starina, 1879, I. 552.

[2] I was once the witness of a very similar scene at Valarshapat, when a detach-
ment of cavalry took possession of the Armenian convent in order to carry off
two harmless and aged monks, suspected by the Russian Government of favouring
the election as Armenian Patriarch of Monsignor Ormanian, Armenian Patriarch

Cornelius made no attempt to resist, but took the keys of his house and laid them on the table, whereupon Zosimus took them up and went towards the church to unlock it; but a crowd had collected in the porch and barred his way, while others sounded an alarm on the big bell, crying: "Help, Help!" Zosimus was not authorized to resort to force, so he retired with his officers to the town and wrote a minute of the affair to his superiors.

In February a large posse of officials, with gendarmes to assist them, repaired afresh to the monastery, and found a crowd of some 500 gathered inside the precincts, ringing the bells to attract their fellows outside, and once more the officials retired after making a few arrests. Information was conveyed to Saratov, and now the Governor himself appeared on the scene, only to find some 2,000 sectaries mustered inside the convent, who fell on their knees in a circle round the church, clasping each others hands and vowing that it should only be entered, if at all, across their dead bodies. Thereupon the Governor returned to Saratov and wrote to the ministry accusing the poor people of sedition and riot.

The inevitable in Russia, then ensued. The Governor appeared once more with a force of Cossacks and artillery. A rumour was set abroad that the Raskolniks intended to burn down the monastery, so a fire engine was brought on the scene, and streams of water pumped over them as they lay on the ground, with clasped hands. It was a glacial day, and presently, unable to stand the cold water, they proceeded to flee inside the buildings. In the melée which followed the soldiers beat them with the butt ends of their muskets and arrested many of them, after which the monastery was handed over to Zosimus. At the same time the women's convent of Uspenski was closed, and such of its inmates as were registered obliged to migrate to the Pokrovski convent in Upper Irgiz, the rest being sent to their homes. But not a single monk or nun turned Uniat. All of them were scattered far and wide,

of Constantinople. It was a time of interregnum, when the old Patriarch was dead and the time drawing near for the election of a new one by all the Armenian congregations of the entire world. The Russian Government dreaded the election of a Turkish prelate, and had a creature of their own for the post.

some to the Ural, others to the Don, many to the deserts of Siberia, where they spread the tale which enhanced the propaganda of their sect. Nor did Stepanov gain anything by it, for, as is usual with despotisms, the sins of the system were atoned for by the unsuccessful instrument. He was cashiered and one Bibikov sent to take his place, but not without a direct admonition on the part of Nicholas I on no account to lose sight of any opportunity that might offer itself of annihilating the Spasopreobrazhenski Monastery of the Raskolniks.

In 1841 its conversion to the Uniat body was actually effected under the new Governor Thadeev. A sudden descent was made on the place, and bursting into the church, the authorities with the Uniat clergy in their train sprayed it with their own holy water. The monks were ordered to join the Uniats or quit the place, and all but two quitted it. The monk Trifilius, a creature of the Bishop of Saratov, was then made Abbot. With the same secrecy, suddenness and violence the Pokrovski nunnery was assigned to the Uniats, but not a single nun apostatized.

Such measures in Irgiz contributed enormously to the spread of the Raskol, and they were related in verse all over Russia. They revealed what Tsardom was capable of.

I have outlined from Macarius' and Ivanovski's pages the Uniat movement initiated at Starodub by Nicodemus. We are not surprised to learn from the same author that after his death it made no way, and that the true Raskol waxed stronger and stronger under Alexander I. The Tsar Nicholas Pavlovich on his way to the Crimea in 1847, halted at a Starodub village named Dobryank, whose inhabitants proffered him the usual bread and salt of old-world hospitality. He declined it harshly and addressed the village deputies as follows: "I regret deeply to see you all in error; whenever you make up your minds to go to church, I will accept your bread, and will myself build you a church." And to suit the words a Uniat Church was instantly built and consecrated in the presence of the commandant of Starodub; and a Uniat priest named Timothy Verkhovski was sent thither from Petersburg. On his way back the Tsar finding the church built accepted bread and salt.

In Moscow also under Nicholas an attempt was made to implant the Uniat faith in the Raskol centres of the Popovtsy and Bezpopovtsy (Thedosievtsy) sects, known respectively as the Rogozhski and Preobrazhenski cemeteries.[1] In the former one Vladimir Andreevich Sapelkin acquired some influence, and according to Ivanovski he neither shared the doubts still entertained by many of the Popovtsy of the validity of orthodox orders nor tolerated the ordination by the stray bishop they had procured of peasants and tradesmen who had no learning or sense of vocation. In 1854 accordingly he addressed himself to Philaret the metropolitan with a view to the reconsecration of one of the oratories of his sect as a church, and this was effected much to the indignation and surprise of the faithful who in the course of the vigil of the eve of the ceremony surrounded his house crying: "Let us burn down Sapelnik's house!", a demonstration of hatred which the latter's faith in God and the Russian police combined qualified him to bear with equanimity, and the entire convent was handed over to the Uniats. In 1856 the old rites were resumed, priests being provided of Austrian ordination. This led to the closing of the Popovets Church and the altars remained sealed until May 3, 1883. In 1854 the priestless cemetery of Preobrazhen, which Haxthausen visited ten years before and has described, was similarly invaded with the magnificent result that sixty-four persons became Uniats. One chapel was then consecrated by the metropolitan, and another in 1857. In 1866 an Uniat Monastery for men was established under the archimandrite Paul of Prussia and the library of the merchant

---

[1] The right to possess these cemeteries and to construct in them hospitals and chapels and monastic buildings was conceded by Catherine in 1771, and as Leroy-Beaulieu remarks (iii. 405), they remind us of the Roman cemeteries of the early Christians. They were and are vast compounds in the suburbs surrounded by walls; round them were grouped the houses and workshops of the two sets of sectaries; inside them were their chief bureaux for the management of their affairs all over the Empire. Each establishment had its directors, its treasury, its own regulations, its charter, its seal. Each, as the same author says, was at once a convent, a seminary, a sort of chamber of commerce and a bourse. Nicholas I. suppressed the one and the other; the altars in the Rogozhski were still sealed when Leroy-Beaulieu visited Moscow and only released on the occasion of the temporary fall from power of Count D. Tolstoi, procurator of the Holy Synod.

Alexis Ivan Khludovo deposited therein. Paul had come to
Russia in 1847 and had written many books about the Raskol.

In 1848 a skete of the Popovtsy had long been sealed and
sequestrated by the Government in the province of Semenov
in the Nizhegorod Government. Tarasius, formerly prior,
tired it would seem of the nomadic life inflicted on him, had
promised the local bishop to become a Uniat, if he might be
readmitted with his monks, of whom a certain number shared
in his submission. It would seem as if the policy of the Russian
Government all through was that of which Pobedonostsev
under Alexander III secured the ratification by law, namely
that if any member of any family, man, woman or child, anywhere in the Russian dominions, joined the Orthodox Church,
the entire family should be regarded officially as such. One
can conceive of the hatred for the Church engendered by such
legislation. It is obvious that the Popovtsy recognition of the
validity of the orders of fugitive priests who came over to
them from the Orthodox Church furnished the latter with a
certain pretext for its use against them. The Bezpopovtsy
held a more logical position and one less assailable by a persecuting Government such as until yesterday was Holy Russia.

Beside the few centres in which the origin and fortunes of
the Uniat Movement have been detailed, it was pushed far
and wide over the whole country between 1825 and 1854, as
many as one hundred and fifty Uniat Churches being built in
that period, largely in consequence of the zeal and energy for
the cause of Jacob, Bishop of Saratov, and Arcadius, Bishop
of Perm. Yet the historian Ivanovski seems dubious of the
ultimate success of the movement. Many of the Uniats, he
states, having obtained a clergy and permission to keep up the
old rites, set themselves to emphasize their peculiar status
and their independence of the Orthodox Church. They took
no pains to conceal their leanings towards the Raskol, and were
careful to convey to their neighbours the impression that they
were genuine Raskolniki. Here and there they even refused
to accept the popes sent them by the Synod without first
subjecting them to "correction or amendment"; they did so,
for example, in the village of Krivolych (in the Nikolaev region

of the Saratov Government). Occasionally they refused to allow an orthodox bishop to officiate in their churches. In the Kostroma Government many professed themselves Uniats, yet remained Raskol, and subjected the popes sent to minister to them to every sort of oppression, indignity and servitude. Others continued to clamour for a bishop of their own, for free permission to be given to the orthodox to join them and for the annulling of the anathemas of 1667. A leading Uniat agitator of this kind was the priest, Joan Verkhovski of Petersburg, who as late as 1885 was on that account unfrocked by the Synod and found it consonant with his personal safety to retire across the frontier to the Raskol abroad.

Palmieri (Chiesa Russa, 1908, p. 456), whose opinion carries weight, is equally convinced that the Uniat movement or *edinovierie*, as it is called, has no future before it. In spite of the mild flattery of the Synod, he declares it to be a hybrid organism in Orthodox Russia. "Its separatist tendencies, inherited from the Raskol, are accentuated every day: it would form alongside of the official Church modernized, a second official Church on ancient lines." He reviews the Uniat attempts to secure a hierarchy, so nearly successful under Alexander I in 1824; and he gives an account of the debate held in the Holy Synod in 1864, when some members shewed themselves favourable to the institution of an Uniat bishop; Plato, however, the bishop of Kostroma, insisted that it would diminish the prestige of the Orthodox Church, violate ecclesiastical canons by placing two bishops in one eparchial jurisdiction, confuse parish and administrative records, alienate Raskolniks still more completely from Orthodoxy, lower the episcopal dignity, and encourage the founding of an independent Church. Other bishops feared it would pave the way to a fresh schism and strengthen the Raskol argument that the Church is infected with error. It appears, however, that in spite of these arguments ten bishops against twelve upheld the Uniat plea, as the only method of strengthening the Uniats in their struggle with the Raskol hierarchy. In general, says Palmieri, the Uniats are viewed with contempt by the Orthodox, with hatred by the Raskol. It is a half-way house that disgusts both, and most

Raskolniks would prefer to go straight back into the Church. What the influence of the present revolution will be, in case it permanently succeed, we must wait to see. The immediate result will be that the Raskol everywhere will enjoy the same privileges as the Orthodox Church, in which case the Uniats might well rejoin the Raskol; but as the white or parochial clergy will inevitably assert themselves against the monkish higher clergy, it is possible that the lines of demarcation between Raskol and orthodoxy may be more or less obliterated and a return be made to the state of things that prevailed in the XVth Century when the Popes were the servants of the Mirs.

On the other hand Ivanovski notes a tendency among sincere Uniats to draw nearer to the Orthodox Church, and he ascribes this tendency to the spectacle of bishops officiating in their churches and using there the old rites, the two fingers, etc.; for such incidents prove to them that the Orthodox Church no longer regards them as heretics. In Moscow and Kazan the rival clergy have even gone so far as to officiate together at the same altar, so proving that they really form a single Church. Owing to the complaint of some Uniats that the condemnation in 1666-7 of the old rites weighed upon their consciences, the Holy Synod in 1886 issued an 'Explanation' to the effect that these censures and ancient polemics reflected nothing more than the personal opinions of over-zealous writers and "were neither shared nor upheld by the Orthodox Church itself." This explanation evinces a laudable regret for its past on the part of the Orthodox Church and Synod, and an anxiety not to commit such follies in future as Nikon was allowed to commit; but historically it is a direct contradiction of the events which led to the schism as related by Ivanovski himself. In 1890 the Uniats appealed afresh to Government to be granted their own hierarchy, but Pobedonostsev opposed the scheme, although in 1905 some of the members of the Synod favoured the institution of a Uniat see at Uralsk near Orenburg where 55% of the population were Raskolniks. This was after the proclamation of liberty of conscience, which encouraged the Uniats to renew their demand for a bishop of their own.

Late in the same year they founded a journal for the defence of their interests.

The Uniat movement was due to the widespread desire of the Popovtsy to secure a hierarchy of their own. It is now time to narrate a less equivocal endeavour towards the same end, which was crowned with comparative success.

The Austrian Hierarchy

It is worthy of remark that the Empress Catharine was more tolerant in spirit towards the Raskol than any of the Tsars, except perhaps Alexander I, no steps being taken in their reigns to cut off the supply of runaway popes upon whom the Popovtsy depended for the administration of the Sacraments; this enabled them to hold as many services as they liked and to spare nothing to make them as elegant and elaborate as those of the Orthodox Church. But Nicholas I after his accession, in 1827 abruptly cut off the supply both at the Rogozhski Cemetery in Moscow and elsewhere, subjecting to dire penalties popes who quitted the orthodox fold in order to minister to heretics. In 1832 all older laws mitigating the fate of the Raskol were repealed, and by the new law the Popovtsy could only retain popes who had joined them before 1826.

Those who remained were perpetually dwindling, if we may believe Ivanovski, and, being able to magnify their office as they pleased, shewed much disregard both for the holy rites and for their congregations. The latter could not afford to dismiss them for private irregularities nor for negligence in their ministrations. One priest would baptize several children at once,— a justifiable procedure of old when a St. Gregory was converting a whole nation of pagans on the spur of the moment, but illegitimate in a Christian age. He would also marry several couples in a group and confess the faithful not individually and privately but collectively, the deacon reading out a list of sins from the Euchologion, while the people cried *peccavi* — a scandalous procedure since it involved the admission by women and children of sins consistent with neither their sex nor age. Instead of going about in the open the dissenting clergy under Nicholas I had to steal hither and thither in secret, always in fear, and, says Ivanovski, often drunk,— a vice which, if they really had it, was also not unknown among the orthodox clergy and monks at that time as attests the proverb popular with the muzhik: "The pope is drunk and his cross a bit of wood"!

It was in vain that the Popovtsy of the Rogozh Communion agitated for a return to the tolerant law of March, 1822, which had outraged the Holy Synod by allowing the Raskol openly to employ runaway popes, in case the latter before joining them had committed no criminal offence. Meanwhile the old dreams of a genuine clergy somewhere surviving in the East revived; and Heraclius, prior of the Kurenev monastery in the Podolski government, dispatched several of his own monks to join in a search for a hierarchy with the Old believers of Moldavia. Sixteen in all started and roamed through Turkey as far as Egypt. Only four lived to return and they had found nothing suitable.

Next the settlers of Irgiz were induced to go on the same quest by one of their persuasion, Athoni Kuzmich Kochuev, a man of affluence with a hobby for collecting old books and MSS. So much was he esteemed as a bibliophile even outside his sect, that he was elected in 1847 a member of the Moscow Society of Antiquaries. When the idea was mooted in a Synod held in 1832 at the Rogozhski Cemetery (or hospice) in Moscow, the merchant Tsarski scouted it; but it had the support of the rich family of the Rakhmanovs, and eventually it was resolved to consult the Old believers in Petersburg. There the Popovets family of the Gromovs, timber merchants on a large scale, members of the Korolevski congregation, had influence, and Serge Gromov even consulted on the point Count Benkendorf, head of the police, who assured him that, although the Tsar would never allow of their resumption of deserters from the Orthodox Church, he might not object so strongly to their setting up a hierarchy of their own. In the end Serge Gromov resolved to seek a bishop himself, but said nothing about it for the moment, because he distrusted Rakhmanov's loquacity. He took steps however to find a man

suitable for the prosecution of the quest. Such a one he met
with in Peter Vasilev Velikodvorski, son of a notary of a
village among the Valdai Hills, a man of inflexible will and
untiring energy, qualities which were written in his face, if we
may judge from a photograph taken of him in old age and
preserved in Chernovitz.

It is related that on one occasion St. Nicholas, patron saint
of this young man, had appeared to him attired in full canonicals in order to reassure him as to the future of the Popovtsy
Church of which he was an adherent; and the tale fits in with
the report that he was a mystic, an ascetic enthusiast and a
devout student of hagiology. It is probable that at any time
dreams and visions were more in vogue among the Old believers
than in the bosom of the Orthodox Church, of which the
leaders had the police at their disposal, and were not so much
in need of spiritual and inner aids to faith and confidence in
their future.

Though we may distrust the tale, repeated by Ivanovski,
of how Peter went a-hunting for a church treasure and failed
to find it, we may well believe that he entered as a youth the
Old believers' monastery at Starodub, assuming in religion
the name of Paul, that he cherished lofty but correspondingly
vague aspirations and that he felt an inward assurance that
Providence had assigned him a lofty mission — he did not
exactly know what. He was in this state of exaltation when
Gromov met him in 1835 and launched him on a quest for a
real bishop. He forthwith chose another enthusiast as his
fidus Achates, to wit, Gerasimus Kolpakov, in religion Gerontius, of the Serkov convent in Bessarabia, son of a peasant
near Moscow and more practically minded than himself.

When the Emperor Justinian closed the schools of Athens,
certain of the neo-Platonic and pagan philosophers of that
city set out in search of a purer air and more liberal environ-
ment for Persia, whence they afterwards returned shocked
and discouraged by the vices of polygamy and worse which
were rampant in the dominion of the Great King. Like them
in 1836 our two seekers after a genuine episcopate turned
their thoughts and their steps to Persia; but they were not

destined to reach that ecclesiastical elysium; for, having incurred the suspicion of the authorities, they were arrested in
the Caucasus and sent back under police surveillance, the one
to the Valdai, the other to Bessarabia.

But hope springs eternal in the human breast. The summer
of 1839 saw them re-equipped for their project; they had not
abandoned as their guiding principle the old motto *ex oriente
lux*, but they took care to start this time by way of Austria,
with the intention of making their way to the Far East along a
route on which the Russian Government would not be able to
lay hands on them. In due course they came to the Popovtsy,
and other Raskol settlements at Bielo (white) Krinits in
Austria.[1] Here their co-religionists had enjoyed liberty of
worship ever since 1783, thanks to the liberal laws of the
Emperor Joseph II; and the thought now struck Peter Vasilev
that it would be safer to establish his episcopate in this home of
freedom than in Russia. He therefore urged the authorities
of the Lipovan[2] convent to supplicate the Austrian Government to permit them to appoint a bishop. The local Austrian
authorities (Kreisamt) consented, but the Government refused,
possibly because they realized even then that any step taken or
allowed to be taken in Austria in mitigation of the iron religious
oppression of the Holy Synod would in due time call down
upon them the wrath of the Tsar Nicholas I and furnish him
in the future with an additional incentive for wresting Galicia
and the Ruthenes from that connection with the Austrian
Empire with which they were perfectly content. The Orthodox Church, which till yesterday pulled all strings of government and international policy in Russia, would be certain to
resent it, if the Emperor of Austria allowed a focus and hearth
of Raskol propaganda to be established on Austrian soil.
The convent moreover, had only been allowed to exist there

---

[1] Liprandi: (*Short sketch of Raskol*, 1853) describes the routes from Russia
into Austria and Bessarabia taken by Raskolniki in his age and bitterly assails the
Austrian Government for allowing them horses and guides! This was in the days
before railways.

[2] This was a general name given by their neighbours to Raskolniki who had
taken refuge in Transylvania.

on the assumption that its inmates were of a purely contemplative order.

But there were those in Vienna who were quite ready to do the Holy Synod a nasty turn, among them the Minister of the Interior, Count Kolovrat, and the Arch-Duke Ludwig; and to them Peter and his companion turned, with the result that, after all formalities had been complied with, the Emperor Ferdinand in 1844 gave permission for a foreign bishop to be imported into his dominions by the Raskol and established at Bielo-Krinits, where the monastery was to be under the charge of himself and his successors.

The two emissaries, it will be noticed, had passed several years at Bielo-Krinits, during which time Gerontius had been elevated to the dignity of Superior of the monastery there, in succession to the monk Joel. He now returned to Russia, only to find Serge Gromov dead. The latter until now had financed the enterprise, but the Rakhmanovs stepped nobly into his place and undertook the expense, computed at 200,000 roubles, of installing the future prelate, if one could be procured, in due style and of rebuilding the monastery, for the church of which the faithful were already providing ornaments and plate.

Having as it were built the nest the enthusiastic Peter now started afresh for the East in order to find a phoenix bird to fill it choosing as his travelling companion another monk named Alimpius. He was minded, if he could not discover a genuine Old believer, to be content with a schismatic bishop whose orders and ordinances the canon law of the Church allowed him to regard as valid. For generations there had been, as we saw, communities of Old believers in European Turkey, refugees from Russian violence and cruelty, and to these the Raskolnik in quest of a bishop naturally first turned his steps. In our own generation we have examples of Poles who, to avenge wrongs done by the Russian Government to their compatriots have taken service under the Turkish Government. Already in 1844 there existed at the Porte a Polish section led by a *Pan* or member of the Polish nobility, by name Tchaykovski, and known in Turkish circles as Saduk Pasha. To him the Raskolniki obtained an introduction from the Ataman of the Nekra-

sovtsy Goncharov,[1] and found him only too willing to render
a disservice to the oppressors of his native land. He seems
even to have had a list of stray bishops of the Greek rite
resident in the Turkish capital and in want of employment.
Peter, however, determined to try further afield before adopting one of these, and, filled with high hope, continued his
quest in the East, where he met with the debris of Nestorians,
Eutychians and Severians, but with no Old believers. But he
was able to satisfy himself that the Greeks shared his own
meticulous distrust of baptism by aspersion and insisted on
trine immersion, regarding the former as no baptism at all,
but only a Roman tradition. Accordingly when he had found
his way back again to Constantinople, he wrote to his friend
Gerontius that he could find no suitable candidate in the East,
but that they could, without violating their consciences, acquiesce in the choice of a Greek.

Among other candidates his Polish friends especially com-
mended to him one Ambrose, who had formerly been metropolitan of Serajevo in Bosnia, but whom for political or other
reasons the Turks had expelled from his see. He was a Greek
from Enos, a widower, and he was living in Constantinople
in great poverty. Peter got hold of a dragoman, a Serb,
Constantine Ognianovich by name, who could talk both
Greek and Russian, and through him opened negotiations with
Ambrose, but failed, it would seem, to convince him at first
of the canonicity and orthodoxy of the Popovtsy communion.
Ambrose, according to Ivanovski, was dismayed at the prospect of being constrained, in order to take up his new episcopate, to anathematize an orthodox body of believers like the
Russian Church and himself to submit to the indignity of
being re-anointed as if he were a schismatic.

Henri IV found Paris worth a mass, and orthodox scruples
have too often yielded to cupidity; and this proved to be the
case when Peter turned from the Bosnian prelate to his son
George, and dangled before his eyes the prospect of a country
residence with ease and emolument on Austrian soil. He

---

[1] Nekrasov was chief of a tribe of Don Cossacks who fled from Russia in the
days of the Streltsy revolt. The Turkish Popovtsy bore his name.

yielded and undertook to procure his father's assent to the
scheme; Ambrose gave way, much against his instincts and
better judgment, if we are to believe Ivanovski. What, according to this authority, most awoke his religious scruples, was the
Raskol use of two fingers in blessing instead of three; however,
Peter proved to his satisfaction that this usage went back
behind Nikon; and, his last scruples overcome, Ambrose on
April 15th, 1846, accepted the position on condition of receiving
500 ducats a year with a country house for his son George.
Perhaps the promise that he should appoint his son successor
and so found a hierarchy flattered the native pride seldom
absent in modern Greeks, and it is anyhow better to begin even
a spiritual lineage than to end a carnal one. His happiness
must have been complete when he was put on board a steam-
packet *en route* to Austria. On his way he was exhibited to the
Old-believing congregations settled on the Duna (Danube);
then resuming his disguise, and successfully avoiding detection by Russian agents, he reached Vienna, and was at Bielo-
Krinits on October 12th, 1846.

Ivanovski gives a somewhat splenetic account of the ceremony arranged a few days later, October 27th, for the reception of Ambrose into the true Church of the Popovtsy. It
was held in their church of the Theotokos, Gerontius presiding
with many outward embellishments and much pomp, but, if
we can believe Ivanovski, not without internal misgivings on
the part of the main actors in the scene. The Popovtsi could
not agree among themselves on the point whether, as was
usual with runaway popes, Ambrose should be re-anointed
with the holy *myron*. Peter had written a book about it,
but had failed to create unanimity; and finally the discussion
became so acrimonious that the congregation had to be ad-
journed, without Ambrose, who knew no word of Russian,
realizing in the least what the uproar was about. They
eventually agreed to consult Ambrose himself on the morrow
about which rite of reception he preferred. Anointers were
in a majority, but Peter who urged the use of the third rite
for the reconciliation of schismatics as found in the old Slavonic
Euchologion, visited Ambrose by night and represented to

him that in order to quiet the conscience of the weaker brethren
he should submit to the rite most in vogue. "You mean your
own conscience, you idiot," was Ambrose's reply.

Finally the hieromonachus arranged the rite for the following day, and Ambrose who only understood of it such passages
as his Serbian interpreter translated for him, offered no resistance, reciting with much *éclat* — as he stood before the
royal entrance of the Sanctuary or Bema—the Slav anathemas
against all heresies which had been written out for the purpose
in the letters of the Greek alphabet. This much achieved, he
retired behind the screen into the Sanctuary together with
Hieronymus, to whom he was to make his confession, a religious
act none the easier of accomplishment because one of them
knew no Greek and the other no Russian. The monk Onuphrius, who was present, has testified, according to Ivanovski,
that the entire rite was uncanonical. Presumably he was a
votary of re-anointing with *myron*, but was outraged at the
fact that Hieronymus, having stared for a couple of minutes at
Ambrose who returned his stare, — this under the rubric of
confession — anointed him, not with *myron*, of which they
had none in stock, but with common oil. Next Hieronymus
proclaimed that Ambrose was worthy of his new dignity and
deposed in writing that he had searched the secrets of the
candidate's heart. Ambrose now issued forth through the
Royal Gate in full canonicals and, grasping in his hands
the three and two-branched candlesticks, proceeded to bless
the people.

Ambrose was now a Raskol prelate or metropolitan and
proceeded to celebrate the liturgy and ordain a clergy of every
grade, reading the prayers in his own native Greek, the deacon
making the proclamations in Slavonic. In the following year,
1847, on January 6th, Ambrose consecrated a bishop for the Old
believers settled at Maenos. The canons of course required
the presence of three bishops at the ceremony, but the Raskol
justified the irregularity on the score of necessity. This was
the day of Epiphany when Eastern Churches celebrate the
Baptism of our Lord by a solemn blessing of the waters. For
this rite the Popovtsy produced on this occasion two archpriests.

Ambrose read the gospel, Cyril, the newly consecrated bishop of Maenos, the prayers; he had been secretary of the place under the lay name of Kiprian Timofeev. The imminence of the ceremony had been noised abroad all over the Bukowina and the commander of the local forces as well as the civil Governor attended, a banquet being given in their honour by the monks.

The Austrian Government was clearly glad of an opportunity of sticking pins into a Schismatic Church like the Russian which had nursed for centuries a sleepless hostility to Rome; and the dismay and irritation of Petersburg is voiced by Liprandi (*Short Sketch of Raskol*), who insists that the Popovtsy by their connivance with the authorities of Bielo-Krinits in erecting an alien hierarchy in Russia had ceased to be a religious body and constituted themselves a source of grave political danger to the Tsar's Government. Liprandi was an inquisitor appointed by Nicholas I and the right hand man of Protassov, the hussar officer appointed by that Tsar to keep the Holy Synod in order, so it could hardly occur to him that a little religious toleration was a better and more dignified way of exorcising the imaginary menace than to expostulate with the Austrian Government. In their self-assumed rôle of protectors of orthodoxy all over the world the Tsars constantly addressed reprimands then and later to foreign governments through their Procurators; for example in December, 1886, Pobedonostsev assailed Austria for favouring Catholicism, and Rumania for negotiating a concordat with Rome. Turkey, Greece, Servia, Bulgaria, were equally regarded by the Tsars as in a way amenable to their religious jurisdiction. Meanwhile any foreign criticism of pogroms was actively resented in Petersburg.

In August, 1847, Ambrose ordained a second bishop, Arcadius, for the Nekrasovtsy or Raskol diaspora of Turkey. He was called the Slav bishop, and the Popovtsy now had the minimum of three bishops needful to assure the future of their episcopate.

It would be interesting to know how far the affair of Bielo-Krinits helped to bring about the Crimean War, just as ortho-

dox propaganda of the Russian Government among the Latin
Uniats of Eastern Galicia and the counter propaganda of
Vienna amongst the inhabitants of the Ukraine were among
the causes of the recent war.

On this occasion the Tsar Nicholas felt that he had been
outwitted and outraged by his Latin opponents, and he
promptly arrested Gerontius when, in the guise of a merchant
under the name of Leonov, he entered his dominions with the
help of a false passport; he next sternly demanded of Vienna
the removal of Ambrose from the Austrian dominions, and at
the same time called on the Greek Patriarch of Constantinople to take the necessary steps for his reconversion or, in
default, his condemnation. The Greek Patriarch, subservient
then as always to the Moscovite, sent through Austrian chan-
nels an intimation to Ambrose that he must repent and return.
The Austrian Government in its turn had no desire to compli-
cate the internal difficulties of the moment by quarreling over
such a matter with Nicholas I; so Ambrose was summoned to
Vienna and given to understand that he must either go back
whence he came or retire into some more convenient exile;
and his monastery was closed and officially sealed on March
3rd, 1848. But before he had set out for his place of exile,
Tsill in Styria, revolution broke out in Vienna and a popular
Government was established at the head of which was Count
Kolovrat, the protector of the Old believers in Austria. Alimpius was returned to the new house of representatives as deputy
for the Bielo-Krinits monastery, and at once took steps to get
it reopened, and Ambrose went back to it. The Government,
however, refused and Alimpius, more immediately concerned
in aiding the revolution in Prague, was too busy to prosecute
the enterprise. Later on, however, he got back to Vienna and
succeeded in obtaining the release of Ambrose who was allowed
to go and live at Tsill (Tzill). Lest the Popovtsy hierarchy
should fall below the canonical figure of three bishops, Cyril
Bishop of Maenos now consecrated Onuphrius, Bishop of
Braila, and Sophronius, Bishop of the Popovtsy in Russia, on
January 3rd, 1849. These two bishops in turn consecrated
Cyril to be metropolitan of Bielo-Krinits, with the full grade of

archihieratic dignity. The monks at Bielo-Krinits now opened their monastery afresh without consulting the Government, but with the assent of the local authorities. They continued on sufferance until 1859 when the Government once more openly extended its patronage to the institution. In the interim the Crimean War had been fought and Nicholas I had departed to a better or a worse world.

The rest of Ambrose's career possesses a morbid attraction for Ivanovski. He continued for a time to draw his salary from the Old believers, but he shewed his contempt for them by refusing to confess to the bishops and hieromonachi of their denomination who continued to visit him in exile. He was deeply incensed to find his stipend abolished in 1859, and made it an occasion for anathematizing Cyril who had taken his place, along with all the priests whom he had ordained and all who had accepted their ministrations. "Henceforth," he is reported to have written, "I will make Bezpopovtsy of the whole lot of you." He died in 1863 not — we take it for granted — without receiving the viaticum from an orthodox Greek priest, and he was buried in Trieste. His son George is said to have written later on, that his venerable sire had often blamed him for pushing him into the Lipovan heresy, of those who baptised with aspersion only,— a statement which need not be taken seriously.

Ivanovski gives many details of the success of the Bielo-Krinits hierarchy in Turkey and Rumania. In the XVIIIth Century settlements of Popovtsy, fleeing from the Russian Government, had been formed in the Dobrudja along the lower Danube, and here they were known as Nekrasovtsy, after the Cossack ataman Nekrasov who escaped thither from Russia together with his troop. Another settlement had, as we saw above, been established about 1750, between the Sea of Marmora and the Archipelago; a third, that of Maenos in Asia Minor on the Sea itself. In all three there lived some 10,000 of the sect. They had all taken an interest in the search for a prelate, and it was the ataman Goncharov himself who had introduced Peter to Saduk Pasha the Pole. They had contributed money to the scheme and formed a separate see, although, it is said, a minority repudiated Ambrose because they felt a doubt whether he had not received in baptism aspersion instead of trine immersion — a doubt which, if it really existed, might one would suppose, have been got rid of by conditional rebaptism.

These congregations had selected for ordination as their bishop Arcadius Shaposhnikov, hegumen of the monastery of St. Laurence; but Ambrose displayed his zeal for canonicity by rejecting him on the score of his having married a widow in his pre-monkish days. Instead of him he ordained in August 1847, another Arcadius, also called Dorotheus or Lysias, who was subjected to some annoyance by enemies of Ambrose, for they declared him to be no better than a Greek or a Bulgarian agitator, and essayed on that ground to arouse against him the suspicions of the Porte. In consequence Arcadius was arrested and imprisoned for half a year and only liberated by the efforts of Goncharov and the Poles. The latter were now rewarded by a firman granting to the Nekrasovtsy as loyal subjects of the Sultan full liberty, the use of their own clergy, and immunity from annoyance by any other religious body. Taking advantage of the favours thus accorded them the Popovtsy of Turkey treated themselves to bells on their churches, a luxury forbidden to other religious sects, but no doubt accorded to them because of the irritation it would be sure to arouse in the breast of Tsar Nicholas I and his successors. Arcadius was known as the Slavonic or Slavianski bishop; and, as the Popovtsy of Turkey at Tulcha in the Dobrudja also asked for a bishop of their own, Arcadius and Onuphrius, Cyril's suffragan, consecrated Alipius for their special edification with the title of Bishop of Tulcha.

This was on September 27th, 1850, but neither of these bishops occupied their sees for long. In 1853 the Russian armies invaded the principalities of the Lower Danube and by the advice of the Porte most of the Nekrasovtsy families fled from their settlements into Turkey proper. The two bishops, however, stuck to their posts; and the fugitives claimed and obtained this time as their archbishop the very Arcadius whom Ambrose, because of a technical flaw in his sanctity, had refused to consecrate. He was known as the bearded bishop, and was a man of rough tongue and great energy. He duly shepherded his flock of refugees to the shore of the Bosphorus where he remained during the war.

It would clearly then have been a miracle if in 1853 the Tsar had spared the two Popovtsy prelates who bravely stood their ground on the Lower Danube, and he did not. Both of them were arrested by the advancing Russian army, deported and, on the strange ground that they were absconding Russian subjects, imprisoned in the Spaso-Euthimiev monastery at Suzdal. At the end of the war the Popovtsy through the Turkish Government, and with the sympathy of Napoleon III, though not, apparently, of the British Government, interested himself in their fate, but in vain; and the settlers persuaded Arcadius Shaposhnikov to leave the Bosphorus and come to them as Slav-bishop, while Alipius the Bishop of Tulcha was replaced by the lay-brother of Arcadius, Justin, a native of the Volokolamski district of the Moscow Government, a wise, temperate and learned man.

This assured the future of the Popovtsy hierarchy in Turkey. For the service of the 20,000 of them settled in Moldavia and Wallachia Ambrose ordained as bishop a pope named Nicephorus who had his seat at Jassy. Subsequently one Onuphrius was made suffragan of Braila to attend to the congregation in that neighbourhood. In 1853 they obtained a bishop of their own, Arcadius, with his see at Vasluya in Moldavia. He was a native of Saratov and a learned fanatic who ordained a great many priests. To begin with the Turkish Government was somewhat severe on the Raskolniks of Moldavia and Wallachia, and Arcadius had to go about his diocese in secret. Probably the Porte suspected these fugitives from Russia of being Russian agents. After the Crimean War, when Rumania received independence under Prince Kuza, the protégé of Napoleon, they were more liberally dealt with and enjoyed complete religious freedom. Their prelate Arcadius was treated by the civil authorities with all the respect due to his position; and when the metropolitan of Jassy complained of the presence of a schismatic prelate in his diocese, the Government told him curtly that Rumania was a free country; and in 1860 Arcadius was officially recognized as Archbishop of Moldavia. It is pleasant to think that the hierarchy of Bielo-Krinits so completely succeeded in the nearer East. It was a triumph at once of Austria and of religious liberty. The Rumanian Government also deserved much credit.

In Russia proper the Bielo-Krinits hierarchy was also a success in spite of governmental opposition and of the doubts entertained by a few of the Popovtsy, notably by the runaway pope Paul of Tula, as to Ambrose's baptism. Gerontius had first carried the news into Russia of the episcopal ordination of Ambrose and Cyril, and the congregations of Rogozh and Kerzhen under the influence of the Rakhmanovs received it with enthusiasm, and sent two priests in disguise, Borisov and Zhigarev, to Bielo-Krinits to obtain holy chrism. In January, 1849, Cyril consecrated as bishop of Simbirsk Sophronius, in the world Stephan Trifonov Zhirov, a peasant of Maloyaroslav and afterwards a citizen of Moscow, whose business had been to smuggle fugitive priests to their destinations. He was now appointed head of the Russian Popovtsy. Ivanovski accuses him of having been a rapacious brigand, selling ordinations, exacting from his popes in Moscow half their pay and more still from the country ones. Perhaps this was the reason why in 1853 his congregation removed him to the see of Simbirsk and obtained in his stead a new prelate Antony, who had been a Bezpopovets of the Thedosyevski communion, and whose name in the world was Andrei Larionov Shutov.

In 1855 a see of Saratov was founded under a bishop Athanasius, who had been a merchant. In 1856 were created sees in Perm and Kazan and Kolomna, in 1857 a see for the Caucasus.

In fact within twelve years the Austrian hierarchy spread all over Russia, ten sees in all being founded and priests ordained everywhere. In Moscow a supreme board of control was established for the transaction of all the ecclesiastical affairs of the sect. It consisted, however, too exclusively of bishops and priests, and for that reason aroused the jealousy of some of the laity, who petitioned the Tsar to allow runaway popes to minister to them by way of healthy competition with those of

Austrian origin. The layman party was known as the *Vino-kurovski*. In opposition Paphnutius, Bishop of Kolomna, petitioned the Tsar to recognize the existing Popovtsy clergy as Alexander I had done in 1822; this he was not likely to do, inasmuch as the Austrian clergy, at any rate outside Russia, were accused of refusing in their liturgy to offer up prayers for the Tsar.

About the year 1860 the Raskol took root in London among emigrants headed by Herzen and Kelsiev, who took in hand there the publication of the reports concerning the Old believers collected in the course of various inquisitions by the Russian Government. The firm of Paul Trubner published five volumes of these between 1860 and 1870; it is to be regretted that the English Universities took no pains under the Copyright Act to acquire copies of documents so precious for the historian. Copies, however, are in the Widener Library at Harvard University, and in the British Museum. Paphnutius of Kolomna also tried to found in London a school and church for his co-religionists, a seminary for the training of missionaries and a Russian press. But the emigrants there offered very poor soil in which to try and plant his faith. They were, and still are for the most part, people who, as far as religion is concerned, have been completely sterilized by contact with the orthodox Church of their native land.

In 1863 the Russian Government began to tolerate the Bielo-Krinits clergy, only continuing to punish converts and repress all public manifestations of the sect. In 1908, according to Palmieri (p. 421), the Bielo-Krinits hierarchy numbered fifteen bishops, twelve governing dioceses, and three *emeriti*. Their archbishop resided in Moscow, and bishops resided at Izmail, Kazan, Perm, Uralsk, the Caucasus, Smolensk, Samara, Tomsk, Nizhni-Novgorod, Petersburg. Their Synod meets once or twice a year, when all bishops must attend or, if sick, send substitutes. The Synod nominates bishops to vacant sees; the archbishop can judge of complaints against them, found new sees, and settle controversies of an ecclesiastical character. In each see there exists a consultative house of convocation open to priests and laity. In 1861 this Russian Popovtsy church declared itself autokephalous and independent of Bielo-Krinits. With this the Russian Government hampered communications; moreover it was a monkish settlement and ill-qualified on that account alone to exercise jurisdiction in Russia. Since Russian orthodox publicists continued to deny that the Bielo-Krinits ordinations were valid, the Popovtsy appealed in 1875, 1892 and 1896 to the Patriarch of Constantinople to recognize their orders. In 1899 a commission was appointed there to study the matter, which reported that the Metropolitan of Serajevo was *not* by the mere fact of his quitting Constantinople disqualified to administer as a bishop ecclesiastical censures and canonical punishments. This was a tacit recognition of the Austrian hierarchy by the supreme Greek orthodox Patriarch, and Pobedonostsev when he heard of the decision was greatly disturbed. Since the proclamation of liberty of conscience on April 17th, 1905, the Popovtsy have redoubled their energy, and in a Synod held on August 25th of that year decreed that that day should be for ever feasted as a holy day in their Church.

The General Character of the Popovtsy

In their religious convictions, remarks Uzov, the Popovtsy are closer than the rest to the orthodox Church, their relation to which is well set forth in a 'petition' written in the name of the Uniats and circulating from hand to hand in manuscript among the Popovtsy. In the words of this document Orthodoxy is not Catholic Orthodoxy but only "a Russian Nikonian, Muscovite, Synodalist, fiscal system, based on the use of three fingers and on the withershins form of procession." "Such orthodoxy outrages Apostolic orthodoxy, because it is naught else than a botched and retouched ceremonial, in other words a sort of ritualistic faith, an ignorant condemnation of the old national ritual customs of the Church, is, in a word, Greek ritualism." "Orthodoxy, so far as we mean thereby antagonism to the old ritualism, is no more than slavish belief in ritual, belief in the dogmatic importance of certain ceremonial details; it involves the principle of ritualist exclusiveness or the restriction of orthodox opinion exclusively to certain

ceremonial details. Hence the clownish condemnation by a
supreme pastor (Nikon) of ceremonial usages consecrated by
age-long usage. And, lastly it raises to the rank of dogmas
mere peculiarities of Greek ritual. Orthodoxy is just one of
the sects into which the Russian Church has fallen asunder,
a sect which lays stress on the necessity for the Russian Church
of Greek ritual." "The Raskol (by this word, which signifies
religious dissidence, the Raskolniks mean the Orthodox Church)
is an apostasy on the part of the Supreme Shepherd (i.e.,
Nikon) from the usages and ceremonies or rites elaborated by
the Church of our fathers; it is antagonistic to the spirit and
traditions of the Holy Apostolic Church, and has tyrannically
usurped the prerogative of ordaining such rites and usages
in our Church; it stands for ritualist intolerance, iniquitous
expulsion from the Church and persecution of those who cling
to older rituals and older custom. It is not the Holy Catholic
and Apostolic Church moulded by councils and commemorated
in the symbol of faith; it is not even a Russian Church; it is
merely an archpastorate illegal in its procedure, and circumscribed by a Synod whose members are appointed by the Government itself." "What can we say," write the Popovtsy,
"of a Church which, it is pretended, is invincible, because it
rests upon the support and sword of the powers of the earth?
What has it to do with the Truth when it resorts, not to
persuasion in a spirit of evangelical gentleness, but to civil
statutes, to influences of which the flesh alone is sensible, to
fetters and prison cell? Eternal Truth abhors such arguments,
disdains to subserve and stoop to methods as vulgar as they
are sanguinary. Truth has power in herself to conquer all
who think; the lie, on the contrary, because its authority only
rests on the violence of a despotism which fawns on it, is
beholden to external might and must approve all its measures.
The methods upon which the domination of the new ritualism
is built and reposes are good evidence of its inward insufficiency."

These are noble words, all the more striking when we bear
in mind that they were penned in a Russia still sunk in Cim-
merian darkness, and anticipate the dawn by at least two hun-

dred years. They might very well have been addressed by
Sir Thomas More to his sovereign. But we must not forget
that it was the Pope of Rome who sent to Henry VIII, along
with the title of Defender of the Faith, not a copy of the
Gospel, but a sword.

"Is it the Raskol," ask the petitioners, "that stands fast or
if it does move, then only along the path of hand-in-hand examination and consent,— or is it the man who after overthrowing
the age-long decisions of our Church hurls recriminations at us,
blocks our path with lies and calumnies, vomits against us
curses and anathemas, destroys all liberty of conviction, insults
the people in their most sacred feelings of attachment and veneration for all that concerns the Church of our ancestors,
thereby bringing ruin on all?" "Old ritualism in itself, in its
own conception, is neither heresy nor Raskol (dissent), but
above all things faith in a piety that reflects our ancestral and
national holiness; and so far forth it is the legitimate and justified protest of the people, of the veritable flesh and blood of the
Church, the guardian of the religion of our sires against the
wilful bias entertained by the Russian Supreme Shepherd
(Nikon) in favour of alien rite and usage, to the outraging of all
who love their country,— it is a protest against his autocracy,
against his pretensions to dictate to us our conscientious convictions, a protest against his efforts to import into the practice
of the Russian Church the discipline of Papistry." Old ritualism then is 'popular orthodoxy.' "Our supreme pastorate by
foisting on us a monkish discipline and subservience to a con-
ventual 'rule' in what appertains to the rites and usages of
our Church, and by lording it in practice over ceremonials and
ecclesiastical affairs, has by brute force introduced in our
national Church Greek ritualism instead of the old ancestral
ritualism, so despoiling the people and its clergy of their right
to a voice in the affairs of the Church and in the control of
matters of faith and ritual, arrogating to itself alone the rôle of
Church, nay more of the Apostolic Church and of its infalli-
bility. In all these respects our Supreme pastorate has
declined from the spirit and traditions of the Holy Apostolic
Church, has fallen into *Latinism*."

Regarding the anathema pronounced against the Raskol in the Council of 1666, the petitioners speak thus: "This condemnation was pronounced by the supreme pastor (Nikon) alone in despite of the Russian Church itself, in other words, in despite of the people who are the very flesh and blood of the Church and guardians of its piety. And as the supreme pastorate does not of itself and alone constitute the Church in its true sense, so this condemnation was not only not pronounced by the Apostolic Church, but not even by the Russian. By consequence it is not valid, because it is no expression of the Church's own convictions."

We are reminded, as we read the above, of Tertullian's noble plea for the rights of conscience, when he wrote that the Christian Church is not a *numerus episcoporum*, a mere tale of bishops.

"The Apostolic Church," continued the petitioners, "has never invested, nor now invests, ritual with the unchangeability of dogma, nor conceded to it an ecumenically binding uniformity; but each particular Church according to the measure of its independence, has been allowed to construct its own ordinances and ceremonies, customs and rites, as suits the age, the position and the spirit of the people." "A decision in questions of faith," they add, "indisputably belongs to the supreme pastor — yet is not given to him apart from the consent of those he shepherds; for in antiquity the consent of the people was declared by the presence at the councils of its representatives in the persons of rulers and senate. In questions then of mere ritual, no decisions are valid and effective without the mutual consent of the Supreme Shepherd and of his flock." [1]

"In respect of Church Government it is clear to all that the single head of Holy Church is our Lord Jesus Christ; but in the code of rules of the Russian Church it is affirmed that the head of the all-Russian Church is the Emperor of Russia..." "And a meeting of bishops is convened not in the form of a Council, but at the arbitrary will of a member of the world, which implies nothing less than debasement." "Similarly

[1] *Strannik*, 1866, No. 3, art. of Tverdynski, pp. 90–110.

there are selected for the priesthood not men known for the purity of their lives, but youthful domestics who have not attained the canonical age, who are not graced with good works, and have as yet no knowledge of the seductions of life, men unknown for goodness of character to the parishioners. How can such persons feed Christ's flock?"

"And who is there in the all-Russian Church to deal with dogmas and faith? According to the example set by the Apostles, we ought to deal with them in a council, but in this Church what councils are there? A Synod held under an officer's commands can only manage affairs of the outer world."

"We," say the Raskolniks, "recognize a single head, the Lord Jesus Christ, and as directors of the Church we recognize such bishops as will govern it not as autocrats, but in accordance with the rules of the holy councils; not applying the holy canons merely at their good pleasure, but in accordance with conciliary deliberations concerning them; and among us bishops are chosen not at the good pleasure of any and everyone, but by a council from among respectable men, known for their zeal for the faith and for the purity of their lives, and in the same way the presbyters." [1]

---

[1] Hegumen Parthenius, *The Spiritual Sword*, pp. 27–44.

CHAPTER IV

THE BEZPOPOVTSY OR PRIESTLESS SECT

The Various Settlements of the Bezpopovtsy

1. *In Kostroma and the Viaznikov region of the Vladimir Government.* Kapiton led this colony of which the members were at first known as Kapitonians. He was a native of the village of Danilovskoye in the uyezd or district of Kostroma and became a monk in the Kolesnik hermitage. Illiterate, he gathered about him followers as early as the reign of Michael Theodorovitch, attracted by his asceticism which discarded all sustenance except bread, berries and fruit. He eschewed, even on the great feasts, butter, cheese and fish; and he encouraged his admirers to paint onions and eat them instead of Easter eggs. To escape the Government when the persecution of the Raskol began he quitted Kolesnik and sought refuge in the Viaznikov forests, already full of religious fugitives. These he organized and ministered to, and in spite of ukases and soldiers died there in peace. One of his followers, a peasant, named Podreshetnikov founded near Kostroma in the Kineshemski and Reshemski regions a community whose lay members boldly performed their own rites of baptism, penitence and eucharist, each for his own family.

2. *In Siberia.* Thither five disciples of Avvakum fled. The most prominent of them was Oska (Joseph) Astomen from Kazan, an Armenian convert to orthodoxy. Banished in 1660 to the Yenisei he spread Raskol tenets there for 24 years; but when summoned in 1684 to Tobolsk by Metropolitan Paul of Siberia he pretended to repent and died there in the Znamenski Monastery in 1693. Some 1700 of his followers, led by one of his successors, Vaska or Basil Shaposhnik burned themselves to escape the cruelty of the Government.

3. *In the Novgorod and Pskov Country.* Here, as also in parts of Sweden and Poland, the Bezpopovtsy came to be known

as the sect of Theodosius. In 1682, there was a great exodus from Novgorod into Swedish territory, whither one Timoshka had already fled with fifty families to Narva. There in 1692 Ivan of Kolomna, himself a dissident, proposed to the settlers to return to orthodoxy and Theodosius Vasilev was sent from Novgorod to check the backsliders, who at a Raskol council in 1694 were excommunicated. In the same council were condemned the improprieties inseparable from the attempt of men and women to live together as monks and nuns. Presently Theodosius left the Swedish settlement and founded one of his own in Poland. He was related to the Boyar Urusov and his fame attracted many to his camp. He agreed with the rest of the Bezpopovtsy in most things, e. g. in teaching that Anti-Christ was reigning, in rejecting all priesthood, in rebaptizing the orthodox; but he differed in respect of how the title of Christ should be written on crosses and he recognized as valid ties of wedlock contracted by people in orthodox churches before they joined the Raskol. On the other hand he was stricter with his food taboos than the sect of the Pomorians, for he would not permit food bought in the market to be eaten without being previously cleansed by prayers and prostrations. Harried by the Poles he at one time returned to Russia and settled in the district of Velikoluts in the Vyazovski volost. After arrest and imprisonment he died at Novgorod in 1711. His followers settled at Ryapin in the district of Yurya Livonski. There his two communities flourished greatly, and overflowed into Novgorod, Yaroslavl, Staraya Russa, Pskov, Riga, Austria, Prussia and Poland. One of their counts against the Pomorian sectaries was that the latter from fear of the Russian general Samarin, who raided them in 1735, consented to pray for the royal family.

4. *Moscow.* The chief centre of the Theodosiev sect was founded in Moscow in 1771 by a merchant there, Ilia Alexsieievitch Kovylin, a clever and practical, if illiterate, man. It was the year of a great plague, and Kovylin got leave to start a hospital and cemetery for the poor, the sick and the dying, at Cherkizov on the River Khapilovok outside the city. His fellow sectaries, numerous in the city, loyally assisted, and

thousands resorted to his hospice to be fed and solaced. There in his chapel he prayed with them before the old ikons, held the legitimate services of every kind, and preached to willing ears that the plague was God's judgment on Moscow for forsaking the ancient faith. "The credulous," writes Macarius, archbishop of Kharkov, "weakened by hunger and disease, blindly submitted to the voice of the lying teacher, and were rebaptized in the nearest tub." Many left him their fortunes and the hundred horses that the philanthropic merchant used ordinarily for carting about his bricks (he was a brick merchant) were busy transporting the goods bequeathed to him and his associate, Zenkov. One asks what was the Orthodox Church, of which Macarius till lately was a chief ornament, doing in order to keep pace with Kovylin.

The new refuge at Moscow was dedicated to the Transfiguration, and before 1800 it contained 500 inmates, and 3000 adherents in Moscow frequented the services held there. In the school were 200 pupils. Gradually other Theodosiev settlements affiliated themselves to it, e.g. in Novgorod, Petersburg, Yaroslavl, the upper Volga, Riga, Tula, Saratov, Nizhninovgorod, Kazan, Simbirsk on the Don, Kuban, Starodub. All these procured from it their overseers, choristers, service books, ikons, and sent in return ample offerings year by year. A triennial meeting was held there for deciding all contested points of faith or discipline.

5. *The Pomor.*[1] The first Colony in the Olonets region was founded by Paul, bishop of Kolomna, and its history survives in a book written by one of its leaders, Ivan Philippov, in 1774. Paul was succeeded by Dositheos, hegumen of the Nikolski Besedovski Monastery three versts from Tikhvin on the Yaroslav road founded by Vasili Ioannovich in 1510 on the spot where the Virgin and St. Nicholas appeared to the monk George.

One Cornelius succeeded him. Early in the siege of Solovets, and still more after its disastrous termination, colonies of refugees from it settled in various parts of Pomor. Thus

[1] Pomor means 'sea board'; hence in Germany Pomerania means the shore of the Baltic, in Russia it means the shore of the Arctic.

the deacon Ignatius, after a halt near Kargopol, fled to the isle
of Pal in Lake Onega, and was there joined by Emelian Ivanov
from Povyenets. In Sept. 1787 they won over to the cause the
Paleostrov monastery, an ancient foundation of the twelfth
century, situated on the Pal island in lake Onega, 15 versts
from the village of Shung, and defied the Novgorod authorities for a while, but in March 1687 were reduced to burning
themselves, monastery and all. Ignatius and 2700 of his followers perished in the flames, but Ivanov escaped. Before
long the latter, reinforced by another monk of Solovets,
Germanus, again obtained possession of Paleostrov, and
defied the Government for nine weeks, when they were over-
powered and 500 of them burned alive. A third Solovets
monk in July 1693 seized the church of Pudozh, reconsecrated
it after its contamination by Nikon, and converted the villagers
to his cause. The Government sent a force, and 800 Raskolniki burned themselves alive rather than yield.

On the river Vyg, the chief settlement was formed by the
four Raskolniki saints, Daniel, Peter, Andrew and Simeon,
with the coöperation of the Cornelius and Ignatius already mentioned. Of these Daniel Vikulich was a church scribe of the
Shumski parish and teacher of the Raskol hegumen Dositheus.
After escaping from Paleostrov he joined an already existing
community of fugitives on the Vyg. These with the aid of
the Elder Cornelius he organized about 1695 into a regular
skete or monastic community, of which he remained abbot
till 1734. In 1692 he had already been joined by Peter Proko-
piev, a convert of Ignatius, who being a learned canonist and
singer was made ecclesiarch and conducted the cult until he
died in 1727. But of the Vyg leaders, Andrew and Simeon
Dionysievich (Denisov) were the two most famous. They
belonged to the princely family of the Mushetski of Novgorod,
and took over with them their sister Salomona, who later on
headed a female convent. Andrew presided over the monastery 35 years, until 1730, in association with Daniel Vikulich.
Disguised as a merchant he conducted long missionary expeditions to Kiev and all over Russia. His brother Simeon was
less of a practical genius, but accompanied his brother in his

peregrinations, and in the course of them he made himself an expert in rhetoric, grammar, singing and philosophy, writing many books in the library he formed inside the monastery. He succeeded his brother as abbot in 1730 and survived him ten years. The Monastery was given the name of the Theophany.

At its foundation in 1695 the Vyg settlement comprised only 40 men and women, who built wooden huts, a granary and a refectory. The sexes, as is usual in Russia, sat apart in church services. Soon entire families joined them, the convent had to be enlarged, and a dividing wall across it separated the sexes. Presently a special convent was built for women, on the River Leksi, called of the Cross, and presided over by Salomona, who died 1735. About 1703 fresh settlements began to group themselves around the original one with chapels of their own. At first Cornelius, as we saw, conducted religious worship, baptized, or rebaptized his new monks and nuns. Later on he was assisted in this by the Elders Paphnutius, Paul, Barlaam and others. There was a corps of singers, psalmodists, cellarers, kanonarchs; and matins, vespers, vigils of feasts and other services were duly held in the settlements. In the refectories religious books were read out loud at meals. All were kept busy, hewing wood, planting fields, tending the flocks and herds, working the corn mills and fishing.

The Archangel climate is harsh, and occasionally the harvests failed. Then many would flee back to the province of Novgorod, and Andrew and Simeon would set off to collect food and alms in Pskov and elsewhere. In 1710 they bought a large pasture 16 versts square near Kargopol on the River Chazhenga and built huts there for shepherds and tillers of the soil. In time they also began to eke out their scanty living with trade in Petersburg and elsewhere, and their dealers returning from Russia brought with them old books and gospels from sacristies and libraries containing the handwriting of princes and upper clergy of an earlier day, together with crosses, ikons and church vessels of the older fashions which the Raskol venerated. Nor were they behind hand in controversy, as the *Responses* of Andrew and Simeon prove. They compiled a new martyrology for church use containing the lives of martyrs newly slain by the Russian Government. They had schools for the education of missionaries and others who spread their tenets in the city and country side. Before 1800 there were 2000 males and 1000 females in the Vyg monasteries.

An offshoot of the Pomorians was founded by a monk Philip in 1737 some versts away from the Vygovski settlement. Philip was a deserter from the Strelets force in Moscow, in civil life named Photius. It is said that after the death of Daniel Vykulin he desired to succeed him. Disappointed in his hopes he began a skete of his own with fifty families, assailing the Vygovskis because they had been terrorized by Samarin into praying for the Tsar. Attacked by Samarin thirty-eight of the Philip community burned themselves alive, and in 1742 and 1765, when Philip's sect had spread far and wide in the Archangel Government, in Novgorod and in Finland, there were fresh burnings on a much larger scale. The sect for its rigour was singled out by the Government for persecution and that explains why they came to be known par excellence as the self-burners. In strength of numbers this sect ranked third among the Priestless ones.

It was not the only offshoot from Vyg. Under the régime of Andrew Denisov another colony was led forth by a shepherd of Vyg who condemned the use of money and passports, pavements and payment of the double poll tax imposed on the Old believers by Peter I. This sect was known as the Pastukhovo or Adamantovo; it respected marriages contracted in the orthodox church and, according to Macarius, deprecated self-burning.

The Stranniki

An incipient reconciliation in the last quarter of the XVIIIth Century of the Raskol with civil society explains the fact that there arose about that time among the Rigorists or followers of Philip, a teacher named Euthymius or Eufimius, a native of Pereyaslav in Poltava, who regarded any accommodation with normal society, with State or Church, as backsliding and impiety. Pressed into the army, he deserted and hid himself first in Moscow, then in the Philipovski sketes of Pomor, last of all in the forests of the Yaroslav Government. The time came when, repelled by the overfacile compliance of Philip's sect with Church and State, he set himself seriously both to write a book and to found a sect of his own. He got together in the village of Korovin in that Government a number of sympathizers; and, assuming for the gathering the dignity of a council, he solemnly condemned other Raskol groups, and embodied his complaint in a work called *The Peroration*. In it he condemned the act of inscribing their names in the registers as Raskolniks as tantamount to abjuring the name of Christian and as subservience to Antichrist. One who so registered himself and his family deified the Antichrist. His philippic against those who simulated orthodoxy was of the sternest, and brings before us in a lively manner the disabilities to which dissenters were subjected. They as good as admitted themselves, he says, to be adherents of a heretical body, and condemned themselves to go cadging for favours to the state priest, e.g. for the *billets de confession*, without which they could not obtain passports, they had to seek his permission to dig graves for their dead, to receive him into their houses on feastdays and give him alms. Such people, he writes, have prostituted their children to the Great Russian Church, have made their confession to the Devil, have disavowed Christ, presented themselves at an unholy altar (trapeza), bowing and scraping before it; they even invite the priest to enter their houses, when on festivals he comes rapping at their doors and windows and calling for the master of the house to give him something for church purposes, thanksgiving offerings, and the rest; they debase themselves by stuffing his bag with bread, pastries, cakes. What, he indignantly asks, is all this but to crucify Christ afresh, to pretend to love heretics and be at peace with them? Piety is extinguished, he laments, and impiety reigns everywhere. All the Old believers had bowed the knee to Baal and no longer had the baptism of Christ.

He accordingly baptized himself a third time, for he had been first baptized in the Orthodox Church, next when he joined the

Philipovtsy, and now in despair of finding any real baptism on the face of this earth he performed the rite first on himself and then on his followers; and he made it his principle to wander abroad on the earth, because we have here no abiding city. The true Christian, he taught, must either conceal himself and flee away, or wage open war with Antichrist. He must be literally an outcast and in an alien world break every tie with society. He has nowhere to lay his head, but is a wanderer (strannik), a fugitive (begun), a stowaway.

This sect has above all others distinguished itself by its fierce denunciations of the Tsars and Tsardom, and of the orthodox priests as lying prophets of Antichrist. They have obstinately refused to register themselves, to pay taxes, to bear passports. Their doctrine is the last word of the Bezpopovtsy against the regime of Antichrist. Certain of the sectaries of the Pomorians who pray for the Tsar were careful to justify their action by citing the precepts of St. Paul in favour of praying for Gentile or infidel sovereigns. So also the Thedosyevtsi or sect of Theodosius were careful to indicate that they only paid the Tsar's taxes, because the New Testament inculcates submission to the Powers which be. The 'Wanderers', however, were guilty of a very disrespectful comparison of the Tsar with the heathen rulers, obedience to whom was counselled by the Apostles. They were no better than servants of the Devil, but the Tsar is Satan himself. You can do nothing but make war on him.

No permanent community or society higher than gypsies can be founded on the mere precept to wander and hide. The early followers of Jesus soon found that it was not enough to wait for the Second Coming, and that even to keep the faith alive they must organize. Euthymius' tenets excluded all idea of settlement; but presently, after his death, when the bond of his strong personality and preaching was removed, it became an urgent question how to assure to his Church any sort of stability or future. Continual vagabondage through 'desirable deserts' afforded no bond of union, nay rendered permanent ties between its members precarious. A number of poverty-stricken, homeless itinerant friars might attract to themselves fugitive criminals, but not people with settled notions of life and anything to lose. The members of the sect therefore met to consider whether in future they should continue to wander or settle down in fixed homes. An elder named Yakov Yakovlev urged that no one could be regarded as a member who did not imitate the master, but a lady named Irene, who had been Euthymius' companion in travel, as also the Elder or 'director' Krainev, proposed a compromise, by which they should only receive as members of the society those who took a vow to become *Stranniki* some day, even if for the present they kept their homes and went on living in them. After warm discussion the compromise was accepted, and a distinction was henceforth drawn between imperfect members who might live in town and village and only vow themselves to become adepts in the Christian faith later on, and those who pursued the original ideal of Euthymius in its entirety. It was stipulated however that those who lived in fixed abodes should maintain shelters or asylums of refuge for the true wanderers and extend their hospitality to them whenever they appeared.

The student of early Christianity will at once recognize the parallelism of the *Strannik* society with the earliest Church. Ivanovski describes in detail the life of concealment led by the *Strannik* missionaries with evident gusto, as if they reflected no discredit on the persecuting Church of which he is so distinguished an ornament. The refuges, he tells us, of these sectaries are furnished with secret ways in and out; they mostly consist of underground cellars or garrets constructed in courtyards, kitchen-gardens and so forth. There are also hiding places for the missionaries under staircases, in closets, in cupboards; sometimes they are concealed behind walls or under the roof, sometimes under the stove. Whole secret villages of Beguni have been discovered, in which each house communicated with the rest by secret passages, and the secret entrance of the last in the street opened into the garden or into a thicket or somewhere out on a highroad.

This twofold organization of the *Stranniki* into those who live as wandering monks and those who, remaining in the world, are under a vow to become true wanderers ere they die, closely

resembles that of the Cathars. The Elect Cathar cut himself
or herself off from the world; while the laity, if we may so call
them, continued to live in the world, fed and sheltered the Elect,
but ever cherished the hope and intention of being themselves
elected before they died. For Election implied the reception
of the Holy Spirit, whereby they became incarnations of Christ,
Christs themselves, adopted sons of the Heavenly Father. In
Catharism no doubt there survived the deferred baptism of the
early centuries, and the same rite has lived on in the Catholic
Church in the form of extreme unction. The Cathars knew the
rite under the name of *Consolamentum*, or reception of the
Comforter or Paraclete.

The *Stranniki* then who remain in the world and maintain
these refuges for the spiritually perfect, the initiates, are under
a vow themselves to adopt the wandering life before they die.
In old age or in case of sickness felt to be mortal they retire
into a wood, and there live till death overtakes them. The
excuse for their disappearance from the ranks of society is
usually that they have set off on a pilgrimage. Sick children
are rebaptized, and baptism is usually performed in all cases
in a lake or a pond, either because they have no fonts or, more
probably, in deference to the preference for *living* water so
strong in the early Church and in other ancient forms of lustration. Ivanovski also states,— though this like some others
of his statements must be accepted with caution,— that the
rite of initiation is often arranged in a merely formal and
hypocritical fashion. The relations of a dying *Strannik*, he
says, inform the police (in the last degree improbable!) that so
and so is in hiding,— this in token of the fact that he has broken
off all ties and relations with society. The sick person is withal
removed to a neighbouring house or into a hiding place where
he spends his time 'in concealment and salutary fear,' till
presently he is received, baptized and installed a 'perfect'
Strannik. His vocation is then complete.

The dead are buried in obscure places, in a forest, a field;
children often under ploughland or in kitchen-gardens. A
Strannik's grave is unrecognizable, for no mound ever marks it.
We are reminded of the account of the recent persecution of the

Uniat Catholics in the Polish province of Kholm given in that dreadful book *L'apostolat du Knout* published at Paris in 1913 by the Diocesan Society of Tours. In Kholm the Catholics would hide the fact that anyone was dying, and bury him secretly in their gardens, and wait till they could get a Latin priest to read their rites over the extemporized grave. If it was known that a man lay sick to death in a house, the agents of the Russian Government would wait round the house ready to burst in and carry the corpse off in triumph to the 'orthodox' Church, there to be submitted to 'orthodox' burial rites. New-born children similarly were torn from their mothers' breasts and carried off to the Russian Church to receive 'orthodox' baptism; and any but 'orthodox' marriages being forbidden and repudiated as illegitimate along with their fruit by Pobedonostzev's law, young couples, desiring to marry, would escape across the frontier to Crakov in Austrian Poland, and get married by a Latin Priest. By such means, in the years preceding this war, the Holy and Orthodox Church of Russia had converted as many as 400,000 Uniat or Latin Ruthenes.

We have seen that numbers of the Priestless Sect, just because they regarded marriage as a sacrament, needing a priest to administer it, tried for a while, and here and there, to live as monks and nuns, and presently, following Uzov, we shall discuss this aspect of their life in more detail. How far Euthymius revived this strict ideal in his sect, is not clear, but we need not doubt Ivanovski's statement that his adherents followed monastic usage so far as to assume in their 'religion' monastic names, such as Niphon, Eustathius etc., and that they lived as monks and nuns under strict rule, for violation of which rigorous penalties were exacted, especially for infringement of the seventh commandment. Ivanovski states, however, that, in spite of their lofty pretensions, revolting scenes of debauchery were common among them, accompanied with great cruelty. Beginning with Euthymius, every one of their leaders or elders kept a mistress; and theft, brigandage, even assassination were not unknown in the bosom of the sect. He attributes this partly to the fact that many exiled criminals joined them, no doubt to secure shelter under the cover of piety. Kelsiev in his *Sbornik*, vol. IV, 288 foll., prints evidence of such irregularities from the lips of members of the sect, most of them renegades. But it is possible that the 'mistress' of Euthymius was a 'spiritual' wife, a relationship common though often reprobated in the Early Church from the time of St. Paul onwards for about four centuries. The Stranniki certainly regarded marriages contracted before a Nikonian or orthodox priest as mere fornication, just as the mediaeval Cathari regarded marriage inside the Catholic Church.

Such relationship led to grave scandals in the Early Church: they could not do otherwise in Russia a hundred years ago, and one of the first questions that rent asunder the Strannik Society after the founder's death was that of marriage. The institution was plainly incompatible with the idea of religious vagabondage, of inhabiting neither city nor village; and yet the conditions of human life had to be met, and in the sixties of the last century the followers of Euthymius found themselves suddenly compelled to make their decision, whether or no a *Strannik* after initiation could or could not continue to lead a family life.

A convert, Nicholas Ignatiev Kosatkin in the Government of Novgorod, had fallen sick and sought 'perfection' ere death should overtake him. But in making his confession prior to being baptized he avowed no intention of parting from his wife, and even declared he would abandon the sect if its statutes and if scripture were so interpreted. Nevertheless the prior or spiritual authority, deputed to 'receive' him, admitted him to baptism, because he was so grievously ill, and so he became a full member of the sect. Then he recovered after all, but refused to abandon his wife and children, nay, begat a new child. Thenceforth he began a propaganda in favour of marriage in the sect.

He found an ally in one Miron Vasilev, and it was resolved by most of the society under their guidance that marriage was allowable, along with the two other sacraments of baptism and penance, until the second advent — a sensible conclusion. Forthwith members who were married before they joined the sect began to live together again, where they had not done so all along. There was a minority however that held out against marriage, and met the argument that the early Christians allowed it with the counter argument that these only fled into the desert to escape persecution and hoped to return when the persecution was ended, whereas they, the *Stranniki*, had fled into the desert for good and ever, never meaning to return and live in an unregenerate world. In view of Uzov's account of the sect one suspects that Ivanovski somewhat over-generalizes and accepts as valid and significant for the entire sect of Stranniki events and quarrels and decisions that only really concerned a section of it.

There were other questions also which led to dissensions in the society, for example the trivial one whether a Strannik should carry in his pocket coins that bore the stamp of Antichrist. Euthymius had avoided this 'Archimedian problem,' but one of his stricter followers Vasili Petrov raised it, and an insignificant minority followed him in his objection to money, and were known as the 'moneyless' ones. They got over the practical inconvenience by getting novices to carry money for them and make their disbursements, just as the Manichean Elect ones carried their scruple against taking life so far as to make their novices cut their salads for them, shriving them afterwards for the sin they had committed. Nicetas Semenov, one of their best known teachers, raised his voice against such nonsense, and also against the scruple felt against the use of prayer books printed for the Uniats. These bore on the title page the imprimatur of the Tsar-Antichrist and of the Holy synod, and it was impossible to procure the old printed service books anterior to Nikon, because they had become so rare. In a Begun Council it was agreed to get over the difficulty by tearing out the title pages!

Another cause of dissension was a sensible attempt made by this same Nicetas Semenov to organize the society better and keep it more together by appointing superior and inferior clergy in some localities. Semenov published a tract on the subject, but was accused by some of his brethren of being a second Nikon and of wishing to establish a hierarchy. His supporters however chose him to be supreme head or director of the society. In the early church the episcopate did not get the better of the itinerant prophet without a struggle, and, we may be sure, some heartburnings. It was so with the Stranniki; thus does religious history repeat itself.

Latterly, according to Ivanovski, the *Strannik* elders or initiates have compromised with Antichrist in yet another matter. In order to roam about and propagate their tenets with greater security they apply for passports, not in the names they bear in 'religion,' but in the lay names which they bore in the world, before they were converted.

The Netovtsi and the Self-Baptizers

Macarius and Ivanovski distinguish among the priestless sectaries who assert that the advent of Antichrist has brought about the demise of the Church with its priesthood and sacraments, the *Netovtsi* or *Nothingites*, as a separate and self-contained sect whose members repudiate baptism altogether, because they cannot reconcile it with their consciences that laymen should administer it, for that is a violation of the second of the Apostolical Canons contained in the Kormchei (conciliary) Book, which rules that "those who snatch at gifts not vouchsafed to them offend against God, as did the sons of Korah and King Uzziah. Not even a deacon is worthy to offer the Sacrifice or to baptize anyone or to celebrate the little or great benediction."

An offshoot of the 'Nothingites' are, however, the self-baptizers, who get over the difficulty by baptizing themselves. Their converts immerse themselves in a lake or river, and instead of a priest, as in the orthodox Church, using over them the formula:— "This child of God is baptized," they repeat over themselves the words:— "I, a child of God, baptize myself." Similarly they repeat over themselves, when they marry the formulas:— "I betrothe myself," and "I crown myself," for in Eastern marriages a crown is placed on the head of each of the parties. This sect sprang up in the last years of the XVIIIth Century, and flourished exceedingly in the Saratov Government, according to Veskinski's notice of them in the *Orthodox Review*, of 1864, No. 8. A member of it, Timothy Bondarev, composed a work called:—'A true and faithful Way of Salvation,' from which K. Kustodiev in the *Russki Vestnik* (for 1862, No. 9, p. 420) adduces the views of the Sect with regard to the history of religion, which views, as he says, approximate in a remarkable degree to western rationalism.

Bondarev started from the position that everything in the world grows old and decays, and out of what has lived its day springs up a new growth, which in its turn will grow old and give way to new. This thesis he applied to the many laws which have successively been vouchsafed by God to the human race, namely to those of Adam, Noah, Abraham, Moses, Aaron, Solomon, and lastly to ourselves in the law of the Gospel. All these revelations, he says, were given for everlasting fulfilment unto all eternity, and the first six of them were part of the old covenant. Yet by divine destiny all has been changed, and no one any more observes the first six, nor has their abrogation displeased the Lord God. The seventh and last, that of the Gospel, can only hold good until the glorious second advent on earth of Christ. Yet he will come, not as the profane imagine, to the eye or senses, but spiritually and intellectually; not in brutal fact and sight to all or any, but in the form of righteous mind, and true preaching and in no other. It is clear, adds Kustodiev, that in strict accordance with his fundamental idea, Bondarev's rebukes smite the external side of religion, not only in the Church, but in the Raskol Sects themselves, in so far as they tolerate presbytery and preceptorate. He is an enemy of every kind of hierarchy, and his opinions connect the teaching of the *Stranniki* with that of two unreservedly rationalist groups of Old believers, the Prayerless and the Sighers (*or* Aspirants), who very likely owe much to his work.

The Prayerless and the Sighers

These two bodies virtually agree in their tenets and are the extreme champions of the religion of the inner man, and V. S. Tolstoi in a communication to the Imperial Society of History and Antiquities in the year 1864 (bk. 4, p. 123) gave an account of the Founder of the *Prayerless* Sect. He was a Don Cossack, named Gabriel Zimin, an inhabitant of the Thedosievskaya Stanitsa. In his childhood a Popovets, he subsequently joined the opposite Sect the Bezpopovtsy, as a member of which he gave himself up to the reading of old printed books, in order to ascertain their interpretation of various points. Presently he elaborated a doctrine of his own, of which, though based on Scripture, no sect had ever dreamt. This new teaching exposed him to the reprisals of the Government, which banished him in 1837 to Transcaucasia, where what became of him is not known. The thoroughness with which he carried his creed into life, is shewn by an incident narrated of him. The moment proceedings were taken against him for joining the Sect, he took off a cross of St. George which had been conferred upon him for valor and restored it to the Government.

It was to be expected that this sect as being the *ne plus ultra* of 'Old belief' would attract to itself more Old believers than Orthodox, and it is so. The former are perpetually routing about among their old books. This sharpens their wits, and not seldom they find among the rubbish treasures of value, as they think, even for the modern world.

How closely Zimin's sect connects with the Old believers is seen in their general attitude. They regard all the corrections made by Nikon as so many 'perversions of the truth,' and esteem Nikon himself 'as a pioneer in that path of corruption' which led up to the age of the spirit, and along which the mass of Russians are moving to-day.

They base their religious philosophy on a division of the past into four ages; of these four, the first lasted from creation until Moses; this was *Springtide*, the age of the fore-fathers of our race, i.e. the Patriarchs: the second extended from Moses to the birth of Christ, and is called *Summer*, the age of our Fathers. The third from Julius Caesar to 1666 was *Autumn*, the age of sons; from 1666 to the present day is *Winter*, the age of the Holy Spirit.

The Sighers put it somewhat differently, holding in a manner in some ways reminiscent of Marcion, in others of Montanus, that in the Old Testament we have the kingdom of God the Father, in whom men then believed; in the New Testament that of God the Son, which began with the birth of Christ and continued to the 8,000th year from Creation, and is now ended. With the 8,000th year begins the reign of God the Spirit, or the Age to Come; and in the present it behooves us to believe in the truth of the Spirit, by means of sighing or aspiration or out-breathing, according to the saying: Glory to the Father, and Son, and Holy Spirit.[1]

The *Prayerless* teaching then in general inculcates that Truth is utterly extinct, faith suppressed and hidden; but as the age of the Holy Spirit is nigh, there remains but a single chance of salvation, the attainment namely of such ideals and ends as it is ordained for us to fulfill in *the spirit*, but not at all through the flesh or any material modes. Not even oral services to God are permissible, for they involve use of the tongue of the body. Impressed with the belief that they are living in the age of the Spirit, they are minded to take everything, holy Scripture not excepted, in a spiritual sense. They do not shrink even from evaporating off in the same way the birth of Jesus Christ in the flesh, his passion, death, resurrection and ascension. For example, the Virgin Mary was good counsel, out of which was born the Word of God, and he is Jesus Christ, the Son of God. His coming in the flesh they do not preach; but by way of explaining it they fall back on the idea that in Jesus' age, divine rites and services were performed in the flesh, and that this flesh, after the advent of the age of the Spirit, is completely set aside and abrogated. Ecclesiastical authorities, after the 7000 years had elapsed, no less than Church Services and all external rites, came abruptly to an end; and since then all grades of clergy, from deacon to patriarch are on a level with the ordinary layman; nor are pastors and preceptors or rectors any better, for they usurp their authority instead of receiving it by direct succession. A church or orthodox temple is nothing

---

[1] This information is given in an article in the Supplement to the Journal of the See of Kaluga, for the year 1873, No. 3, entitled "A few words about the *Sighers of Kaluga*," pp. 53–4. Cp. Albrecht Dieterich, *Eine Mithrasliturgie*, p. 14, l. 20 for a curious parallel.

more than a simple house, and sacraments performed therein
were only pleasing to God before the term of 7000 years expired.
All rubrics are antiquated; external modes of veneration of
God no longer have any significance. All this is a thing of the
past. The age to come is upon us, and no Church is left on
earth. It is not wanted any more; no more are priestly functions or offerings or outward ceremonies. The true temple is
within us each, in the heart; for it was said: "Ye are the
churches of the living God," and "Are ye not a temple of
God." [1]

If the old Manichean faith had not lain buried for a thousand
years at least under the sands of Central Asia, awaiting dis-
interment by scholars and explorers like Sir Aurel Stein,
Grunwedel, W. D. Müller and others, one could almost suppose that Zimin had drunk of its inspiration. He shares with
Mani, and Mani's spiritual father Marcion, the docetism which
gets rid of the flesh and historicity of the Messiah; he also
betrays the same abhorrence of material cults, which was
carried so far among the Cathars and Manicheans that they
would not even use water in baptism or the human hand in
ordination. In their abrogation of ecclesiastical orders the
Prayerless have also reached the same goal from which Marcion
and his Cathar and Manichean progeny perhaps started, the
conception namely of a single spiritual grade of election by the
spirit, first exampled in Jesus and accessible to all alike who
follow in his footsteps. From such a standpoint the difference
between a pneumatic or inspired laity and a charismatic priesthood fades into nothingness; we are back in a stage of the
development of Christian speculation and practice earlier
than any separate priesthood at all, in which priesthood had
not emerged; such a stage has barely left any trace in the
Great Churches of East and West, although it survived into
the middle ages among the Cathars and even into the XIXth
Century among the Thonraki heretics of Armenia described
in my 'Key of Truth.'   The orthodox clergy, according to
Zimin's followers, are ministers of Antichrist, and the priestly
functions exercised by them are a tissue of fraud and avarice.

[1] *Kaluga Journal* 1873, No. 2, p. 32, and No. 3, pp. 53–55.

God asks nothing of us in return for his grace and loving kindness; and if the priests were truly his ministers they would take nothing for their rites. Seeing that they take money for every prayer, we have, they say, no use for them.[1]

The scriptures, they maintain, must without exception be understood in a spiritual sense, especially today. Everything revealed in them refers to this age; of the Heaven to be, of the bliss of the just ones, of the departure of the spirit from the flesh, no one, in their opinion can know aught, for it is all an incomprehensible mystery. The Father, to quote their language, denotes the Paternal principle or rule which lasted until Jesus Christ; the Son, the filial principle that held sway from the birth of Christ until 1666; the Holy Spirit the principle that dominates this age, the last.[2]

They will not hear of prayers offered with lips of flesh, whence the name by which they are known of the *Prayerless*. In their opinion we must not offer up to God, prayers written in books, but prayers that come from the worshipper's own heart and soul, and emanate from the spirit of wisdom. And in proof they appeal to the saying of the Gospel: "Enter thy chamber, shut thy door and pray in secret." "Enter thy chamber," they argue, is a precept of silence; "shut the door" means to close the lips; and of the same purport is the maxim: "True worshippers worship in spirit and in truth." It is an evil thing to liken oneself to the heathen, to utter or recite any sort of prayers at home or in meetings, for there is no salvation in vain repetition. Nay more, to supplicate in one's mind for anything definite is superfluous and useless, for our Heavenly Father knows, without our asking, what we need.[3]

The Cross they utterly reject; as a visible or material object it is of no avail, at any rate in the present, the age of the spirit. Baptisms they have none, and only give a child a name in accordance with common custom.

The marriage union is accomplished among them without any religious rite; they only insist on a mutual agreement of

---

[1] *Kaluga Journal* 1873, No. 3, p. 56.

[2] Tolstoi, *op. cit.* pp. 127–131.

[3] *Istina*, 1875, 41, *Missionary Information about Raskol.*

bride and bridegroom and parents; but one party must not abandon the other without there has been open violation of the marriage tie to excuse it. "What do you want with marriage?" they say. "Choose your wife, as you please, and live with her as you please, and you commit no sin." They bury the dead without any hymns or prayers and in the simplest manner possible, for they hold that a dead body is earth and returns to dust. They therefore reject all rites performed over the dead and allow no commemoration of them. If they occasionally conduct a burial in accordance with the regulations of the orthodox church, they only do so to escape the vexations of the police.

Holy relics discovered before the 7000th year, they admit to be efficacious; but all later ones they repudiate on the ground that, since the age of the Spirit began, there is no use for them, while even genuine ones are deprived of any further miraculous efficacity, inasmuch as the fleshly or carnal age has expired. The second advent of Christ, they say, is already past, and they alone had understanding to recognize the event in accordance with divine revelation. The day of judgment they do not believe in and appeal to the saying: "The Father hath given judgment to his Son," but the Son is the Word, and the Word has already delivered his judgment in his time, that is before the expiration of the 7000 years. So they await no further advent of Christ nor attend his dread judgment. And they say, "after death there is nothing of the sort; we shall not answer for our deeds to anyone."

Feasts and fasts they equally reject. "You think," they say to the orthodox, "that you are gratifying God by eating mushrooms and radishes. You are not. You only exhaust yourselves and enfeeble your strength."

They have put aside everything visible, and along with it priesthood, nor among themselves have they a presbyterate resting on selection, although they make much of those who have a turn for explaining in a spiritual manner texts of scripture, perverting, says Ivanovski, their meaning to their own ends.

Their attitude to the State is narrowly connected with their theological views. They shew respect for the Lord, the Tsar and the Government, as well as for the civil laws, because they cannot avoid doing so; but in reality they hold that all established authority, being based on ignorance of the age and season, must inevitably be neither valid nor just, and for that reason they decline to obey as they ought. Imbued with such ideas, opposed to sound common sense, as Ivanovski thinks, they reject oaths taken no matter with what object, and are convinced that an oath in particular is not only unavailing but intrinsically absurd, all the more so because an ecclesiastic has to administer it. "In any service of the Government, they say, no matter what, even if you could take part, don't, except in so far as the Government drives you to do so by force, so that you cannot help yourself. Should you find yourself face, to face with enemies with arms in their hands, that is no excuse for you to rush to arms. Remember the words of the Gospel, Mat. 26, 52: "All that take to the sword shall die by the sword." They reserve the appellation of Christian warrior for the man who is at issue with infidels, understanding by the latter term those who do not share their beliefs in the succession of the ages nor realize that the age of the Holy Spirit is already come. Such is the picture of the tenets of this remarkable sect, so closely allied to our own Quakers, given in the two sources named, viz: Tolstoi's articles and the Kaluga diocesan journal.

Uzov admits his ignorance with regard to the strength and diffusion of the Prayerless Sect, but has evidence of their being found all over Russia, e.g. in the territory of the Don Cossacks (Voiska Donskago); in Odessa as early as 1845, as testified by Andreev; in the Vyatka Government in 1867, in the province of Sarapul. Here entire villages belonged to it, and the Government in the hope of extirpating it proceeded about that time to imprison its leading members. Thereupon the members of it presented themselves *en masse* before the local authorities and besought them to imprison them as well; but the jails were not large enough, and many of them were turned away disappointed.[1]

Gatsisski asserts in *Old and New Russia*, 1877, No. 11, p. 274,

[1] V. Popov: *Secrets of the Raskolniks, Old Ritualists*, etc. pp. 15, 16.

that seven years before that date they were diffused in the
trans-Volga districts of the Nizhegorod Government, in other
parts of which they already existed; in many villages the soil
was turned up ready for the seed of the new faith to spring up
on it. In the Kaluga Government, we learn from the Kaluga
diocesan Journal of 1873, Nos. 2 and 3, p. 39, that the "lying
propaganda" of the 'Sighers' had already reached a great
extension. In *cabarets*, taverns, in the streets on feast days,
you heard them preaching. Near the Tula Gate in Kaluga
in a certain class of 'establishment,' their disputes with other
sectaries often threatened to degenerate into fisticuffs. According to reports they had appeared in the Borov and Maloyaroslav provinces. In the Kostroma Government they were,
according to Gatsisski, scattered about in the district of
Varnavin; and their presence in that of Korchev was also
recorded. Such was the diffusion of this sect in 1880, when
Uzov wrote; since then it is likely to have multiplied itself
on the same scale as other forms of dissent.

The Intellectual Development of the Bezpopovtsy

In general and especially during the XIXth Century the
Bezpopovtsy have shewn a more liberal tendency than the
Popovtsy. All their sects have evinced the same determination
to supersede, or at least not to accept without careful examination, the authority even of their own writers of an earlier
generation. Thus the Theodosian sect at Riga in 1826 drew
up a code for the regulation of their refuge or house of mercy
in that city in which it is pointed out that "their ancestors'
prescriptions were often wrong." It was therefore felt to be
necessary "to examine attentively the publications and decrees
of former generations, to uphold such parts of them as are
consonant with law and scripture, to supplement what is
defective, to make clear what is obscure, and exhibit before the
community whatever conflicts with principles and holy writ,
so that it may be altered." [1] Long ago the members of this
same sect, in their discussion of burning questions with the

[1] Nilski: *Family Life in the Russian Raskol*, pt. 2, p. 139.

Pomorians, refused to be bound even by texts from the Epistles of the Apostles unless these could be shewn to be applicable to the circumstances of the age;[1] and a well-read monk Paul of the priestless sect in his work: *The Royal Road*, which enjoyed extraordinary vogue among his people, repudiated the assumption that authority attaches to *all* the works of the Fathers.[2]

And the same independence of mind is revealed by the leaders of the priestless sects in their discussions with the orthodox clergy sent to convert them. Confronted with citations from ancient books they answer: "Well and good; but these books, my father, were written in an age when the ancient piety existed, and were true to fact when they were penned. But that old piety is past and done with and now there is nothing to which you can apply what the book contains."[3] "These were books of great men," others will answer, "but they have passed through the hands of heretics who have doctored them."[4]

It was in vain, remarks Uzov, that orthodox doctors adduced passages from the New Testament to the Fathers to prove that the Church of Christ must endure to the end of the world, that the gates of Hell shall not prevail against it, that the hierarchical order is similarly perpetual, because, as Cyril of Jerusalem wrote: "Christ's priesthood after the order of Melchizedek shall never cease," and so forth. The Bezpopovtsy replied that such promises could be annulled by the sins of mankind and that the Scripture offered many examples of promises *for ever* which were never realized. "God," they argued, "promised David that his throne should stand *for ever*, and yet long ago the Hebrew priesthood and kingdom ceased to exist."[5] Dire necessity turned these Raskolniks into higher critics and their agility in controversy led an orthodox publicist, K. Nadezhdin, to write of them as follows: "It is true they often borrow proofs of their lying teaching

---

[1] K. Nadezhdin: *Disputes of the Bezpopovtsy of the Preobrazhenski Cemetery and of the Pokrovski Chapel about marriage.*

[2] M. Stebnitski: *Among the People of the Old Religion*, 2nd. Edition p. 12.

[3] T. Tverdynski: *Conversations of an Orthodox Priest*, p. 28.

[4] *Istina* (Truth) 1877, Bk. 51, *Preaching of the Truth*, p. 181.

[5] *Istina*, 1877, Bk. 53: *Preaching of the Truth in the See of Pskov*, p. 67.

from holy writ, but at the same time no sooner do they see that, in spite of their garbling, it does not bear out their assertions, than they are ready to deny the sanctity even of holy writ itself, frequently adding that it was given us as much for our ruin as not." Scripture, according to the Bezpopovtsi, is no other than a two-edged sword; out of it springs every sort of heresy.[1]

In the conferences which were held at Kazan in 1871 the Bezpopovtsy commenting on the proofs from Scripture laid before them by N. Ivanovski, professor in the seminary there, answered: "Scripture is a trackless abyss; that only to one that has understanding is the advent of Antichrist palpable, and men have advanced interpretations out of their own imaginations, based on nothing at all." Ivanovski replied that though on the one hand the Old believers pretend to be champions of the letter, yet wherever it suits their doctrine they have no scruple in violating its obvious meaning, and concocting interpretations of various kinds, half rationalist, half mystical, which they dignify by the name of the 'inward meaning.' To the plainest and simplest passages of Scripture and the Fathers they attribute one allegorical sense or another, all equally strange. A monk named Barnabas, formerly one of the Bezpopovtsy, who in 1880 had joined the Orthodox Church, wrote of them that "by preference they interpret everything spiritually." [2] In this connection the question of Antichrist occupies the first place. In their reasonings about his person and time of appearance we always hear one and the same thing said: "We must understand the Scriptures allegorically, and conceive in a spiritual manner of spiritual matters"; "no, no, it does not help us to understand things carnally; we must understand Scripture, not according to the ink, but allegorically." But their commonest watchword is: "To him that hath shall understanding be given." [3] And they appeal to a passage of Ephrem Syrus to this effect, to be read in his tract on the *Dread Judgment and on Antichrist:* —

[1] *Istina*, Bk. 6: *Controversy among Bezpopovtsy.*

[2] *Chronicle* (Letopis) *of Events among the Raskol*, by N. Subbotin, p. 32.

[3] *Orthodox Companion*, No. 12, art. by N. Ivanovski, pp. 475-8.

"To anyone gifted with divine wisdom and understanding, the advent of the tormenter will be intelligible, but for him that is immersed in the things of this world and loves the earthly, it shall not be so; for if we be wedded to interests of this life, we may hear the Word, but will have no faith; nay, they who preach it will excite our hatred."

The Bezpopovtsy in view of the endeavours of Orthodoxy to convert them, if only to the Uniat position (which they term a snare) by a system of missionary preaching, and finding themselves compelled under pain of a fine to send their learned men to hold discussions with the missionaries, say to the latter: "Formerly we were tortured, and without any success; and now you think you are going to convert us to the Church with the help of a few old books." [1] "You can find no arguments now to lay before us by way of exonerating yourselves but what you find in our own old printed books; but you yourselves have cursed these books and abused them and confiscated them and relegated them to your lumber-rooms: and we are on our guard. Just as you used to torture us for an old book, so now you will make us pay dear; and if we give you nothing, you will carry off our book straight away; nay, will lock us up in the casemate as well. Of course you eulogise the old books now, you even appeal to them for everything, as if, my brother, we had not read them a thousand times and long ago." [2]

Uzov pertinently observes that, so long as the old books were the sole property of the Old believers, they naturally took good care in citing them to pass by passages that contradicted their position; but as soon as orthodox missionaries that had belonged to their sect began to use them, as weapons of attack, and so revealed what double-edged tools they were, then the Old believers' enthusiasm for them, as we saw above, began to evaporate, and they proclaimed that "to him that hath understanding, more shall be given."

We have already glanced at the doctrine of the Antichrist so widely current in the Raskol, and Uzov gives some account of a book entitled *About the Antichrist, Testimony from Holy*

---

[1] *Istina*, 1876, bk. 45, *Records of Conversations*, p. 654.

[2] *Conversations* of the psalm reader Paul, p. 6.

Writ. He was to appear according to it at the very end of the XVIIIth or rather at the beginning of the XIXth Century, and it is explained that: "he is not a man but the spirit of our world, an heretical condition of the Church, an apostasy of Christians from the Truth vouchsafed by Christ, a spirit of sacrilegious impiety and eternal perdition. By the woman of whom he is to be born we are to understand a society of unclean people; by his birth, their apostasy from Gospel truth; lastly by the three and a half years which is to be the period of his reign is signified an indefinite lapse of time"; "the idea of the Antichrist as of something imperceptible, ideal, spiritual, arose among them long ago, at the very beginning of the Raskol movement, but by reason of its abstract character it had at first little vogue among them and was never formulated clearly and definitely; [1] nowadays it has become a favourite topic of Bezpopovtsy conversations." "As a spirit of sacrilegious apostasy a spirit of eternal perdition, it lives, so they teach, and operates principally *in the governing classes who hold power in their hands.*"[2] For the rest: "There exist among them at present two opinions about the person of the Antichrist: some of them understanding by the name an antichristian spirit in society, an apostasy of men from Christ and from the teaching he bestowed on us, an heretical condition of the Christian Church; others conceiving of Antichrist as the last of a series of persons pursuing one and the same teaching opposed to the truth of the Gospel." The latter "understand by the woman from whom is to be born the Man of Sin to mean an earthly kingdom of some sort, concentrated as it were in a single body; the birth of Antichrist is the issuing or provenance of such persons out of this kingdom or their manifestation therein." They point to the passage of the apocalypse about a whore, whose name Babylon, they declare (following Andrew of Caesarea), is derived from the woman, who is nothing but a kingdom of earth, and in especial the Roman Kingdom, called in Peter's epistle Babylon, and the Russian Kingdom called by the patriarch Jeremiah the third Rome. Antichrist is to be

---

[1] I. Nilski: *About Antichrist*, p. xxxiv.
[2] I. Popov: *Sbornik* for history of Old believers, t. 1, p. xi.

born, that is, manifest himself in this kingdom or issue therefrom; consequently he must appear in Russia, which is the third Rome." He "has been reigning in the world for long ages," in Russia ever since 1666.[1] Allegorization of the old legend of Antichrist, as Miliukov points out, rendered it easier for the Raskolniki to compromise with a world which after all had not come to an end, as at first they had expected it to do. The logic of events had falsified their early anticipations of his advent, and allegory furnished them with a means of readjusting them.

"In the old legends of the Antichrist, Enoch and Elias the prophets were also to appear, and the Bezpopovtsy found as little difficulty in dissipating their personalities by means of allegory. Enoch was the natural law, Elias the written law, John the law of grace." [2] "Others declared that Elias and Enoch are symbols of zealous men in general, and that anyone who argues from the written letter is no better than a Jew." [1] Such glosses as the above reveal that the Dissenters had grown out of their early belief in Antichrist, with its implication of the imminence of the end of the world. The world had stood the test, and they had after all to live in it. Hence the new orientation of old beliefs.

At this time one can hardly refrain from asking oneself if these opinions have not had much to do with the present upheaval in Russia. In their crude way these simple people had apprehended the truth. That the present catastrophe is a result of the neglect by all the Governments of Europe of the elementary moral truths enunciated in the Gospel, who can doubt? These truths avenge themselves, if they are flouted and ignored, as surely as would the axioms of mathematics, if they were set at naught; moral principles are no less infallible and certain, remarked Leibnitz long ago, than the postulates and axioms of geometry; and if the latter got in the way of our passions and cupidity as much as does morality, Euclid and Archimedes would be denounced as dreamers and hopelessly impracticable people.

[1] I. Nilski: *About Antichrist against the Raskolniks*, pp. 1, 100–1, 107, 108.

[2] *Edifying Reading (Dushepoleznoe Chtenie)* 1869, *On the Advent of Elias and Enoch*, by the Priest Paul, pt. 2, 137, 138, 140, 147 and pt. 3, 10, 12.

The identification of Tsardom and of the late Russian polity
with the reign of Antichrist was naturally little conducive to
the loyalty which finds expression in prayers for the Sovereign.
A minority of the dissenters, especially in the cities, tried by
unsparing use of the allegorical method to reconcile such
loyalty with their conscience, especially in times when the
Tsar's Government betrayed the least tendency to tolerate
their existence; but these fits of toleration were always of
brief duration and due to the personal enlightenment of a Tsar
or Tsaritsa. Behind the sovereign there ever stood the Holy
Synod with its 'short method for dealing with dissenters.'

It was mainly the Thedosievtsy and Pomortsy who lived in
cities that shewed a tendency to compromise and admit a
détente in the sway over Russia of the Antichrist, but the more
extreme sect, the wanderers or Beguny, remained intransigent,
and indeed the vast majority of the Raskolniks held by their
convictions, as is shewn by the fact that in the XIXth Century
the sects which spread and multiplied were mostly those which
regarded prayers for the Tsar and the royal family as the worst
form of blasphemy, an actual verification of the legend which
represented the Antichrist as forcing his way into the temple
and deifying himself. Nor was this tendency confined to the
priestless dissenters. The less extreme Popovtsy shared it,[1]
and in 1868, in a council held in their Austrian centre of Bielo-
Krinits, they solemnly decreed that any who pray for the
Powers that be shall be excommunicate. 'How will you ever
find grace at the hands of the Beast?' asked such partisans.[2]

In every country trade and wealth engenders the instinct
to uphold Church and State. One is therefore prepared to
learn that it was chiefly among dissenting shop-keepers in
Russia that an inclination to pray for the Tsar shewed itself.
The Russian peasant, on the other hand, remained obdurate.
Thus on January 23rd, 1864, when division of opinion about
the matter revealed itself in a general meeting of the Popovtsy,
held in their Moscow headquarters, the so-called Rogozhski
cemetery, only ten persons were in favour of offering up in the

---

[1] *Russki Vestnik*, 1869, No. 2, art. by Subbotin.
[2] *Edifying Readings*, 1869, Pt. 3, art. by Paul the Priest, pp. 365–6.

liturgy a prayer for the Tsar, the peasants and poorer citizens going against it *en masse*, according to Subbotin's articles in the "Russki Vestnik" for that year (No. 2, p. 775; No. 3, pp. 407, 413) and for 1869 (No. 10, p. 605). The vast majority of the Popovtsy were during the sixties of the last century at one in such matters with the Priestless Sect, into whose ranks of every shade of opinion there was a constant tendency for them to drift, as we read in the "Russki Vestnik" for June 1865 in I. Belliyustin's art: *More About Movements in the Raskol*, also in I. Liprandi's contribution to the Proceedings of the Imperial Society of Antiquaries of Russia, for 1870, Vol. 2. Another author notes how the majority of dissidents used in their hymns such words as 'Vouchsafe to true believers victory over all opposition.'[1] But the so-called *Stranniki* or *Wanderers* were the leading propagandists of an intransigent attitude towards the Imperial Government, and accused those of their co-religionists who prayed for the Tsar of gross inconsistency with their principles, inasmuch as victory for the Government meant victory of devil and Antichrist.[2] And another writer, I. Dobrotvorski, has justly remarked:[3] "Among the Priestless dissenters the belief in Antichrist colours their view of all that appertains to the State, of its laws, of its judicial procedure, of everything that reminds them of Authority, in a word of all governmental usages. The stamp of Antichrist is on it all; and it is all equally hateful to the Raskolniks, all equally impregnated with anti-Christian spirit. Some of them, no doubt, are less extreme than others and only go half-way, but the leaven has been there always and is ever at work."

The elementary intellectual independence of the Bezpopovtsy was shewn in their repudiation 'in case of need' of everything in Holy Scripture that conflicted with their religious aspirations. Antichrist has annihilated the genuine priesthood, therefore they have none. "This," they cried, "is the last age, in which everyone must judge for himself what is best."[4]

---

[1] *Istina* for 1875, Vol. 38: '*Internal Disputes among the Dissidents.*'

[2] *Vestnik Europy*, 1871, No. 1, art. by Rozov, p. 287.

[3] *Orthodox Review*, 1862, Pt. 1, p. 386.

[4] T. Tverdynski, *Discussions of orthodox principles with old ritualists*, p. 437.

The Church, they hold, is an union of the faithful, and can dispense, if need be, with a hierarchy for the best of reasons, to wit, because it has Christ himself for its head. A priestless believer will point his finger to his own breast and say: "Here is the true Church, here, in my heart! Not in the timbers of a church, but in my ribs." The Apostle Paul wrote: "Ye are the temple of the living God," according to the divine utterance: "I will dwell in them etc." [1] In them therefore is fulfilled the teaching that every man is a temple of God not built with hands, that in each of us God lives and gives ear to the heart's prayers.[2] You can hear the Bezpopovtsy to-day using such words as: 'I am the Church.' [3]

Opinion on Priesthood and Sacraments

There are even Bezpopovtsy, according to the Hegumen Paul, who maintain that "the priesthood itself and the Sacraments of the Eucharist and of anointing with Chrism are innovations. They declare that in the earliest age they never existed and were all introduced by Nikon. Before his date there was nothing but what the Bezpopovtsy now possess, namely an order of teachers, whom they also call popes." [4] This opinion, remarks Uzov, which seems merely absurd to the hegumen Paul, rests nevertheless on firm historical facts. Before Nikon's age the relations of clergy to people were not what they are to-day. "The parish churches in Russia had long been accustomed to see in their priests elected representatives of the people's will. At the close of the XIVth Century they were judged by laymen even in ecclesiastical matters, each parish instituted any particular priest it preferred, and his election depended on his receiving from the Commune a diploma of approval to which the parishioners must subscribe their names."

Moreover, it is notorious, writes Andreev in his work on *the Raskol and its significance in popular Russian history* (pp. 93,

---

[1] T. Tverdynski, *Discussions of orthodox principles with Old ritualists*, p. 115.

[2] Istina, 1874, bk. 35: *Propaganda of Truth in See of Pskov*, p. 3.

[3] Hegumen Paul: *Description of a Tour among Litovski* (Lithuanian) *Old-believers* in 1869–70, p. 20.

[4] *Op. cit.* p. 18.

94, 95, 135, 136), that "in the pre-Muscovite period Novgorod often transacted its ecclesiastical affairs without the benedictions of hierarchical authorities. Their spiritual lords Arsenius and Theodosius were never consecrated by any higher church authority; popular choice, it is clear, was of more importance in their eyes than consecration by a metropolitan or patriarch. Even as late as the beginning of the XVIIth Century in central Russia the priesthood was an elective dignity; in Pskov and its neighbourhood in 1685 as many as 160 churches were in the hands of peasants, who, without recognizing archpriest or bishop, paid the priests whatever prestimony or annual stipend they liked. Of old the parishioners regarded the church as an appanage of their own."

In that age and even later on the inhabitants of Pomor often dispensed altogether with a priest. Accordingly Barsov relates "that the people of that region finding it not infrequently impossible to visit their parish churches by reason of want of good roads and the great distances, confined themselves to building oratories in which all the services, except the liturgy, were performed by any common person. This explains why the laity of Northern Pomor so easily asserted themselves in ecclesiastical affairs, regarding them as no less the concern of villagers and local authorities than of the clergy. Individual village communities, for example, in the revolutionary epoch, with the consent of their zemstvos or county councils, undertook certain arrangements on their own initiative, drew up religious rules and regulations. When, later on, the institution of the popes by the people on the spot, by peasants and even by serfs, was declared irregular by the canons of the church authorities, and strict ukases were issued dealing with candidates for ordination and registers to the newly appointed popes and deacons,— then the clergy began at once to lose their moral influence and power over the zemstvos in the Pomor region; conversely the latter began to sit loose to clergy and church, began to trust more in the intellectual and religious influence of the learned than in that of the popes. In this condition of things we have, in fine, one of the main reasons, if not the main reason why in the Pomor region the priestless

Raskol spread with such rapidity." [1] Ivanovski, we saw, takes a similar view.

When the Raskol began in the XVIIth Century its teachers had none of them any idea of abandoning priesthood and sacraments. It was only gradually that circumstances reconciled them, at first to dispensing with them at need, and later on to abandoning them altogether, and adopting the idea that every man is a priest. This truth was fully enunciated early in the XIXth Century by Nicephor Petrov: "all are on a level; for pastors we have no use; all have received one and the same *cheirotonia* (laying on of hands); Confession also should consist in the taking of counsel with the inner self and not in the power to remit sins." [2] In 1841 Sidor Kutkin "preached in the Kurlyandski (Courland) Government, that any and every Raskolnik may himself fulfil the needs of the Church without having to resort to elder or teacher." [3] Such teaching was widespread within thirty years, and in 1875 the teachers of the sect, if asked on what ground they regarded themselves as pastors, would reply with a text from the Apocalypse: "He created us to be kings and priests." [4] At other times they would answer: "The Mir (village commune) has chosen us as pastors." When Paul the hegumen objected that this was not enough, and that Divine Ordination by means of prayers appointed to that end was necessary, he was met with the answer: "The voice of the People is the voice of God." [5]

In the discussions held in the Government of Pskov the Bezpopovtsy also declared as follows: "Among us today exists the priesthood of Melchizedek; every man is his own priest." [6]

The author of a work entitled *Ritualists of the Church Hierarchy* (the Orthodox are meant) writes: "The spiritual sacramental Priesthood of Christ belongs to every Christian, who has hallowed himself with the gifts of the Holy Spirit." [7] In

[1] Nikolaï Barsov, *The brothers Andrew and Semen Denisov*, p. 41–2.
[2] Vestnik Evropy, 1871, No. 4, art. by Kostomarov, p. 531.
[3] *Orth. Review*, 1865, No. 3, Art. by A. Veskinski.
[4] This text is ever on the tip of a Raskolnik's tongue.
[5] *Bratskoe Slovo* (Brotherly Word), 1875, bk. 2. *Journal of Hegumen Paul*, p. 123.
[6] Istina, 1873, Bk. 35, *Preaching of the Truth in Pskov*, p. 7.
[7] *Edifying Readings*, 1870, pt. 1, Art. by the Priest Paul.

another work entitled: *Doctrine of the Christian Church about the Keys*, it is shewn that the Keys of Priesthood belong not only to ordained persons, but to the whole Church, which can therefore very well exist without any priesthood at all. This is quoted in a "description of sundry works written by the Russian Raskolniks for use of the Raskol," among the memoirs (*zapiski*) of Alexander B. pt. 2, p. 332.

Renunciation of priesthood carried with it that of most of the sacraments; and the Bezpopovtsy, as we saw, were left with baptism and penance only, because these could be administered by laymen. "Jesus Christ," they argued, "commanded many of his apostles to baptize without their possessing priesthood, and apostolic perfection is attained, not by a graduated hierarchical promotion, but by moral improvement, purity of heart and freedom from passion." [1]

We see how the lack of a priesthood gradually awakened the mind of the majority of the Raskol to the truth that every man is a priest, and this step in religious reasoning has inevitably led to a new idea of the sacrament of communion. Accordingly it is commonly urged among them to-day that "a man who lives by the sweat of his brow, communicates every day of his life." [2] "If I live a good life, then I am saved even without communicating in the holy mysteries. [3] Live you a life of good works, they say to the orthodox, and God will not forsake you; only set your hope on communion with him. [4] Communion is reached in a life that imitates Christ's, according to his saying: If a man loveth me and keepeth my word, my Father will love him and come unto him and make his dwelling in him." [5] It is the merit of the Bezpopovtsy to have seen this truth, when they appeal to Augustine's saying that he who eats his meal with faith already communicates in the divine mystery. Let a man, they say, but sit down to meat after a prayer, and cross himself before he begins to eat, and

[1] *Ibid.* pp. 115, 117.
[2] *Ibid.* 1871, No. 7, art. of Hegumen Paul 143-5.
[3] *Ibid.*
[4] *Istina*, 1870, bk. 15: *Conversations with Bezpopovtsy of the monk Prokopius*, p. 58.
[5] *Edifying Readings*, 1870, pt. 1: Art. of the Priest Paul, p. 170.

then his common bread shall be for him the equivalent of holy communion.[1]

In exemplification of this conviction Uzov reproduces a fragment of a conversation between an orthodox priest and a Bezpopovets elder as follows: —

Elder: Here you see my church (*leading the way to his cottage*).

Priest: And how do you communicate in this pretended church of yours?

Elder: (*pointing to his homely table*): There we have our altar, at which we communicate day by day.

Priest: And how can you communicate at this table?

Elder: How? In what? Surely in the bread of Christ. Behold the bread that Christ has given us.[2]

The scene reminds us of much in early Christian literature of the κλάσις ἄρτου 'Breaking of Bread,' of the Acts and Epistles; of that ancient *Teaching of the Apostles* in which the Lord's Prayer was used as *the* prayer for the consecration of the Eucharistic meal; reminds us also of the fact, attested by Socrates the historian, that still in the IVth Century in parts of Egypt the eucharistic rite was celebrated by a layman, the head of a household, sitting with his family round his own table; of the fact, attested in the 'invectives' of a Byzantine Churchman against the Armenians, that the same pristine simplicity still prevailed in primitive Christian circles among them. Late into the Middle Ages, as the Inquisitors' records prove, the Cathars consecrated their Eucharist by repeating, before they partook of the sacred food, the Lord's Prayer and no more. Under stress of Orthodox persecution the Bezpopovtsy have wandered back unwittingly into a paleontological phase of the Christian Church.

The Bezpopovtsy take up an equally free and unconventional attitude towards other Sacraments, and betray no little agility in finding scriptural texts to bear them out, and where they cannot find any, leap lightly over the *letter*, to shield themselves behind the necessities of an age in which Antichrist dominates the world.

---

[1] From the Priest Paul, *Edifying Readings*, 1870, pt. 1, p. 170.

[2] *Istina*, 1868, bk. 6, *Vsyachina* (Miscellany).

Uzov admirably summarizes the religious development of the Raskol during the XIXth Century in these words: "Marching under the banner of Holy Scripture, at the same time admitting a 'higher' or spiritual interpretation, they are little by little reforming and recasting their outlook on the world, are drawing ever nearer and nearer to religious rationalism. They are as a rule condemned for their slavish adherence to the letter, to ritual, to forms, as compared with the rest of the populace that remains orthodox. This is a huge mistake, based on the tactics formerly — and still occasionally — followed by them in their assaults on orthodoxy. They began by finding fault with the orthodox because the latter used three fingers in crossing themselves instead of two, because they used the spelling *Iesus* instead of *Isus*, used a four-cornered cross instead of an eight-cornered one, repeated the Alleluiah thrice instead of twice; reduced the seven *prosphorae* or wafers of the liturgy to five, and so forth. We must not overlook this, that such argumentation was fashioned in an age when the supreme shepherds of the Orthodox Church had anathematized the Raskolniks for adhering to these trifling points of ritual, stigmatized the two-fingered signature as an Armenian jest, denied that *Isus* could be a title of God, because in Greek it means *equal* ($\mathrm{\ddot{\iota}\sigma o\varsigma}$), and so on. The Raskolniks successfully assailed the Orthodox on such points, and they attained their object, which was separation from the Orthodox Church and independence of the orthodox clergy. The latter left nothing undone to keep up a purely ritualist antagonism; for example in an Ukase of the Holy Synod of May 15, 1722, we read among other things the following: 'If there be any who while obeying Holy Church and accepting all her sacraments, nevertheless in signing themselves with the Cross employ two fingers instead of three, no matter whether they do this with the subtilty of opponents or out of ignorance or out of obstinacy, all such shall be inscribed in the Raskol and regarded as nothing else.' " [1]

In the past the orthodox clergy, no less than the Raskolniks, were characterized by an excessive adherence to the letter, by extreme formalism; but in any case this characteristic was

---

[1] *Collection of ordinances as touching Raskol*, bk. 1, p. 33.

less developed in the Raskolnik than in the orthodox clergy, as is shewn by later history. To-day it is the turn of the orthodox to find fault with the Raskolniks, not for their insistence on the letter, but for the wrongheaded liberties they assume in interpreting Scripture. The vast majority of them, consisting of Bezpopovtsy, are beginning, as we have seen, to champion the rights of private judgment and freedom of interpretation. Among them a book circulates, in which the Orthodox are termed 'the ritualists of the Church hierarchy,' a sign that they regard hierarchy as a vice in the Orthodox. "Almost all the Bezpopovtsy sects allow, like the Protestants, complete liberty of research, and base their teaching not upon tradition, but upon logic and reasoning." [1] "So called orthodox faith," has remarked one of the Bezpopovtsy, "is an appurtenance of the Crown and Treasury, an official badge. It rests on no basis of real life or sincere conviction, but just does duty as a Government weapon for the defence of order." [2]

The Hegumen Paul also reports a conversation he held with Markian Gerasimov, a hermit who wielded a great influence in his circle of Dissenters and who told him in a discussion that, in his opinion, we have no need to believe in an ink-written volume of the Gospel, such as belonged to Father Paul, even if it did belong to the time (c. 1609) of the Patriarch Hermogenes. It was better to believe in the volume of the Gospel which is stored up in the heart, and he called Father Paul a necromancer, [3] by reason of his adherence to the dead letter.

The germs of such opinions had made their appearance long before. Thus early in the 18th century Hierotheus, a member of the Anufrievski (Onufrius) sect of Old believers, put together on the basis of Avvakum's writings twenty-five points of which the tenth runs thus:— "To venerate the Gospel story, because it is written down in ink, smacks of the manners of the Tartar." And when the rest of the Old believers of Kerzhen (his own sect excepted) asked for proofs from holy writ, he, along with those who shared his views, instead of furnishing them, answered:

---

[1] Kelsiev, *Sbornik*, vol. 1, p. viii.
[2] *Russian Archive*, 1866, No. 4, art. by I. Aksakov, p. 633.
[3] *Bratskoe Slovo*, 1876, bk. 2, M. Makarov, p. 156.

"You are gross minds and do not understand how to handle the Scriptures." This is related by Esipov in his work on the Raskolniks of the 18th century, vol. 2, p. 236.

A talented teacher of the Stranniki (Pilgrim or Wanderer) Sect, Nicetas Semenov Kiselev, remarked to a certain Kosharin, "that the reasons given for separating from the Church indicated in the *Pomorski Responses* were, in his judgment at least, insufficient; for there existed others incomparably weightier, but unknown to the ancestors of the Old believers." [1] He taught that "the cross of endurance, borne by the *pilgrims*, which cross is the *strannitchestvo* or wandering life itself, is weightier than the Cross of Christ, and that by it alone the sins of humanity are redeemed and atoned for."

K. Nadezhdin in 1866 deplored the infidelity and atheism of the Bezpopovtsy in general, and stated that "it had gone so far of late years as to reject the pure and life-giving cross on which Christ suffered for our redemption. They refused to bow down before it and abused it, calling it a log of wood like any other log."[2] Another observer summarizes their teaching thus:—"It is indubitable that Antichrist came long ago, so that by now all divine promises about the Church are made vain and at an end. We are living *in the age to come,* that is, *in the new heavens and new earth.* The resurrection of the dead is past, or rather it is incessantly being accomplished in each of us according to the degree of his merit and piety." [3] Such an outlook is no unique case. Thus in a "conversation which was held in the *stanitsa* or Cossack Colony of Ust-Medveditskaya, the Bezpopovtsy defended their way of living without any divinely established sacraments by the following argument among others. They said that in accordance with St. Peter's prediction (II Peter III. 7.) the heaven, by which they understand the Church, is already consumed by fire, and the elements, meaning the sacraments, are abolished, so that they are now living in the new heavens." [4]

These opinions, says Uzov, that we are living "in a new

[1] Contemporary Chronicles (Sovrem. Letopis), 1868, No. 16.
[2] *Orthodox Review*, 1866, No. 7, p. 317.
[3] *Orthodox Convers.* 1869, No. 10, art. by N. I., p. 130.
[4] *Bratskoe Slovo*, 1876, bk. 2, *Chronicle of Raskol Events*, p. 226.

heaven," and that all "the promises of God" are already fulfilled and so forth, reveal the range of the individual believer's
speculation and feelings. All that was written by Evangelists
and other holy men refers to the past; in the present the
individual believer's conscience constitutes the sole norm of
what is right. Orthodox missionaries of to-day find themselves
confronted with a mental attitude which they can only describe
by saying that the peasants of a particular village openly
avow their disbelief in a future life.[1]

[1] *Moscow See's News-letter*, 1874, p. 161.

CHAPTER V

THE QUESTION OF MARRIAGE

THE question of marriage has rent asunder the Priestless or
Bezpopovtsy society from the very first, with the result that
there are two groups among them, each numbering millions of
souls, one known as the married, the other as the marriageless
(bezbrachniki). It is evident — as Uzov remarks — that
an agricultural population cannot renounce the institution and
essay to live, men and women together, as brother and sister.
Notwithstanding so obvious a truth, a polemic has raged for two
centuries among these good people about the matter and gen-
erated an infinity of tracts for or against marriage, and the
issue seems as far as ever from being settled by any common
agreement. Both parties of course appeal to Scripture, but,
after all, as the Bezpopovtsy are not brutish, ignorant people,
besotted with antiquated superstitions, we shall err if we dismiss their various solutions as unworthy of serious study, the
more so as their conception of the place of woman in the social
scheme is involved.

Marriage Among the Stranniki

"The Society of the Beguny," says Shchapov," [1] has emancipated — as have certain other Bezpopovtsy communities —
the poor woman from the position she occupied of a chattel,
imprisoned as it were and restricted to a life of unending toil";
they have raised her to one "in which she is as fundamentally
important in the Society as the man." [2] In places where the
influence of the Beguny has made itself deeply felt it is become
impossible to speak to wife or daughters rudely, or even to
reprove them in a boorish fashion. The man who did so would

[1] *Vremya*, 1862, No. 11, p. 280.
[2] *The Raskol and its Significance in popular Russian History*, p. 251.

be left without housekeeper or companion to help him in his daily toil.[1]

A member of the priestless sect has described the true position which belongs to women. "Family life," he writes,[2] "is based on the consciousness of mutual love in husband and wife, of their equality of rights in every enterprise. All this involves, as all know, mutual aid in counsel, and is the reward of the natural capacities of both. The wife must not claim to give up the task of bearing children and bringing them up in order to become a knight errant. She must not abandon the cares that centre in her children, and set out to interest herself in the remote ties and interests of nations or of trade. So on his side the husband cannot claim to bear children or bring them up or look after the household, to the abandonment of public and industrial matters. In all this they must both keep to the balance prescribed by nature; and the true path leading to mutual life is loving counsel in all enterprises." The same author contrasts the positions which woman occupies among the infidels (he means the upper classes), among religious people (the poorer but Orthodox population), and in his own Society respectively. In the first she is a target of vain infidel fancies: in the second she is an unfortunate servile creature, condemned to perpetual subjection by man: in the third category, that of the Raskol, which he terms orthodoxy, she is the precious helpmate of the man and the half of his soul. Among them she is no victim consecrated to pleasure, as she is among infidels, but is reverenced as the half of the human race, and is treated with the deference which the honest love of a true believer and a pure well-regulated relationship inspire. The infidel does not regard woman from the point of view of her moral beauty, for he does not look forward to a lifelong union with her and to the requirements of a well-ordered family life; he only thinks of her outward beauty as an object for the gratification of his lusts, and only courts her until it is extinguished, and no longer.

[1] Kelsiev, *Sbornik*, iv, 161.

[2] *Istina*, 1867. Art. *Fruit of Life*, pub. in Johanisburg. Those who know Russia must accuse the writer of considerable exaggeration.

Varieties of Opinion among the Bezpopovtsy.

Various solutions are met with among the Bezpopovtsy of the marriage problem, but all agree in regarding the sexes as having equal rights one with the other.

Those among them who retain marriage argue that where no priest is to be found marriages may be celebrated without any clerical rite; at the same time marriage is a sacrament, holy, ordained by God, and upheld by Christ.[1] The sacrament of wedlock was created by God, but the ceremony of crowning is an invention of the civil powers.[2] True marriage consists not in crown and prayer, but in the dispositions and inclinations of bride and bridegroom. Priestly rites do not make a marriage, but mutual and *eternal* concord of man and wife.[3]

In our opinion, they say, it is enough if father and mother bless their child's union with anyone and if the couple live a godly life, that renders the marriage legitimate. The paternal blessing is precious above everything; and in this connection they point out that the Patriarchs, for example Abraham and others, were not married after the manner of the Church with aid of popes; and yet no one can say that they lived with their wives illegally.[4] Already in 1838 the marrying sect of the Government of Kostroma took young women to wife merely with the assent of the parents, for which reason they were known as 'self-binders,' and in doing so they followed the example of their co-religionists of the Vyatka Government.[5]

We can conclude from such passages that the married sect of Bezpopovtsy, while denying the necessity that the sacrament of marriage should be performed by a priest, equally assert the essence of the sacrament to consist in an agreement of the parties to the marriage, in their consent to a *perpetual* union,

[1] *Istina*, 1873, March, April.

[2] *Among the People of Ancient Piety*, Y. Stebnitsi, 2nd. ed. p. 17.

[3] Notes (zapiski) of Alexander B. Pt. 2, p. 305. The *Crown* is the nuptial wreath kept in an Orthodox Church and laid on the head of the bride and bridegroom by the Pope before the altar.

[4] *Conversations of orthodox priest, with Old believers*, by Tverdynski, pp. 322–4.

[5] *Christian Readings*, 1869, No. 6, Art. by Nilski, p. 895.

and that they regard the will or intention to contract the marriage as sufficient consecration of their union. While rejecting the rites of the Church, held by the Church essential to any marriage, this sect preserves the substance of Church teaching, that is to say the perpetuity of the marriage union.

There is great difficulty in getting at the truth about the family life of these people owing to the calumnies spread abroad about them either wilfully or from pure ignorance by Russian publicists. When I first visited Russia in 1881 in company with the late Mr. William John Birkbeck, and made inquiry, I was told that the Government was tolerant of the Old believers as a whole, but drew the line at those sects which rejected marriage and lived promiscuously. It never occurred to me at the time that what they really rejected was the Church ceremony and sacrament of marriage, with which, having no priests nor being allowed to have any by the Government, they had no choice but to dispense. Most students of the Raskol, says Uzov, have maintained that the marriageless group of the Priestless ones reject the institution of the family and affect asceticism. The sectaries, he points out, are themselves largely to blame for this, because they use words, not in their natural and ordinary sense, but in an artificial one of their own. This has led investigators to argue as if the fundamental principle of their doctrine was the preservation of 'virginity.' If it were really so, they would eschew family life and live as monks and nuns, which they certainly do not. The problem is no doubt obscured by the way in which they preach 'virginity' as a religious ideal, and yet accompany the teaching with permission to men and women to "love one another" as they like, so long as they do not marry.[1] The obvious inference is that, under the cloak of asceticism they practice debauchery and go about to destroy all family unions; yet the inference is wholly wrong.

The requirement of 'virginity' is usually based by these sectaries on the circumstance that "the hands of priests have crumbled into dust," in other words, no priests survive to

[1] i.e. in a Nikonian Church. See *Family Life in the Raskol*, by Nilski, Pt. 2, p. 83.

perform the rite of marriage. No man or woman therefore can any more be 'married' in the old sense, and all must remain to that extent unmarried or technically 'virgins'; but this does not preclude the existence broadcast among them of permanent family unions. Uzov raises the question why, as they allow laymen to celebrate sacraments of baptism and penance, they do not allow them equally to celebrate marriage, and continue to regard it as a sacrament. That they do not is apparently due to the exigencies of debate and discussion of the matter with other rival sects. In such debates it has been customary with both sides to make the Bible the referee — though not always; for one of the sect, Ilia Alexieiev Kovylin,[1] defending his position against the marrying sect, who recognize the legitimacy and sacramental character of marriages contracted later than 1666, is said to have exclaimed: "I will not accept from you any bookish evidence, so do not quote to me the seven ecumenical councils or the nine local ones, or the apostolic canons. If you do I shall answer you that even if Christ descended with the angels from heaven and bade me accept in my communion such 'new' marriages, I would reply to him: I won't listen to you, Christ." This elegant extract is from a debate on the subject of marriage held between the Bezpopovtsy of the Transfiguration Cemetery and the members of the Pokrovski oratory in Moscow, cited by K. Nadezhdin, *op. cit.* p. 38.

There have been, says Uzov, among the section of the Raskol that rejects marriage, plenty of teachers who preached and practised the monastic ideal; but it is certain that they never led opinion nor lead it now. The mass of adherents formed family unions from the first without attending to them. They listened rather to such of their teachers as, under the emblem or cloak of 'virginity,' inculcated among the people the form of family life to which they aspire in obedience to their instinctive feelings for freedom and independence. The 'marriageless' sectary may not approve of unions concluded for the whole of life, but find it a burden. He aspires to another type of conjugal relationship, a type which more

---

[1] President of the Preobrazhenski cemetery in Moscow. He died in 1808.

nearly approximates to the ancient Slavonic free union, dissoluble by the will of either party. He has scanty regard for the Byzantine type of family which has only gained currency in Russia during the last few centuries. He does not derive his notions of family obligations and felicity from the canon law, but from living principles engrained in the character of the people. But at the same time that he insists on family freedom, he is far from discarding the family as students of the Raskol imagine, misled by their terminology. It all comes of the mistaken endeavour of the exponents of the 'marriage-less' doctrine to justify the life and practice of their brethren from Scripture, instead of basing it on sociological principles common to all peoples. Their teachers committed and commit this solecism of trying to find in Hebrew literature a scheme of social organization for their sect, because in Russia (as among ourselves) the religious point of view was *the* point of view of the people, who were on a plane of culture that was not ripe for any other mode of apprehending social phenomena. The Raskol teachers had no books save those of traditional Christianity, and naturally sought in these an explanation and justification of everything. In spite, however, of their lucubrations the life and institutions of the Raskol masses have developed along the lines of human nature, in accordance with the feelings and affections of the common man and woman. No theological cobwebs could hamper these. In Russian upper classes writers scientifically trained have approached these subjects from a secular point of view and written books about them; but neither these nor the culture they represent, have yet penetrated to the people, and the circumstance that they are written by and for a class theoretically hostile to the masses, is enough to hamper their circulation among the latter.

Such is Uzov's view. Students of Greek history will recall the feeling in ancient Athens against the reforms of Kleisthenes immediately after the Persian wars; yet all he aimed at was to base popular representation on arithmetic instead of upon tribal units descended in popular imagination from eponymous and legendary heroes, if not from totems. The feeling was so strong against touching the religious unit that it was left alone, and the deme or canton reserved for purposes of political organization.

In proof that the 'marriageless' Raskol did not repudiate family life and unions, even long ago, when ascetic teaching was much more highly esteemed than it is to-day among them, Uzov appeals to a 'canon' or rule of life which was in vogue in the Theodosian sect, by which the faithful were instructed "not to hold shameful the living in one house or home with wife, stranger and children. Even if generation be accounted abominable, it is yet not to be regarded as forbidden. Virgins who have borne children are to pass muster as virgins even if their offspring number fifteen. "Let this be the rule you observe," runs the canon "but do not marry on any account. You can always repent and do penance and become afresh the virgin (male or female) you were before."

The idea of penance here involved is that which became normal in the Great Church towards the end of the second Century. According to it the sin of fornication can be atoned for and obliterated by confession and absolution. The sin being thus wiped out, the man or woman who was guilty of it becomes once more sinless, in other words, becomes a 'virgin' and chaste as before. By this device a sufficiently indulgent confessor can dovetail family life into the somewhat rigorous ideal of enthusiasts prone to believe that with the carnal hand of the ordained priest the *charisma,* or sacramental gift of marriage from God has been for ever lost among men. If we desire proof that this controversial maintenance of virginity interfered little with family life and propagation of children among the 'marriageless' Bezpopovtsy, we have it in the fact that in the third, eighth, and tenth registers compiled and revised in the XVIIIth Century by Imperial authority we find inscribed the names not only of the wives of the 'marriageless' Bezpopovtsy, but of their children as well, together with the names of the husbands and fathers. The information on which these registers were based was supplied by the sectaries themselves and shows that family life was universal among them as far back as the time of Peter the Great.

These considerations are necessary to correct and supplement the pages of Ivanovski, who labours under the common delusion that the attribution to marriage of a sacramental character can alone guarantee its existence and permanence. Yet unless people were independently and by old racial tradition (as are most of the Indo-Germanic peoples) imbued with respect for the marriage union, it could not be kept sacred; if people had not the instinct to marry one wife and live exclusively with her, no sacramental system or theory would make them do so.

Theodosius Vasilev

Ivanovski relates that the earliest Priestless settlement at Vyg was founded along monastic lines, and that it was not before 1696, when Theodosius Vasilev, formerly a deacon of Novgorod, seceded from it and formed a colony of his own on the northwest limits of Polsk or Poland, that wedlock was allowed, and Theodosius even then only admitted of conjugal relations between men and women in his colony who had been married before 1666. These unions, we gather, were termed *old* marriages in contrast with new marriages of a later date. Avvakum had laid it down that, if you can get no priest to marry you, then you had better live single; and rather than break with the Pomorian communities Theodosius had refused to recognize other than old marriages, and would not recognize new ones as sacramental unions at all. After his death, says Ivanovski, the Theodosian congregation refused to recognize even old marriages. These communities were thus definitely committed to abrogation of marriage and chastity made obligatory for all.

But *naturam expellas furca licet, usque redibit*. It was not long before human nature asserted her rights, and there were Raskol writers who complained loudly of the declension from moral standards visible both in the Vygovski desert (or hermitage) and among the followers of the deceased Theodosius. The entire community was filled, according to the testimony of upholders of the monkish ideal, with fornication and obscenity. In order, however, to estimate aright such assertions we must bear in mind that the abrogation of the sacrament of marriage for want of priests in itself placed all relations between the sexes in the category of fornication in the eyes of members of the straiter sect. To remedy the evil, Vyschatin, a member of the Pomorski colony, set off to the east in hope of finding a genuine priest to return with him and regularize unions, but he failed and died abroad.

Ivan Alexiev

Nature and religion had in some way to be reconciled, and the most brilliant attempt was that of a young and energetic member of the Theodosian Settlement, Ivan Alexiev, who raised his voice against the fiction of virginity, boldly advocated the restitution of marriage and urged his brethren to resort to the Orthodox Churches for the purpose of getting married, arguing that, as heretics and even non-Christians went to be married in them, the faithful might do the same.

Ivanovski remarks that this solution found favour not only with the 'old married' members of the Theodosian Pomorski colonies, but also with the 'newly married,' and gave great relief to both sets.[1] He also records that the elders or leaders of the communities which Alexiev thus tried to reform, denounced him as a dangerous libertine and drunkard. In 1752[2] a council of the Theodosians decided not to admit his 'newly married' followers to their public prayers, not to live or eat with them, not to wash in the same bath, nor even admit them to repentance, even if they were in peril of death, not to baptize their children or even kiss them. Even their wives were not to be assisted in the throes of childbirth. This sentence was practically one of excommunication, but in practise it was abated by permission, after repentance and rebaptism, to live apart in the community. The result was the elimination of the reformed. Many, says Ivanovski, passed into other sects, others left their wives and chose for themselves cooks and so-forth as companions. This last statement that they forsook

---

[1] By the 'old-married' he must mean those who had sought the Sacrament at the hands of Orthodox priests, fugitives or others.

[2] Acc. to Macarius in 1751.

their wives barely agrees with the canon of the Theodosian sect adduced by Uzov and cited by us above.

Reading between the lines one can see that the orthodox historian is too anxious to magnify the rôle played by his Church in the developments of the Bezpopovtsy sect and that he has no such clear apprehension of the true state of affairs as has Uzov. It is probable that the canon adduced by the latter is one of those fixed by the Theodosian assembly of 1752 and that it was the rough handling of the semi-orthodox 'reformer' at this council that led him to secede and form a sect of his own in 1757. Of this sect Ivanovski records no further details. What he next relates, however, of the Pomorian elders is thoroughly credible and confirms Uzov's conclusions. For he states that they also rejected Alexiev's reform of sending the faithful to get married in orthodox Churches; but that they were more indulgent to the 'newly married,' admitting them to penance for their offence and to prayers and baptizing their children. Obviously 'newly married' here means men and women who, in spite of the ideal of enforced virginity, maintained regular, but non-sacramental, conjugal unions; for he has declared, immediately before, that marriages by orthodox priests were abhorred in Pomor.

We can also well believe his next statement, that what was at first only allowed by way of exception under protest, and as a *pis aller* in the Pomorski congregations, gradually became the rule, and that married life was in that society so much more thoroughly legitimized than among the Theodosians as to become in the second half of the XVIIIth Century the dividing line between the two.

Paul Miliukov's account of Alexiev's contribution to the marriage controversy in his Outlines of Russian Civilization (ed. 4, pt. 4, Petersb. 1905) is valuable. It took precedence, he says, over all other matters in dispute, not merely personal, such as rebaptism, prayers for the Tsar, submission to the extra taxes and to registration; for the austerest of the sectaries had to admit the impossibility of avoiding all contact between the 'fire' and the 'hay.' As a matter of form they continued to insist on male and female chastity, sexual unions being no better than

fornication in the absence of priests and after abrogation of the
marriage sacrament; but in practise they were reduced to
winking at such unions. Theodosius, the scribe of the Kres-
tetski village, though on other points he was more intransigent
than Andrew Denisov (d. 1730) and had therefore forsaken the
settlement of Vyg, forming new ones in the S. W. of the province
of Novgorod and in Poland, was nevertheless more compliant
in regard to marriage, and recognized as legitimate 'new'
marriages celebrated in Nikonian churches, which to his mind,
of course, were heretical. Andrew Denisov, though addicted
to compromise in such a matter as praying for the Tsar in his
community on the Vyg, insisted to the end of his life on con-
tinence. Even he, however, as we saw, was obliged to confine
his principles to the monastery and permit unions in the *sketes*
around it.

Ivan Alexiev's remarkable work on the Sacrament of marriage only appeared in 1762, thirty-four years after he had
first broached his solution to Andrew Denisov. In the
interval he had busied himself collecting material and spreading his views. What in this work he chiefly insists upon is
this, that the primitive Church never repeated the marriage
sacrament in the case of couples who joined it after having
been married according to the usages and formulae of other
religions. It recognized therefore the validity of unions contracted in other circles of faith than its own, so evincing the
truth that the charisma of marriage is not bound up with
the use of any particular rite. In this respect, he argued,
holy wedlock differs from other sacraments, and he appealed
to the Russian *Greater Catechism*, which defines it as a sacrament "by and in which man and wife out of pure love in their
hearts frame an agreement and mutual vow. The agent and
author thereof is God himself who implanted in living creatures
the instinct to increase and multiply; and this instinct coupled
with loving agreement between the wedded" constitutes the
essence of the sacrament. All else, he argued, is mere formal-
ity. The priest is only a witness to the union in behalf of the
public, and the church ceremony is at best a popular custom,
giving popular assent thereto, ratifying it, and investing it

with civil validity. True, in order to safeguard its durability marriage needs a rite, but the rite is a mere form, of later manifestation, in written law. The thing itself is a part of natural law, independent of and earlier than any ceremony or rite. Here, he argues, we have a reason why the Bezpopovtsy Church should, in imitation of the primitive, recognize a marriage celebrated in a Nikonian Church, for it is merely a public testimony to the union, whereas the sacrament itself is administered by God and consummated in the mutual affection of man and wife.

Such a novel argument naturally shocked extremists, but Alexiev defended it on the ground that the Raskol were no longer living, like their progenitors, in the wilds of the desert. They were now living in the world, and had to protect the young against its temptations. His work therefore marked a fresh stage in the reconciliation of the Dissenters with the actualities of life, which could only be escaped by fresh flights into the wilderness and even by self-immolation as of old. But the question was not settled by his book; it even became a more burning one than that of ritual reception among the Popovtsy of runaway members of the orthodox clergy. Over both questions the moderates were at issue with the extremists. The more accommodating of the Popovtsy were approximating to the teaching of the dominant Church; the Priestless ones were in principle challenging the very bases of established religion and embarking on the uncharted main of free religious creation. The victory of moderation among the former on the point of reanointing was only a partial return to the admission of a clergy whose orders they began by rejecting; the victory in the matter of marriage was a recognition of a law of nature behind and paramount over Church traditions and supposed Christian revelation. In neither case however, was the victory complete, but followed by fresh struggles and even wider breaches of unity.

It is doubtful whether Ivanovski does not all through confuse cohabitation with debauchery and wilful concubinage, owing to his prejudice that marriage is nothing else, unless it be contracted on sacramental lines; and the Bezpopovtsy, in so far as they formally rejected marriage on this very ground, while materially they accepted the institution, were themselves responsible for the confusion. Sacramental rigorism inevitably leads to such paradoxes in other countries than Russia. Thus the Protestant Churches in the eye of Latin doctors have no orders, no priests, and therefore no sacraments, with the possible exception of baptism. They cannot therefore marry men and women; Protestant married couples to one who literally accepts the Latin view, are living in mere concubinage. This however does not prevent Catholics from living on terms of the closest friendship and purest charity with their Protestant neighbours; though they would ostracize people, whether of their own faith or not, who were simply living together without having been married in Church or before a registrar. This means that in spite of the rigour of their doctrines they accept marriages duly contracted according to the law of the State in which they live, and so far assent to the doctrine *cuius regio, eius religio*. But the Bezpopovtsy had never heard of any form of marriage but the sacramental and religious one. Under stress of circumstances they invented civil marriage, and Ivanovski and others have as little right to say that they reject marriage and live in debauchery or concubinage as Catholics would have to say the same thing of their Protestant neighbours.

I. A. Kovylin

Such sacramentalist prejudice probably colours Macarius' and Ivanovski's account of the Thedosievski teacher, I. A. Kovylin. Owing to the tolerant policy of Catharine II this sect, we saw, as also the Pomorians, were allowed to establish centres in Moscow in the year 1771; and the Thedosievski colony over which Kovylin presided was, as we saw above, known under the unassuming name of the Preobrazhenski or Transfiguration Cemetery. In spite of want of education Kovylin was a remarkable man whose reputation extended from Riga to Astrakhan, and his own adherents went on their knees to him and kissed his hand out of reverence. In Petersburg as in Moscow his interest and influence extended far beyond his own religious circle. He was true to the tenets of the founder of his sect Theodosius Vasilev, in that he condemned marriage, carrying his prejudice against it so far, according to Ivanovski, as to condemn as lecherous unions 'old marriages,' i.e. marriages contracted in the Nikonian Church, of which, as savouring of Antichrist, Kovylin would naturally not approve. At the same time, says Ivanovski, Kovylin was most severe "upon the violations of moral purity inseparable from the obligation not to marry." Until his time (1776) these declensions had been regarded in the sect as deplorable incidents requiring healing treatment. But the fact that innumerable persons had taken shelter in his asylum or hospital settlement who had been married in that church seems to have driven Kovylin to adopt a new point of view. He was merciless to those caught *flagrante delicto*, in open sin, but lenient and consoling to those who knew how to conceal their sins, and so he connived at their secret immorality. "Sin committed in secret, is in secret to be judged. Without sin there is no penitence, and without penitence, no salvation. In paradise are many sinners, but no heretics." Such is the express teaching which Ivanovski attributes to Kovylin, accusing him of replacing the moral obligation of chastity by the doctrine that people in view of the denial of married life had a moral license to sin, only encouraging his chartered libertines to become hypocrites as well. He adds — what is incredible —that Kovylin's followers were shocked at their leader's cynicism, and yet adopted his conviction that casual and secret unions were better morally and religiously than open and avowed married life, because the hero of gallant adventures sins and repents, while the avowed husband and wife complacently acquiesce in their open and avowed sin. This recalls the doctrine that wedlock is the *maius adulterium*, put forward by the Cathars, who, like the early Christian Encratites, condemned all sexual unions licit or illicit.

It is, however, easy to discern that all Kovylin was really guilty of was a desperate attempt to reconcile the innocent needs of human society with the sacramentalist conception of marriage which the Raskol had carried in its bosom into exile.

He was not advising his followers to live promiscuously and sin the more in order that grace might the more abound. There were, no doubt, fanatics inside the sect who condemned all sexual unions as being impossible and wrong in the absence of genuine priests who should sacramentally consecrate them; and in Moscow, Petersburg and other cities in which Catharine II had allowed the sect to settle, there were plenty of orthodox critics ready to accuse the Raskolniks of debauchery, because they contracted unions which could not, even from the Raskol point of view, much less from their own, be termed marriages. Kovylin may perhaps have advised his followers not to expose themselves to orthodox attacks, more than they need, by flaunting their non-sacramental unions before the eyes of their orthodox neighbours. That he applied the sacrament of penance to help his followers out of the religious dilemma in which they found themselves and to soothe the perplexed consciences of the weaker brethren among them,— that much we can safely gather from Ivanovski's uncertain paragraphs, but no more.

New marriages in the sect were not, as might be supposed, those for celebration of which the sectaries repaired, according to the counsels of Ivan Alexiev (1750), to orthodox churches; the so-called 'newly married,' were rather those who regarded themselves as married in spite of the circumstance that real priesthood had come to an abrupt end in 1666, those, namely, of the sectaries who held with the Apostle that "marriage is holy and the wedding couch undefiled." Two bourgeois members of the Pokrovski Oratory (as the Pomorski called an establishment which Catharine allowed them to found in Moscow about 1770), bearing the names Vasili Emelyanov and Gabriel Skachkov, drew from the Apostle's very sensible doctrine of wedlock the corollary that it might be celebrated not by priests alone but by laymen as well, in the same way that laymen could confer baptism and admit their brethren to repentance after confession of their sins.

This was a beneficent reform, for it removed from Pomorski unions the stigma of being irreligious. It was, as Ivanovski says, "a great step in the development of Bezpopovtsy doctrine," but such an innovation startled the Vygovski commun-

ity of the Pomorskis and they challenged Emelyanov to justify
it. Their elders adhered to the old sacramental prejudice and
Emelyanov submitted to their decision for a time; but when
Catharine II granted civil rights to the Old believers and they
took to living in cities, the need to regularize the situation was
felt so acutely by the whole Pomorski sect that the Vygovski
authorities gave in to him.

The new compromise was, according to Ivanovski, this:
Marriage unions were legitimately contracted, if the bride and
bridegroom agreed to join their lives indissolubly. The
approval and blessing of their parents was essential, and the
wedding was accompanied with prayers and hymns expressly
composed. This rule was adopted by the Pomorski of Moscow
and presently by those of Pomor, Archangel and elsewhere,
and all schism was thus avoided on the question — a splendid
victory of common-sense. Ivanovski is right in saying that
hereby the Pomorski had really elaborated a new sacrament.
He gives an interesting picture of the circumstances of such
weddings, under the impression apparently that they were
peculiar to this sect. Matchmakers were sent in advance to the
bride's house, the bridegroom's visits and handshakings were
arranged, and the betrothed interchanged their rings. Then
each party promised to accept the other for life, and finally the
union was celebrated by the Elder in the chapel or oratory.

The Theodosian sect, however, in Kovylin's settlement,
seems to have adhered to their old view of 'no popes, no marriages,' a *dictum* of Avvakum, reminding us in form at least of
Disraeli's answer to a latitudinarian Anglican divine who,
aspiring no less to livings than to immortal life, solicited a fat
deanery at his hands. His answer was: No dogma, no deans.
In Moscow the representatives of the two sects seems to have
sustained a lively polemic on the subject, each being anxious
to secure its predominance in the Bezpopovtsy world, and the
Theodosian sect who owned the Bezpopovtsy cemetery made
themselves disagreeable to their rivals who shared it with them
and lacked one of their own. Kovylin relegated them to a
damp corner of it where their graves were flooded. At times
the Pomorski were not allowed into it, and found that the

rigorous adherents of sacramental marriage took the plaques on which were inscribed their epitaphs as well as their crosses, and used them as fuel. In the end they had to summon to their aid the police of Antichrist.

It is possible that Ivanovski exaggerates the petty bickerings between the two groups; but he allows that Kovylin was so struck towards the end of his life by the triumph of priestless marriage among the Pomorksi as to relax his ascetic ideal and consent to couples married before they were rebaptized and joined his sect living together in 'chastity,' i.e. as "virgins," only punishing their breaches of chastity and childbirth by a short term of penance.

In Petersburg, then the Theodosian teachers already during Kovylin's lifetime winked at quasi-matrimonial unions and raised no difficulty about baptizing the offspring of them; after his death his followers did the same. They continued to regard non-sacramental marriage as an evil to be tolerated, a compromise between the inculcation of celibacy for all and the exigencies of human life. The Thedosievski wife is a wife before the world, but before God a fornicatress. She was formerly known among the sectaries, not as a wife, but as housekeeper, manageress, cook, companion, hostess — occupying therefore very much the same position as was held in the middle ages by the priests' concubines, when the priests enjoyed every imaginable license so long only as they did not marry. The Thedosievski couples also, according to Macarius and Ivanovski, are not full members of the congregation; they are admitted nowadays to divine service, but only given a place behind the congregation, and instead of joining in the prayers, only allowed to listen to them. When the Elder censes the congregation, they do not hold out their hands to catch the perfume, like the faithful; in a word they are treated as half believers, half excommunicates, as *auditores* or penitents in the early church. For the sin of child-birth the wife is subjected to penance or ἐπιτιμία; except in grave sickness they are not admitted to confession, and then have to promise not to cohabit any more.

Ivanovski describes the peculiar and original type of mar-

riage formerly in vogue in this sect, and seems to regard it as
due to the fact that marriage is only tolerated among them,
is on suffrance only as a concession to human weakness. By
common convention the men, he says, carried off the girl from
her parents to their own dwelling; sometimes the girls ran away
themselves carrying with them goods belonging to their parents.
The latter as a rule were quite prepared for this, but pretended
to know nothing about it, and went through the form of
making out that it was done against their will. The end of it
all was that the parents of bride and bridegroom met and
agreed about the dowry, and then went to their respective
homes. Nowadays the matter is conducted more simply;
the marriage festivities are openly held, to the exclusion of
course of religious rites, though in cases there is a blessing of the
young couple by the ikons.

Tolstoy has given us a charming picture of a peasant wedding
which no doubt is identical in outline with these; and it is
recognized that the old institution of marriage by capture has
left numerous survivals on Russian soil. The ceremonies,
therefore, ascribed by Ivanovski to the Thedosievski sect are
not peculiar to it, but are racy of the soil.

The Present Situation

The Bezpopovtsy have thus arrived at a double solution of
the marriage problem. One sect frankly recognizes it and have
tried to establish a new religious basis for it. The other only
tolerates it as a sin to be expiated by penance; and has split up
into fresh sects as marriage is tolerated more or less. A
Thedosievski council was held in 1883 in Moscow in order to
re-establish the stricter ideal of non-marriage, but it only
roused fresh internal dissensions and divisions of which the
Bratskii Slovo for the years 1883–5 gives details. The straiter
sect does not baptize the children or only does so when they are
found exposed, in which case they are called God's gifts, it
being unknown who exposed them. This sect is probably not
very numerous, and the majority of its adherents, as has been
noticed in the sees of Vyatka and Kazan, recognize marriage
outright as thoroughly legitimate.

Uzov relates that in his day, that is about the year 1880, a former monk of the Pomor 'married' group, named Barnabas, summed up the 'subtilties' of the 'marriageless' sect as follows: "There is no longer any sacrament of marriage, but all agree upon free life in union with each other, and by this expedient the world is being filled up with people." [1]

Among the dissidents of the Philippovski and Thedosievski groups, although marriage does not exist, married life goes on all the same.[2] The tendency of the 'marriageless' is brought out in relief in the teaching that there must be no monkery, but that everyone must live a family life. Naturally this doctrine, like the rival one, tries to find its justification in holy writ; and accordingly the monk Barnabas taught that, as in their philosophy 'no priest' involved 'no marriage,' so also it involved 'no monkery';[3] for without a clergy you cannot receive the monkish habit. On this principle two monks, Joasaph and Ioanikii gave up the monkish habit, and the former took to himself a cook, the latter returned to his former wife, or, to use the 'marriageless' terminology, his cook.[4]

An account of the actual practice of the sect furnished by the *Orthodox Review* for 1865 (No. 3, art. by Veskinski) bears out Uzov's conclusions: "The Thedosievski of the districts of Liontsin, Rezhits, Drys and Dinamin in their doctrine of marriage approach most nearly to the regulations of their founder; and though they practise cohabitation, yet only admit it as a necessity, and perform no ceremonies in connection with it; but among the Thedosievski of the Polotsk, Vitebsk and Lepelsk districts, before a man and woman can begin their cohabitation, certain rites are observed, such as benediction by the Elders or religious leaders at a gathering of the parents of the girl and bridegroom, special prayers being recited and so forth, all which imparts to it outwardly the aspect of a sacrament." [5]

The above account apparently refers also to the 'married'

---

[1] *Chronicle of Raskol Events* by I. Subbotin, p. 49.
[2] *Istina*, 1874, Bk. XXXII *Sketches of Old rit. Life*, p. 37.
[3] *Istina*, 1872, Bk. XXI, *Voyage of Monk Barnabas* p. 60.
[4] *Ibid.*, p. 106.
[5] *Orthodox Review*, 1865, No. 3, art. by Veskinski, p. 280.

sect of the Vitebski Government. How then in the matter of family organization do the two halves of the Bezpopovtsy differ from each other? Uzov replies that the 'married' sect impart to their marriages the significance of a sacrament in order to procure divine sanction and intervention for the union; the rival sect under stress of a counter tendency accomplish the union in a purely secular fashion: a man first betrothes himself to some woman or girl and receives her consent, he then goes for her to a place agreed upon and, after making a pretence of ravishing her away, takes her to his own home, and their cohabitation lasts until or unless family jars put an end to it. To give the transaction due publicity the parties who have thus taken to cohabitation visit the bazaars and other places of popular resort again and again, hand in hand or with a single cloak cast over both of them, by way of manifesting to all the fact that they now live together.[1] Such idyllic simplicity reminds one of a Scotch marriage in the presence of four witnesses, to which it would impart a picturesque touch of Highland romance if a semblance of marriage by capture were added as in Russia.

The 'marriageless' sectary of the Varnavinski province of the Kostroma Government, when the time comes for him to form a household, merely takes home a girl of another family with the consent of her parents and lives with her as his wife.[2] The conditions of town life, especially for the labouring classes, impose a somewhat different type of family life than is possible in country villages and lead to greater frequency of divorce.[3] The poorer parents in the cities are working in manufactories and mills, and have not the same economic facilities for themselves bringing up their families as they would have if they lived in villages. In the country the child can help a little

---

[1] *Orthodox Review*, 1865, No. 3, art. by Veskinski, pp. 288–9.

[2] Kelsiev *Sbornik*, IV, 300.

[3] Nicolas Popov thus describes the mode of divorce of a couple who had lived together only a few months: "Pelagia Michailovna collected all her dowry chattels together and then bowed low thrice, according to their custom, at her husband's feet, laid her hansel before the ikons and after that bade farewell to her mother-in-law and to the witnesses present." (From *Materials for a history of the Bezpopovtsy congregation in Moscow*, p. 152.)

with the animals and in the fields, whereas in the city it is merely in the way and the parents are not at home to look after it. In towns this problem was met even before 1880 by the parents handing their children over to asylums or crêches built by the Thedosievski sect in Moscow and Riga.

In doing so they had not, as too often supposed, any idea or intention of cutting themselves off from their offspring. It can be proved that this was so from an incident which occurred in 1830. The Government had decreed that the children in these crêches should be registered as Cantonists, i.e. the mostly Jewish children stolen by the Russian Government to be turned into soldiers like the janissaries. Thereupon a crowd of work-people and labourers, having discovered that the children whom women of the 'Cemetery' (or Raskol Settlement in Moscow) and others had born to them, were to be carried off 'for torture,' gathered in a crowd at the gate of the Cemetery and raised an uproar crying out: "Here is an inhuman Tsar who would rob our children from the very arms of their mothers." All the children were promptly picked out and taken away by their parents, and even such as had lost both parents were taken charge of by the well-to-do members of the sect to be brought up in their homes, rather than allow them to be taken and reared in a battalion of military cantonists.[1]

We see from the above that the 'marriageless' sectaries in the cities, finding themselves constrained to adjust their lives to conditions of mill and factory, were very nearly organizing them on a better basis than the rest of the population that worked in the same institutions. Whereas the 'orthodox' mother, when she went off for the entire day to the factory, had to leave her children without anyone to look after them, the sectaries handed them over to a crêche in which they could rely on their welfare and education being attended to by responsible persons of their own way of thinking. Except for the interference of the Government, we should probably, says Uzov, find among them a regularly organized public system of bringing up and educating the younger generation. Not long ago there was a notice in the Russian Gazette (Vedomosti) of secret institutions

---

[1] Nilski *Family Life in Russian Raskol*, pp. 103, 133.

or refuges in Moscow for the education of the children of the
'marriageless' Pomorski sect. Any government worth the
name would have welcomed such efforts on the part of the poor
to do the best for their offspring, but that was not the way of
Tsardom.

Marriage Among the Stranniki

We have related in some detail from Ivanovski the rise and
development of the *wandering* sect called *Beguny* or *Stranniki*,
more uncompromising in the hostility to the present order of
things than any other sect, and in consequence the object of
malignant persecution by the Government. The vast majority
of them, says Uzov, live a family life and 'for fear of the Jews'
as they call the Government, are even 'crowned,' that is, married in orthodox churches, though they attach no significance
to the rite. He agrees with Ivanovski in saying that the
majority of this sect, who marry and have families, are denominated by themselves "people of the world, entertainers of
wanderers, domiciled Christians." The minority make it
their business to spread their ideas, and undertake the 'apostolic labour' of roving from village to village.

They may be said to have no families, but all the same they
do not preach asceticism and non-marriage in our sense, and
even essay to harmonize their vagabondage with the satisfaction of family instincts and leanings. In theory, as sacramental marriage has disappeared along with the priests of the
ancient order, all men and women are now 'virgins,' monks and
nuns. Thus a married member of the sect has explained that,
whereas a wife is the gift of the devil, i.e. of the priest of the
church, the virgin with whom he lives is the gift of God. He
who lives with a wife lives in sin; he who lives with one that is
not his wife, *out of love*, commits no sin.[1] The Stranniki thus
allow irregular cohabitation instead of marriage, on the principle that they are to be regarded in this age of Antichrist as

[1] Kelsiev, *Sb.* iv, 124, from evidence given by women brought before the
Government commission of 1852. The Strannik repaired with his "virgin"
before an ikon in his forest cell and there recited to her this formula of the matri-
monial code.

the only people that are just and righteous, and the Apostle Paul has declared that the law is not laid upon the justified.[1] On this ground the Beguns of the Desert (which means not necessarily a forest or wilderness, but in general a place of hiding, be it only their own homes), live, each brother with a sister of one spirit with him in a common cell.[1] The Begun sire allows his daughter to fall in love with whomever she likes and as long as she pleases, delighted if an obedient daughter remains a bride of Christ and adds to the home a new future worker, male or female.[2] "Bear children once a week if you like, only do not go and get 'crowned' in church," is his advice to her.

It is rare, says Shchapov in the *Vremya*, No. 11, p. 293, for the teacher to go unaccompanied in his travels by his mistress. So Euthymius wandered about with Irene Thedorovna, who after his death played a great part in the dissemination of his doctrine, and he never changed her for another all his life, says S. Maximov in an article in the *National Records* (*Otetchest. Zap.*) for 1876, No. 7. Nicetas Semenov Kilesev in accordance with Euthymius' rule, out of two converted sisters that were become his friends, chose the one that was a virgin, the elder sister, Barbara Dmitrievna, according to the same source of information. Vasili Gorbunchik wandered in company with Maria Vasilev, his mistress, who had twice saved him from the hands of the ministers of Antichrist, in other words from Government officials.

These missionaries understand well enough that children born of their unions would hamper their activities, since they have to be brought up; and in order to bring them up they would have to abandon their 'apostolic' labours, a thing which the propagandist zeal of the sect cannot allow. In this, and no other sense, is their doctrine a denial of the family; and the denial, such as it is, was never due to ascetic impulses, but to their passionate ardour for propaganda which forbids them to live in any one place for long. Accordingly they either leave the children they have begotten in the family of their mistresses

---

[1] *Edifying Readings*, 1863, pt. 3: Athanasius Petrov, a Stranniki teacher, p. 117.

[2] Kelsiev, *sb.* iv, 160, from the same class of evidence.

or hand them over to a crêche or asylum. "According to a rumour gathered on the spot by a member of an expedition sent out with a view to a persecution of the Raskol, there existed in the Yaroslav Government in the Poshekhonski Sykhotski forest an inaccessible underground skete where the virgins of the sect repair for their confinements." The existence of this skete was affirmed in 1834 by a person brought up in it, and according to Kelsiev (*Sbornik* iv, 75) children remained in it up to their 20th year.

Thus it is not uncommon, remarks Uzov, for family instincts to get the better of propagandist zeal with members who have undertaken 'Apostolic' work. On the whole however, the tendency is for those who eschew marriage to deride those who do not. They ask: Why bring your children into the desert? How are you going to hide yourselves with a pack of children? They anyhow do not repudiate family ties in the name of asceticism, but because they are incompatible with their vocation. One might say the same of the Latin discipline of celibacy for parish priests. Yet, he continues, all the facts adduced tend to prove that the overwhelming majority of the 'marriageless' sects live a family life, only the family is precarious and easily dissoluble at will by either party. There are no generally recognized rules limiting the facilities of disruption; it is enough for the parties to desire to terminate a conjugal relation which is felt to be onerous to both. The minority that really have no families have avoided having them, not on religious grounds, but because for other reasons they cannot tolerate them.

Many observers hold that so loose an organization of family life must be specially hard on the woman, and Nilski [1] expresses his wonder that it has been preferred not only by the Thedosievki, including those of Riga (Rizhski), but also by the women of the uniat and orthodox persuasions. Uzov on the contrary urges that family happiness does not depend on the external forces upholding the family union, but on affection and mutual respect, and very often on economic necessity. He argues that the best and most moral section of the population is averse from

[1] *Family Life in the Raskol*, by Nilski, p. 152.

applying constraint in the case of family disagreement, and that such constraint only benefits crude, egoistic and purely animal natures. He points out that such hard and fast union does not *de facto* exist for the husband, so that the whole burden of it falls on the woman, whom we cannot expect to forego a right freely conceded to the man. Where unions are as free, as they are among these sects, a man dares not beat his partner, dares hardly to raise his hand, for fear she may say "I know my way home," and if he exclaims: "I defy you to," she answers: "I never married you!" [1]

[1] *Conversations of an orthodox priest with old ritualists*, T. Tverdynski, p. 334.

CHAPTER VI

THE ORGANIZATION, LEGAL POSITION, AND NUMBERS OF THE RASKOL

THE merit of Uzov's work is that he exhibits so clearly the close connection between the Raskol and the original constitution and development of Russian peasant society, whereas Ivanovski and most foreign publicists have superficially tried to explain its rise and duration from purely religious and theological considerations. Uzov devotes an entire chapter to this aspect of his subject, which he begins by remarking that, as the corner-stone of the edifice of Russian society has always been communism, it was but natural that the so-called Old believers, as representatives and champions of the independent and home intelligence and feeling of the Russian people, should withal exemplify in their settlements the prevailing communistic instinct. He illustrates this contention by the constitution of a Raskol Priestless settlement in Prussia described in the *Istina* for 1871, No. 18; for this exhibited the sharp contrast between genuine Russian life and the institutions of Western Europe. The description is from the pen of one of the Raskolniks, who using the familiar jargon of the sect, calls it a monastery, although it was neither more nor less than a mundane collection of Russian peasants immersed in family life.

The Prussians inhabiting the locality, he says, were filled with wonder at the example of solidarity and cohesion shewn by the immigrants from Russia. They held all the pastureland in common. Notwithstanding the seeming rudeness of their Russian agricultural implements the tilth was manured and got ready with extreme rapidity. All operations went easily among them because of the spirit of mutual union and friendship which bound them up together. The Prussian individualists of the neighbourhood were strangely interested in this exhibition of the Russian instinct of mutual goodwill and charity. The author says that this moral coherence was imputed by the Prussians to the ignorance of the settlers. This reminds one, he adds, of the language of our own *intelligentsia*, who, like the Prussians, have broken society up into loose pawns upon the board, and like them impute to crass ignorance and lack of understanding the charity which is engrained in the Russian nature, in the *anima naturaliter Christiana* of the Slav peasant.

The Raskol was recruited from the most energetic and intelligent section of the people, and it is a matter of regret that so many who thirsted for a spiritual life had no other alternative but to adopt it. All other avenues to a better life were closed juridically or *de facto*. The result was that the Raskol throve by absorbing into itself all the best living juices of the Russian people, and the results are visible in the singular capacity it has shewn for communism.

The Communes of the Vyg

Already at the close of the XVIIth Century the bond of communism held together their earliest societies, and its force was exampled in the society formed on the River Vyg in the Olonets Government. This consisted of an entire group of communes, cohering among themselves as well as with the rest of the other Raskol communes scattered all over Russia. One of the teachers who helped to found it predicted that it would disseminate itself and be celebrated all over the land, and be the salvation of many who were doing the will of God and walking in his ways; and the work of multiplication lay in the future with those who settled down along with their matrons and maidens, their cows and cradles.[1]

His testimony, says Uzov, proves that it was a purely secular foundation, like the other Vygovtsy settlements which also styled themselves *sketes*. It is true they were gathered round an Epiphany convent, of which the inmates followed the ascetic ideal; but both before and after this convent was founded in their midst, the inhabitants of the *sketes* around it eschewed the monastic ideal, married and had families; they only depended on the monks for conducting their religious

[1] *Christian Reading*, Nos. 7, 8, art. by Barsov, p. 52.

ceremonies. Such is the testimony of the same Raskol teacher Barsov in an article upon vexed questions of the earliest history of the Bezpopovtsy in the same journal for 1876 (Nos. 11, 12, p. 708).

The founders of this convent, the brothers Andrew and Semen Denisov, made an honest attempt to enforce in it monastic discipline, but failed, so that the former of them was constrained in 1719 to admit that, although the rules and regulations were still those of a monastery, yet the brethren were vigorously pursuing a practical and purely secular ideal, and modelled themselves on the economy of an old Novgorod parish. The principles of their confraternity, to wit, life in common and regulation of their affairs by monastic chapter, remained in force as their charter. All the same there was not visible among the brethren, so he complains, any distinction between the ecclesiastical and civil life.[1] And Barsov in his volume on these two brothers (pp. 84, 108) writes that the inmates of this Monastery never really entered it by way of freely avowing their need to isolate themselves for the practice of religion, nor because they had leanings towards the monastic life; their motive was either to conceal themselves and escape persecution, or because they were fired with enthusiasm (for the Raskol cause). Furthermore, he says, they were all of them people accustomed to family life, to rustic pursuits and agriculture, and of a grade of spiritual development that did not much incline them to contemplation or monastic life. Of it they had no idea, nor could it be expected of them that they would keep vows of celibacy. Accordingly, when, one day, the father or prior was holding a conclave of the brethren who had returned from their labours here there and everywhere, and asked them if they had in their absence and during their travels kept to the rule of Church and cell, they had to acknowledge that whether from stress of labour or weakness of the flesh or pure negligence they had neglected what was so salutary and inestimable.

The end of it was, as Barsov remarks, that the rigour and

---

[1] N. Aristov, *Structure of Raskolnik Commune*, in *Library of Reading*, 1863, No. 7, p. 5.

discipline of the Denisov brothers was not appreciated. Several of the monks fled, others after a brief stay in the monastery migrated into the Sketes in which they enjoyed much more liberty; occasionally there was a revolt against Andrew and his discipline. The monastery itself was organized on a basis of free communistic tendencies, all the brethren being on an equality, and each member enjoying the same rights as every other.[1] Thus, although Andrew Denisov was superior prior, his views in matters affecting the brethren as a whole were always laid before the rest.[2] Even rations of bread could not reach the monastery without all the members being notified of it.

In the commune the powers and capacities of each member were ascertained by overseers who conjointly with the cenobites assigned to each his occupation. In this manner the entire Vygovski community was organized in different groups of labourers and mechanics; to each group or guild was assigned quarters of its own, and their collective affairs were transacted by bailies and directors annually elected. Special officials also supervised the education of the children and looked after the teachers. The churchwardens and religious fathers were at once teachers and authorities for such purposes, and were appointed by reason of their gentleness of character and of their gifts of insight and discretion in everything to do with children. The divines thus chosen were for the most part of middle age, distinguished for their disinterestedness and learning and for their labours in behalf of the community and for their tender care of infants and orphans.[3]

The independence of the individual, his aspirations and convictions, were scrupulously respected, and each thought and taught exactly as his understanding led him to do.[4] Religious tolerance was such that even foreigners of the Lutheran faith were admitted into the community. Thus the assistant of the chief Raskol teacher Kapiton, was an individual named Babila, by birth, according to Denisov, a German, and of the Lutheran

[1] Aristov, p. 6.
[2] Barsov, pp. 93, 106.
[3] Aristov, pp. 7, 12, 13, 14, 11.
[4] *op. cit.* p. 28.

faith. He had taught reading and writing for some years in the
Slav Academy at Paris and was well trained in rhetoric, logic,
philosophy and theology. He also knew Latin, Greek, Hebrew
and Slavonic.[1]

Property in Vyg was of two kinds, public and private. The
former, says Uzov, included land, buildings and everything
indispensable for the common economy. Private property
consisted of part of the moveables or furniture which were
known as goods of the cell. At death many left by will all
their 'cell' property to their kinsfolk; but the majority bequeathed all their private effects to the public chest; others
divided it between the community and their relatives.[2]

The other sketes which formed part of the Vyg system and
were diffused over the wild forests of Pomor looked to the
Epiphany Monastery as their centre. As early as 1703, says
Aristov, there were not a few sketes and separate 'cells' — *kills*
as they were called in ancient Ireland — in Pomor; all the
Raskolniks were linked with one another, all paid their visits to
the Vygovski community and took part in its *councils*. In this
connection, be it remarked, it was not merely affairs administrative and economical that had to be settled by all the members; religious concerns and problems of church government
were equally under the control of the entire community. In
cases of grave crime the decision equally rested with a council,
which could condemn the offenders to banishment from the
community. It is to be noticed that female offenders were not
subjected to corporal punishment. No drunkenness was
allowed in the sketes; drunkards and beggars were cast out
without any ceremony.

The Communes of Sopelok

Uzov passes from the consideration of the Pomor communities as they were already organized early in the XVIIIth Century to the group or 'concord' of the Stranniki or Beguny
which, as we saw above, pp. 156 ff., grew up towards the close of
the same century under the impulse of that remarkable reli-

[1] Shchapov, *Russ. Raskol*, p. 175–6.
[2] Aristov, p. 18.

gious reader Euthymius or Euphimius, as the Slavs spell it; and he has much to say about them which supplements Ivanovski's account. He illustrates from Shchapov's article in the *Vremya* of 1862, No. 11, p. 279, the gradual growth of the movement. It began about 1770 in the village of Sopelok, on the right bank of the Volga near Yaroslav, and from it radiated in ever larger circles to embrace vast tracts of Russia and Siberia. Wherever it extended, asylums or hospices, resembling the rest-houses or μοναί of early Christian missions and equally those of the Jewish Essenes, and the *Vanq* of Armenia, were established.

These far-flung settlements formed a confederation of which Sopelok was the metropolis, keeping them all in touch with one another. Each provincial or local 'hospice' however formed a separate flock, was an autonomous and self-governing unit with its own directing council and tribunal, but not so independent that, when necessary, the common and supreme headquarters council and tribunal of the Beguni, was not recognized to lie at Sopelok, whither members repaired even from Siberia. Uzov states that in his day (1880) the sect found more difficulty in gathering together a representative board for the settlement of unavoidable questions. Nevertheless in July 1864 as many as a hundred *nastavniks* or 'rectors' met in the village of Vakhrushevo, of the Damshinski *volost* (circle of villages) in the province of Vologda. This council was convoked to decide about the 'articles' of Nicetas Semenov, one of their own elders who for ten years from 1854 had interested the police.

Uzov raises the question whether the internal structure of this sect can be described as genuinely communistic, as A. I. Rozov[1] asserts the founder Euthymius to have intended it to be. He denies that the Beguny themselves so interpret their founder's projects; they only refer his words to agrarian property, to fisheries, salt deposits and so forth. He admits indeed that Stranniki are met with who preach communism, and in favour of it appeal to certain of the founder's writings, especially the work entitled Tsvetnik (flower-bed, florilegium) in which

[1] See the three articles printed in the *Vestnik Europy*, Nov. and Dec. 1872 and Jan. 1873.

the registration of people and their separation into distinct classes, the partitioning of lands, forests and waters, are stigmatized as triumphs of Antichrist. This sort of confiscation and unfair division was, in Euthymius's opinion, a heathenish abuse, possible only because one man was envious of another, and because mutual hostility ended in the apportioning of much to one, of little to another, of nothing at all to the residuum compelled to hew wood and draw water for the wealthy. The passage is quoted by Kelsiev in his history of the Government's inquisition into the Raskol (*Sbornik pravitelstvennykh svēdēnii*) vol. 4, p. 260. But it is hardly conclusive as to the founder's opinions.

Anyhow, soon after his death, which befell in 1792, Vasili Petrov, one of his peasant disciples, took to teaching that no Strannik has the right to own property, but must give up everything he has to the uses of the community.[1] And in the Poshekhonski province Ivan Petrov, and in the so-called Plyosovski region, which comprised three provinces of the Kostroma Government, Antip Yakovlev, proclaimed that Euthymius's dictum that "the phrase 'mine-thine' is accursed and profane, for God created everything among you common"; refers not only to landmarks, but to all property alike. On this ground, says Rozov in the *Vestnik Europy* (1873, No. 1), they demand a rigorous communism and complete renunciation of the rights of property.

It comes to this then, says Uzov, that among the Old believers the extremists of the different groups do not shrink from the same impossible abrogation of *mine* and *thine*, as the extremists among the "spiritual christians," who carry the principle of communism to excess. In all probability the intransigent communism of these Beguny teachers met with no better success than it did among them; it is to be regretted, he adds, that we have so little information about them, and how contemporary Begunism lives is, it may be said, completely unknown.

---

[1] Orthodox Review, 1864, No. 8, Art. by Veskinsky, p. 315.

General Organization

Uzov maintains, however, in regard to the Raskol as a whole that Formakovski's statement that it is a sort of federation of politico-religious societies is borne out by facts; not only was it true long ago, but it can be demonstrated in quite recent times. And this is so, although the various groups differ widely in social ideals, and among all of them the tendency and leanings to independence are much more pronounced than in the rest of the population.

It is quite rare, says a writer Vitkovski in the *National Memorials* (1862, No. 5, p. 355), for the members of the Raskol to prefer a complaint in the course of their mutual disputes to the local authorities or to go to law with one another. Such is the unity of spirit, such the feeling of fraternity among these intelligent people, that they find themselves able to do without invoking any outside protection. And Uzov illustrates the point from the case of one of the Strannik teachers, Athanasius Petrov, who in 1850 was detected in the act of hoarding a quantity of money in an ikon. The next day, says one who had belonged to the sect, a council was held at which Athanasius, as a lover of money, was deprived of his title of teacher, his emblems of apostolic dignity taken from him, a rough garment assigned him, and a decision come to, to keep him under strict supervision. However the delinquent made good his escape and very soon was caught in a second misdemeanour, for he had taken to wandering about pretending he was a proto-hiereus with a mission from the Vyg desert or hermitage. Thereupon sentence was pronounced upon him by 'a general court of the Old ritualists.' This court was instituted in 1850 in the settlement just named in consequence of altercations and assassinations among the different groups. It was commissioned to examine and deal with all suits which arose between them. Three representatives were chosen from each group, in all 27, and three of them presided over it.[1] Such an institution absolutely confirms Formakovski's statement.

But, as the same author observes in the *National Memorials*

---

[1] *Edifying Readings*, 1863, pt. 3, pp. 120–5.

(1866, Nov. Dec., p. 641), of all the factors which lend to the Raskolnik federation irrefragable stability and strength, the capital one is the feeling of brotherhood among its members and communities. Nothing else can explain such facts as the existence in Russia of an Old ritualist hierarchy, whose leaders the police, in spite of all their researches, have never been able to get hold of. Thus, to give an example, in Moscow, one of the lower officials was enjoined to occupy himself exclusively with the task of collecting information about bishop Sophronius, what he was doing and what had become of him. In this task he displayed a rare zeal. Petersburg was full of 'secret' or 'very secret' items of information about him, one bit of news came flying after another, and more than once the authorities entertained the consoling hope that the moment was approaching when they would catch him. It was destined never to be realized. The strength of the Old believers' organization may also be judged of from the following incident: Measures had been taken to arrest a foreign emigrant, one of the Raskolniks, who had been residing a long time in Moscow; but before the plan could be carried out, the Old believers there had received exact tidings of it, and had got in their ecclesiastical council a copy even of the confidential circular on which the whole manoeuvre was based and which was intended only for the eyes of the very highest personages.[1]

The Raskol communities hold together by means of a close and constant intercourse among themselves and have their own post office. In their communications they employ a cipher and conventional language. They usually send their letters by confidential messengers and not by post. On how considerable a scale this correspondence goes on, one can judge from the fact that in the inquisition of the year 1852, the dissenters of Moscow, Grusia (Georgia) and Siberia were found to be communicating with one another.[2] They have their own post, and by means of it circulate necessary information all over the provinces in the course of a few days.

The Raskolnik communities, says Bellyustin, are so arranged

---

[1] "Contemporary Chronicles", 1867, No. 23, art. by N. Subbotin.
[2] Kelsiev, Vol. IV, p. 341.

that the lowest beggar has a voice in them. The following, for
example, is a description of the rich boot-making village of
Kimry in the Korchevski province of Tver, inhabited by
Popovtsy.

"The relations of employers and workmen are altogether
peculiar and characteristic; the latter form unions usually of
30 to 60 persons, and these possess so much moral influence,
that they not only hold their own in all that concerns their
religious convictions against the patron, in case he is inclined
to oppose them, but they can oblige him to adopt their point of
view. It was our good fortune to be present not only at their
deliberations, but at a discussion of the 'faith' between an
employer and his guild; and it contrasted strongly with the
usual relations between an employer and his workmen. Una-
bashed by anything or anyone the humblest worker, if he be
their most instructed man, corrects the patron's arguments;
let a question be put, and they insist on an answer to it. They
often leave the employer in a dilemma; he is obliged either to
capitulate unconditionally to the body of workmen — and let
us not forget the unbroken solidarity that prevails among
them in all that borders on religion — or to antagonize them,
and that means to antagonize the whole society." [1] Not that
we must even among the Raskolniks regard the relations of
labour and capital too optimistically, says Uzov. For however
strong the organization of the community, the capitalists
manage to make their power felt; and a latent antagonism
is revealed by the fact that latterly the Old believers have discovered that the number of the Beast, i.e. the title of Antichrist, is contained in the word *Khozyain*, which means
employer.[2] If the latter in their idea becomes a tool of Antichrist, that is of evil, then we can no longer entertain any hope
even among the Raskolniks of friendly relations between capital and labour. The ideal of a Russian revolutionary is to
manage a workshop or a manufactory along the communists
lines of the *mir* or village commune.

The ideal of life common to them all is expressed, concludes

[1] *Russki Vestnik*, 1865, June, p. 762.
[2] *Istina*, 1877, bk. 51, p. 29.

Uzov, in their so-called *Belovody* (white waters). Long since they have had aspirations for this land, that to many seemed a dream and fable. "In this region," says the monk Mark Topozerski, "theft, larceny and other offences against the law are unknown." Its inhabitants who number over half a million, "pay taxes to no government whatever." [1] From the information communicated by Yadrintsev, we gather that the accounts given among the Raskolniks of Belovody contain much truth. Among the Altai mountains is a spot which the Russian bureaucrat has only lately discovered; there in very truth flow the white (mountain) streams, and there is to be found a Russian settlement, which until yesterday knew not the heavy hand of any intrusive authorities. At their advent, then, and not before, the myth of White waters was revealed to have been more or less of a real fact; but they had not been there long before, alas, the myth became a real myth.

Legal Position of the Raskol

Ivanovski in a chapter entitled 'External Relations of the Raskol to the Government and the Measures undertaken by the Clergy in order to achieve its enfeeblement,' summarizes what has been in the main 250 years of dreary religious persecution, broken only occasionally by brief lucid intervals of semi-toleration. He justly divides these 250 years into four periods, viz:

1. From the beginning of the Raskol to the reign of Peter I, that is approximately to the beginning of the XVIIIth Century.

2. The Reigns of Peter I and his successor to the beginning of the reign of Catharine II.

3. The Reigns of Catharine II and Alexander I.

4. From death of Alexander I until the end of the XIXth Century.

To these four epochs, let us hope that the present Revolution may add an altogether new and happier one.

[1] P. Melnikov, *Hist. Sketch of Popovtsy*, pp. 41, 43.

Before Peter I

No ukases were hurled directly against the Old believers until Tsar Alexis Mikhailovich issued one, which the patriarch Joseph countersigned, as well as his Metropolitans and archbishops, bishops and the entire holy synod; this condemned to the stake any and all who should insult Jesus Christ, the Virgin or the Cross. Under this law provision was duly made for hunting down and burning alive such as confronted the inquisitor with firmness and courage, while those who promptly made their peace with the church were only to be subjected to what was understood in that age as spiritual admonition, no doubt of the kind that Claverhouse administered about the same time to Scotch covenanters.

The above ukase, however, was too indefinite and too gentle for the Empress Regent Sophia, who as soon as she had disarmed her rebellious praetorian guard, the Streltsy, issued a new one proscribing the very existence of the Raskol, and making it illegal; the teachers of the Raskol were condemned to be burned alive as heretics, as were all whom they had rebaptized. The repentant, who saw the error of their ways, were to be sent to convents and enlightened by application of the knout, as also were any who sheltered them, unless they did so in ignorance, in which case they were to be heavily fined.

Peter I

The above law continued in force under Peter I, called the Great, but was not put in force by him very thoroughly, because he was preoccupied with other concerns. He was intent on opening his window towards Europe, the new capital of Petersburg, as he called it, rechristened by the late Tsar Petrograd, a change of name which, though it pleases the Panslavists, is not likely to be permanent. Peter I was too busy at first building a fleet of ships and developing the system of bureaucratic concentration begun a hundred years before, to turn his attention to the persecution of heretics. What is more, he may even have sympathized a little with them, for he had himself to bear the odium of abolishing the patriarchate and installing himself in its place, of tearing the veils off the faces of high-born ladies, of cutting off the curls of the Jews and the beards of Russians. Such an emperor was not, at any rate at first, disposed to make martyrs of people who were to his mind, as they would have been to Frederick the Great's or Voltaire's, cranks and ignoramuses. As long as they did not hinder his pet designs, he had little fault to find with them, and was ready to consider them as good citizens, just as he regarded the many Lutherans who put their wits at his disposal. The settlers on the Vyg even earned his good will by assisting him in his enterprises; so did those of Starodub, and he rewarded both for a time by allowing them liberty to worship as they liked.

Later on, however, Peter discovered their fanaticism. Most probably their orthodox enemies discovered it for him. Anyhow in 1714 unfriendly laws were made against them of a kind to facilitate their exploitation by the Government. As Sophia's edict stood on the statute book with its menace of rack and stake, any official could blackmail them, and they were naturally ready to bear any burdens of taxation or corvée provided only they were allowed to retain their convictions.

Peter the Great therefore began by obliging them to inscribe themselves as Raskolniks on a state-kept register and to pay double taxes. Now they regarded themselves as the Orthodox Church, and indeed had as much right to the name as Nikon and his time-serving prelates. It is not surprising therefore that many refused to register themselves in the ledgers of Antichrist, as Ivanovski explains, "partly to avoid the extra imposts but still more *from fanaticism.*" The result was that Peter I invented ingenious penalties alike for those heretics who concealed their identity and for those who revealed it. The avowed dissenter was not to be actively molested, but to be made ridiculous in the eyes of all, *monstrari digito praetereuntium.* To that end they were, like our convicts, to wear clothes of a special cut marked with the agreeable lettering H. R. A., i.e. Heretic, Raskolnik, Apostate. They were to be denied any, even the humblest, of public offices. Their evidence could not be accepted in a court of justice except as against members of their own sect. The only function of a public kind left to them was that of collecting the double tax of their fellows in misfortune. This last improvement in their position was sanctioned July 7, 1725. Already, however, in May 1722 a fresh edict had been issued against their teachers and against any who sheltered the latter; and on July 13 of the same year another forbade runaway priests, as well as Bezpopovtsy elders, to hold any sort of religious services anywhere. The children of dissenters were to be baptized by orthodox priests, while the settlers on the Vyg, who still enjoyed certain immunities because of the services they had loyally rendered to Peter I, were in 1724 forbidden to quit their residences without passports.

The reason for all these restrictions, alien to Peter's original conceptions of his duties as a ruler, is to be sought in the hostility of the holy synod, which waxed ever more intense as the propaganda of the Raskol spread. They had hoped to extirpate it by the Draconian law of Sophia. They now demanded of the Government fresh powers to hunt down and capture the malignants.

All the above regulations applied primarily to the avowed dissenters. The task of discovering the unavowed ones was now entrusted to the clergy; the maxim 'set a thief to catch a thief,' seeming no doubt to Peter thoroughly applicable. But here the Government met with difficulty. Very many of the clergy were secretly in sympathy with the Raskol, as is shewn by the constant leakage from their ranks into those of the adversary. Many more, as underpaid men with families to support, were open to bribes. It was held necessary therefore by the Synod to frame edicts against its own clergy in case they sheltered or connived at Dissent. Those who did so were liable to forfeit their orders, to undergo corporal punishment, forced labour, etc. Civil and military officials were in turn appointed to hunt out the orthodox clergy who were lax in their duty — *Quis custodiet ipsos custodes?* — and to assist them in discharging the same, in case they were loyal to their bishops. Even the landowners were found to be infected with the Raskol poison, and were made liable to capture, and to 'admonition', as it was tenderly called, by the spiritual authorities; and if that failed of effect to punishment and exile. The punishment — according to the old trick of the Roman inquisition — was nominally levelled, not against religious opinion, but at those who opposed the civil Government, in this case the Ukases of the Tsar. Secret police were sent to Starodub, Novgorod, Nizhigorod, Livonia and elsewhere, to keep watch not only on the quasi-orthodox clergy, but upon the landed proprietors as well. Such was the legislation of Peter the Great, and it furnished a model which succeeding Governments as a rule followed only too faithfully.

We have seen that for a time the settlers on the Vyg enjoyed exemption from the double tax along with a few other privileges; but not for long, since one of the first acts of the next ruler, Catharine I, was to impose it on them in June 1726. The new Government even entertained the plan of extirpating that community and removing its members to their original homes by force. It was eventually decided however in 1732 to pass a law or ukase condemning all members of the Raskol to be interned in monasteries, there to undergo clerical 'correction.' They were by the same ukase to be taken regularly to divine service and in case of resistance to be handed over to the civil authorities and secular arm. In 1734 they were forbidden to erect chapels or oratories for themselves, and finally in 1734 under Anna Ivanovna took place the first great hunt. The Cossacks in the course of a campaign in Poland descended upon the settlement of Vetka which had till now been out of range of the Russian Government, and 40,000 of them were driven back across the frontier into the grip of the Moscovite.

Peter III to Alexander I

3. We now approach the second half of the XVIIIth Century, an era of greater freedom lasting from the accession of Peter III in 1750 to the end of the reign of Alexander I in 1825, seventy-five years in all. The former monarch tried to assimilate the status of the dissenters to that of cults recognized in

the empire as legitimate though not orthodox.   He did not live
to carry out his plan, and it devolved on Catharine II to execute
so sensible and humane a project.   She began by issuing an
edict inviting members of the Raskol who had fled across the
borders in the previous reigns to return to Russia, where such
orderly and industrious people could ill be spared; she promised
them in return an indemnity for any wrongs they might have
committed, and instead of being shorn, as together with the
Jews, they had been by Peter the Great, the right was conceded
to them of wearing their beards, to the disgust of the many
German barbers whom Peter's legislation had furnished with
remunerative jobs.   Catharine also engaged to spare them the
indignity of wearing a distinctive dress not unlike that assigned
by Latin Inquisitors to the victims of an auto-da-fé.   Over and
above these indulgences, the returned Raskolniks were allowed
to become proprietors of land, 'royal peasants,' or, if they preferred it, tradesmen and merchants.   They were however condemned to continue to pay to the Government double taxes for
a period of six years.   There still remained a considerable number of settlers at Vetka in Poland, and, as she was conducting
one of the perpetual campaigns against the Poles, Catharine
seized the occasion to transport thence to their old homes
another 20,000 of them.   This second enforced migration gave
the *coup de grace* to this once flourishing colony of Old believers.
The date of the granting of these exemptions was 1764.   At the
same time Raskolniks who remained confined in monasteries
were liberated.   Five years later they were admitted to the
witness box in legal cases; in 1782 the double tax was abolished.

Hitherto this had been levied on avowed Raskolniks, and
pressure had been used to force them to inscribe their names
in the official registers, in consequence of which and from abhorrence of the name Raskol — for they considered themselves
to be the Orthodox Church — they had concealed their qual-
ity.   There was no longer the same reason to do so and some
began even to see an advantage in being put on the register,
for once they were inscribed upon it they were exempt from
the exactions which the authorized clergy were authorized to
levy upon their flocks.   Not a few even of the orthodox

inscribed themselves upon the register in order to escape these. The Government thus found itself in a dilemma; certain of the provincial governors moreover, e.g., those of Perm and Tobolsk, represented that the retention of the double category of Raskol and Orthodox confused the census and taxation lists and made the collecting of accurate statistics more difficult than need be. The end of it was that the Tsarina expugned the very name Raskol from all juridical and official documents. The Senate approved of this step, and by an ukase of 1783 the name was discarded in ecclesiastical lists and records as also in verbal communications. The next year, 1784, the holy Synod was induced to assent to this reform, and in 1785 the dissenters had all their disabilities removed by a fresh ukase which admitted them to public positions in all towns and cities. The most enlightened of all female sovereigns in Russia and perhaps the whole world, had won, and all the oppressive regulations of Peter I were abrogated. At the same time permission was given to the members of the Raskol to settle in Siberia.

After Catharine's death succeeded the brief reign of Paul (Nov. 1796 to March 1801), and then Alexander came to the throne, a man of liberal and humane instincts. His policy towards the Raskol however was a perpetual seesaw, according as his native disposition or the sleepless hatred of the orthodox prelates prevailed. Even under Catharine the law against orthodox popes who joined the Raskol was maintained in all its severity, and ukases of November 1765 and January 1776 condemned them to ecclesiastical degradation and deprivation of their orders, and it was not safe for them to appear in public in their true colours. At the beginning of Alexander's reign, although the laws were not changed, the Government shewed itself more indulgent; and in many places, e.g. Gorodets in the Nizhegorod Government and at Starodub, they were in 1803 openly discharging their spiritual offices. Nine years later however the Synod interfered to prevent the Popovtsy of the village of Uvanov in the Vladimirski Government from employing them, and their veto was upheld by Alexander in February 1812. Later on, in March 1822, the Sovereign crowned his inconsistencies by sanctioning the use of runaway popes in case they had been guilty of no crime and were not quitting the church in order to evade the consequences of their actions. The prelates expostulated against such mildness, but this time in vain.

The right of having their own chapels and oratories was conceded or denied under Alexander to the Raskol with similar waverings. Before Catharine II had finally lightened their yoke, the old laws forbidding them to have places of worship of their own had been reaffirmed in ukases of July 1769 and April 1778. Subsequently, it is true, the Government winked at their existence and the law was not carried out. In one case (1817) the cupola of a church would be pulled down, but the rest of it left intact. In other cases the raising of a church was allowed, but the right to hold services in it denied. It was a real triumph, however, for the Raskol in Moscow when in 1809 the legality of their Transfiguration Cemetery was upheld, and when the Minister of the Interior authorized the rebuilding of churches in the Vyatka Government and in the district of Sarapul. The Holy Synod of course fumed at the least show of tolerance, and appealed to the ukase of 1803 which, while disclaiming any desire to violate men's consciences, forbade any open exhibitions of apostasy; and in 1816 they managed to get the chapels in Fatezh in the Government of Kursk destroyed, especially any that presumed to have a bell. In 1817 the Tsar issued instructions to local authorities to forbid the erection of chapels. In 1822 a fresh edict allowed old structures to remain, but forbade the raising of new ones.

Under Alexander's régime the open celebration of their rites was also winked at, and the Raskol were freely allowed to baptize and to bury their dead until 1818, in some cases even to ring a bell to summon the faithful to worship. But stronger measures were enforced in 1820, especially against Raskol propaganda. Any public manifestation of their religion, even the conducting of a burial by a priest attired in canonicals, was forbidden in 1824. They might bury their dead, but without hymns or candles.

Nicholas I and his Successors, to 1903

We have already seen how the accession in 1825 of
Nicholas I, a bigot and martinet, was marked by a return to
the system of persecution. Raskol communities were placed
afresh outside the law, their members denied the right of will
and testament, no churches or schools were allowed to be put
up, no hospitals or rest-houses. The title of *Raskolnik* had
been expunged from official documents: it was now revived,
and all public offices and employments were closed afresh to
them. No dissenter might engage in trade or become a merchant of the first or second *guilds* or categories. New oratories,
of course, or chapels were disallowed, and it was forbidden to
repair those which already existed. Most of their charitable
institutions were closed or pulled down. The dissenters were
also obliged by ukase to take their children to an orthodox priest
for baptism; their marriages were declared invalid. The
object of such legislation was to allow members of the sect to
live on as such till death overtook them, but prevent their ranks
from being recruited either by inheritance or by propaganda.
To facilitate the project Nicholas had a list made of the names
of all living Raskolniks, with an inventory of all their churches,
monasteries and sketes so called, between the years 1840 and
1853. Everywhere the police were set on to see that all these
oppressive regulations were carried out, and garrisons were
located in the chief Raskol centres. In 1847 a special police
was created to exact the extra taxes levied upon dissenters.

Any system which reposes on policemen, especially in Russia,
is insecure, for they are generally no less venal than unobserv-
ant. In spite of Nicholas' campaign therefore the Raskolniks
went on building their chapels and increasing their numbers.
When an extraordinary inquisition was to be made in any
centre, the people were always forewarned. Now and again,
as at Semenov, sketes were destroyed, but the inmates were
regarded as martyrs and the hatred of the Orthodox oppressors
waxed more intense. The exiled and transported managed to
correspond with their coreligionists and inflame what Ivanovski calls their fanaticism. The mockery to which church

consistories condemned them served, he says, to harden their hearts, and, if they repented, it was only in semblance.

In 1855 Nicholas I was succeeded by Alexander II Nikolaevich, a man of more liberal tendencies. The question of the best way to deal with the Raskol was laid before him in 1858, and he was at first in favour of applying the law as it stood, but impartially and equally all around; for a member of the Raskol never knew beforehand how a court of first instance would decide his case, and was the victim of all sorts of caprice on the part of police and judge. Later in the same year, Alexander decided against persecution, but agreed to forbid any propaganda amongst the Orthodox and any public manifestations of Raskol faith, such as processions with cross and banners, hymn singing outside a place of worship, solemn celebrations of baptism or marriage, funeral processions in which the clergy wore vestments and cowls, monastic habits, outward emblems of religion on churches, bells, etc. On the other hand Raskolniks were permitted to trade in November, 1863, and to earn medals and orders from the Government in 1864, unless indeed they belonged to the most noxious sects which eschewed marriage and prayers for the Tsar; they were allowed in 1861 with the consent of the Minister of the Interior to be admitted to public offices. In 1874 their marriages were legitimized, if duly registered in the records of the police and commune, and their licit character was made to depend not on the use of religious rites, but on the act of registration. The law obliging them to go through the mockery of baptizing their children in an orthodox church was now abrogated.

As early as 1864 the Tsar Alexander projected a revision of all the laws affecting the Raskol, and in 1867 charged his council to undertake new legislation. Committees of investigation were formed in consequence and men of special knowledge, like Melnikov, consulted. A new scheme of law was prepared and laid before the Holy Synod; but the political events of 1877, the war with Turkey, and the assassination of the Tsar in 1881 arrested the whole scheme, which was not resumed until 1883, when by Ukase of May 3 the new Tsar Alexander III gave sanction to the views of his council in favour of recogniz-

ing the civil rights of Dissenters and their liberty of worship.
But the proscription of any outward signs or evidence of Raskol
faith was kept up, and every measure taken to prevent propaganda and protect the Orthodox Church from being attacked.
The general principle of religious liberty and toleration was
admitted and even paraded in the new law, but in application
sadly curtailed. The Orthodox Church was recognized as
having a monopoly of religious truth and Government protection. No other religious body could make converts from other
faiths, while no Orthodox person could leave the Church and
enroll himself in the ranks of the Raskol. The statute forbidding any public manifestation of Raskol faith and opinion was
to be vigorously enforced, and exile awaited any member of it
who converted an Orthodox to his faith. Any who printed
books with a view to Raskol propaganda, or gave lectures or
distributed tracts for the purpose were liable to be imprisoned.
Any who overtly spoke ill of the Orthodox clergy or vilified the
Church were liable to the same penalty. The printing of the
liturgical books of the Raskol was likewise forbidden, and any
one selling them might be fined 300 rubles. No new churches,
nor restoration of old ones, was to be attempted without the
fiat of the provincial governor, and all Government officials
and bureaucrats were pledged to assist the Orthodox bishops
and clergy in the sacred duty of repressing the Raskol. The
inferior clergy had to keep the bishop informed of any considerable defection on the part of the parishioners, in accordance with the principle that "the dominant Church, Orthodox,
Catholic and Oriental, is invested with the right, as is no other,
within the frontiers of the Empire to induce the heterodox by
way of persuasion to embrace its doctrine." [1] The Government
rewards those who assist in the work of converting Raskolnik
by conferring the decoration of the third grade of the order of
St. Anna on any missionary who is so fortunate as to make, with
the aid of the police, one hundred converts among the Raskol
or the infidels.

---

[1] Skvortsov, *Zakony o raskolnikakh* (Laws concerning the Raskolniki), Moscow,
1903, p. 166, cited by Aurel. Palmieri, *La Chiesa Russa*, Firenze, 1908, to whom I
am much indebted in this section.

Mixed marriages between the Orthodox and members of the Raskol were only legal if celebrated in an Orthodox Church, with Orthodox rites, and if the Raskolnik party 'verted' to the Orthodox Church. Minors perverted to the Raskol or to any heresy were placed under the charge of the Minister of the Interior. All prosecutions directed against the Raskol had to be initiated by the ecclesiastical authorities, and the parish clergy could do no more than report cases to the bishop of the diocese. A request for a prosecution must be precise and clearly formulated.

Such in brief were the regulations in force before the year 1903. They purported to be inspired by goodwill and toleration, and the Imperial Senate in its commentaries on them mitigated them in a few particulars. For example, public vilification of an orthodox priest was to be condoned, if the latter by insolence or altercation had provoked it; and the mere performance of a rite by a Raskol priest for orthodox persons, especially if the latter were not of an age to appreciate dogmatic distinctions, was not to be classed as an attempt at religious perversion. Commenting on the clause forbidding Raskolniks to officiate for the Orthodox at baptisms, marriages or funerals, the Senate held that, in such cases, the ministrant alone be held responsible, and not the parents and other parties, even though they consented. In Russia it rests or rested with the bureaucracy, lay or spiritual, to enforce the laws of the Empire, very much as they please; and it can well be imagined, writes Palmieri (p. 411), that, under the superintendence of an intransigent Procurator of the Holy Synod like Pobedonostsev bureaucrats continued to use against the Raskol the weapons of an earlier legislation. To the protests of the Raskolniks no attention was paid; their chapels continued to receive the visits of the police who closed them when and as they chose; for it was this fanatical functionary's idea to beat down Catholicism, to suffocate the Raskol, and by such means bring about the religious unity of Russia.

The Reforms of 1903

A better epoch seemed about to dawn when on February 26, 1903, after the fall of Pobedonostsev, the young Tsar, Nicholas II proclaimed liberty of conscience; and in an Ukase promulgated by the Senate on December 12, 1904, a revision was promised of all the laws directed against the Raskol. Official persecutions, remarks Palmieri, far from having enfeebled the religious feelings and the spirit of abnegation of the Dissenters had only made them more tenacious of their beliefs, readier than ever to sacrifice everything rather than stoop to apostasy. Accordingly they formulated the following demands:—

1. That in official documents the offensive epithet *Raskolniki* or dissidents should be cancelled, and that of Old believers or Old Ritualists — the latter first used in Catharine II's rescript of August 13, 1775 — should take its place. These substitutes the Orthodox objected to as implying that they themselves were the innovators in 1667.

2. They demanded juridical and religious autonomy for their parishes, and a corresponding right to possess what places of worship and charitable institutions they liked. Till now they had had mainly to meet for worship in private houses.

3. Liberty of cult, and a recognition of the legality of the so-called *metriki* or registers drawn up by Raskol ministers. They asked that there should be inscribed in these the names of those who, though they figured in the registers of the orthodox priests, had nevertheless declined their sacraments for a period of ten years. The law of 1883 only allowed Raskol chapels to be reopened which had been founded before 1826, when there were 1257 of them. Since 1883 and up to 1904 the number of their chapels had increased by 283.

4. The right of those, who in spite of their really being Raskolniks, figured as orthodox in civil documents, to inscribe their children in the Raskol registers. Members of the Raskol inscribed against their will in orthodox ledgers and lists generally refused on that account to report their births, marriages and deaths to the police. For example over fourteen years, 1889–1903, according to a fairly accurate estimate, out of

29,431 Raskolnik marriages only 1840 were reported to the police; out of 131,730 births, only 552.[1]

5. Lastly the Raskolniks asked in 1904 for liberty to open elementary schools for their children in which their own catechisms should be taught; liberty for Raskol students, *not* to have to listen in secondary schools to a catechist's lectures *against* their religion; exemption of their priests from military service to which no orthodox priest is liable, and free access for their laity to all civil and military duties and offices.

Their demands, owing to Pobedonostsev's sudden fall from power and the disasters of the Japanese War, received some satisfaction, and an imperial Ukase of April 17, 1905, suppressed the offensive *Raskol,* and distinguished among Russian dissenters three categories: 1. of Old Ritualists who recognize the sacraments and dogmatic doctrines of the Orthodox Church, but differ therefrom on points of ritual; 2. of Sectaries, e.g. the Molokani, Stundists and Dukhobortsi; 3. the 'pernicious' sects, e.g. the Khlysty or Flagellants and the Skoptsy or Self-mutilators.

The first-named were henceforth to be allowed to organize themselves into a corporate Church and enjoy such rights as the Lutherans or Catholics already enjoyed; they were to divide themselves into parishes under rectors (*nastoyateli, nastavniki*), their clergy were exempted from military service, they might found schools of their own and move about without that machinery of passports which made them the special victims of police oppression and blackmail. The Council of Ministers, glossing the Ukase, furthermore gave them the right to *own* their churches, hospitals and cemeteries, the right of admission as students in military and naval academies, of receiving decorations and of printing their liturgies.

These concessions excited great hopes in the breast of the Raskolnik, while the orthodox journals also pretended to be overjoyed at so signal a proof that the Russian people is hostile to religious persecution. Skvortsov wrote as follows:— "We know by experience that police measures are repugnant to our

[1] These figures from the *Pravoslavnyi Putevoditel* or "Orthodox Guide," an organ of the Russian Church, 1905, t. ii, p. 39.

aims. Religious errors are maladies of heart and soul, and it is best to use against them nothing but the gentle words of love and conviction. Government protection of a church by dint of law generates supineness in the pastors, somnolence and apathy; and it is all for the good if the Government, by withdrawing its aid from the Orthodox, constrains them to count on themselves and their own forces and to combat with their own weapons." [1] Yet Skvortsov had been, as Palmieri remarks, the hammer of the Raskolniks, the loyal henchman of the arch-persecutor Pobedonostsev. "When the devil is sick, the devil a saint will be."

The real feeling of the Orthodox and of the Holy Synod was revealed in the organ of the latter, the *Kolokol* or *Bell*, which objected particularly to the liberty accorded to the Raskol to have its own parishes, and declared that before long the best energies of the official Church would pass into the ranks of the Raskol, seeing that the Orthodox Church in spite of the support, protection and tutelage of the State was unable to defend itself. The young Tsar's Government impressed by these wailings of the Holy Synod took a fresh tack, and a new Ukase of April 17, 1905, enacted a year's imprisonment for anyone who tries to seduce an orthodox person into any of the rival confessions by means of sermons or dissemination of written works or images.

The Number of the Raskol

What were the numbers, asks Uzov, of the Dissidents thus driven by the folly and cruelty of the Moscovite Government to the extremes of Russia and even beyond them? To this question he devotes considerable research, and his pages though written as far back as 1881 cannot be ignored even to-day, for as he remarks their number is an important factor in the historical rôle they have played, perhaps even in the revolution of 1917.

For a long time, he points out, Russian society and no less the Russian Government had no exact idea of their numbers,

[1] *Mission Review*, 1905, Tom. 1, p. 542.

and relied on the figures assigned by local officials to those who, registering themselves as Raskolniks in the course of the XVIIIth Century (1715–1782), paid double taxes. "These figures," writes Melnikov, "in some districts underwent no change for forty years, no account being taken of the excess of births over deaths. Here and there the police commissaries even reduced them artificially year by year in order to gain credit with the government for their own efficiency as persecutors. In many cases, however, especially by young officials new to the task, attempts were made to attain statistics closer to the facts by comparing the lists either with the records kept by the clergy,— in whose computations the numbers were almost everywhere larger than those given in the police bureaus,— or with independent observations. In such cases the numbers were apt to shew a sudden rise, and on reception of them the Government would demand of the local officials an explanation of the fact, posing such questions as: why had the Raskol strengthened its position in such and such an uyezd or district? who was responsible for so marked an increase in their numbers? what steps were being taken with a view to the prevention and destruction of Raskol propaganda? why had the Government not been warned earlier of their growth? and so forth. A rescript would then be sent to the local officials couched in no friendly tone and usually ending with a reprimand for the inconsistency of their informations or their want of firmness in repression of the sect. After once experiencing such consequences an official was naturally careful not to betray too much zeal in future, and his successors profiting by his example were equally careful not to bring down on their heads reproofs which unsolicited zeal for fact and accuracy provoked. The result was that the old figures held the field, annually diminished by a small amount. Nevertheless any diligent head of police possessed formerly, and still possesses, more or less credible figures of the dissidents settled in a district, and sometimes the Governors take them into account; but they are kept fairly secret and are as a rule described as unofficial figures.

On the other hand there have been cases where the Governor

has furnished for his entire province numbers more consonant with reality, but with similar result. Questions at once were rained upon him as to how and why there had come to be such an increase of sectaries in his Government, fresh notes were written, and after that everything relapsed into the old routine.[1]

"Not only the police, but the clergy had to keep lists, and these in some dioceses presented higher figures than those of the Governors, in others lower. If it be asked why different estimates could be supplied by the Government of one and the same region — the answer is simple: the Governor and the Archpriest alike rendered to their superiors fantastic figures, based on those of bygone years and on nothing else." [2]

"The parish clergy," continues Melnikov, "in drawing up their reports paid as little regard to actual facts as the bureaucrats, and, like them, kept to the figures of earlier years; for if they ever thought of laying before the consistory anything like the truth, they exposed themselves to still harsher reprimands than they did. Routine and red-tape was as engrained in the ecclesiastical as in the civil administration."

"Above all the clergy in parishes where there are many sectaries have — we regret to say — special reasons of their own for hiding the actual figures. The registered Raskolnik is a lost man as far as the priest is concerned, for he gets no kopecks out of him. On the other hand the unregistered one is a regular gold mine for his household, since he pays very dear to the pope for the privilege of being excused his ministrations, much dearer than does the most assiduous of his parishioners for submitting to them."

By such methods, writes Uzov, in 1850 the number of Raskolniks was officially calculated as 829,971. Yet in this year the Minister of the Interior, Count L. A. Perovski, laid before the Emperor a report concerning them denying the

[1] *Statistics of the Raskol* by P. Melnikov in *Russkii Vestnik* of 1868, No. 2 (?), pp. 416–8. Reprinted in Melnikov's collected works, Peterb. 1898, xiv 368, in which I have read it.

[2] *Ibid.*, pp. 416, 420, 422. In the reprinted edition p. 371, *faktitcheskuyu* seems to be a misprint for *fantastitchkuyu*.

reliability of the official figure and fixing the true figure at nine million; and the latter was taken as the basis of a study of the Raskol in the Moscow Government by an official of that ministry, the Councillor of State Liprandi.[1]

Perovski's report led to the nomination in 1852 of two statistical expeditions for the study of the Raskol on the spot, one in the Government of Nizhegorod, the other in Yaroslav. Soon afterwards officials were also dispatched for the same purpose to the Kostroma Government. "The following are the results of the census thus instituted in 1852 in these three Governments:—

"In that of Nizhegorod according to the Governor's figures, the number of sectaries of both sexes, 20,246. According to the statistical commissioners sent to examine the facts on the spot, 172,500.

"In that of Kostroma, official figure 19,870. The commissioners Bryanchaninov and Arnoldi counted 105,572.

"In that of Yaroslav the numbers were 7,454, and 278,417 respectively.

"In these three Governments then the real figures were five, eight and a half and thirty-seven times the official ones, and the official total for the three taken together one-eleventh of the true. It follows that the real total for the whole of Russia in 1852 should have been not 910,000, but nearly ten millions. "What is more," remarks Melnikov, "910,000 had already before this time been accepted in governing circles as the true figure."[2] There is no reason, argues Uzov, to suppose that the members of the Statistical Commission exaggerated; indeed Liprandi asserts that "attempts so conducted to ascertain the numbers of the Raskolniks were far from satisfactory, as a first essay of the sort was met everywhere not so much with sympathy and coöperation, as with hostility and all kinds of opposition and impediments."[3] The Commission, continues Uzov, reduced rather than exaggerated the figures:

[1] id. pp. 416, 420, 422.
[2] id. pp. 426–7.
[3] Imperial Society of History and Antiquities in Moscow Univ. for 1870, bk. 2, art. by Liprandi, p. 115.

e.g. in the Yaroslav Government it reckoned 278,417, where one of its members J. Aksakov estimates "the orthodox as being but a fourth of the population, with the result that, as there were in 1852 as many as 943,583 [1] persons in this Government, the true proportion of dissidents must have been 672,687. Another member of the Commission, Count Stenbok, reckoned the orthodox to be only a third of the population,[2] in which case the dissidents numbered 629,056, against an official record of not more than 12,000.

In the Nizhegorod Government the Commission only counted 172,000, where in the sequel the Bishop Jeremiah found 233,323.[3]

We are justified therefore, says Uzov, in concluding with Liprandi, that the real number, if more carefully calculated than they could be by the members of the Commission of 1852, must have been "immeasurably greater"[4] than was allowed by them. In 1853 the Government began an inquisition on a much vaster scale based on a coöperation of the officials of the Ministry of the Interior with the clergy. The results of the two sets of investigators were compared, and the "general conclusion was that the Raskolniks were ten times as numerous as had been supposed."[5] The sectaries themselves, "though very reserved in their confidence estimated their number at ten millions."[6]

In proof of the huge hiatus there was between the real and official numbers may be cited, adds Uzov, the case of the Archangel Government, where "officially 4,428 persons were allowed to be dissenters, though the Hieromonachus Donatus counted 90,000, or twenty times as many.[7] In the Povenets district of the Olonets Government the official figure was 2,383, out of a total of 24,628 inhabitants.[8] Here Mainov avers

---

[1] Russian Archives, 1866, No. 4, p. 634.
[2] Sbornik by Kelsiev, t. iv, pp. 24, 329.
[3] Sobranie Postanovlenii (collected regulations) for Raskol, bk. 2, p. 673.
[4] Liprandi in Imperial Society of Antiquities l. c.
[5] Russkiya Vesti, 1868, No. 2, art. II. of Melnikov, p. 435. In edition p. 381.
[6] Liprandi, op. cit. p. 115, and Statistical Tables, p. 211.
[7] Records of the Archangel Govt. for 1863, art. of Donatus, p. 80.
[8] Records of Olonets Gov., 1866.

that in reality no more than five hundred orthodox inhabitants or rather five hundred lukewarm sectaries could be mustered in the same district.[1] In other words the Raskol have exceeded the official estimate by ten times.

There is another way of arriving at the figures of the Raskol, namely the following:

In the census of the Ministry of Cults for 1859 the number of orthodox believers in all Russia is put at 51,474,209. Of these

1. Confessing and receiving the Sacrament   35,081,097
2. Confessing but not receiving the Sacrament   2,196,714
3. Infants not confessing   9,232,234
4. Not confessing for other satisfactory reasons   819,951
5. Not confessing by reason of negligence   3,417,231
6. Not confessing through leaning to the Raskol   726,982

These six categories include the entire population under the care of the orthodox clergy, but not the registered Raskolniks. Obviously the sixth category, however, belongs to them entire, and in secret almost the whole of the fifth, say three millions, as also the second, say two. Lastly we must subtract a proportion of the third and fourth, say ten per cent. or in all about one million. Then again we must bear in mind that many Raskolniks, especially those who belong to the sects furthest removed from orthodoxy, go to confession and communion punctually, because this is their only way of deceiving the police and avoiding incarceration. Among these we must reckon, says Uzov, "the entire body of the Spasov sect, very numerous on the Volga and reckoned by Melnikov in his *Numbers of the Raskol* at 700,000. We have no means of computing the number of the latter, so we will confine ourselves to the approximate figures exhibited above, and assume the total of the Raskol openly registered to be seven millions, and will include the secret Raskolniks, who discharge all the rites of orthodoxy, say as many as eight millions. Most probably we may take 10% of the entire population or one-sixth of the

---

[1] Mainov, *Tour in Obonezh and Korel.*

orthodox population."[1] It follows, remarks Uzov, that in 1859 there were 8,579,034 of them.

For reasons, he adds, which we do not grasp, Bushen in his computations completely ignores the registered Raskolniks, who according to Melnikov were in 1859 reckoned at 875,382. Adding these to the sum of those taken account of in the *Statistical Tables*, we reach the figure 9,456,416.

Thus, concludes Uzov, if we combine the figures drawn up by the officials of the Ministry of the Interior with those of the *Statistical Tables*, we may fairly assume that in 1859 there were nine and a half millions. Assuming the annual increase of population to be 1.3%, the figure nine and a half millions for 1859 would in 1878 have altered to twelve millions. But we cannot rest at this figure, for the number increases *pari passu* not only with the birth-rate, but with the propaganda. According to Bellyustin the peasants are being converted to the Raskol ' *en masse.*' [2] "At the present time (1880) it wins adherents even in parishes where it was unknown." [3] The priest Tverdynski declares that, "to his sorrow, he must agree with the apologists of the Raskol, that the number of its converts from orthodoxy goes up by thousands." [4] "I have seen," says Mackenzie Wallace, "large villages in which by the testimony of the inhabitants, there was not fifteen years ago a single Raskolnik, and now fully half the people are Molokanye." He also says of the Stundists that "according to the latest information the number of the sect increases," [5] in spite of official castigation with birch twigs.

Apart from the above testimonies to the increase, Uzov points to the articles of the priests Blagoveshchenski in *Strannik*, 1865, No. 7, p. 23: Gromachevski in *Zarya*, 1871, No. 9: C. M. B. in *Strannik*, 1871, No. 2, p. 93: and to an article entitled: "How explain the longevity of the Raskol?" in *Christian Readings* (*Khrist. Chteniya*), 1871, pt. 1, and also

[1] *Statistical Tables of the Russ. Empire.* Published by Ministry of the Interior, 1863.

[2] *Russkii Vestnik*, 1865, June, p. 761.

[3] *Orthodox Conversations (pravosl. sobesyed.)* 1866, pt. 3, art. by E. L. p. 264.

[4] Strannik 1866, No. 3, p. 129.

[5] *Vestnik Europy* 1877, No. 5, p. 340. See edition of New York, 1880, p. 304.

to the evidence tendered by officials that have studied the Raskol as well as by the other persons already mentioned. He warns us that we must furthermore distinguish between real and only nominal conversion, understanding by the latter the passage from secret to open adherence, which with the relaxation of persecution has become a daily phenomenon in Russian life. Orthodoxy incurs no loss thereby; it only reduces the takings of the orthodox clergy. In all allusions to conversions we have had in view real conversion and no other.

To sum up, writes Uzov, if we take into consideration the vigour of Raskol propaganda during the last twenty years,[1] we may raise the figure of twelve millions to thirteen or fourteen in 1880.

Uzov next attempts to estimate the distribution of the total according to the different groups or concords as they are called. According to the figures of the officials of the Ministry of the Interior in 1852 in the Yaroslav Government, the number of dissidents (Uniats) was $1\frac{1}{4}\%$; Popovtsy $16\frac{1}{2}\%$; Spasov group $8\frac{1}{4}\%$; Pomortsy $1\frac{1}{4}\%$; Thedosyevtsy 30%; Philippovtsy $12\frac{1}{2}\%$; Khlysty and Skoptsy $\frac{1}{4}\%$; total $67\frac{3}{4}\%$; for the remaining $30\frac{1}{4}\%$ no data.[2]

In the Kostroma Government there were found of those who prayed for the Tsar (chiefly Popovtsy, though there were here Bezpopovtsy also of the Pomorski Communion) 39%; of those who did not, chiefly Thedosyevtsy and Philippovtsy, $28\frac{1}{2}\%$; of the Spasov group $31\frac{1}{2}\%$; Khlysty and Skoptsy $\frac{1}{2}\%$.

Comparing these figures, Uzov deduces that the Popovtsy make up about 28%, the Bezpopovtsy about 55, Khlysty and Skoptsy $\frac{1}{2}\%$, leaving $16\frac{1}{2}\%$ unknown. And dividing up the 13,000,000 Raskolniks in the corresponding proportions, Uzov reaches the following figures:

Popovtsy,   3,640,000;
Bezpopovtsy,   7,150,000;
Khlysty, etc.,   65,000;
Unascertained, 2,145,000.

Of the last, one million he claims are 'spiritual Christians.'
That there are as many is attested by the facts: firstly that,
according to the Government inquisition of 1842–1846 into
the Molokan sect, its adherents, secret or overt, numbered
200,000 in the Government of Tambov alone; secondly, he
adduces the testimony of Mackenzie Wallace that there are
some hundreds of thousands of them, and that latterly their
diffusion has increased on a vast scale. Besides that we must
remark, he says, that we are reckoning among the Spiritual
Christians the Evangelicals (Stundists), who, notwithstanding
that they are a relatively new sect, already can count a formidable number of adherents.

The figures here assigned by Uzov to the Popovtsy and
Bezpopovtsy, are based on those of 1852; but since that date
up to 1880, when he wrote, they both increased by leaps and
bounds. All who are familiar with the Raskol testify that the
sects without a clergy gain at the expense of the sects who
retain it. Thus already in 1853 Liprandi noted that "the
Bezpopovtsy heresy is spreading among us with incredible
rapidity," and that "for some time past they have won over
to themselves members of the rival sect." [1] Bellyustin
writing in 1865 says that "among the peasants the diffusion
and acceptance are ever deeper and stronger of such teachings
as amount intellectually to a denial of all that even savours
of priesthood." [2] Taking into account the leakage of the
sects with clergy into those without, we could reckon the
number of the former in the year 1880 at three millions, of
the latter at eight.

M. Anatole Leroy Beaulieu in the third volume of his
L'Empire des Tsars, published in 1889, p. 377 estimates the
number of Old believers (to the exclusion of other sects) at
twelve to fifteen millions, but omits to state in detail the bases
of his calculation, which is unduly cautious, but he justly adds
that no figures can impart a fair idea of the importance of the
Raskol. The influence of this Russian Schism cannot, like

---

[1] Imperial Society of History in Moscow University for 1870, bk. 2, art. of
Liprandi, pp. 78 and 119.

[2] Russkii Vestnik, 1865, June.

that of most established religions, be measured by figures. For it exists not merely as a Church, a confession adopted by so many millions of souls. It is often a simple tendency, a bias to which many incline who have not openly quitted the official orthodoxy. Its strength lies less in the overt adepts than in the masses who mutely sympathize with it. This sympathy is intelligible if we bear in mind that it issued spontaneously out of the heart of the people and is a product no less than a glorification of popular customs and ideas. Instead of loathing them as rebels and heretics, the peasants and workmen, who remain within the fold of the Church, often regard these old-believers as most pious and fervent people, as Christians resembling those of antiquity who were persecuted for their faith. In many regions, among the *petit peuple* we meet with the singular opinion that official orthodoxy is only good for the lukewarm, that it is a worldly religion through which it is barely possible to attain salvation, that the holy and true religion is that of the old-believers.... A high functionary, charged, towards the close of Nicholas the First's reign to conduct a secret enquiry into the Raskol, tells an instructive anecdote on the point: "When I entered a peasant's *izba* or hut I was often received with the words 'We are not Christians.' 'What then are you, infidels?' 'No,' they would answer, 'we believe in Christ, but we belong to the Church, for we are worldly frivolous people.' 'Why are you not Christians, since you believe in Christ?' 'Christians,' they reply, 'are those who stick to the old faith, and they don't pray in the same way as we do; but as for us, we have no time to imitate them.'"

Uzov concludes that the 12 to 13 millions of Raskolniks alive in 1880 could be apportioned as follows:—

Popovtsy	3,000,000
Bezpopovtsy	8,000,000
Spiritual Christians	1,000,000
Khlysty, etc.	65,000
Total	12,065,000

There remained a million over, but there were no data of a kind to indicate to which of the above sects they belonged.

Uzov's statistical researches here given are of singular value; for, as I point out later on, the figures given some twenty years later by the Russian State and Church authorities were, to put it mildly, misleading. Allowing for growth of population alone, there must have been some twenty millions of Raskol in 1900; if we allow for their active propaganda many more. In 1917 their numbers must have approached twenty-five millions at least. Yet at the end of the century Russian Authorities, after twenty years of Pobedonostsev's régime, reckoned them at only two million and a quarter, a figure fantastically small.

Controversial Propaganda against the Raskol

It remains to say a few words about the missions organized by the Russian Government for the conversion of the Raskol. They began with Peter the Great, who deputed Pitirim, Bishop of Nizhni-Novgorod (1665–1738), whose figure has already crossed our pages, to find arguments against the dissidents. His arguments were not so potent that he did not very soon realize the necessity of sustaining them with the secular arm; and in 1715 an Ukase decreed death against any who should traverse them. Peter also, as we saw, sent the monk Neophitus, chosen for the task by Pitirim in 1722, to convert the Raskolniks of Vyg in Russian Pomerania or Pomor. He was no match for the dialectic of the two brothers Denisov, and speedily invoked the stake to second his arguments. It is to the credit of Tsar Alexander I that in his reign the Raskol were left alone even by missionaries, but under Nicholas I the various sees were warned by Government of the necessity of missionary enterprise, that of Perm in 1827, Penza in 1828, Saratov in 1833, Chernigov in 1838, Irkutsk in 1839. The missionaries were well paid and armed with Raskol books lest they should not know what they had to confute. In 1853 chairs of anti-Raskol history and confutation were directed by the Synod to be created in seminaries, and printed counter-

blasts began to be prepared.   In 1882, 4,000 roubles were voted
for the printing expenses of a single year; all episcopal and
parish libraries are furnished with such books free gratis and
for nothing.   In 1886 confraternities were organized for combating the Raskol, especially among women.   Two years before
an older regulation was revived obliging seminarists to study
the Raskol,— a most dangerous ordinance.   In 1888 also the
corps of missionaries was organized on a more ambitious plan
than ever before, and new arrangements made for public
debates with Raskol teachers.   The missionaries themselves
regularly met in conclave to discuss their successes with the
orthodox prelates.

Palmieri gives some interesting details (p. 443, foll.) of recent
missionary literature directed against the Raskol.   The
Bratskoe Slovo (Fraternal words) is a journal which began in
January, 1875 under the editorship of N. N. Subbotin, professor
of the Church Academy in Moscow, one whose name has often
figured in our pages, a man of learning and large minded.   It
came to an end in 1899 for want of subscribers, but contains a
multitude of articles of great value.

In 1888 the Moscow clergy started a weekly journal under the
direction of Protohierei I. T. Vinogradov, called the *Drug
Istiny* or "Friend of Truth."   It was more militant in tone
than Subbotin's journal and came to an end in 1890.   In 1896
appeared at Kiev a new journal, the *Missionerskoe Obozrenie*
or "Missionary Review" under the patronage of Pobedonostsev, with the ardent collaboration of B. M. Skvortsov, professor
of Raskol history in the Kiev Seminary.   In 1899 it was transferred to Petersburg, and in it has been published much of
importance; but in tone it was fanatical and reactionary, full
of hatred of Catholicism and ever demanding a crusade against
the Raskol which it wished to see suffocated in blood.   Even
the orthodox clergy learned to detest it.   In 1903 a new
monthly journal the *Pravoslavnyi Putevoditel* or "Orthodox
Guide" appeared at Petersburg.   In 1906 it became a bi-
monthly journal, and its tone was more liberal than Skvortsov's
journal.

Successes, however, have been microscopic, and, if under

Alexander III they claimed to convert annually eight or ten thousand persons, this was to be attributed more to the intransigent ferocity of Pobedonostsev than to genuine missionary effort, although over 400 missionaries were at work. The moment freedom of conscience was proclaimed by Nicholas II in 1903, there was no more talk of conversions to orthodoxy but only of defection *en masse* among *soi-disant* Orthodox. Palmieri attributes the futility of missionary effort to the fact that not a few of the missionaries and most popes are not educated enough to reply to their adversaries, who have a rich literature of their own, and do not scruple to silence them, often by simply talking common sense. Zealous partisans of orthodoxy, like Ivanovski himself, have been the first to recognize that fresh blood is needed in orthodox seminaries, if the clergy are ever to exert any influence on the Raskol. The lives of the parish priests, their drunkenness, avarice and servility to Government, in themselves constituted a mighty stumbling-block. Nor have the public debates which Raskol teachers have been compelled to hold with orthodox missionaries borne fruit. As often as not they ended in the ridiculous discomfiture of the spokesmen of orthodoxy, and only served to inflame religious passions. In many cases the paid missionary of the Holy Synod ended by invoking the aid of the police and he was everywhere regarded as a spy in the service of the State. If the missionaries had been real students of the Raskol, they could have spent their time better, says Palmieri, in combating the Raskol in periodicals. Nor were the orthodox schoolmasters appointed in Raskol districts ideals of Christian virtue; the net result was that Raskol youth subjected to their teaching shewed little inclination to profit by it.

The orthodox press has ever been prone to resort to calumny and talk of the moral decadence of the Raskol; but the facts in this field belie the reports of the missionaries. A mother of a family who noticed the change wrought in her husband from the first moment he began to frequent Raskol meetings, in particular that he gave up drink, became herself an apostle of the doctrines that had regenerated the domestic hearth.[1]

[1] Kalnev in *Mission. Obozrenie*, 1906, t. ii, p. 62, foll.

Liprandi, though as we saw above, a persecutor, acknowledges the virtues of the Raskolniks in his *"Short Sketch of the Raskol"* (1853) as follows:— "Russian people delight to listen to stories and in particular to readings of Scripture. The Raskol are more literary than the Orthodox and make the most of the case. They are ever ready to tender their services to a village neighbour, and by reading the Gospel and other religious books and interpreting them to them, insensibly win them over. The Orthodox envy the affluence of their Raskol neighbours. They do not reflect that they never spend a farthing at the grog shop, that they keep sober and work hard every day. The Raskolnik wife when she goes to town wastes no money on ribbons, whereas the Orthodox one purchases all she sees when she goes there or visits her friends, goes to weddings, baptisms or church, all of which the Raskolnik finds superfluous. The Orthodox person without reflecting sets all this down to the superiority of the Raskol religion and *nolens volens* is predisposed in favour of it,— all the more so because, in case she does join it, she finds herself actually able to better her position."

We have seen how impossible it is to calculate its numerical strength. We can only guess at it. But whatever its real figures may be they do not represent the limits of its influence, for several reasons. Millions of peasants, nominally Orthodox, look up, we saw, to their Raskolnik neighbours as champions of the true ancient faith of Russia and secretly condemn themselves as backsliders. This popular reverence for the dissenters is enhanced by their superior standard of morality and of education and by the wealth which accompanies these. To their eminent sobriety I have already cited the testimony of several writers. I add two more such tributes. The first is from a well-informed Russian who published anonymously a work on them entitled *Le Raskol* in Paris in 1859. He is hostile to them, yet he writes thus (p. 99):

"In general you meet to-day with more morality in the masses of the people than you do in certain exalted circles of Russian society. Among the Schismatics the Popovtsy, the most (?) numerous, often practise virtues unknown to those who are loyal to the State Church. Even among the Bezpopovtsy, whose doctrines deliver man wholly to the caprice of his passions, it is not rare to behold regularity of manners result from the very cause which ought to ruin and degrade them. Thus among them marriage is in principle only a temporary union, and its duration depends on that of the mutual affection of the parties. And yet these unions seemingly so fragile are often solid, and offer remarkable examples of conjugal concord and peace. Husband and wife, being in love, avoid mutual provocation, fear to alienate each other's goodwill, make allowance for one another's faults, and live in the most exemplary manner."

M. Volkov in his *Lettres de l'Etranger* is equally loud in praise of the purity of life he witnessed among these sectaries when he lived among them. "In general, he says, they are also less ignorant than the adherents of the Orthodox Church. Most of them can read and write, but they read only the Scriptures, being of opinion that the human intelligence needs no other reading." Elsewhere he writes (p. 122): "If the Raskol reject the official religion, it is because the priests are servants of an administration which oppresses them, which claims to enslave their consciences, which despising the most sacred rights of the individual violates his domicile, tears from him the symbols of his faith, his venerated images, mute witnesses of his religious transports, snatches them from him on the sole ground that they do not conform to the orthodox model. If then the Russian people has affirmed its liberty of conscience until to-day, it has done so in the way of religious opposition. With them the activity of the free spirit has never manifested itself through abstract writings, but in and through an uninterrupted series of religious sects...Every day the people's protest against the fetters fastened on the conscience becomes more patent and general...Since Peter the Great's brusque reforms, beneficial as they were in some respects, the leaven of revolt has been fermenting in the masses of the people. His reforms have ever figured in popular imagination as an attack on their traditions, their ways of life, as a vague and undefined aggravation of their state of servitude...They submitted to these reforms, but never acquiesced in them. They took refuge in a tacit and passive resistance which endures to-day. The German and bureaucratic civilization these reforms imposed on the peasant annoys, wearies, stifles him. It is as if a cloud of government *employés* had alighted on a conquered land and were exploiting it."

Let us remember that the above was written before the serf was emancipated. Can we doubt that he found in religion a freedom of the soul and conscience, a spiritual antidote and anodyne of the slavery to which the Proprietor and the State subjected his person?

The Publications of the Raskol in Modern Times

Owing to the censorship Raskol writers were seldom able to print anything, but their works circulated in manuscript. Similarly when I was in Tiflis twenty-five years ago I was surprised to hear how many works of Tolstoy and other religious authors were circulating in copies all written out by hand. The Raskol were able, however, to print books in Austria and it was there that Uzov, to whom I am so much indebted, published his important work: *Tserkov Khristova vremenno bez episkopa* "The Church of Christ temporarily without a bishop." In Prussia and Rumania the Raskolniks also had presses and, as we saw above, Kelsiev's monumental work was published in London by Trubner as early as 1870. In 1878 the *Staroobryadets* or "Old Ritualist" appeared in Austria and ran for eight years, the regular organ of the Raskol, circulating far and wide, but in secret, in Russia. A similar journal, the *Slovo Pravdy* began to be published in 1896 at Braila in Rumania, but the Russian police got hold of the editor the following year and he went to prison. In 1905 at Klimutz in Bukovina was begun the *Staroobriadcheski Vestnik* or *Messenger of the Old Ritualists*, which boldly took the line that, if the Russian-Orthodox Church desired any reconciliation with the Dissidents, it must unsay and undo the last two hundred and fifty years of its history. In January, 1906 for the first time they were allowed to print their books in Russia, and a monthly was begun at Nizhni Novgorod called *Staroobriadets*, in the supplements of which have appeared many old monuments of the movement, e.g. the *Diakonovskie Otviety* or "Responses of a Deacon," written by the Deacon Alexander of that city, who was burned at the stake in 1720; also the *Vinograd rossiiskii* of Simeon Denisov, a collection of lives of leading Raskolniks. The Moscow *Narodnaya Gazeta* or "PopularGazette" published twice a week a supplement called the *Golos Staroobryadtsa*, a chronicle of the Old believers, and once a month appears the *Isbornik*, a splendidly illustrated supplement dedicated to the history of the sect, and of much value. The Molokani, since 1905 have issued a monthly at Tiflis called *Dukhovnyi Khristianin* or "Spiritual Christian."

"The influence among the Raskol," writes an orthodox publicist Vishnyakov,[1] "of monks and nuns is still very great, and is seen not so much in their asceticism, as in other points in which they excel, in their literary aptitudes, their books, their book-trade, their educational system, etc. All this requires spare time, which the lying ascetics procure at the expense of the village commune." In the great annual fair of Nizhni Novgorod the manuscripts etc. for church use of Raskol monks and nuns are remarkable.

Palmieri gives a striking summary of the teaching inculcated in the *Old Believing* journals, especially in the *Staroobryadets*. Politically they stand for respect of all nationalities and all religions; they support the constitutionalist party, urge economic reforms, work hard to settle the quarrel between capital and labour and to improve the conditions of the proletariat.

The Church, say the Dissenters, must undertake all these problems. It is not an infallible clergy, but consists of the whole people freely choosing its priests and supervising its own ecclesiastical affairs. The supreme government of the Church is not vested in any monarch but in councils. In Russia they say there is no fear of clericalism among the adherents of the Raskol; for that is only possible where the church is not separate from the state, or is hampered in its life by conventions and concordats. Freed from the support, political and material, of the State, the Church becomes once again the free society of

[1] *Nevskii Sbornik*, 1867, p. 91.

the faithful, a Christian brotherhood, a body whose mission is always spiritual and whose influence is propagated in souls by means of persuasion and charity. For this principle of liberty and independence the Old believers have undergone martyrdom for two centuries and a half. In their political program also figures the abolition of death and life sentences, as a barbarous custom contrary to divine laws. On the intellectual and moral side they would educate the people, and they combat drunkenness and the use of tobacco, as diabolical inventions for the destruction of mankind.

In religious matters they do not conceal their hostility towards the official Church, which they blame for the complete divorce there is in Russia between pastors and people. The orthodox clergy, enslaved by Government, never raise their voice to defend the rights of the Church. The latter should stand above political factions and limit its action to the field of morals. The orthodox clergy are devoured with avarice. In peasant families children are left seven or eight months unbaptized, because the parents have no money to pay the pope the sum asked for the sacrament. Parents often live in concubinage, because the popes demand fifteen, twenty or twenty-five roubles before they will bless their unions. Often a corpse remains for days unburied because the pope asks five roubles before he will inter it in the cemetery.

The official Church in Russia is dead, exhausted, under the thumb of lay bureaucrats, subject to the Powers of the world, vending the heritage of Christ for a morsel of bread, with no faculty of self-reform from within, and without the aid of the Government. In its relations with the police you behold it sacrifice sincerity and authority and enslave itself to Babylon. Russian orthodox Christianity is wholly official, a mystic Byzantinism barely to be distinguished from pagan formalism. The Russian clergy preach to the people the indissoluble union of autocracy, orthodoxy and nationality, and deny the form of government to be a thing both human and mutable. This is why the clergy has made itself hated of an oppressed people and has pardoned all and every act of violence. The Church has really transformed itself into a political institution, and its pastors, mere *employés* of the Government, by their conduct sow incredulity and atheism and slay faith in the people's heart. The faithful perceive that the religious life of Orthodoxy is reduced to a legalistic formalism, a mechanical asceticism, that the Russian Church is no longer a society consciously bound up in itself by a spirit of love and brotherhood; they know that hierocratic despotism takes for its device the formula: "I am the Church, the Church is I," and intolerant of such oppression they abandon the temple.

To remedy such a condition of petrifaction and putrifaction the organs of the Old believers propose a series of measures that would restore to the Russian Church its primitive and pristine splendour; they insist on decentralization, the institution of Councils, the suppression of the system which puffs up and aggrandizes the orthodox clergy by loading them with secular honours and medals, etc. But the ills which beset it are no merely passing ones. Its entire framework is weakened by the marasma which besets one who for long years languishes among tombs. Like a parasitic organism it nourishes itself on the living juices of the civil power alone, and its life will fade away as soon as it is refused such diet or refuses it of its own initiative.

In such criticism one catches the glow in the sky which heralded the dawn of the Russian Revolution. *Quod felix faustum sit.*

William Palmer writing in 1871 the preface to his *Replies of the humble Nicon*, p. xxiv, penned the following remarkable words:

" It is possible, too, to imagine such changes in the world at large, as might make it the policy of the Russian government to return towards faith and piety.

"Supposing that before long, the Turkish empire should come to its end, without Syria falling under the exclusive dominion or protection of Russia, and that the Jewish nationality reappearing in Palestine, a part of that nationality should, from Infidel become Christian, just as now a part of the Italian nationality have, from Christians and Catholics, become as infidel Jews. Suppose then that, within a century, St. Peter, in his successor, should go away from the Italians, become Jews at Rome, to the Jews become Christians at Jerusalem; a supposition which, after the experience at Avignon, cannot be rejected as absolutely impossible.

Suppose too that, in spite of great social changes, such as the cessation of all coercion in matters of belief or unbelief, and of the former union of church and state, there should still exist in Russia a government leaning rather on the orderly and religious, than on the anarchical and irreligious part of the nation, when the pole of Christianity is shifted from the West to the East, 'the time of the Gentiles' and of the desolation of the Holy Land being fulfilled. Under such circumstances it might perhaps be as much the interest and policy of a Russian emperor to heal the Greek schism, as it was before the interest and policy of the Turkish Sultans directly, and of the Russian sovereigns indirectly, to maintain and perpetuate it."

So much of this curious forecast has lately come true that it is not, we hope, impossible that someday the Christianity of the West, duly purged, may link up with an equally purged Christianity of the East. But is it impossible that it will be, not, as Palmer imagines, the orthodox of the two hemispheres, but the heretics and dissenters who will point the way and by their example shame formalists into true charity?

INTRODUCTION

The three sects which I have next to describe are as characteristically Little Russian in their origin and provenance as the Raskolniks are Great Russian. They are those which Russian publicists have agreed to call Rationalists[1] or Mystics. It is somewhat of a misnomer, but it calls attention to the fact that they are the outcome, not of reverence for the traditions and ritual of the Great Churches, but of inward illumination; of the spirit that quickens rather than of the letter which killeth. They are Montanist rather than Catholic in tone and tendency, and, if in the Early Church there was, as in old Israel, an antithesis between prophet and priest, so in these sects prophecy is first, priesthood second; they are a protest against the latent tendency in human nature for the seer to develop into a formularist. I shall begin with the twin sects of Dukhobortsy and Molokanye, both indefinably ancient and branches of one and the same stem and pass on to the Stundites, in whom German influence is more visible.

The origin of these 'heretical' sects of Russia is obscure; it is probable however, that the Dukhobortsy and Molokanye, as well as the Khlysty, antedate the Old believers by many generations. The *Intelligentsia* of Russia, when they first became aware of these 'protestant heretics' in their midst, jumped at the conclusion that they were, like themselves, an importation, from the West. They had already made the mistake of regarding the Raskol as a party of religious stagnation, a litter of ignorance and obscurantism, of blind adherence to the letter, of petrified superstition, of routine and respect for an outworn past. Ever since the reign of Peter I, who first encouraged

[1] Ivanovski like other Russian publicists means by rationalism rejection of ecclesiastical authority, a "protestant" claim to think out one's creed and interpret Scripture without the aid of a priest. To his mind also the Raskolniki whom we have so far dealt with are only, like the Latins, schismatics; the sects we now approach, like the churches of the west that have broken with Rome, are heretics. On the whole, we shall see, his charge of rationalistic interpretation of the Scripture means no more than that these sects try to take the Gospel in the sense in which it was meant to be read.

them, these 'superior' people of Russia have imagined that they alone tread the path of progress. They derived their illumination and infidelity from the West; was it possible that sects which rebelled against the yoke of Orthodoxy with less ceremony even than the Old believers should draw their inspiration from any other quarter? Accordingly this explanation was taken on trust and unexamined, found to be not only credible, but a compliment to the Genius of the Russian people. Yet it ignored the leading characteristic of these sects, which was that their revolt was rather moral than intellectual, of the heart rather than of the head. Their cry was 'Back to Christ,' and away from a Church which, affecting to believe the Gospel to be a Divine Message, has ever since the nominal conversion under Constantine of the Roman Empire, ostentatiously set it aside. True Christian piety,— they contended — passed underground in the fourth century to emerge afresh in the bosom of their own and similar congregations.

They were not far wrong. And the remarkable thing in Russia is that this movement back to Christ has ever been an indigenous impulse, a direct result of putting the New Testament in the hands of Russian peasants, the spontaneous echo which the book awoke in an *anima naturaliter Christiana*. With them there is not even the antecedent provocation to become Christians which there was in the case of the Raskol. The latter was in origin a protest on the part of a few who saw their ancestral customs and convictions assailed, not by Poles or alien Latin influences, but by their own countrymen, whom they expected to defend and champion them. Perhaps the contest with Nikon took shape as a spiritual one and was fought out with the weapons of controversy, because the numerical insignificance of the Raskol and the deeply engrained, almost instinctive, capacity of the Russian poor to endure violence humbly and patiently at the hands of their own rulers rendered it out of the question to employ the crude material methods of resistance with which they had encountered Tartars and Latins. The Raskol then was a reaction against violence, a defence of old convictions doubled with local patriotism in opposition to a civil authority as cruel as it was arrogant.

Dukhoborism, Molokanism and Stundism on the other hand savour more of pure conversion to simple Christianity. There underlies these sects little except a conscience responsive to the teaching of the Sermon on the Mount. While admitting all this, we can yet recognize that the first two of these movements exhibit certain traits which remind us of the Cathar or Albigensian sects, and it is probable that the Bogomilism of Bulgaria and of the Balkans, still vigorous in the crusading epoch, was the germ out of which they developed. The foreign elements they hold in suspension are anyhow more likely to have entered Russia from Bulgaria than from Germany or even from Armenia and Asia Minor where from the earliest centuries was diffused a type of faith, the Paulician, closely related to Catharism, as I have pointed out in my edition of the *Key of Truth*, the manual of the Armenian Paulicians.

Such elements must, like Byzantine orthodoxy, have penetrated Muscovy across the Ukraine by way of Kiev. For Little Russia was in close contact with Muscovy long before Peter the Great broke his window into the Baltic Sea and paved an open road along which the stately German influence could advance. It has been noticed that the religious folk-songs of Little Russia agree in presenting variants met with sporadically in Bulgarian, Serbian, Czech, Moravian, Polish, even German Hussite sources, and it would be an interesting study to compare the Dukhobortsy hymns with those of the early Anabaptists. If the above considerations be valid we must regard this sect to some extent as a continuation on Russian soil of the primitive semi-gnostic, perhaps Marcionite and Pneumatic, Christianity of the first centuries. As it radiated from Asia Minor through the Balkans to South Russia, so from Rome it spread by way of Milan, Marseilles and Lyons throughout western Europe. Widely diffused in the west under the crust of dominant Catholicism, it emerged into the light in the great upheaval of the Reformation; latent equally among the Slavs it came to the surface when the Raskol movement and the so-called reforms of Peter the Great stirred Russia to her depths.

But from whatever sources and by whatever means they

penetrated Russia, the Dukhobortsy emerged clearly into view according to the historian Novitski (Kiev, 1832), about the year 1785. They were then met with as an organized sect in the village of Nikolski in the Ekaterinoslav Government, under a teacher named Silvan (Siluyan) Kolesnikov. There they attracted the attention of the local bishop Ambrose, who is said first to have stigmatized them as a sect of Pneumato-machi that "fought against the Holy Spirit." The sectaries interpreted the title to mean that the Spirit fought *in* them. The people at first called them Ikon-wrestlers, because they rejected ikons.

Dukhoborism demanded of its adherents so lofty an ethical level that it spread little before it accommodated itself in the form of Molokanism to the mentality of Russian peasants. Even so transformed, its propaganda only began on a great scale about the year 1860. It must to-day count its adherents by millions.

Stundism is the only one of the trio which can even in part be identified with a German evangelicalism or methodism, trans-ported on to Russian soil. It probably owes more to Molo-kanism. If its adherents claim a Teutonic origin they do so, because as such they acquire a title to toleration not accorded to sects of purely Russian origin. They allied themselves in the closing years of the last century with the Molokanye of the Don, and the difference between them and any form of Lutheranism has constantly increased. That German settlers in Russia for years rarely talked any but their own language, in itself mili-tates against the facile hypothesis of a purely German origin for this or other Russian sects. German missionaries no doubt furnished the Stundist impulse, but it is mainly a product of the Russian religious genius.

Ivanovski, overprone to shallow explanations of religious facts, exaggerates German influence among his countrymen, and is inclined to date the rise of these three sects in the reign of Peter the Great, because that monarch allowed Russian translations to be made of the Latin, Lutheran and Calvinist catechisms; and he makes much of the fact that a Russian of Moscow named Dmitri Tveritinov, anathematized by the clergy for heresy and imprisoned in a monastery — one of his followers was burned alive — had studied medicine among Germans and imbibed protestant ideas in doing so. He found fault with the ridiculously severe fasts of the Orthodox Church, rejected the veneration of relics and ikons, denied tradition and authority. He even went the length of saying: "I am the Church myself." He seems also to have expressed himself boldly in public, advocated freedom of speech and distributed hand written tracts setting forth his tenets. In his own chamber he hung up in the corner not an ikon, as Russians do, but a placard inscribed with the first two commandments, and his walls were adorned with various other texts. All this brought down upon him the wrath of the metropolitan Stephan Yavorski who assailed him in a book entitled "The Rock of Faith," which however was not printed during Peter's reign because it insulted the foreigners whose presence that monarch valued and encouraged. When it was published after his death in 1728, it provoked a counter-polemic from Theophan Prokopovich who accused Yavorski of Latinizing and under Anna Ioanovna the book was prohibited.

The annexation of Kiev and the Ukraine had more to do with the spread in Great Russia of these sects; the facilities given in 1701 to the merchants of Little Russia to travel with their goods to Moscow and the opening of a Russian fair in Azov at the mouth of the Don (captured by Peter in 1696 from the Turks) were decisive factors. Peter's conquests along the northern shores of the Euxine led to the diffusion throughout Moscovy of ideas already fermenting in the Ukraine.

CHAPTER I

THE DUKHOBORTSY

I have availed myself of the following sources in my description of the Dukhobortsy:—

1. A description of them penned in 1805 by a friendly observer and Englished by Vladimir Tchertkoff in 1897, (The Brotherhood Publishing Co., London), from a text printed just before in *Russian Antiquity* (*Otetch. Drevn.*). I refer to this source as V. T.

2. An article on *Russian Rationalists* by E. P. in *Vestnik Evropy*, 1831, Vol. 1, p. 650, foll. and Vol. 4, p. 272.

3. Uzov's description of them. This is based on several Russian sources, viz: i. Novitski's work upon them printed at Kiev in 1832. To this I refer as N. The Dukhobortsy accepted this work as a manual of their tenets. It was intended as a criticism from an orthodox standpoint, but sinned by its impartiality. ii. An article in the *Orthodox Conversationalist* (*Pravoslavnyi Sobesyednik*) for 1858, pt. 3: referred to as P. S. 1858. iii. An article in the same journal for 1859, pt. I = P. S. 1859. iv. An article in the *Review* (*Obzor*), 1878, No. 237. v. An article signed A. F. in the *National Records* (*Otechest venniya Zapiski*) for 1828, pt. 33 (= A. F.), and an article on the Molokanye by Anna Filbert, 1870, No. 6. vi. Articles in the *Transactions of the Imperial Society of History and Antiquity:* by I. V. Lopukhin, 1864, bk. 4 and by the Archimandrite Eugenius, for 1874, bk. 4. vii. An article by Shchapov in the Dyelo, 1867, No. 10 (= Sh.).

4. Liprandi, *Raskolniki*, Peterb. 1872.

5. Ivanovski's description. He uses Nos. i, ii and vi of the above list and also D. Varadinov's *History of the Ministry of Internal Affairs*, Vol. viii (= D. V.). For the doctrine of the Dukhobortsy he also used the *Orthodox Conversationalist*, 1859, t. 1, the *Studies* (*Trudy*) of the Kiev Academy for 1875, pt. 1, and the monumental volumes of Livanov, *Raskolniki i Ostrozhniki*. C. Hahn's volume *Kaukasische Reise*, Leipzig, 1896, contains a chapter on the sect (= C. H.)

Of the works enumerated I begin with Vladimir Tchertkoff as the oldest of our sources; it is convenient to summarize it apart from the rest and supplement it from them later on.

The Dukhobortsy suddenly appeared in the second half of the XVIIIth Century, surprising all by their brusque repudiation of the ceremonies and ritual of the Russian Church. An active persecution of them began in 1792 in Ekaterinoslav where the Governor, Kohovsky, reported to the authorities that "those infected with the movement merited no mercy," and were all the more dangerous because "of their exemplary good conduct," because "they avoided drunkenness and idleness, gave themselves up to the welfare of their homes and led a moral life." Their virtues were all the more odious because they attracted the masses. As regards their relations to Government he stated that they "paid their taxes regularly and fulfilled their social duties, often even to excess, as compared with other peasants." The net result was that instead of being left in peace they were victimized by every priest, police agent or magistrate, hailed into court, knouted and sent to prison, burnt alive or exiled as state offenders. They were made to appear as "monsters and breakers of the general peace." Notwithstanding, they carried their propaganda, says Novitski, "with feverish zeal all over the south of Russia, and gained crowds of adherents in the Governments of Ekaterinoslav, Kharkov, Tambov and in the country of the Don Cossacks. They shewed themselves in the Caucasus and overran Saratov, Voronezh, Kursk. They also penetrated to the centre of Russia, to Moscow and Kaluga, and made their way to the north, into Finland, the island of Esel and the Government of Archangel. Eastwards they reached Siberia as far as Irkutsk and even Kamchatka. But wherever they went it was not the rich but the poor and humble, the peasantry and the workers that welcomed their teaching. The educated knew them not and it was rare even for a merchant to join them."

They won a respite from suffering, continues V. T., in 1801, when under the mild and peaceful reign of Alexander I, the Senators Lopokin and Neledinski were directed to report on

them, and exhibited them to the Tsar in their true character.
Anxious in any case to isolate them, the Tsar allowed them to
emigrate to the so-called "Milky Waters" in the Taurid province near Melitopol, north of the Sea of Azov. In 1804 those
who lived in Tambov and Ekaterinoslav were also allowed to
join their brethren in that settlement, where on one occasion
Alexander himself paid them a visit. They called themselves
Christians and nothing more, says V. T., knowing others as
'men of the world.' "Their origin was unknown even to
themselves, for being common people and illiterate, they had
no written history; nor had tradition preserved amongst them
any information upon the subject."

They held all externals, for example, images, the sign of the
cross, fasts, to be useless as a means to Salvation. The external
Church, by reason of true Christianity having lapsed, was
become a den of robbers. They were all that was left of the
one sacred, universal and Apostolic Church, which the Lord
at his advent assembled, consecrated and filled with gifts of the
Holy Ghost.

Their manner of meeting for prayer will be described later
in my chapter on the Molokanye; here I only note that the
author of 1805 describes them as singing psalms and explaining
the word of God in their meetings "without books and from
memory alone." They had no priests and acknowledged as
such only Christ, uplifted above sinners and higher than the
heavens.

Their cardinal tenet was mutual love. They had no private
property, and the goods of each were those of all. In their
settlement at Milky Waters they practised real communism,
had a common treasury, common flocks and herds, and in each
of their villages common granaries, from which each was supplied according to his needs. Their hospitality was great, and
from travellers they would accept no remuneration; but in
order to isolate them from the brethren they kept a special
lodging house in which also they entertained Government
officials and kept the common funds. Their compassion for all
they extended even to their animals, which they refrained from
killing as much as they could.

Respect of children for parents and of young for old was inculcated, but not in a way to give the idea that those of the older generation were anything more than the spiritual equals of the younger. No one was punished except by such admonition as the Gospel allows. Those who wished to quit the society were allowed to depart in peace, even if they were wives of members, and permitted to take away with them such means of life as they could carry. Deserters who had left the society because of their evil propensities were readmitted if they repented.

Every member plied his craft; some were traders, but the great majority agriculturists. They had no rulers or elders specially entrusted with authority by the community, for all were equal; and in spite of there being no written rules and regulations, there was no disorder. Three and even five families would live together in one large cottage. The father had authority over his household and was responsible for the education of his children. If he died his authority passed to his eldest surviving brother.

As soon as a child reached the age of understanding, he was taught prayers and psalms and something of Scripture. These they were encouraged to recite in the meetings. By such methods the spirit and ways of thinking of the parents were passed on to their children.

Vladimir Tchertkoff gives seventeen of their tenets. All of them are summed up in the precept to worship God in Spirit and in Truth. They did not deny the *Credo* of the Church and, indeed, used it as a psalm. The One and Ineffable God is in three persons, Father, Son and Holy Ghost. Through our Memory we are one with the Father, through our Understanding one with the Son, through our Will one with the Spirit; and the three persons are separately symbolized as Light, Life and Peace. Thus every Doukhobor is the Trinity incarnate.

They accepted the Gospel story of Jesus, but insisted that his spiritual experiences must be re-enacted in each of us. He must be begotten, born, grow up, suffer, die, revive and ascend into heaven in each of us. In a word each of us has to become Christ. That is what is meant by Salvation, second birth and renewal. Jesus himself was and is the eternal living Gospel, the Word to be written in our hearts. They rejected the Orthodox dogma of the Incarnation, for according to N. they said: "The divinity of Jesus Christ our Saviour, as shewn in the Old Testament was nothing but wisdom revealed in nature, but in the New Testament he was the spirit of Piety, Purity, etc. incarnate. He is the Son of God; but in the same sense in which we also are sons of God. Our elders know even more than Christ did; go and hear them." Of miracles they said: "We believe that he performed miracles; we ourselves were dead in sin, blind and deaf, and he has raised us up, pardoned our sins, and given us his commandments; but of bodily miracles we know nothing. For our salvation, it is not essential to have an external knowledge of Jesus Christ; for there is the inward word which reveals him in the depth of our souls." A reader of Döllinger's *Sectengeschichte* recognizes here the mysticism of the medieval Cathars. Leroy Beaulieu is surprized that ignorant peasants should interpret Christian mysteries "in a manner analogous to that of Hegelians." If it was Hegelian, then St. Paul was Hegelian from the first, and after him the Cathars and Paulicians.

Mere invocation of God cannot save us, unless we are pure in heart. Faith in Christ is necessary indeed, but implies corresponding works. The Dukhobortsy know no monstrous antithesis between the two.

Like the Molokanye they reject water baptism; a man is baptized in that he repents with a pure and willing heart, and calls upon God. "An adult," writes N. "baptizes himself with the word of truth, and is then baptized, indeed, by the true priest, Christ, with spirit and with fire." Then his sins are remitted, and he turns away from the world. New birth and baptism are one and the same spiritual process. It unites us and reconciles us with God, lends us spiritual eyes to see him with. They ask forgiveness of God for their sins, but confess them before the brethren, asking their forgiveness also. But they do not encourage men to parade and boast of their sins out of sham meekness. Their only form of Communion is forgiveness of sins and inward acceptance of God's Word; bread and wine, entering the mouth like common food, avail not the soul. Nor is it true fasting to abstain from certain foods, but to abstain from gluttony and other vices, to practise purity, meekness and humility. "True confession," writes N. "is heartfelt contrition before God, though we may also confess our sins one to another when occasion presents itself. The external sacraments of the Church are offensive to God, for Christ desires not signs but realities; the real communion comes by the word, by thought and by faith."

The Saints they do not invoke, though they try to imitate them. Rejecting sacraments, they cannot recognize marriage as such. It is enough if the young people consent and promise to live together. The parents allow mutual love and attraction to dictate the union, and no preference is given to wealth or rank. Some abstain from marriage for the sake of purity, and such abstinence is regarded as a lofty virtue.

The dead they commemorate by good deeds, not otherwise; for they hold that they are safe in God's hands and that he will remember the righteous in his kingdom. Therefore they do not pray for those who, in their phrase, have not died, but are only changed. But their idea of heaven is no vulgar one. The Kingdom is in man's own will; Heaven, like Hell, lies in his soul; and righteous souls are in the hands of God. There is no more a material Hell than a material Heaven. The Dukhobors of Tambov in the 18th century, when asked at the Alexander Nevski convent to define the heavens, answered that they are seven,— humility, sobriety, abstemiousness, clemency, good counsel and charity. The wicked after death merely walk in the darkness, expecting soon to perish, and Hell consists in evil feeling and ill will. After death there is no repentance, but each man is judged according to his deeds,— an unusually harsh tenet to be held by such gentle people.

But Salvation is not confined to members of their sect. It depends on conduct, and all who imitated Jesus in all ages or countries, knowingly or not, have been saved. "The Church," writes N. "is a society selected by God himself. It is invisible and is scattered over the whole world; it is not marked externally by any common creed. Not Christians only, but Jews,

Mohammedans and others may be members of it, if only they harken to the inward word. The scriptures must be understood symbolically to represent things that are inward and spiritual. It must all be understood to relate in a mystical manner to the Christ within."

They are careful to keep their houses clean and tidy, and adorn them with pictures of remarkable men or saints, but they do not worship the pictures. The tract concludes with two characteristic specimens of their prayers, imitated from the Psalms. Such is our earliest account of this sect.

The tenets of the sect are written in no books, but, according to P. S. 1859, are contained in a tradition, handed down from father to son, which they term the *Living Book* enshrined in the memory and hearts of the faithful in contrast with the Bible which is written in dead letters. The tradition includes psalms, consisting partly of detached sentences selected both from the Davidic psalms or from the rest of the Bible, and from the prayers and sequences of the Orthodox Church; but in a still higher proportion they are original compositions. The mass of these devotional exercises, the *vox viva* of the Church, is so large that no single man can remember them all. A father usually teaches his children all he knows between the ages of six and fifteen, and this curriculum they call baptism.

In the last quarter of the XVIIIth Century their chief teacher was one Hilarion Pobirokhin, a rich wool merchant, of the village of Goryel in Tambov. He enjoyed the reputation among the people of being a well-read man, and is accused by Ivanovski of having carried extravagance to the length of proclaiming himself to be Son of God and future judge of the world, and of surrounding himself with twelve disciples whom he called archangels. A second set of them he called angels of death. His bold propaganda attracted the attention of the authorities and he was exiled to Siberia along with his family.

Another famous teacher in the same age was Sabellius Kapustin, a retired corporal of the guard, supposed by many to have been a son of Pobirokhin who had enlisted and subsequently deserted. He was a man of great stature, handsome and majestic in bearing, an eloquent and attractive speaker.

The story is that he knew the Bible by heart. He was the object of such reverence that his followers when he went out of his house kneeled before him and sought his blessing. We are reminded of the veneration shewn in the Celtic Church to its saints while they were still detained in the flesh.

Pobirokhin, according to P. S. 1858, taught that God has no independent existence, but is immanent in the righteous; and on the strength of this notion of the Divine Being he called himself, *qua* righteous, a Son of God. Silvanus Kolesnikov, according to N. held that "one believer must bow to another, on the ground that we are the first fruits of God's creation, and among all creatures in the world the living impress of his hand, an image of God on earth." Thus, having no proper feast days, they reckon that day a festival when one of the sect visits another. Such guests they welcome and escort with spiritual songs.

Thus, says the writer in the *Obzor*, they identify God and man; for the two are indivisible and God is a Trinity of Memory, Understanding and Will. Starting from this idea, says the same writer, they reject the life beyond the tomb. They join at death the 'Choir Invisible' which consists merely in being remembered. The next life consists in the memories which the deceased leave behind them. For them Paradise and Hell exist not, and the former is *lived* here on earth. "The living," they are fond of saying, "are helpmates of God." It is not easy to reconcile this view with other sources, which admit another life.

The sole difference for the righteous, writes P. S. 1859, between this and a future life is that they will live alone, apart from sinners; otherwise, birth, labour and death go on as now. There will be no resurrection of the flesh, nay the very end of the world can only be defined as an extinction of sinners; yet the world does not end, but persists forever as we see it now. The orthodox idea of there being another world than this is false. There is no heaven apart from the earth; the world is one, and the word heaven merely signifies the chosen race of God in contrast with that of the Devil.

But these ideas, according to the same informant, are held

in conjunction with a belief in the transmigration of souls.
Men's souls, they say, after severance from the flesh, migrate,
not into some other world, but into the bodies of other men;
and they are convinced that the migration takes place into the
other body when the latter is between the ages of six and fifteen,
that being the age at which the child is being imbued with the
Living Book.

The tradition of adoration, prayer and praise is thus conceived of as a spirit perpetually realizing itself or reborn in
successive generations of the young. This is a more subtle doctrine of transmigration than that of the Cathars of the middle
ages. One asks oneself, however, whether the Dukhobortsy,
having inherited that teaching did not volatilize it in this manner. The Cathars also refused to distinguish between this
and the next life, and taught that Heaven and Hell are within
us here and now, so that we have not to wait for them.

In the Confession, for example, of a Cathar of Aix (Ax),
named Arnald Cicred charged with heresy in October 1321
(given in the *Dokumente der Valdesier und Katharer* of Ignatius
Döllinger, München 1890, p. 152), we read that "the heretic on
being asked whether the souls of bad men did not after death
drop into hell, answered that there was no hell apart from this
visible world, in which the said spirits by way of doing penance
migrate from body to body and from tunic to tunic. And, he
added, the world will not end until all the spirits created by
their Father have been incorporated in the bodies of men and
women of their own (i.e. Cathar) faith, in which they will be
saved and return to the Heavenly Father."

In the *Confessio Johannis Maurini* of Mte. Alio in the same
collection (p. 188) we have a summary of the tenets of a famous
Cathar leader, Guilielmus Belibasta. He taught that "true
rebirth consists not in the baptism of the heretics, but in that
of his own sect. He held that a man's soul on quitting one
body, enters another, and so passes from body to body until it
reaches one in which it is converted to the sect and in that
manner saved. The world will never end until all the erring
souls are gathered up again and converted to Catharism.
That done the world will come to an end, and after that sun

and moon and light will not go on any more." Such was the teaching of Belibasta.

The parallelism between these passages — which could be multiplied — and the tenets of the Dukhobortsy is striking, and cannot be accidental; especially if we take account of other features which they shared with the Cathars, e.g., the honour in which those are held who eschew matrimony; the rejection of baptism and the eucharist, of the sign of the cross, of relics; the conviction that the faithful are so many Christs or incarnations of Christ, by reason of which they ceremonially bow one to another when they meet to worship; their zeal not to slay even an animal; their exaltation of the Holy Spirit above Scripture, perhaps akin to the Marcionite and Cathar rejection of the O. T. Read, for instance, in the same collection of Döllinger's the following from the Acts of the inquisition of Carcassone into the Albigois, (p. 4):

Item nullo modo occidunt aliquod animal nec volatile, quia dicunt et credunt quod in animalibus brutis et in avibus sunt spiritus illi, qui recedunt de corporibus hominum, quando non sunt recepti ad sectam nec ordinem suum et quod transeunt de uno corpore in aliud corpus. Item non tangunt aliquam mulierem . . . Item docent credentes quod exhibeant eis reverentiam, quam vocant melioramentum, nos autem vocamus adorationem, flectendo genua et inclinando se profunde coram ipsis super aliquam bancam et usque ad terram, junctis manibus, tribus vicibus inclinando et surgendo et dicendo qualibet vice: benedicite, et in fine concludendo: boni Christiani benedictionem Dei et vestram, orate Deum pro nobis, etc.

In addition to these ideas and practices among the Cathars, we also meet with the same argument against the Eucharist which the Molokanye use, as we shall see below.

Item quod (hostia) mittitur in latrinam ventris et per turpissimum locum, quae non possent fieri, si esset ibi Deus.

To meet this objection, as is well known, the Church holds that the consecrated morsel ceases to be the body of God as soon as it passes the gullet.

Von Haxthausen in 'The Russian Empire' (English translation, London, 1856, i, 289) has left us an interesting account of the doctrine of Kapustin:— "The most interesting man of this sect of whom we have any knowledge is J. Kapustin. I heard much respecting him from the Mennonites (German) on the Molotchnaya, his nearest neighbours. Complete obscurity veils his birth, name and early life: when he began to disseminate his views among the Molokanye, it caused a schism in their body; and as about that time the majority of the Dukhobortsy in the Government of Tambov emigrated to the Molotchnaya Vody (Milky Waters), in the Government of Taurida, he and his followers accompanied them and settled there."

Of his teaching he writes: "He attached peculiar importance to the doctrine of the transmigration of souls, which was already known among them: he also taught that Christ is born again in every believer; that God is in everyone; for when the Word became flesh, it became this for all time, like everything divine, that is, man in the world; but each human soul, at least as long as the created world exists, remains a distinct individual. Now when God descended into the individuality of Jesus as Christ, He sought out the purest and most perfect man that ever existed, and so the soul of Jesus became the purest and most perfect of all human souls. God, since the time when he first revealed himself in Jesus, has always remained in the Human Race, and dwells and reveals himself in every believer. But the individual soul of Jesus, where has it been? By virtue of the law of the Transmigration of souls, it must necessarily have animated another human body! Jesus himself said, 'I am with you always even to the end of the world.' Thus the soul of Jesus, favoured above all human souls by God, had from generation to generation continually animated new bodies; and by virtue of its higher qualities, and the peculiar and absolute command of God, it had invariably retained a remembrance of its previous condition. Every man, therefore, in whom it resided knew that the soul of Jesus was in him. In the first Centuries after Christ this was so universally acknowledged among believers that everyone recognized the new Jesus, who was the guide and ruler of Christendom and decided all disputes respecting the faith. The Jesus thus always reborn again was called a Pope. False popes however soon obtained possession of the throne of Jesus; but the true Jesus had only retained a small band of believers about him, as he predicted in the N. T. 'Many are called but few chosen.' These believers are the Dukhobortsy, among whom Jesus constantly dwells, his soul animating one of them. 'Thus Sylvan Kolesnikov at Nikolsk,' said Kapustin, 'whom many of the older among you knew, was Jesus; but now as truly as heaven is above me, and the earth under my feet, I am the true Jesus Christ your Lord! Fall down therefore on your knees and worship me!' And they all fell on their knees and worshipped him." These later leaders of the sect seem to have appropriated to themselves a doctrine of the Christhood of the believer which at an earlier time envisaged all the faithful, or as the Cathars put it, all the elect ones alike. It is to be regretted that Haxthausen never published the fuller account of the Dissidents of Russia which he promised in this work. He states that he had collected much material, and where he came into almost personal contact with sects, as in the case of the Dukhobortsy, he would have been reliable. Where he had not such an opportunity of arriving at the truth, his narrative is fantastic, as in regard to the self-immolators.

Another link between these two sects is the rejection of oaths. Moreover the Molokanye, like the Cathars, deny that Jesus was of real flesh and blood, and the Dukhobortsy come near to doing the same. The conclusion imposes itself upon us that Pobirokhin, Kapustin, Kolesnikov and the other heresiarchs, who suddenly appeared in the South of Russia between 1750 and 1800 represented a genuine Cathar tradition, probably that which in the middle ages in Bulgaria and among the Balkan Slavs was known as Bogomilism.

The Dukhobor doctrine of the soul, of its fall and redemption, resurrection and future life, as summarized by Ivanovski, wears an equally Cathar complexion: "The human soul is the image of God, a heavenly likeness. The Divine image consists of memory, reason and will, i.e., of the very same elements of which the Trinity consists. In a word man is the Trinity and the Trinity is man. The soul already existed before the creation of this visible world; then it was it fell. But it fell in spiritual wise, and because of its fall it was driven out into the visible world, as into a prison, by way of punishment." "Our bodies are cages restraining and confining our souls" writes N. In Adam's story we only have an allegory of the fall. His sin does not pass to his descendants, but each man has sinned for himself. In point of fact the fall is going on now and here, whenever man seeks not God's glory, but his own. The sin of Adam, being only a manifestation of a past fall of the soul, is not handed down to posterity; each of us sins or is saved by himself.' There is no original sin."

In such teaching Ivanovski detects what he terms the characteristic dualism of the Khlysty; but in fact the Dukhobors are no more dualist than other Christians, and we may fairly connect them with the so-called Monarchian Bogomilism, which also was not dualist, and which was known in medieval Italy as the heresy of the Concorregio and Bagnolo. In any case the teachings ascribed by Ivanovski to the Dukhobortsy equally characterized the Cathars. Thus in Döllinger's collection, p. 88, we have ascribed to the latter the belief that "Adam and Eve were fashioned by God and placed in paradise to keep his commandments, but because of their transgression they were clad in bodies of clay and given over to death." And in general the Cathars, whether they regarded the Evil principle as coeternal with the Good or Heavenly one or no,— whether, that is, they were dualists or monarchists — agreed in this, that human souls, created by God, enjoyed a pristine glory in heaven, that they lost it by an act of rebellion or by succumbing to the temptations of the Evil One, and were by way of punishment confined in tunics of flesh within the limits of the visible world. That glory, they held, can only be recovered by the gift of the Holy Spirit, a sacrament peculiar to the Cathar Church and not shared by that diabolical counterfeit of Antichrist, the so-called Catholic Church, which had centuries before denied and apostatized from the true Christ.

Like the Molokanye, "the Dukhobortsy, on the strength of the text: 'He made us kings and priests,' (Rev. 16) regard each believer as a priest. To become a priest of the invisible Church a man's own spontaneous act is not enough, nor even the assent of his fellows. Still less need he be of any special calling or class; no outward preparation of himself, no intellectual education, is indispensable. The true priest is he who receives a call from above, he whom Jesus himself elects; and he may be drawn from the ranks of the common people, may be one of the priests of the external Church, or even one of the rulers of the world. Christ, the unseen agent, prepares him by immediate direct illumination of his mind and heart. Accordingly, the call, the election, nay the very preparation for and to priesthood must needs be not external, but internal grace, within us and not without." So writes Novitski, and adds this: "Jesus Christ alone, the inner agent, is our true High priest and Sanctifier, and therefore we need no outward clergy; in whomsoever Christ himself works, he is his successor, and of himself he becomes a priest."

As, moreover, the children of God are bound to worship him in spirit and in truth, there is no call for external divine service, and external sacraments produce no real effect upon men. We have to understand and accept spirituality. Rites, whatever their significance are not only superfluous, but often pernicious so far forth as they are only dead tokens of the inward; too often they bar our approach to God. "Ikons," says A. F., "are idols; Christian saints we may revere for their virtues, but we must not pray to them. Facts should consist in avoidance of appetites and abstinence from excess."

Their conception of God, says P. S. 1859, as a being not self-subsistent nor enjoying individual and independent existence, but as continuing to be and residing conjointly and inseparably in and with the race of the Elect, in such wise that without that race He cannot reveal himself nor be glorified,— this conception is instilled into us out of an infinite condescension, so we may call it, towards human personality. A. F. reports them as saying: "There is a God, He is spirit. He is in us, *we are God.*" And they explain (says P. S., 1859) their bowings of one to another in their meetings by saying that "they are bowing to the inestimably precious living image of God, to man."

We need not stay to inquire how far the Dukhobortsy conception of God avoids the difficulties of nominalism and realism, and steers clear of the fallacy of an universal divorced from particulars, the *caput mortuum* of theological abstraction. We can only praise them for the morally wholesome concreteness of their thinking. In religion it is a first step to a better life to realize that God is or can be immanent in us as in Jesus. These Russian sectaries take humanity seriously, and really endeavour "to adjust their social relations to their fundamental conception, to the truth that lies at the bottom of all Christian theology, even if few theologians know it,— the truth that man is a living image of God. They, more than most, recognize its implication that all men are equal; they therefore ignore outward distinctions of man from man and hold that by nature all are alike and equal, for all have fallen and all alike are exposed to temptation. It follows that in the eye of a true bondsman of the Lord there are no servants in all the world; the Christian is servant in all and of all, in the sense in which Jesus Christ was. We enjoy their help, but in such cases he that assists us is not our servant but our brother and equal" (N.). Among the Dukhobortsy, says the same writer, "children, instead of calling their parents father and mother, give them the titles of elders; and parents do not speak of their children as *mine*, but as *ours*. The women term their husbands brothers, and men call their wives sisters." "Imagine" (writes a tourist in the *Obzor* (1878, No. 237), who had visited the sect not long before) "an old man of eighty and a boy of ten calling one another by diminutives or pet names, like *Stepa*, *Victorushka*, *Lusha*, *Dasha*, etc. Father, mother, wife, husband, brother, sister, children, all these call one another, as we should say by their Christian names. Only the tiny children call their mother *nanny*. At first you have no idea of the degrees of kinship in which the members of families stand to each other; for, as far as names go, and for a stranger, it is all the same. When they meet they all salute one another with exactly the same degree of deference and respect, whether young or old, males or females. In virtue of this equality, whatever is allowed to the men is allowed to their women. On holidays, or better, in their leisure time, they have just as much right to drink or smoke as their husbands and brothers. "The freedom which characterizes the relations of husband and wife as compared with the people who live around them is occasionally carried to excess," says F., "and husbands have been known to quit their wives and consort with other women without the former shewing any jealousy and without discredit attaching to the circumstance." But this is the exception, not the rule.

"In their dealings with strangers," says N., "the Dukhobortsy are courteous, though they do not bare their heads, unless out of exceptional respect for someone or because they cannot help it. In their society they recognize no superiors governing and disposing thereof; their society is administered by each and all."

By the same ideal of profound respect for the individual and by consequence of entire equality for all they would like also to regulate their attitude towards society at large and towards the Government; but they realize how dangerous it might be if they shouted such principles abroad, and therefore they shew some hesitancy and circumspection in the matter. Whenever, says Haxthausen, in his *Studies of the Russian Empire*, (p. 279), conversation began to touch upon the lofty but dangerous teachings of their sect, they began to talk ambiguously and accumulate on my ears such high-flown and fantastic expressions as would have done credit to a sworn sophist well equipped with dialectical arts.

Notwithstanding their reserve however, their sociological views are more or less certain. Thus "they attribute royal dignity to God alone," says D. And N. writes thus: "Silvanus Kolesnikov taught that we ought to submit to authorities and lords of this world, not only to those who are good and gentle, but to the perverse,— obey all in fact, even in evil courses, under durance vile. But his adherents at Ekaterinoslav held a somewhat different language. Human societies, they said, are full of evil people, moved by faction and malignant passions. A community of bad men could not stand, for they would exterminate one another; for this reason the wise ones have set up among themselves distinct authorities to curb the forces of disorder. So far authorities are beneficent and ordained by God himself on earth for the good of the children of the world.

But the Lord said: "I am not of the world and mine are not of
it either"; and worldly authorities are not needed for them that
are not of the world.   The children of God (the Dukhobortsy)
themselves shun evil not from fear, but in order to be regener-
ate.   They try to live as Jesus Christ preached we should do.
He freed us as touching our wills from all human laws.   He has
given us his Holy Spirit and created in us a new heart, leaving
us free to comply with all royal demands according to the
spirit and perform acts pleasing to God in the spirit without
any constraint."

"The Dukhobortsy of Tambov claimed to distinguish
between good and bad authorities and to differentiate their
origins.   Kind and good rulers, they maintain, are from God,
the harsh and unkindly ones we know not whence.   Those of
Melitopol do not discuss the origins, but roundly assert that
there ought to be no authorities on earth.   You may have,
they argue, a sovereign set over reprobates, thieves and
brigands, in order to repress them, but not over good people.
Consequently, although they refrain from rebellion, they
make no wholehearted submission to established authorities.
If they submit to them, they do so in semblance only; while
inwardly and among themselves they regard all subordination,
and in particular the government of a monarch, as contrary to
their ideal.   Even judicial courts are needless for sons of God.
What, they ask, does he want with law courts who never in all
his life dreamed of injuring another?   If a man strike you on
one cheek, resist him not, but turn the other to him, and if a
man would rob you of cloak, withhold not your coat also.
They would observe the same pacific spirit even towards public enemies, for they look on war as unlawful, and appeal to the
Gospel precept to love your enemy (Mat. 5, 38–9).   Oaths
equally are forbidden among them, and they refuse to take
them under any circumstances.   Regarding war as wrong and
forbidden, they make it a rule not to carry weapons.   For the
rest, if they do not pray for enemies, because each must pray
for himself, neither do they for their friends; that is one reason
why they pray neither for the Tsar nor for the authorities which
be."

At the present time, remarks Uzov writing in 1880, they behave meekly and comply with all demands of Government; though they still refuse to bear arms or make oath. As early as 1817, so we learn from the collected regulations regarding the Raskol (p. 75, bk. 3), a committee of ministers made a rule to take members of the sect as recruits, but without forcing the oath of allegiance on them; it was resolved to send them into a special corps stationed in Grusia (Georgia). Later on, January 8, 1820, the Government[1] decided on the one hand not to acquit members of the sect from any state obligations, on the other not to force oaths upon them. This statute also applied to the Molokanye, and as both these allied sects obstinately refused to bear arms, it was further decided, according to L. P. to allocate recruits from among them to sanitary work, hospitals and transport. But according to the same informant the fanaticism of the Dukhobortsy was such that in the first Turkish War those who were enrolled from Wologda threw away their arms near Perekop. It is evident therefore that the Russian Government did not adhere to its own statues.

In N. we meet with several examples of their obstinate but passive resistance to Governmental tyranny; and as early as Catharine II are reported several cases of the kind; also under Paul I in 1799 they came into collision with the Civil Powers. In Little Russia on that occasion they were accused of proclaiming that such Powers are not wanted. On August 28 of that year, in consequence, it was resolved that all persons convicted of the heresy should be banished for good to the mines of Ekaterinburg. They were to be kept in chains and put to heavy labour, "to the end that, since they reject the authorities instituted on earth by divine sanction, they may be made to feel and realize that there exist on earth Powers instituted by God with a view to the firm defence of welldoers and withal to the intimidation and punishment of evildoers like themselves." The 'conscientious objectors' who actually suffered under this edict were comparatively few, and so harsh a sentence, continues the Russian writer of nearly a hundred years ago, did not daunt their fellow heretics, and the next

---

[1] *Russian Mir*, of Nov. 5, 1876, art. on *Raskolniks in the Army*.

year, 1800, the Governor of Novgorod made a fresh discovery
in the village of Chude of men who repudiated the Church and
refused to recognize either Emperor or authorities set up by
him. In the Government of Astrakhan in 1802 whole crowds
of Dukhobortsy invaded the market-places and openly began to
disseminate their heresy; when hailed before the local tribunals they refused not only to give up their errors, but even to
submit to or recognize the authorities. Very much the same
scenes occurred in Siberia in 1807. N. remarks that, in all
probability, it was only want of opportunity and means that
prevented the Dukhobortsy from re-enacting the horrible
mutinies and bloody disputes which characterized the rising
of the similar sect of Anabaptists in Westphalia; but, as Uzov
remarks, the subsequent fortunes of the sect are far from justi-
fying this surmise. Shchapov in the *Dyelo* (1867, No. 10)
shews that in his time they were much less intent on quarrelling
with the authorities than on works of social reform and recon-
struction and on creating a type of community at once just and
sensible. Their superior morale marked them out among the
surrounding population as ears of corn among tares. They
were equally distinguished by their comfortable circumstances — this being due to the aid they rendered to each other
in misfortune. In their teaching and conduct brotherly love
was inculcated above all other virtues, and charity and socia-
bility characterized their mutual relations. They were as N.
attests, sober, hardworking and hospitable; their homes and
dress were ever clean and neat, and they gave themselves up
entirely to the cultivation of their fields and the tending of their
flocks. The only punishment known among them, says
Shchapov, was exclusion from the Society and it was reserved
for open and notorious offenders.

They excel the populations round them, he says, no less in
physical health than in morality; their women are known for
their superior stature and robust constitutions, and according
to F. excel in intelligence and beauty. This fact, remarks
Uzov, can only surprise observers who take account of what
they have suffered for their opinions; for no sooner are they
settled in one district than they are chased out of it into

another, into strange horizons where, broken and ruined by enforced migration, they have to adapt themselves to new conditions of the nature around them.

In the Caucasian settlements, whither Nicholàs I relegated them in 1841, they are environed by Armenians, Georgians, Persians and other tribes. Here, says N., they cannot fulfil what they deem to be their duty, the dissemination, namely of their doctrine. Children of God as they are assured they are, they have received God's behest to teach one another. Servants of the Lord, they strive ever and punctually to discharge their debt to the poor and to give away to others, their talents, all that they themselves received from on high, to each according to his several ability (Mt. 25, 15). But under the conditions, says Uzov, which prevailed in his day, they found it difficult to harmonize their efforts to build up their communities with the sacred duty of propaganda.

But we must not suppose that the Dukhobortsy, because they regard themselves as children of God are wanting in the large charity which admits the salvation of those outside their fold. There is no narrow sectarianism about them, as Ivanovski himself attests when he writes as follows: "Their Church is the gathering together of those whom God himself separates from the people of the world. These elect ones are not distinguished by any special symbols, not united in any special community, with distinct doctrine and divine service. They are scattered all over the world and belong to all confessions, not only to the Christian, but also to the Jewish, whose adherents do not recognize Christ."

In the spirit of a sectary he adds: "In the presence of such indifferentism it is difficult to believe they even constitute a religious sect; while admitting in a large sense the elect of all sorts of faiths into the number of the members of an invisible Church everywhere diffused, in a narrower sense they understand by the word Church themselves in particular." And yet he proceeds to set before us their ideal of a Church. "We are the living temples of God, the altars, the throne of God. In us the Holy Trinity is made flesh; the Dukhobor is at once priest and sacrificer and sacrifice. The heart is altar, the will is offering, the priest is the soul."

It is now a hundred years ago, that in 1819, the English Society of Friends sent a mission to Russia to acquaint themselves with a society so akin to their own; its members were shocked at the Dukhobor admission that they looked upon Jesus in no other light than that of a good man, and therefore had no confidence in him as a Saviour from sin. These good Quakers expected to find ordinary evangelical orthodoxy, but did not. Long afterwards the Friends, in 1895, rendered them all the help they could in the persecutions which waxed ever crueller. A good and clear account of this *via dolorosa* which ended in the removal of several thousands of them to Canada by the kind offices of the Quakers, can be read in Vladimir Tchertkoff's tract, *Christian Martyrdom in Russia*, London, 1897, in Aylmer Maude's *A peculiar People*, New York, 1904, and in many other English publications. For the details of these persecutions at the hands of the late Russian Government I refer my readers to these sources. Their later history, especially in Canada, is adequately related by Mr. Maude, to whom I owe many of my citations of N. I have been concerned mainly to recount the early history and tenets of so remarkable a spiritual movement, perhaps more expressive of the true soul of the Russian peasant than any other, with the exception of Molokanism.

CHAPTER II

THE MOLOKANYE

The Evidence of their Confession of Faith

In Geneva in 1865 was printed in Russian a manual of this Sect called 'The Confession of Faith of the spiritual Christians called Molokanye.' It is an account of the Sect by its own members, and having been written in 1862 deserves to be summarized.

"Before we begin to set forth our confession of faith, we have wished to refute certain false impressions that exist about us and to clear ourselves of the baseless calumnies circulated against us, chiefly by the Greco-Russian clergy."

"They tax us with being innovators, with having invented some sort of new confession, and they even call us renegades from Christianity."

"In justification of ourselves we answer that even if our faith were a novelty, that can be no sufficient cause of reprehension; for the excellence of a faith is measured not by its antiquity, but by its truth. Christ's own teaching was not revealed prior to all other creeds; it is new by comparison, for example, with Chinese, Indian, Greek and many others, and yet no one hesitates to give it a preference over these, and the preference is assigned not on the score of its antiquity, but because it is true teaching."

"If anyone is to be accused of arbitrary innovations, it is not us, but the Greco-Russian Church, since it has introduced many alterations in Christ's teaching, whereas we strictly observe holy writ; and when we abandoned that communion, far from creating any new faith whatever for ourselves, we reverted to the pure Christian doctrine, far older than that of the said Church and — what is capital — truer, for it was from God and consequently comprised in itself all truth."

"As regards our being renegades from the teaching of that Church, or what is the same thing, as regards the revival in

Russia of true Christian worship, we have preserved among us the following tradition. During the reign of Tsar Ivan Vasilevich the Terrible, a certain English physician was called to the court of Moscow; they regarded him in the capital, such was the temper of the age and the savagery of the people, as Antichrist, proclaiming him accursed and barring him out of their houses and homes. Of his family there remains no trace in tradition, but by some chance he had formed an acquaintance with a well known proprietor of Tambov who was then at court. Enjoying his hospitality, and also finding him to be a lover of holy Scripture, he conversed much with him about the Bible, which was at that time in Russia a book forbidden to anyone who was not a member of the higher clergy. This proprietor had a favourite servant, a man of intelligence and reflection, a certain Matthew Semenov, who grasped Biblical truth more quickly than his master, and therefore without delay conceived a contempt for the rites of the Greco-Russian Church and for prostrations to ikons; having procured a Slav Bible, he began to instil into his neighbours the unadultered truth about the worship of God in spirit and in truth. Now in those times it was very dangerous, nay almost wholly impossible not only to utter, but even to conceive anything in opposition of the Church. Consequently Matthew's abandonment of it was no sooner noticed, in particular his refusal to prostrate himself to ikons, than he was denounced to the ecclesiastical authorities, and the unfortunate, but true worshipper of God was sentenced to death and broken on the wheel."

"Some of the martyr's disciples, peasants of the aforesaid proprietor, on their arrival at their birthplace in the Government of Tambov, began with the help of the Bible they had brought with them quietly to propagate the worship of God in spirit and in truth. A considerable number of people followed their teaching in different villages; but the teachers themselves,— such was the rigour and unbridled power of the clergy in those days — were quickly discovered, handed over to the tribunals and cruelly knouted by the hangmen, after which they were sent for ever to prison with hard labour."

"Their followers did not cease in secret to propagate their

teaching; but the common people, failing to comprehend the truth and sometimes surprising them when they were bowing during their religious services to persons in their chambers, took it into their heads that they were bowing to chinks, and so nicknamed them the Chinkers. The clergy went to work more intelligently, and observing that during Lent, they always partook of milk which is then forbidden, nicknamed them *Molokanye* (from *moloko* — milk)."

"The teaching was spread from the Tambov Government by Semen Uklein to the Voronezh Government, to the Mikhailovsky Cossack settlement on the Don and to the Saratov Government, for which cause the adherents of the doctrine were in these localities for a long time known as Semenovtsy; by Isaiah Ivanov Krylov to the line of the Caucasus and across the Volga; by Peter Dementev to the Governments of Nizhegorod and Vladimir; by Moses the Dalmatian to that of Ryazan. Many of their successors in these places were delated by the clergy and haled before the courts, many of them punished and exiled either to Siberia or the Caucasus or the Tauric Chersonese. By these martyrs for the truth, the true Christian doctrine was diffused in those regions."

"Meanwhile some of its adherents conceived it to be superfluous to read the Bible and determine Faith by what is written in it; they separated off from the Spiritual Christians or Molokanye, and formed a separate sect, who were known as Dukhobortsy. Others considered it best to fulfil the Mosaic law alone, and they do not read the New Testament, and feast, not Sunday, but the Sabbath, for which reason they were called Sabbatarians."

Here we pause, to ask what is the value of the account here given by the Molokanye of their origin, and in particular of their statement that a Matthew Semenov, servant of a proprietor of Tambov, first sowed the seed from which they are sprung in the reign of Ivan the Terrible. As we note below (p. 305) the historian Kostomarov identifies him with a Matthew Semenovitch Bashkin who in 1553–4 was tried and condemned by a council of bishops in Moscow for heresy. Nicholas Kostomarov, however, in his *Historical Monographs*, Petersburg, 1863,

p. 454, casts legitimate doubts on his heresy. He relates the
trial from contemporary documents and shows that there was
nothing to incriminate Bashkin save his own confession extorted
by fear and agony of the rack. He was accused of denying the
Church and its sacraments, because he taught that the Church
is the union of the Faithful and not a mere building of brick
and stone. But this is an orthodox opinion, though so often
put forward by Armenian Dissenters (See *Key of Truth*,
Introduction p. clxiv) and by European Cathars. He was
accused of slighting the Son and the Holy Spirit, because in
prison he wrote a prayer addressed to our Father in Heaven.
The same heresy attaches to the Lord's prayer. Also of denying the Sacrament of penance, and yet what led to his trial was
the circumstance that he went to confess to a priest and dis-
closed to him that he took the Sermon on the Mount as his rule
of life, had therefore emancipated his serfs, and held that other
slave owners ought to do the same.

It was no doubt such opinions as these that got him into
trouble, and they may have survived him. The Molokan
statement that the Church withheld the Scriptures from the
people and that Bashkin put them into their hands needs quali-
fication. Copies even of the New Testament were in Russia
rare in that epoch and to be had in manuscript only. It
reminds one of the similar accusation, equally vain, brought by
Lutherans and Protestants against the Latin Church.

In the rest of their manifesto the Molokanye point out that in
their preaching they rely solely on the Bible, wherefore their
tenets are not vain imaginings and dreams, nor rightly esteemed
pernicious by the Government, whose action they attribute to
the ill will of the clergy which spares no calumnies in order to
blacken them and make out that they are enemies of public
order and tranquillity. They are specially accused of not
respecting the Tsar and the powers which be, of concealing
fugitives and of manufacturing false passports and money.

As to the last accusation they do not deny that in their ranks
may be found swindlers and wrongdoers, but they point out
that they are also met with in other confessions in as large a
proportion. But their religion, far from encouraging such

forms of villainy, is based on Christ's teaching which condemns all sorts of lying and deceit. They admit furthermore that in the past when their brethren were exposed to persecution for their steadfastness in the true faith, they concealed their martyrs and put them out of danger; but they never hid criminals and rogues, nor do so now. On the contrary they follow the Apostle's precept (Peter ii, 13–14) and obey the Powers which be. In matters of faith, however, they submit to the Lord God alone. In particular they revere Alexander II as an inspired monarch, sent from God to heal old wounds inflicted formerly on the confessors of their faith and later on themselves. The accession of this Tsar, they say, inaugurated a new era for themselves and for all Russia. War was stopped, and the peasants were emancipated from the yoke of a sinful serfdom which contradicted the will of God who created all men in his image and likeness, equals and brethren. Their own families had been liberated from recruiting and formed into a guild with provisional laws; their wives and children were legitimized, where before they were held illegitimate; by the laws of 1858 they were freed from all interference on the part of the Greco-Russian popes with their religion; finally by the circular addressed to functionaries in 1861 they were no longer prevented from sending their children to any schools they liked. The while they hail these reforms with gratitude, they yet complain that the Law subjects them to certain disabilities not inflicted on other subjects of the Tsar, and they gave the following instances.

In common with all who do not belong to the orthodox Church, they are subject to a statute of 1857, No. 82, to the effect that all Judaizing sects, Skoptsy, Molokanye, Dukhobortsy and members also of the priestless Raskol, who neither pray for the Tsar nor accept marriage, and are therefore to be reckoned peculiarly noxious, are forbidden to receive into their families under any pretext whatever persons of the orthodox persuasion.

By Statute 83 they are forbidden on any pretext whatever to have in their houses, fabrics or institutions orthodox persons as servants or workmen; nor are Molokanye in their turn to

enter theirs.   The police are charged to see to the carrying out
of this law and for violation of it to inflict the penalties laid
down in Statute 307, *Ulozhenie*.   A note or gloss on this
Statute 83 excepts orthodox persons, original inhabitants of the
Trans-Caucasus, from its operation, and it is only Molokanye
who are forbidden to receive the orthodox Russian inhabitants,
to live with them or be their servants.   By Statute 84 local
authorities, so far as possible, are to prevent Judaisers from
holding intercourse with the orthodox, and to that end are to
refuse to any infected with the heresy passports allowing them
to remove to other districts.   This restriction applies equally
to Skoptsy.

In the circular of the Minister of the Interior of January 25,
1836, officials were warned not to grant passports to Molokanye lest they should change their places of residence; and in
another of January 23, 1839, it was stated that "inasmuch as
certain Molokanye and Dukhobortsy of the Tauric Government
possessed lands, the Governor of Novorossiisk and the General
Governor of Bessarabia sought advice on the point whether
members of these sects could own land acquired by purchase
or otherwise.   The matter was referred to the Emperor who
gave instructions: (1) that by a regulation issued January 17,
1836, it was laid down that Molokanye were not to have orthodox persons in their houses, etc., nor to be given passports;
(2) that, since passports are necessary for removal to any
distance exceeding 30 versts (a verst = a kilometer), in order to
impede the diffusion of noxious heresy, the adherents of these
two sects shall not be left in possession of lands situated more
than 30 versts from their residences, nor of any that lie in more
than one circumscription or Uyezd.   Accordingly on February
17, 1839, officials of Governments in which these sectaries live
were secretly instructed to adopt the above rule as their guide
in future, but those already owning lands beyond the prescribed radius were to be left in possession."

In addition to the above the Molokanye complain that they
are not allowed to get members of other confessions to undertake military service as substitutes for themselves and so buy
themselves out.

Such disabilities, they complain, prejudice them in their professions and trades, and deprive them of opportunity to earn an honest livelihood; they serve no useful purpose and do enormous harm to the Government by depriving it of the support it should find in truth and justice and in equality of all and each. Deprived of such support all its strength amounts merely to a show of force, and by this very fact it becomes a complete moral failure.

In conclusion they express their conviction that the Emperor Alexander II is unaware of the disabilities here above enumerated; for a sovereign so entirely reasonable and devoted to truth and justice, as his solicitude for the distribution of the Bible as a 'table' book and for its translation into Russian evidences him to be, would, they feel assured, remedy them the moment they were brought to his notice. They particularly express their approval of the new translation of the Bible into modern Russian, in which the Pentateuch was already completed.

This introduction is followed by an *exposé* of Molokan doctrine as it stood in 1862 entitled *The True Christian Teaching or a Confession of Faith of the Spiritual Christians*, presented in the form of a commentary on the Ten Commandments. It begins with a prayer: "Instruct us, Thou who knowest all, in our labour, to the end that we may in no wise tarnish before men the eternal brightness of thy name. Help us, Almighty, to teach the ignorant thy holy truth, that they may recognize thy love and worship thee in spirit and in truth."

The commentary on the first commandment sets forth the Divine attributes of Spirit, Truth, Freedom, Beauty, Goodness, Love, Power, Life, etc. as revealed in all that is without or within us, and especially in the human soul and in the Bible.

They then reject the traditional Trinitarian doctrine and argue that the text Mt. xxviii, 19, is wrongly interpreted by the Greco-Russian Church: "*Father, Son and Holy Spirit* are no more than titles of God which mark the different angles or aspects from or under which we contemplate him, without losing sight of his unity as Creator of ourselves and of the earth, as Life and Spirit of the universe, as the True Spirit by which he reveals himself to us." The relationship of God to his creatures is exhibited in language which might be that of any educated Anglican or Roman divine, and a section follows directed against anthropolatry or the cult of saints and arguing that Christ's own disciples, e.g., St. Paul and Barnabas at Lystra, refused to be worshipped.

There follows a less commonplace section against baptism with water. The true baptism consists of instruction in the word of God. Baptism, whether by immersion or aspersion, is a fond thing vainly imagined in opposition to Christ's own promise that, whereas John only baptized with water, his own faithful should after not many days be baptized with the Holy Spirit (Acts i, 5), a promise fulfilled at Pentecost. They also appeal to Lk. iii, 16: 'He shall baptize you in the Spirit,' and in Fire, and conclude that water baptism was only valid before Christ's advent; that it was not an apostolic practice they argue from Paul's declaration that Christ sent him not to baptize, and that in baptism we share his death. The passage Rom. vi. 3–13 refers, not to baptism of the flesh but of the spirit. In John iii, 5 the words *born of water* were not intended literally and in Mt. xxviii, 19 the instruction to baptize etc., is epexegetic of the phrase 'make disciples of all nations.'

In this repudiation of water baptism the Molokanye agree with the Dukhobortsy, and, like them, exhibit the ancient tradition of Cathar and Marcionite Christianity.

Under the rubric of the second commandment the worship of ikons is condemned. The contention of the Orthodox that the faithful bows not to the ikon but to the saint depicted therein, is met with the reply that God alone should be worshipped and that he cannot be represented in any picture. They argue that the faithful really worship the particular ikon. Else, why carry it about from church to church? Why ascribe miracles to it? Why burn lamps before it? Why, if it be the saint that is adored and not the wood, pretend that one image fell from heaven and was not made with hands, whereas another not? Why as a rule prefer the smoky greasy boards whereon nothing is decipherable to those on which the saint's image is new and fresh? Does not the most popular image of the Virgin

depict her with three hands? Has not each village and city
its special idol? Was anyone ever deterred from sin by such
idol worship? Do not those who prostrate themselves before
them know that an idol cannot punish them for their iniquities?
They know not the true God who can, and worship a wooden
one who does inspire no fear. As for ikon's 'not made with
hands,' is God a man, first to forbid us to worship images and
then set to manufacturing them for our cult? Relics are
equally condemned. Old bones are no substitute as an object
of worship for Spirit. A man's spirit, not his flesh and bones,
is the image and likeness of God. No doubt that is the reason
why the Molokanye in worship bow to those among themselves
who are filled with the Spirit and are literally Christs. In
doing so they again adhere to the custom of the Cathars. To
this practice however there is no reference in this tract save in
the Introduction, wherein it is said that the vulgar, not understanding the reason, nicknamed them *Chinkers*.

Interpreting the third commandment they forbid oaths;
and they inculcate observance of the fourth, insisting however that in Christendom the holiness of the Sabbath has been
transferred to the Lord's Day. Following Mt. xii 1–13, they
insist on the necessity of good works on the Sabbath, that is on
Sunday, and regret the license, frivolities and drunkenness with
which the Orthodox violate the day. They admit as worthy
to be observed in addition to the Sunday the Dominical feasts
of Annunciation, Nativity, Purification, Baptism, Transfiguration, Resurrection, Ascension, and Descent of the Holy Spirit.
Other festivals they ignore, as being days consecrated to trivial
events of no special holiness. Good Friday they observe as a
Fast, eating nothing that day and only praying on it. They
hold a Fast day to be not one on which you stuff your belly
with fish and fungi, but one of complete abstention from food
of all kinds; the distinction between one diet and another was
only made by the Orthodox. All food was given by God and
one food is as good as another. In any case fasts in themselves
are valueless unless they are observed as an aid to the formation
of good character and to holiness of life.

In connection with the fifth commandment the duty of chil-

dren to their parents is illustrated from many passages in the
Bible, and it is also urged that parents in their turn owe it to
their children to win their loving obedience and respect by
their solicitude and self-denial in behalf of them.

The reason of the sixth commandment is declared to be
that man is the image and likeness of God, wherefore murder is
a violation and diminution of the divine glory. Only God has a
right to kill. Men are all brethren in Christ and the brand of
Cain is on the brow of him that slays his brother. The Molokan acceptance of the Old Testament necessitates a somewhat
tortuous interpretation of the Hebrew God's instructions to
his people to slay unoffending Amalekites and others whose
lands they coveted. But the expositor is quite sure that no
man has a right to say to his fellow: ' You must die, you deserve
death.' Nor can murder be justified by the plea: 'I slew him
to save my own life and property,' for Jesus forbade his disciples
to protect him by force of arms; still less is murder justifiable
on the ground that the murdered man was a foreigner or an
infidel. Even if it can be urged that Jehovah permitted the
Jews to slay their enemies, Jesus Christ anyhow bade us love
our enemies.

The Molokanye have ever been classed a dangerous sect by
the Russian Government, and that is perhaps the reason why
in their manifesto the Molokanye append to their commentary
on the seventh commandment a special disquisition upon marriage. It was ordained by God in the Garden, and it is an
union not of body with body so much as of soul with soul and
spirit with spirit, a fleshly union indeed for the multiplication
and increase of mankind, but also an association for mutual
aid and counsel and comfort. Divorce is forbidden except in
case of adultery; but second marriage after the death of one
of the parties is permissible. The prayers and lections of
Scripture with which the sect celebrates matrimony are given
in full. In these the bride and bridegroom pledge each other
to perpetual fidelity throughout life, and the parents on each
side must be present and give their blessing to the union before
God and the faithful meet to attest it. The prayers to heaven
and the angels to protect the newly-married couple and lead

them in the path of peace, goodness and conjugal harmony are
not surpassed for simple eloquence and fervour by those of
any church. There is no crowning of the couple as in the
orthodox rite, which is declared to be unscriptural and invalid.

This is followed by a section repudiating the mutilators or
Skoptsy, who make themselves eunuchs for the kingdom of
heaven. Their interpretation of the text Mt. xix, 12 is rejected
and it is argued, as by orthodox exegetes in general, that it
should be interpreted allegorically and was intended to be so
interpreted, for otherwise both Christ and his Apostles must
have emasculated themselves, which they did not.

They condemn monkery mainly because of the drunken and
vicious and idle lives led by monks, and object to permanent
vows, though they admit the expediency of St. Paul's advice
that at times man and wife should keep apart for prayer and
religious meditation.

The comment on the eighth commandment consists wholly
of Scripture passages nor does the treatment of the last two
call for notice. The concluding section however of the tract
is devoted to the Church and is most characteristic. It begins
by insisting that it is the community of the faithful who accept
the teaching of Jesus and his Apostles, and appeals to such texts
as I Cor. iii, 16: "Know you not that ye are the temple of God
and the Spirit of God liveth in you," and I Cor. vi, 19: "Know
ye not that your members are a temple of the Holy Spirit dwelling within you, which ye have from God." Inspired with such
sentiments the Molokanye deny that any sanctity attaches to
buildings, altars, altar furniture, *Antiminsia*, ikons, relics and
the like." What connection, they ask, can there be between
a temple of God and idols? "For ye, the Apostle said (II Cor.
vi, 16), are a temple of the living God, as God hath declared
saying: I will dwell in them and will walk up and down in them,
and I will be their God and they shall be my people." Is not
the Russo-Greek Church teaching about the temple a destruction of the temple of God? The founder and head of the
Church is Jesus Christ himself: "When two or three are
gathered together in my name, there am I in their midst."
(Mt. xviii 20). "And I will ask the Father, and he will give

you another Consoler and he shall abide with you for ever."
In this context Acts ii, 1, 2, 4, is also cited along with Eph. v,
26–7; I Peter ii, 4–5; I Cor. xii, 12, 27; Eph. ii, 19–22; I Cor.
iii, 11; Eph. iv, 4–6. Fortified with such texts they deny the
Greco-Russian or the Old Ritualists, or the Western Church
to be the true Church. These so-called Churches are in con-
flict with the Teaching and have thus cut themselves off from
Christ.

From many passages of the New Testament, e.g., Hebrews
iv, 15; viii, 1; vii, 23–27; v, 4–6, it is argued that we can have
no High priest save Jesus Christ alone, and that it is vain for
the orthodox Churches to entitle men such. There is one
priest, who is our Lord.

The tract then describes the Molokan cult. It includes (1)
reading of Scripture with, occasionally, interpretation of it to
those who do not clearly comprehend its drift; (2) singing of
the Psalms and other canticles from Scripture; (3) Prayer,
answering to the precept laid down in Cor. iii, 16.

But it must not be supposed that the Molokanye dispense with
organization in their Church. On the contrary in each locality
to supervise their affairs and to lead their services they elect a
presbyter or bishop, that is a supervisor; for after the manner
of the earliest Church they make no distinction between a
presbyter or elder and a bishop. Their bishop has two coadjutors, who in case he is sick or absent, take his place. He is
chosen in accordance with the rules laid down in Tim. iii, 2–5.
They have no deacons. These, they say, were necessary in the
early Church for the keeping of good order. If they found
them essential to the extension of their Church, the Molokanye
would elect them, but so far they have found no use for them.

The duties of a bishop are those prescribed in I Peter v. 1–3.
He receives no salary as do the popes of the orthodox Church,
who exact payment from their faithful for every prayer they
repeat, forgetting that Jesus asked nothing when he suffered
and shed his blood in our behoof.

The Molokanye scrupulously disclaim any sacerdotalism.
Their presbyters or bishops are the equals only of the rest of
the congregation, according to the precepts Mt. xxiii, 8, 10.

In their Church there are no Greater ones, no Lesser ones, all are equal as brethren met together before God. One authority only they possess and recognize, to wit, Jesus Christ; and therefore they are the true Church. The presbyter may be deprived if he offends against the rules set out in Tim. iii, 2–5.

They have no buildings reserved for religious service, and hold that prayer hallows the building, and not the building the prayers offered in it; because God lives not in temples made with hands, and the hour is with us, when true worshippers must worship in Spirit and in Truth. They argue that the earliest Christians similarly met for prayer in private houses.

They reject utterly the doctrine of the Sacrament which has been elaborated in the great Churches of East and West, and to understand their objection we must bear in mind that in the East the word for Sacrament (a Latin word) is mystery or secret cult, the entire doctrine of which was taken over by the early Churches of the East from the old Greek mysteries and clothed with their paraphernalia. They hold that the recitation, standing, of the Lord's Prayer followed by the reading and exposition (if needful) of the Scriptures (the congregation sitting down) and by prayers with genuflexion — this service in itself constitutes communion in the body and blood of Jesus Christ, and in evidence thereof they appeal to such texts as John vi, 47–51; 53, 60–63. The fleshly communion which consists in consumption of material bread and wine, which being swallowed passes into the stomach to be evacuated (Mt. xv, 17) is a vain thing falsely imagined. Neither if we eat it, do we abound in grace, nor if we do not, lack the same (I Cor. viii, 8). The only true communion is in the Word of God. The vulgar Church teaching about the matter insults the body and blood given and shed for our instruction and salvation by Jesus.

The recital and intoning of Scripture in their divine service may last some hours and is followed by prayers in a kneeling posture according to the example of Jesus in Lk. xx, 41 and of the early saints in Acts xx, 36. They do not cross their persons, for to do so is vain and superfluous for those who carry in their hearts the passion and cross of the Saviour; nor is it anywhere prescribed in Scripture. The prayers recited by the Presbyter are given in full. The first begins thus:—

"Protect us, Lord, from the dwelling-place of thy Holiness. Accept our prayers for all men, for the King and for all in authority, to the end that we may live a life quiet and free from turbulence in all piety and purity. For this is acceptable before our Saviour, God, who desireth all men to be saved and to receive the Truth with understanding. Look mercifully and with favour, Lord, upon our offering, as thou didst on the sacrifice of Abel; accept our devotion as thou didst Enoch's; preserve us from a flood of vain imaginings, as thou didst Noe; save us from fire and brimstone, as thou didst Lot from Sodom; and enlighten us, as thou didst Abraham, our father, with thy Holy Spirit"... At the end they pray that "our bountiful mother Wisdom" may come unto them, an antique touch reminding us of "Our Mother the Holy Spirit" in Aphraates.

This prayer is followed by Psalm 50: "Have mercy on me," then a prayer which begins: "To-day we glorify thee, Lord, and bend our knee before thee our Lord and Creator, and magnify thy holy Name, and exalt the fleshless host of thy Angels and Archangels, Cherubim and Seraphim, and we follow the Holy Prophets and Apostles and Martyrs and thy Elect ones; for thou hast designed, Lord, that we should call upon thy all serene and sanctified holy Name. Now therefore make us, thy young men and women, worthy to dwell with thyself in the Kingdom of Heaven for ever and ever."

There follows Psalm 26: "Lord our Illumination," and a prayer:— "To thee, Lord, we bend our knees, who createdst heaven and earth. Lord, remit all our sins. Shelter us under the shadow of thy wings from the fury of the enemy. Lord, deliver us, thy young men and maidens, from eternal torment; save us with salvation eternal; Lord, sanctify us in presence of all nations, for thou hast loved thy saints. Amen."

There follows Psalm 85: "Incline thine ear O Lord," and a long prayer beginning: "Blessed art thou, Lord our God, and blessed is thy holy name for ever..." a prayer for replenishment and illumination by the Holy Ghost. After it they sing Psalm 114: "I delighted that the Lord hearkened unto the voice of my prayer." Then a long prayer beginning: "Lord, God of Heaven, Mighty, Powerful and Terrible, observe thy promise and be merciful to those who love thee and keep thy commandments ... and now, Lord raise thy almighty hand and extend it from on high from thy throne, and gather together all who are thy chosen in the unity of faith. Raise, Lord, around them a rampart of awe like a wall of fire," etc.

Psalm 140 is next sung: "Lord I called unto thee," followed by a brief but characteristic prayer: "Lord, make us worthy, thy sons and daughters, to stand in thine image and make us, Lord, to resemble thy rubies; choose us, Lord, for thy foundations, as if we were sapphires; uphold us and strengthen us in thy sight as if jasper; and cleanse and purify us as crystals. Teach us, Lord, by thy Holy Spirit, and save, our Saviour, our souls henceforth and for ever."

Next is sung Psalm 87: "Lord, God of my salvation" followed by the Prayer of Manasses and the Psalm: "Lord, in thy wrath, deny me not."

The above service of prayer and praise is followed by a love feast, a "*brotherly trapeza*," devoid of sacramental significance. In it they do but satiate their hunger, first thanking God for the food he gives them. It is no part of the service and can be dispensed with as well as not. On the anniversary of the Last Supper they meet, and breaking bread, eat it in memory of the Lord, holding withal holy conversation one with the other; but this meal is not a sacrament in the sense of an arcane mystery. On the contrary they reject all such mysteries, because Jesus Christ at his advent revealed all mysteries as is attested in Mt. xiii, 11 and Eph. iii, 4–5 and 8–10. The mysteries of the Orthodox are idle trifling, since it is the duty of Christians to reveal divine truth to all as the only means to salvation, and not keep it secret and make a mystery of it, as the Russo-Greek popes do, who hide away under superstitious rites the truth that man is a temple of God in whom dwells the Divine Spirit, and that all commandments are included in the one precept to love one's neighbour as oneself, seeing that God is our Father and men are sons of God. This truth lies open to all in the New Testament; no other mystery was revealed to us by Jesus Christ, and he that acknowledges it, shall live for ever. No rites are to be performed, no incense burned, no water sprinkled, no tapers lit. If the Molokanye, when they assemble at eventide light candles, it is only in order to light up their chamber. Do the popes imagine that the candles which their faithful light, when they enter their churches, in any way open their eyes to the Truth of God? Were it not better if they explained the Gospel to them and enlightened their understanding?

The presbyter of the Molokanye wears no special vestments, but leads their prayers attired in his ordinary garb; the orthodox contention that the Apostles dressed up is false.[1]

Members of the sect believe in the future life, and when the spirit quits the body they offer prayer and sing Psalms 23 and 145; and before the open grave Psalm 83. Then follow Acts viii, 2, and Jesus Sirach xxxviii, 16, 17, 22. In the faith that the dead rise again, they pray that their sins may be forgiven in the spirit of II Mac. xii, 44–46. The tract ends with attestations from Scripture of the future life, e.g., Mark xii, 26, 27; II Cor. v, 1; Isaiah lv, 17–18; Mt. xxiv, 30; John v. 28–9; Rev. xx, 12–15, xxi, 1–5.

The accounts of Uzov, Stollov and Kostomarov

This account, given by the Molokanye of themselves and their religion in 1862, harmonizes with that of Uzov, who, following Stollov's articles in the *National Memorials* (*Otetch. Zap.*) of 1870, No. 6, relates that they denominate themselves the truly spiritual Christians, in contrast with all others whom they call 'the worldly.' They are an offshoot of the Dukhobortsy, according to this authority, and were accounted one sect with them until 1823, when they parted company with them in certain matters of doctrine. In particular they are closer to the Orthodox. The common people still in 1870 identified them with the Dukhobortsy. Some aver that they split off from the latter about 1780. Stollov states that the Molokanye date their rise in the reign of Alexis Michailovich,

---

[1] Livanov in Vol. I of his Raskolniki, St. Petersburg 1872, pp. 446–459, prints an order of common prayer in use among the Molokanye.

and that they were then called or called themselves Duk-hobortsy. This title translates the Greek *pneumatomachos*, a term of abuse leveled in the IVth Century at the Semi-Arian theologians who scrupled to set the Holy Spirit on a level of complete equality with the Father and Son in the Trinitarian scheme of dogma. It is probable that orthodox Russian doctors used it in an equally derogatory sense of the ancestors of the Molokanye, who, as we saw above, adopted it of themselves, but interpreting it to mean not those who wrestle against the Spirit, but in whom the Spirit wrestles against the world, the flesh and the devil. Stollov also regards Matthew Semenov as their founder, and he has been plausibly identified by Kostomarov in an article in the same review (1869, No. 3, p. 78) with Bashkin who was condemned at Moscow in 1555. The chief author, however, of the separation of the Molokanye from the older sect was Semen Uklein about 1780, son-in-law of the well-known teacher Hilarion Pobirokhin; and his memory is cherished by the Molokanye, as we saw in their own tract, which fails to acquaint us with the fact that over two hundred years transpired between Matthew Semenov and Semen Uklein. The latter's propaganda attracted, says Stollov, the orthodox as well as the Dukhobortsy, and he began in Tambov and passed thence to the Voronezh and Saratov governments. The success of his preaching exposed him to the reprisals of the State, and I. V. Lopukhin (in the *Transactions* of the Imp. Society of Hist. and Antiquity, 1860, bk. 3, p. 110) records that his followers underwent various tortures and were condemned to hard labour and the cruelest imprisonment in cells so small that they could neither stand upright in them or lie down at full length. They did but increase the more in number, and information collected by the State in the years 1842-6 shewed that there were 200,000 of them in the Tambov Government alone.

In 1880 those of the Don differed somewhat from the other two main divisions in Tambov and Vladimir (who still closely adhered to the teaching of Semen Uklein) in political and religious views. Those of the Don called themselves 'Evangelical Christians.'

Uzov's outline of the common teaching of all three of these divisions, which he bases on Stollov and Kostomarov, agrees well enough with the Molokan tract. There is the Trinity in three persons, and Scripture as the sole source of doctrine. As compared with the Gospel, Christology, they held, was of little importance; and a man may allegorize away the historical Christ altogether, if he likes, provided he practises the moral teaching, which is very much what Marcion did. In any case the letter of Scripture must not be insisted on to the detriment of the spirit. They deny none of the events narrated in the Gospels, but admit a man's right to find a higher moral meaning in them. Holy Writ is anyhow the source of moral perfection, and such perfection is attained by anyone who adopts it as his rule of life. "The letter killeth, the Spirit giveth life," say they. It is no use to believe what is recorded of Jesus, unless you practise what he preached.

"During his life on earth," according to the Molokanye, "Christ founded the Church; at first it consisted of the Apostles and later on of all who believed in him. But the true Christian Church only endured down to the IVth Century, when the ecumenical councils and the teachers of the Church by their arbitrary interpretations of the Bible perverted the religion and imported into it pagan beliefs and rites. To-day the real Church consists exclusively of the truly spiritual Christians, who repudiate the traditions and canons of the doctors by which the conciliar Church sets store, and profess what the Gospel teaches and no more." [1]

For this reason they "condemn as vain and fanciful the Church teaching about Sacraments and deny it to be based on God's word." [2]

"Consider," they say to the Orthodox, "who invented your Church rites and canons and why. They were devised by your popes for their own gain." [3] In the opinion of the Molokanye "the sacrament of Christian regeneration must be understood

---

[1] Stollov, *Nat. Records*, 1870, p. 300.
[2] *Orth. Review*, (*Pravosl. Obozr.*) 1867, t. 1, art. by Z., p. 327.
[3] Varadinov, *Hist. Min. Vnutr. Diel* (*Hist. of Ministry of the Interior*), t, viii, p. 617.

spiritually."[1]   Accordingly baptism consists in the good tidings
of Christ's teaching, and is the spiritual cleansing from sin
along with belief in the three hypotheses or persons of God,
the mortification of the old man and his conversion to a life of
faith without stain.[2]

"Water baptism," remarks Kostomarov in the same journal
(1869, No. 3, p. 69), "has no virtue in their opinion; instruction they say is what is wanted and a hold upon the teaching."
Communion equally consists in "study of the divine utterances
and in the fulfilment and keeping of the commandments;
repentance or penitence must be undergone immediately in the
presence of God himself, and last unction consists in earnest
prayer on the part of the faithful and the sick.

Marriage is no sacrament.   Kostomarov remarks that in
proof of the fact that its essence is love and accord rather than
ritual, they ask whether evil relations between husband and
wife can be hallowed by the circumstance that they were
crowned.   If they give notice that they are going to live
together and begin to do so in harmony and honestly,— is
their joint life any less pleasing to God than that of two people
who, after being crowned in church, straightway begin to
quarrel, lose their mutual confidence and deceive each other?
By his account their marriage is even simpler than that we have
taken from their Geneva tract.   The young man, he says,
makes his proposal to the girl and obtains her assent.   He then
asks the parents for their blessing and they repair, as agreed
upon, to the home of one or the other; here witnesses are summoned before whom they receive the mutual blessings of the
parents of both parties and the marriage is finished.   Nuptial
ceremonies there are none.   According to Stollov, however,
the father leads his daughter by hand, and in giving her away
to the husband says: Here I give thee my daughter to wife
according to God's law, take her away with thee to thy father's
house.   The Elder (or rector) reads passages of Holy Scripture
bearing on wedlock, they sing divers psalms, and the marriage
concludes, with the bridegroom embracing the bride amid

---

[1] *Orth. Rev.* 1867, t. 1, art. by Z., p. 328.

[2] *Nat. Records,* 1870, No. 6, art. by Stollov.

felicitations on their lawful wedlock. Divorce,[1] adds another observer, is allowed; but only after it has first been decided, as it were, in formal debate who was to blame for the domestic quarrel and what was the cause. After hearing the complaint made by the injured party and the defence of the accused, the 'Elder' proceeds to read out biblical texts relative to family life and conjugal fidelity. "A husband should love his wife as our Lord loved his Church," says the Elder. Does then Christ wound and injure his Church? The union of a man and wife must be one of love, a spiritual union. He who loves his wife, loves himself; wherefore a man sins against the Lord's commandment who treats his wife harshly by word or deed. For what love or harmony can there be between people who quarrel? Without it a wife can be no helpmate to her husband, as our Lord himself attested, but only a slave for carnal cohabitation, degraded thereby to the level of a brute without reason, the spirit and image of God in her lost and dishonoured. Unless there be the link of affection to unite them their union is fornication and adultery. Another authority, V. Mainov, (in *Znanie*, 'Knowledge,' 1874, No. 3), cites a definition of the conjugal relation from the 'Faith and Doctrine of the Molokani,' as follows: "Among us a woman is not a beast of burden, but a helpmate and standby, a friend and companion in this vale of misery."

In the Caucasus I have passed through many Molokan villages in early spring and in late autumn. Their dwellings were usually of wood, but sometimes of stone, often built in gardens surrounded by walls. Everything was neat and clean, and everywhere prevailed an air of sobriety and quiet industry. It was a pleasure to see the stalwart tidy wives sitting outside their houses in the sun, working at their sewing, the snow still around their feet at the close of winter, which in the highlands between Tiflis and Erivan is very severe.

Stollov describes the Molokan funeral. The 'Elders' or Rectors read over the grave certain prayers and sing Psalms; after which all present, or at least the older ones, are invited to

[1] Nicolas Popov, "Materials for the history of the Priestless Communions in Moscow," p. 150.

d under another Government is accounted a good deed ...
ten among us, the Molokanye continue, the law prescribes
opposite of good deeds, and forbids what charity and love
one's neighbour demands, and in many cases prevents one
m doing good to one's neighbor. It is impossible, nor is it
's duty, to do what authority decrees, if this be opposed to
demands of conscience and right. Thus they point to the
mple of the early Christians whom the Roman emperors
d to force to bow down to idols. Emperors were invested
all the power of the law; and yet Christians did not fulfil
commands when these violated their convictions. Thus it
hat the three youths, despite the threat of the Chaldean
ce, refused to obey the king who violated their own law.
t, though he bade us render to Caesar the things that are
r's, did so with the reserve that we render to God what is

It is clear, therefore, that even if Caesar himself
es aught of a kind to violate our own law and conscience,
as Scripture teaches, is the true law of God, written on
shy tablets of our hearts, we must not, to please Caesar,
the Divine will, otherwise we are timeservers, respecters
, but reprehensible before God. By reason of this
ce of true welldoing to the rules of convention, the Molo-
go so far as to disdain positive law: authority as the
f law and constraint to fulfil it is in their opinion liable
es, to doubts and glosses.

s Kostmarov's account of the Molokan attitude on
s of conscience, and the writer in the Orthodox Review
e p. 309) sets before us the practical results of their
thereof. They regard it as a first duty to avoid mili-
ice and resort to any means of escaping from it.
they are under no moral obligation to pay taxes.
ot belong to Caesar, but to God, and can recognize
dship of Caesar. Thirdly it is a pious duty to receive
fugitives. Kostomarov states that in their estima-
e best of deeds to conceal deserters from the army;
ot only deserters, but anyone fleeing from the per-
f the Tsar's Government finds a welcome among
ey say that they do not know the wrongs or rights

the house of the deceased person's parents where prayer is
raised to God, while all partake of bread and salt, and offer
vows for the entrance of the dead into the Kingdom of Heaven
and for the happiness of the survivors.

The same author testifies to the Molokan rejection of external ritual and religious gestures, as well as of the invocation of
the Virgin and Saints. A writer in the *Orthodox Review*
(*Pravosl. Obozr.* 1867, t. 1, p. 327) dwells on the absence among
them of a true hierarchy. Every man is a priest; their Elders
are no more than rectors chosen by the community and possess
no superior sanctity. Christ did not choose his Apostles from
among the Levites or priests nor consecrate them to be such;
nor are priests any nearer to God than unconsecrated laymen.
The Molokan Elder is not even an interpreter of religious
truths. The individual among them understands the Scriptures as he likes. In the matter of fasts they recognize that
the Old Testament rule to avoid pork, fish devoid of scales,
etc., is not feasible; but for the rest they abstain from wine and
eat no onions or garlic. They pretend that these are prejudicial to the bodily economy. One would like to know whether
the refusal of onions and garlic is not a survival of some ancient
taboo, like the English avoidance of horseflesh, snails, frogs,
cuttlefish, etc.

Stollov states that the above description is true of the vast
majority of Molokanye, but that those of the Don who call
themselves evangelical Christians are less rigorous in their
practice of Uklein's precept of spiritual worship, in that they
have certain ceremonies devised by themselves. For instance
their 'rectors' are called in to read prayers over a child on the
first day after birth and to bestow a name on him. On the
fortieth day they read prayers for the purification of the mother
and her reconciliation or rather atonement with the Church,
and at the same time baptize the child, plunging it thrice into
the water, after, as a preliminary, they have invoked the Spirit
to descend and hallow the water.

One recognizes in the above rites a mere survival of those of
the Eastern Churches, and they were certainly not devised by
the Molokanye as Stollov supposes. He may also be wrong in

fixing the name-giving rite on the first day, for in all oriental churches, even among the Paulicians of Armenia, it took place on the eighth. This rite replaced among Gentile converts that of circumcision, but was much older than Christianity. An Italian child on the ninth day (counting in Roman fashion that of birth as an entire day and so equivalent to our eighth) was, according to Macrobius (Sat. i, 16) carried to the temple by the friends and relations, cleansed with water, given a personal name and recommended to the protection of a tutelar deity, as in the Great Church a child is to that of a saint. The goddess who in general presides over the rite was by the Romans known as *Nundina* or goddess of the ninth day, and the day was also called *dies lustricus* or the day of lustration. Similar rites were in vogue all round the Mediterranean.

Among the Molokanye of the Don the presbyter, according to Stollov, also receives the personal and private confessions of penitents and reads over them prayers of absolution. Furthermore he celebrates with suitable prayers the breaking of bread. Early in the morning bread is set ready on a table with red wine. After prayers have been recited the 'rector' or 'Elder' apostrophizes the faithful in the words: "With fear of God and faith advance," and then breaks the bread and distributes it to each by hand in a white platter kept specially for the purpose. He serves it round to men and women alike, who remain in their places. The 'rectors' are also summoned to visit the sick, whose confessions they receive, pray over them and anoint them with oil thrice, in the name of the Trinity, on the forehead, breast, hands, feet and spine. Before accomplishing this rite they consecrate the oil with divers prayers and invoke upon it the virtue of healing, reading James, v, 10–16 and Luke x, 25–37. Unfortunately, says Uzov, we lack information as to the peculiar significance attaching to the 'rectors' among the 'Evangelical Christians'; but in view of the survival among them of so many rites, performed by these 'rectors' the latter must be invested with a higher dignity and importance than they have in other Molokan sects.

Kostomarov points out that the Molokan conceptions of civil society are direct inferences from their religious outlook.

Society and Christ cannot be separated; th[...] same, and rest alike on the Gospel precepts [...] in accordance with the text (II Cor. iii, 1[...] where there is the Spirit of the Lord, t[...] follows that we can have no other moral b[...] life than complete freedom and indepen[...] laws and constraint of any sort. The a[...] binding on those who have the inspirat[...] Christ. Worldly authorities are salu[...] appointed by God, but only so for the[...] and the Lord spoke of Christians wher[...] of the world, as I am not of the wor[...] spiritual Christians therefore, who are [...] authorities are not needful. As chil[...] tians strive to live according to the [...] Christ. Fulfilling God's commandm[...] human laws, nor are they under an[...] and by consequence their duty is [...] which violate the doctrine of God's [...] avoid servitude under landowners [...] emancipation of the peasants as l[...] tary service, and oaths as forbidd[...] impossible openly to oppose the [...] their requirements, spiritual Chr[...] Christians, must conceal themse[...] in the faith are under an obligati[...] of the Scriptural precept: 'B[...] little, like unto Abraham wh[...] derers or to the harlot Raha[...] Hebrew spies' (Esdras ii, 22)[...]

In thus repudiating allegia[...] affirm, as Kostomarov rema[...] unique, true law, which has [...] God on the fleshly tablets o[...] adopted by dint of medit[...] acts of charity intimated [...] laws are exposed to temp[...] under one Government i[...]

an[...]
Of[...]
the[...]
for[...]
fro[...]
one[...]
the[...]
exa[...]
trie[...]
with[...]
their[...]
was [...]
furna[...]
Chris[...]
Caesa[...]
God's[...]
requir[...]
which,[...]
the fle[...]
violate[...]
of mar[...]
preferer[...]
kanye [...]
source o[...]
to reser[...]
Such [...]
the right[...]
(see abo[...]
adoption[...]
tary serv[...]
Secondly [...]
They do [...]
no overlor[...]
and hide [...]
tion it is t[...]
and that [...]
secutions [...]
them. Th[...]

of the fugitives, but anyhow the law is frequently unjust and the courts give false verdicts, and the authorities are given over to vanity and make demands opposed to the divine law. The culprit pursued therefore is as likely as not to be just and innocent. They are not judges, nor called on to decide; but they deem it right to help anyone who appeals to them to save him, mindful of the text: Hide between the lesser and greater wall.

Nor have they failed to carry out in practice what they hold as a theory. They did so in 1826 when they refused to pay taxes and to serve as recruits. The Russian Government treated them then as other Governments have treated those who strive to live according to the abstract precepts of Jesus of Nazareth. They were knouted and exiled to Siberia, and many of them sent into madhouses where they perished.

Since 1827 the idea of refusing taxes has not been put forward by the Molokanye who according to Varadinov (*op. cit.* viii 233) punctually pay the imperial taxes. But as they obstinately refuse to bear arms, they are assigned duties in Sanitary units, hospitals, transport etc.[1]

To-day, says Kostomarov, the Molokanye hold this language: "We must recognize the Authorities, whatever they be, as soon as they come into existence. But we deem it impossible and wrong to regard anything they do or say as excellent, in case our own reason convince us that it is not so." "It is," they say, "merely to submit to monarchical authority." But they do not regard as valid any external tokens of its sanctity nor set any store by any monarch as a divine anointed being; they are more inclined in opposition to the monarchical institution itself to point to the history of Saul: "By the lips of Samuel himself the Divine being dissuaded the Israelites from choosing a king for themselves; and the prophet warned his people of the tribulations and iniquities they would suffer as soon as they set a king over themselves"..."Rejecting kingly power, they equally reject every sort of personal distinction; for according to their doctrine all men are equals of one another, all are brethren, and there should not be nobles or plebeians; and correspondingly all outward badges of distinction, titles, rank

[1] *Russk. Mir*, Nov. 5, 1876.

are from their point of view vanities and contradictions of
evangelical teaching."

They regard all war as forbidden, and maintain on the basis
of the precepts of Christ, that we ought not to resist evil, but
rather turn the other cheek to the smiter. They say that
blessed are they who live in peace and are peacemakers, for
they shall be called Sons of God. For the same reason they
refuse to bear arms, says the Archimandrite Israel in his *Sketch
of the Russian Dissenters* (*Obozren. russk. Raskol.* p. 253), and
consider any revolt against the Powers which be, no matter
how unjust they are, as in itself a wrong act. They preach
instead a sturdy endurance and tenacity of purpose. Rebellion and open opposition bring in their train evil to one's neighbours and it is our duty to avoid anything that may do harm.[1]
There are those however who suspect the Molokanye of only
counselling submission to the Authorities because they have no
choice, and say they only do so until the time comes when they
shall have won enough influence and become strong enough to
shake off the pagan yoke.[2] Long ago there appeared to be a
basis for this suspicion, because among other things they sent a
deputation to meet Napoleon in 1812 under the impression
that he would protect them. Its members however were captured on the banks of the Vistula, as Aug. Haxthausen relates
in his *Survey of interior relations* (*Izsledov. vnutr. otnosh.* p. 260).
During the Crimean war the Molokanye, according to the
Orthodox Review (1867, art. 7, p. 337), expressed the opinion
that prayer ought not to be offered up for the Tsar, but on the
contrary for the defeat of those who oppressed the Spiritual
Christians and curtailed their liberties. Prof. Asher however,
who has studied them in our own day, writes as follows in the
European Messenger (Vestn. Europ. 1879, no. 9, p. 371): "The
Molokanye having long ago got accustomed to being referred to
in the laws as a dangerous sect, take up the same attitude to the
Authorities and the Government as did the earliest Christians:
they scrupulously obey them, but regard them as alien to themselves. The established Church they term the Russian and its
adherents Russians, as if they were themselves foreigners."

---

[1] Kostomarov *op. cit.* p. 76–7.
[2] Varadinov *op. cit.* viii, 318.

They condemn, continues Kostomarov, all luxury and elaborate food or dress, in general all expensive habits of life. On this head they reason thus: If we insist on living luxuriously and use up on ourselves a great deal of wealth, we shall only help to disseminate misery among our neighbours. Every superfluity we allow ourselves deprives others of our brethren of what is indispensable to them. It is well to be rich, but let your wealth be for the common benefit of our brethren, and not spent to gratify the caprices of its owner. Let him find his own greatest pleasure in this that, more than others, he can contribute to the welfare of his society; but to do so he must lead a simple life and not go mad about luxuries. After reading the above we shall not be surprised to learn from S. Atav, writing in the *National Memorials* (*Otech. Zapisk.* 1870, No. 4, p. 621-3), that the Molokanye are thrice or four times as rich as the orthodox; the reason being, among them as among our own Quakers, their perpetual and habitual readiness to rescue one another. We have been told, continues Atav, that there never was a case of a Molokan household being ruined. Positively they would never allow such a thing to happen. If a calamity befalls one of them, all are prepared to assist him. Another writer in the same journal (1828, pt. 33, p. 58) records that the majority of the Molokanye love to do good; and even endeavour to banish from their lives anything that in their opinion can corrupt a man. Thus they condemn card-playing and in general any game that aims at making money for the player of it. They argue that such games are a useless waste of time and teach a man to be rapacious; that they generate strife among people because in them one wins at the expense of another. Nothing is so pernicious as play and drink, they say, nothing leads so directly to ruin and sin against the Christian life. Both of these vices are equally to be shunned. Hard work, according to them, is as necessary to man as bread and breath of life. It not only furnishes means to live, but keeps a man out of the way of ruin and depravity; consequently they look upon work as a religious duty.[1] These people, says another authority, Philibert, in the *Nat. Mem.* (1870, No. 3),

[1] Kostomarov, *op. cit.* p. 74-5.

the moment you come across them, rivet your attention by their reasonable modes of personal expression and by the peculiarly sensible way in which they talk. They are distinguished by their sobriety and good manners and morals; by their addiction to labour and enterprise. Their villages are neat and well built. In all branches of household economy they show a gift of organization and attain great success in the production of wool. This is particularly true of the Tauric Molokanye according to a writer in the *Nat. Mem.* (1870, No. 3). The same Heidelberg professor Asher in the *European Messenger* (1879, no. 9, p. 379) declares that you recognize the Molokanye at first glance by their look of honesty, the gentle expression of their countenances, by their frank and open demeanour.

They are keen propagandists, especially among the labouring classes.[1] For a long time stress of persecution made them very circumspect, and it was only when persecutions relaxed somewhat that they went to work openly. Every Molokanin is familiar with the Gospel and overwhelms an adversary in discussion with citations of it. The result is that a village priest seldom risks a controversy with them. "More than once," says Atav,[2] "I have seen priests subjected to resounding defeats, followed most certainly by the conversion of very many of the listeners. Nor do they confine themselves to acquaintance with the Scriptures; for many of them buy or obtain various books, which they devour in the hope of finding in them arguments of some sort in support of their teaching."

The spiritual Christians of the Don Sect, who call themselves Evangelicals, differ somewhat in their political and social views from the followers of Uklein. Thus, to use their own phrase, they have always fulfilled the orders of the Government without a murmur. Their Elders instruct those whom fate transfers into the ranks of the imperial army to accomplish their duties as soldiers and to cherish in their souls the fear of God, bearing in mind the precept of King Solomon: "Fear God, my son, and the King, and oppose thyself to neither of them." Hereby, so they insist to their flock, they are obliged to love

---

[1] *Orth. Review* 1876, vol. I, p. 333–4, art. by Z.
[2] *Nat. Mem.* 1870, No. 4, p. 622.

the Ruler and serve him honestly. If they are required to take an oath, they must tender it in the same form as others, only omitting the words 'before the lifegiving cross.' They would have it administered by an Elder of their own faith before an open Gospel.[1] Furthermore these evangelicals offer prayers in their meetings for the Emperor and the Powers that be.[2]

It is evident from the above account of the Spiritual Christians of the Don that the Geneva tract which we have summarized did not emanate from them, but from the followers of Uklein, who eschew baptism and rites of communion. The latter better reflect the Cathar tradition, or anyhow a tradition closely resembling that of the Albigenses. The Evangelicals of the Don wear rather the air of a much expurgated orthodoxy, and must be remotely derived from the Russian Church, from which they are hardly more widely separated than are extreme low churchmen of the Anglican communion from the Romanizing ritualists.

Ivanovski's account

So far we have described the Molokanye from their own manual of instruction and from the accounts given by Russian publicists, if not wholly favourable to them, at least fairminded. It remains to complete it from the pages of Prof. Ivanovski who is openly hostile. His sources were as follows: "History of the Ministry of the Interior," Suppl. to Vol. viii, p. 232: also Livanov, Vol. 1, art. xii; Vol. ii, arts. vii and xiv; National Memorials" (*Otech. Zap.*), 1867 for March and 1870 for June: "Orthodox Conversations" (*Pravosl. Sobes.*), 1858. In general his conclusions and statements agree with those of the sources I have set before the reader.

He regards the temper underlying this religious movement as a mixture of wilful mysticism and irreverence for scripture, for he cannot conceive of people seriously taking the Sermon on the Mount as their rule of life. He is also very severe on the half divine authority claimed by some of their leaders, such

---

[1] *Nat. Mem.* 1870, No. 6, art. by Stollov, p. 309.
[2] *Orth. Review* 1867, vol. I, art. by Z., p. 331.

as Pobirokhin, who, he declares, pretended to be judge of the world. After all even Orthodox Bishops claim the right, and exercise it, of excommunicating whom they will; so we may pardon the minor extravagances of a fervent Russian peasant.

Semen Uklein, whom the Molokanye reverence as their proximate founder, was a tailor, who in following his trade, moved up and down the Governments of Tambov and Voronezh. He was already married, but falling under the influence of Pobirokhin he fell a convert to the Dukhobor faith, to which his familiarity with Scripture already predisposed him. He now aspired to marry his teacher's daughter and she became his spiritual wife. But presently he came to find fault with his father-in-law's obstinate claim to judge all men and his preference for his own inner lights over the authority of the Bible, and after five years he finally emancipated himself from his influence. Meanwhile many inhabitants of the Tambov province infected with the rationalism, as Ivanovski calls it,— meaning thereby the temper which rejects orthodox accretions on the Christianity of the New Testament — of Tveretinov, had attached themselves to Uklein. They had been marked down by the ecclesiastical authorities as dangerous people, but formed no distinct sect until Uklein organized them as such, and choosing seventy of them as his disciples or apostles made a solemn entry into the town of Tambov, singing hymns and proclaiming his new doctrine. It may be that he was inspired by the story of Palm Sunday and saw no reason why the Orthodox should have a monopoly of Tabors or religious processions and of similar spectacular enterprises.

All this occurred in the reign of Catharine II, whose police now seized and locked him up. He was given a choice of punishment or of returning to the orthodoxy in which he had been brought up. He made belief of returning, but in fact went on with his propaganda, and converted as many as 5000 souls in the provinces of Tambov, Voronezh and (the modern) Saratov. His sect also spread to Ekaterinoslav, Astrakhan and the Caucasus.

As early as 1765 the church consistory of Tambov labelled them Molokanye because of their drinking milk during the canonical fasts. The name stuck, and they interpreted it themselves as meaning that the simple evangelical teaching on which they fed was the Milk of the Word. In general they called themselves as the Spiritual Christians, and they regard themselves as the only true successors of the Church of the first three centuries.

Ivanovski has of course little difficulty in shewing that many traditions, especially that of episcopacy, which they reject, were well established long before the year 300, and pathetically complains of their rejection of the authority of the Fathers. He testifies that they do not trouble their heads very much about minutiae of Trinitarian theology, Uklein being so ignorant as to suppose that the Son and Holy Spirit are not coequal in dignity with God the father. Ivanovski also imparts to us the very significant information that Uklein held a more or less docetic view of Christ and taught, like Marcion and the Cathars and Anabaptists of a still later age, that the Son of the Virgin did not take from her real human flesh, but resembled in this matter Tobit's friend and guide, the Archangel Raphael, who declared as follows: "All these days did I appear unto you, but I did neither eat nor drink, but ye did see a vision." [1] In this semi-phantastic body then, according to the Molokanye, Christ ascended into Heaven, and being endowed therewith, it follows that his death was not the death of ordinary men, but of a kind peculiar to himself. As a rule, however, they set small store by such speculations, reserving all their ardour for the upholding of those tenets wherein they contrast externally with the Orthodox Church, whose sacramental theory, rites, fasts, icon-worship, etc. they summarily reject. In these matters they retain the essential teachings of the parent Dukhobor sect, only differing from it in this that they want to prove everything out of scripture. But in interpreting scripture they explain away as allegory and parable all that stands in their way, e. g. the words 'of water' in John iii, 5, which it may be well noted Justin Martyr, c. A.D. 150, our earliest witness to the said text, significantly omits. Had these Russian

---

[1] From the same docetic standpoint Philo interprets the visits of the three angels to Abraham.

heretics studied the early Fathers, they would have found
much to their advantage and to the discomfiture of their
orthodox persecutors.   In this particular text they argue that
water no more signifies the real water than it does in the text
John vii 38: "He that believes in me, out of his belly shall flow
rivers of living water."   Another example of their exegesis
particularly irritating to Ivanovski is their conjunction of
John vi, 63 with John vi, 51 to prove that the story of the Last
Supper should be taken figuratively and not literally, for "the
letter killeth."   Nor can he excuse them for insisting that our
Lord's petition that his persecutors might be forgiven, as also the
Beatitudes and the precepts of the Sermon on the Mount, are of
universal range and anyhow apply to modern Russians.   Such
texts, says Ivanovski, only apply in their contexts and in view
of the peculiar setting and background of historical events in
which they were delivered.   Called upon to practice Christ's
own teaching the orthodox divine suddenly becomes the most
extreme of higher critics and discovers it to have been a mere
ad interim morality.

Ivanovski devotes a special chapter to the religious services
of the Dukhobortsy and Molokanye, in which he repeats what
Livanov has to say in his first volume, articles XVI and XXIII,
and in his second, articles VII, XI, XIV, and XXVI; also what
he has read in the *Orthodox Conversations* of 1858.   He also
uses two manuals of devotion issued by the Molokanye themselves.   The leading difference in matters of cult between the
Dukhobortsy and the Molokanye is that the former recite in
their gatherings their "living book."   The Molokanye meet in
an ordinary chamber, devoid of ecclesiastical furniture and decorations, with a table in the middle and benches or stools along
the walls.   The other sect prefers to hold its meetings out of
doors.   The men sit on the right hand, women on the left.
On entering the meeting a Dukhoborets cries: "Glory be to
God," and those already present answer: "Great is his name
all over the earth."   Very generally when they thus meet the
men salute the men and the women the women; each takes the
other by the right hand and, after the manner of the medieval
Cathars and of Christians in the age of Tertullian, makes three

low bows, one to another, kissing each the other thrice. The bow is a token that they are *theophoroi*, as St. Ignatius was entitled, or that they bear Christ and the Holy Spirit in their hearts and persons. Children on these occasions prostrate themselves thrice at the feet of their elders and kiss their hands.

It is possible that the prayers I have found in the Geneva manual are those which Uklein certainly composed for sundry occasions. Some of his prayers were to be repeated kneeling, others standing up with hands raised to heaven after the manner of the primitive *oranti* depicted in the Christian catacombs. Ivanovski records, however, that after Uklein's death the addition in some congregations of fresh prayers, unauthorized by him, led to schisms. The Molokanye, as we saw, recognize the chief Christian feasts, so contrasting with the Dukhobortsy who refuse to regard one day as holier than another. Every free day is by the latter equally holy to worship, and they have a jingle in which they proclaim Monday (*Ponedyelnik*) as sacred to God's works (*dyela Gospodnya*), Tuesday to regeneration of man, etc. They equally reject the occasional rites devised by the Molokanye for the events of birth, marriage and death. Ivanovski confirms the statement that the Molokanye in their rite of 'Churching' a child (the original meaning of the ceremony of the fortieth day, see Luke ii, 22 foll.) blow or breathe on the child's lips, as Jesus blew on his Apostles, by way of communicating to it the Holy Spirit. In the rite of marriage he notes that the parents bless their respective children by laying their hands on their heads, they kneeling while the appropriate prayers are read over them. This is done in the respective houses. The families then meet and the girl's father, taking her hand, says to the bridegroom: "I give thee my daughter to wife." The young parties are asked if they love each other, mutual vows are interchanged, and the rite ends with lections of the Apostle and prayers with genuflexion. He notes also that the Molokanye, like the Armenian and many other churches, have separate funeral rites for adults and children.

Ivanovski notes that these sects infer from the fact of believers being equals in religion and before God, that they should be equals in civil rank and dignity. He deplores their confusion of religions with civil and social life. Though he does not accuse them of setting the civil authorities at naught, he urges that their doctrines tend to weaken their obedience to the State and that they set up an impossible ideal, which tends to the denial of the necessity of civil authorities. They even go so far as to deny that the Tsar is the anointed vessel of divine election, and so rob him of his holy and religious character — words which make queer reading to-day.

The Dukhobortsy are sure that theirs is the freedom of the Gospel, and that all legitimate authority is from God. Uklein distinguished less emphatically between divine and human law, laid stress on obedience to constituted authority and insisted on prayers being said for the Tsar. Both sects condemn serfdom, war, and the taking of oaths, and encourage the harbouring of deserters.

Ivanovski makes much of the occasional extravagances of Molokan leaders, and it is inevitable that such incidents as the following should occur amidst a population so devout, humble and impressionable as the Slavs. One of Uklein's successors, Sidor Andreev, a deserter from the Army, fled into Persia. Returning thence after some years into Russia, he settled among the Molokanye of the Government of Saratov and began to preach that God was about to appear and liberate them from oppression by the Russian State, and he promised to lead them into a land flowing with milk and honey in the neighbourhood of Mount Ararat. Just then Russia had annexed Persian Armenia, which included the fertile basin of Ararat, and it is likely enough that the biblical and other legends centering round that famous mountain appealed to the imagination of Russian peasants schooled to regard the Bible as the sole source of religious truth. What would not have been the effect of a similar conquest on the evangelical and methodist sects of England and Wales? Andreev therefore set out to lead his followers to so famous and holy a locality, but under the tutelage of the Russian Government he found his way instead to the mines of Siberia.

In 1815 an English Methodist, Young Stilling, published a

book entitled 'The Triumph of Christian Faith,' of which the
Russian translation achieved great vogue and contributed not
a little to stimulate the growth of mystical dreams among the
Molokanye.   It was a commentary on the Apocalypse, in which
the Church was identified with the evangelicalism which rejects
the sacraments and ritualism of Rome; the Russian sectaries
had no difficulty in applying Stilling's arguments to the Orthodox Church, and greedily welcomed the idea that Christ would
ere long inaugurate the Millennium in the basin of Ararat, the
home of the human race and traditional site of Paradise.   This
was in 1830, immediately after Russia had acquired these regions
by the treaty of Turkmanchai in 1828.   The thousand years
of glory were to begin in 1836, according to Niketas Ivanov, a
Molokan prophet of Melitopol, and others like him.   The
result was a considerable movement of peasants towards the
new Jerusalem, and they began to flock from various Governments to the Caucasus.   An Elias appeared among them in
1833 in the person of Terence Byelozorov of Melitopol, who
even foretold the very day on which at the expiration of two
and a half years Elias would, as apocalyptic story required,
reascend to heaven.   Crowds duly collected to witness the
miracle, and the prophet with desperate leapings and waving
of his arms attempted, like Simon Magus and St. Peter, to take
to the air.   But earth chained his specific gravity, and Russian
officials his further freedom, and he was locked up until such
time as he should forget his apocalyptic privileges.

In 1836 a false Messiah from Moldavia made his appearance,
Lukian Petrov, and chose from among his followers two to
impersonate Enoch and Elias.   Next he persuaded a number of
Molokanye to don their Sunday garb and start for the Caucasus,
so as to be in time for the second Advent.   He is said to have
paved his way with supposititious wonders.   He persuaded two
girls to simulate death like well-trained dogs; then at his magic
word they leapt into life amidst the plaudits of the faithful.
Two other false Messiahs appeared among the Molokanye of
Samara.   Meanwhile new essays at ascension into Heaven
were made in the region south of the Caucasus by an Elder
who had discovered the New Zion at Alexandropol.   He had,

like the early pioneers of modern aviation, made himself canvas wings, with which he attempted flights from house-tops and summits of hills veiled appropriately with clouds.

Ivanovski relates these incidents with sombre joy, and it would not astonish us if they really took place amid enthusiasts hard-pressed by the iron hand of persecutors and thrilled with the perusal of such a weird monument of early Christian faith as the Apocalypse. Let us not forget that the Greek Church, under the influence of such teachers as Dionysius of Alexandria and Eusebius of Caesarea, removed that book for hundreds of years from their canon of scripture precisely because it roused men to excesses of Millenarist enthusiasm. History repeats itself, and these Molokanye enacted over again scenes of which we read in the pages of Irenaeus, Hippolytus and other ante-Nicene Fathers.

We noticed above the anxiety of the authors of the Manual to repudiate the literal keeping of the Jewish Sabbath and the observance of Jewish food taboos, pork, fish without scales, etc. This is explicable from the fact attested by Ivanovski that some groups of the Molokanye, under the influence of the O. T., and perhaps of the millions of Jews who inhabited then as now the South of Russia, set themselves to Judaize. Semen Dalmatov, a partisan of Uklein, led the way, and is said to have really converted his leader to his views. If so, Uklein did not attempt to impose them on his followers. We have seen Bibliolatry lead to many curious movements, so it is only natural it should have had similar results in Russia, and Ivanovski indicates various sources of information concerning them, namely the *Orthodox Conversations* for 1858–9; *National Memorials* for 1828, pt. 33, p. 57, for 1864, bk. 5, for 1867, July, for 1870, June; *Strannik* for 1878, January; Journal of the See of the Caucasus, for 1875, p. 195.

These sources incline us to suppose that Uklein really adopted the Judaism of Dalmatov. But his followers could not agree, and the quarrel spread to the Government of Saratov, where under stress of opposition Uklein's followers went so far as to exalt the Mosaic Law above the Christian, and taught that Jesus was no more than a man born of men, a prophet indeed, but inferior to Moses. Perhaps this was a reaction against the docetic view of Jesus' flesh current among them in some circles. It is exactly the sort of thesis and antithesis which we find between the Gnostics and the future Catholic Church in the early stages of the Christian religion. The Judaizers of Saratov, we learn, rejected essential Christian dogmas and feasted Saturday instead of Sunday under the leadership of a peasant named Sunbukov of the village Dubovsk in that province. These called the other Molokanye who disagreed with them the *Sundayites*. Unlike the true Jews, however, Sunbukov's sect do not look forward to a Messiah. There already existed in Russia before the year 1800 groups of Jewish proselytes, and to them this new sect in time affiliated itself. To-day they deny the Divinity of Christ in the sense that others assert it and repudiate all the external rites and symbols of orthodox Christianity; yet they are eclectics and do not adopt indiscriminately all the observances of Russian Jews; for example, they do not insist on circumcision and the feast of new moons. They interpret, as did the good bishop Archelaus and the Gnostics,[1] the text of Isaiah 'a Virgin shall conceive,' etc. of the Virgin Church, and they deny that the scene of the Messianic Kingdom will be laid on earth. On the contrary the Messiah will be a mighty moral teacher, renovating mankind with his teaching and inaugurating an epoch of freedom and sweet reasonableness. In their dwellings these Judaizers of Russia keep the sacred books under a veil on a shelf in the corner of their room, where the orthodox peasant hangs up his ikon. They are reckoned, or were till yesterday reckoned, by the Russian Government as one of the more noxious sects, because they deny the dogma of the Incarnation. They evidently reproduce many characteristics of early Ebionite Christianity.

Uklein, as we have seen, tried in opposition to the Dukhobortsy from whom he was sprung, to institute among his followers the ideas and practices of the Apostolic age; and his follower Isaiah Krylov of Saratov, a deserter from the army, who had fled into the Caucasus, spread his master's tenets in that region in the first quarter of the XIXth Century. The

[1] Cf. the *Acta Archelai*.

police drove him back into Russia, and he settled in the village of Salamatir in the province of Saratov. He knew the Bible almost by heart, and introduced a rite of the Breaking of Bread, and of prayers partly with genuflexion, partly with uplifted hands. After his death his innovations were, in spite of the opposition of one Pchelin, further developed by Maslov, who wrote prayers and chose lections for the evening rite of the Breaking of Bread. He is also said to have devised the rite of Namegiving in use among the Molokanye along with that of blowing on a child's lips on the fortieth day after birth, and also the rite of marriage. One of his adherents, a Cossack named Andrew Salamatin in 1823 propagated his tenets in the Tauric Chersonese, and his teaching was developed into that of the Molokanye of the Don. The rites and teaching of the latter are described by Ivanovski from three sources, the *National Memorials* of 1870, bk. 6; the *Orthodox Review* of 1867, pt. 22; and a manual drawn up by themselves in 1875. His description agrees in all essential respects with that which we have already furnished. He rightly observes that, of all the Molokan groups, that of the Don approximates most closely to the Orthodox Church.

CHAPTER III

THE COMMUNISTS, STUNDISTS AND OTHER SMALL SECTS

The Communists

This sect is a ramification of the Molokanye, from whom they only differ in details of social organization. It was founded by a well-to-do peasant of Samara named Maxim Akinthiev Popov who about the year 1820 wrote a tract upholding the communism of the earliest Church as described in the Book of Acts, and working out a scheme for a communistic society organized in families, villages and unions of villages. No member was to own anything except his wife and children, all earnings were pooled and stored in a common treasury, or, where they were in kind, in common granaries; all the instruments of labour were common property, and as many as twelve different orders of officials were to be instituted for the regulation of religious services, of social economy and education in common schools of the young. Even the school-books of the children were provided out of the common stock.

The scheme is detailed in an article written by Shchapov in the *Delo* of 1867, No. 10, but it hardly went beyond the limits of theory; and C. V. Maximovich in another article of the same journal for 1867 tells the story of its failure in practice. Popov, who was a Molokanye of the following of Uklein, began by gaining a considerable number of adherents, who were impressed by the manner in which, faithful to his principles, he gave away all he had to the poor. His fame spread quickly among the Molokanye beyond the Volga, and the villages of Yablonovoe (Yablonovoe gay) and Lake Tyagloe went over to him en masse. The inevitable then occurred. Popov was seized by the Government and transported from the Nikolaevski province of the Samara Government to the Caucasus along with a number of his adherents. There, in spite of poverty and distress, they attracted new adherents, with the result that the leader was deported afresh, this time from

the Government of Shemakhin to the Menzelin district of the
Yenisei Government where he was still living as late as 1867
in the Shushin volost or county.

The ideal of the sect was to live in families, but to pool their
work as also their goods and chattels. Twelve 'apostles' were
chosen among them, at whose feet they were to lay all their
property. They built common magazines, and appointed
common treasuries. But the enthusiasm which originally
inspired their renunciation of *meum* and *teum* presently died
down, as it did in the case of the early Church, and they had
to admit to themselves that "they had been carried away by
indiscretion"; at least such is the report of the *Orthodox Conversationalist* of 1859 (pp. 408 and 439). It was too lofty and
exacting an ideal and overtaxed their moral energy. The
time soon came when they judged it best to restore to each
family as nearly as could be what it had contributed to the
common stock and start afresh along humbler lines. Yet the
essay they had made in collectivist communism left its mark
upon them, and they remained after they gave it up on a higher
social and moral level than they were before they attempted it.
They still retained a common magazine, in which each head of a
family was obliged to deposit, for the use of the poor, a tenth
part of all he had, in money or in kind. Over and above that,
each member at the meetings for prayer laid what he could
afford in a plate over which was laid a napkin, so that no one
could criticize his neighbour's benevolence. In all this they
rose, we are told, well above the level of most Russian peasants.

Varadinov, another observer of their communities, relates
in the *History of the Ministry of the Interior*, (Vol. viii, p. 500)
that they chose an official called 'judge' or 'almoner' to whom
they confided the money thus offered for him to distribute it
to the poor and indigent. They chose other officers as well for
the regulation both of their religious services and civil affairs,
bearing such unusual titles as conductors, prayers, clerks or
rhetors, singers, officers *de secretis*, men of counsel or mentalists.
Some of them during service held a sort of spiritual rank and
gave the blessing, expounded the Scriptures when the prayers
were ended, interpreted their meaning for the past and future.

Out of church, however, they became again ordinary members of the community. The choice of these officials was not really popular. They were nominated by their predecessors in office, and their names publicly proclaimed.

The right of the individual to interpret Scripture for himself, so wide in the sister sects, is limited in this one. No one can undertake the task in the meeting without informing the 'judge' beforehand of what line he will take. The founder Popov was not fond of being contradicted, nor are his successors in office; and obedience to officers is a cardinal duty among them. The members of the sect are forbidden all secular literature and only allowed to study the Bible, in contrast with the disciples of Uklein.

The Communists, of course, no longer deserve their name, since they long ago gave up Popov's principles. Maximov in 1867 counted 120 families of them in Nikolaievsk, but if all the Transcaucasian members of the sect could have been assembled in one place there would have been 645 families. This village lies near Lenkoran, surrounded by Armenians, Tatars and other foreigners. At that time they carried on little propaganda, and indeed in their situation were little able to do so, for the Russian authorities prevented their holding communication with European Russia. All their letters, going or coming, were opened by the police.

In matters of creed and cult the Communists differ little from the followers of Uklein, but out of them issued about 1830 a sect of religious leapers, forming as it were a link with the Khlysty. Lukian Petrov was the founder of these. The Communists are reputed by Tolstoy, who described them in an article in the *Proceedings* of the Imp. Soc. of Hist. for 1864, bk. 4, not to pray for the Tsar. Indeed another writer in the *National Records* (*Otetch Zap.* for 1878, No. 10) states that they called the government the Scourge of Antichrist. They are careful about the schooling of their children, but in 1850 their school in Nikolaievsk was closed by the Holy Synod, as a centre of heretical infection. Under a new regulation it was allowed to continue, if the teacher was appointed by the local governor, but the writer in the *Proceedings* just above mentioned does

not know if the sect complied or not. Ivanovski's account of
this sect substantially agrees with that of Uzov and the sources
I have cited, but he gives no estimate of the numbers of the
sect at the end of the last century. Probably they were very
reduced.

The Righthand Brotherhood or Zion's Tidings

Ivanovski describes this obscure sect from the *Orthodox
Conversationalist* of May, 1876, the *Orthodox Review*, June,
1867, and the Perm *Diocesan Gazette*, 1867, No. 24, and from
a MS. book sent him by an examining magistrate. It is
probably a sect as feeble in numbers as its tenets, as recorded
in this work, are violent. Its founder was a Staff-captain of
artillery named Ilin, who was banished in 1856 to the Solovets
monastery; previously he had lived in the Baltic provinces.
At the end of the last century his followers were chiefly encountered in the Governments of Perm and Ural. His book
regarded as a sort of gospel by them is partly in prose, partly
in verse.

The main source of his inspiration is the Apocalypse, and we
have pictures of the destined end of the world and of the
Church and of their present condition. Like the Dukhobortsy
this sect rejects all externals, invocation of saints, relics, ecclesiastical authority. The following verses contain the gist of the
founder's message:—

"Nor churches raise of stone, nor altars rear,
But everywhere God glorify and fear.
    Your priests we own not,— rites away we fling,
    With us each brother is a saint and king."

But he has a higher Christology than the Dukhobortsy, who
in 1816 informed the two worthy Quakers who visited them that
Jesus was mere man, for this book teaches that Jesus Christ
was Jehovah crucified, God-man, after the manner of the
ancient Patripassians.

Ivanovski declares that there is no trace of Christianity
in the book save the name *Isus*, the use of which seems to indicate that it was penned under the influence of the Old believers.

It is, however, strongly tinctured with Judaism, for it inculcates the observance of the Sabbath, circumcision and disuse of pork. At the same time the Jews are called a congregation of Satan, and the author assails the Jews of Paris in particular!

He looks forward to the institution of a Judaism in accordance with the New Testament and believes that Jehovah will soon appear, and, after separating the left from the right among us, gather the latter into a millennial Kingdom in Judaea. In it "all sorts of blessings are to be heaped like mountains on us, woods, green fields, gardens, honeycomb and fruit, gold, bronze and silver, gems. There will be no barbaric studies, no schools for recruits, no violence or tricks, no reports, no flattery of the authorities. All will be equal and of one rank, no police, no judges, everywhere sanctity and common people."

The Stundists

More important is the sect of the Stundists, in describing which Ivanovski relies mainly on the Archpriest Rozhdestvenski's volume, *South Russian Stundism*, published in Petersburg 1889, and the Missionary Troitski's *Refutation of the errors of Stundism*, Kiev, 1890.

It is the most recent of the widespread Russian sects and the only one clearly due to German influences; it is mostly diffused in the South Russian Governments, especially those of Kherson, Ekaterinoslav and Kiev, where towards the close of the XIXth Century it had begun to excite the attention of priests and policemen. Its real founder is said to have been Jacob Spener, a German pastor, who died 1705. He encouraged that form of pietism which delights in meetings where the Bible is read and made the object of meditation, and he insisted on the pious devoting certain hours (German *Stunde*) especially on holidays to such spiritual exercises. But so far there was no separate sect or religious organization, and at the meetings in Hamburg and elsewhere, Lutherans, Calvinist and Baptists mingled together. There was an agreement to do without formal rites, and internal spiritual illumination was by grace divine.

In 1817 Stundism was carried by German settlers to the steppes along the Black Sea into regions where the dregs of Dukhoborism and of the Molokan sect still lingered, in spite of the fact that the bulk of them had been transported beyond the Caucasus. With these dregs Stundism rapidly allied itself.

Ivanovski admits the deplorable religious conditions in those regions a hundred years ago, and adduces in proof the testimony of several Russian divines, e.g., of Bishop Nicanor, who declared that the inhabitants had neither churches nor religion. Children and young people received no religious training whatever, the educated people were libertines, while among the common people vice, drunkenness and dissoluteness reigned unchecked. He admits that here was a soil favourable for the implanting and spread of a sect which laid stress on morality, and that Stundism was such a sect. Its earliest Russian converts and propagandists, Ratushnyi, Tsimban, Ryaboshapka, declared that before they joined the sect they had led a dissolute life and "tasted of vice in all its forms."

But the early Stundists took up no hostile position against the Orthodox Church; their object was merely to moralize its members, just as Wesley, at any rate to begin with, had no idea of founding a separate sect outside the Anglican communion. In the Kherson Government, Bonekemipher, a reforming pastor, exhorted those who listened to his preaching not to desert the Orthodox Church, but only to adapt their lives to the precepts of the Gospel. The earlier preachers of the movement in Little Russia, Ratushnyi and Ryaboshapka, and Gerasim Balaban and Yakob Koval in the Government of Kiev, worked along the same lines; and it was only about 1870 that the new pietists organized themselves into a distinct sect; till then they baptized their children in the orthodox churches, confessed and received the communion in them, and kept the Easter fast.

The separate movement was due to the influence of the Baptists or Mennonites of South Russia and the Caucasus. This explains why they underwent baptism afresh, no doubt because they regarded infant baptism as neither scriptural nor primitive. Ivan Ryaboshapka, already named, was the first to submit to the rite at the hands of Ephim (Euthymius)

Tsimban. Thenceforth they formed a sect and administered their own rites of baptism, marriage and burial.

Ivanovski details their tenets from a manual of the Kosyakovski Stundists, met with in the Tarashchan district or county of the Kiev Government. It contains fifteen sections, and each tenet is clearly expressed and evidenced by texts from scripture. It was translated from a German original. Like the Molokanye, they profess to build entirely on the Bible, and like them are the more difficult to controvert because they interpret a text which *prima facie* is against them by the light of another which favours their views; if hard pressed they even resort to allegory in order to get out of a text. It is not however always apparent what they seek to evade in the examples of allegorization adduced by Ivanovski. For example they explain Gethsemane as meaning the world, the Disciples who went to sleep are those who are sunk in religious torpor till they become Stundists, while those who rejected and crucified Jesus are the orthodox of to-day.

Their tenets are a mixture of the Lutheran, Calvinist and Baptist. Sin was originally due to the Fall of Man and they declare man since the fall to be incapable of good and radically prone to evil. With the Calvinists they hold that certain souls are elect and predestined to Salvation; and these were handed over by the Father to the Saviour, as the reward of his death struggle, nor can they ever be lost or taken from him.

The means, however, by which they will find Salvation are five: the first is the Word of God from which at Baptism they acquire faith in Christ. Baptism is the second, and is the first fruits of faith and love for Christ, a triumphant confession of sin forgiven and washed away. The Breaking of Bread is the third, for in this Holy Supper we spiritually partake of the body and blood of Christ. The fourth is the Communion of Saints, the supreme expression of church unity. Fifth and last is repentance with prayer; but repentance with a pure heart does not involve absolution pronounced by a priest, for prayer is more efficacious as a release from sin than is that; and it is of two sorts, external when attended with sighs, tears, sorrow and uplifted hands; internal as a meditation upon God and the divine verities.

The ecclesiastical organization of the Stundists is simple. They have no bishops, but presbyters are chosen by the faithful to govern and administer their affairs, teachers to preach. These two orders can baptize and serve the Eucharist, assisted by an order of deacons or servers. They have no fixed rites, but church service begins with reading and interpretation, of the Bible, then hymns composed by themselves are sung to popular airs unlike those of the Orthodox Church. In their assembly they sit, but sometimes walk up and down debating the sense of a text. They recognize none but adult baptism, for Jesus (Mark 16 xvi) prescribed faith as the *sine qua non* of baptism.[1] Accordingly the Stundists re-baptize those whom they convert from orthodoxy; and, following the Lord's example, they baptize in a river.

The rite of breaking bread is held once a month, in the presence of all the Stundists of a locality. It begins with the lections of the Last Supper, followed by hymns. Then, all standing, the presbyter prays to the Lord to deign to receive his body in purification from sin. The deacon next brings slices of bread on a plate, which the presbyter breaks into pieces, communicates himself and others in them, the deacon bearing the morsels to the faithful. Next they sing solemn verses about the cup, and read appropriate lections from the Gospel, after which they communicate in the wine. The rite ends with a prayer of thanksgiving.

All other rites they reject; so too fasts, which they say are even harmful, for a man is more likely to do harm when he is hungry, and it is not that which enters the mouth which defiles us. They venerate neither cross nor ikon, nor commemorate the dead. Saints they refuse to invoke, and in particular ridicule the cult of St. Nicholas, so popular in Russia On Good Friday even the poorest among them eat meat.

There is a minority among the Stundists who, like the followers of Uklein and the Dukhobortsy, renounce all rites even

---

[1] Ivanovski appeals to Mark 10 iv: "Forbid them not, for of such is the kingdom of heaven," forgetting that the children in question had certainly not been baptized, and that the text, if it has any bearing on the point at issue, is rather an argument than not for dispensing with baptism altogether.

baptism and the Eucharist, insisting that Christianity is something wholly spiritual. Their teaching is given in a manual compiled by Jacob Koval, and they are found especially in the province of Tarashchan in the Kiev Government. This teacher argued that the baptism of Jesus was a unique event. "We," he said, "do not frequent the banks of the Jordan, but are purified of sin by being baptized into the death of Christ. With him we die and rise again, but not by water. The communion, they argue, of which Paul wrote, stands in the communication of the Holy Spirit through union with Holy Church. In it we are fed with truth and peace. The Saviour was the word made flesh, and if we assimilate the Word, he manifests himself in us."

Part III

THE MYSTIC SECTS

CHAPTER I

THE KHLYSTY

For my knowledge of the mystic sects, the Khlysty and Skoptsy, I am chiefly indebted to the monumental work of Professor Karl Konrad Grass of Dorpat, *Die Russischen Sekten*, Leipzig, 1905–1914, and to his *Geheime Heilige Schrift der Skopzen*, Leipzig, 1904. His account of the Khlysty fills 714 pages of small print, that of the Skoptsi, some 1100, and every page is full of learning. He has ransacked the Russian archives in order to present us with as complete a history as possible; and on dubious or disputed points he sets before us the conclusions of Russian workers in the same field, of whose works he adds a copious bibliography. Too much praise cannot be lavished on a work embodying so much research, patient, exhaustive, clearly written and well-arranged. It was almost superfluous to consult other sources, but I have paid attention to the works of Ivanovski and Liprandi.

The tenets of the Khlysty have no more relation than those of the Dukhobortsy to the stereotyped 'high' Christology of the great historical churches. In the Khlysty hymns, indeed, recur in plenty such terms as the God Sabaoth, God the Father, Christ son of God, the Holy Spirit, the Mother of God — this last a shibboleth, as is well known, of the Council of Ephesus. But in the Christian Shamanism which here lies before us we breathe another atmosphere than that of the speculative doctors of Byzantium, remoulding the messianic ideal according to the categories of Greek philosophy and suppressing, so far as could be, its pneumatic and prophetic aspects. The real parallel to Khlystism is to be sought in some of the earliest phases of our Faith.

In that widespread form of Christianity generally called Adoptionism the Holy Spirit descends from heaven, disguised in the similitude of a dove, to take possession of the 'man born of men,' Jesus of Nazareth, who was singled out for such honour

339

because of his having kept all the precepts of the Law and the Prophets. In him old Jewish prophecy culminated. But the grace of prophecy and of election by the Spirit did not end with Jesus, but only entered in him on a new cycle of development. The same Spirit of which the fullness dwelt in him descended afresh on the day of Pentecost, this time with tongues of fire and even odour of sanctity upon the faithful. They too by this baptism of the Holy Spirit and of fire became elect sons of God, spiritually animated Christs; for Christhood was not the privilege of the Founder alone, but was equally the guerdon of his followers. In this early stage of the Christian religion there was no distinction of the rôles of Christhood, of Spirit, of divine Logos or Word. Like St. Paul, the Adoptionists felt that they had died and risen again with their Master, and in them the Spirit dwelt and spake, not merely in the inarticulate jargon of tongues, but in sober discourse as well.

In the earliest phases of Christianity we have also the same cult of virginity, male and female, as among the Khlysty. The student knows it under the name of encratitism. Tertullian felt it to be incompatible with the spiritual gifts received in baptism for a Christian to continue in carnal relations with his wife, and the same scruples were felt a century later in the age of Augustine. So we read in St. Paul's Epistles of the Apostles taking with them on their missionary travels sister-wives, of the brethren of the Lord doing likewise, of the converted of Corinth aspiring to practise the same continency, though, it seems, less successfully. Everywhere in the Christian literature of the early centuries we come upon the same custom; in Rome, in North Africa, in Syria, in Anatolia where it inspired many of the poems of Gregory of Nyssa, even in the old Celtic church. It underlay the chivalry of the Middle Ages with its idealized mistresses, it inspired Dante's dream of Beatrice. To-day it is spread before us far and wide, up and down, the whole of Russia; and those who practise it call themselves Christs, a title of honour which the population round them has perverted by a pun into Khlysty or flagellants.

As then among the Dukhobortsy, so among the Khlysty, the cardinal doctrine is that of the reincarnation of Christ in the individual; and the doctrine often assumes the form of a belief that at the death of one of their Christs, the Christhood passes into the body of another.[1] But this must not be interpreted in the sense that there is among them no more than one Christ at a time. On the contrary, almost every congregation, every *ship* or *nave* as they call it, has its own Christ, and alongside of him its Mother of God or Theotokos, by whom is signified a female consort of the Christ, like him plenarily inspired with the Holy Spirit.

The Khlysty are not unacquainted with the Old Testament and hold that the ancient Patriarchs were incarnations of Christ, just as Cyrus was a Christ. Even the burning bush in Exodus, Ch. 3, is interpreted as a parable of the flesh tenanted by the Spirit. From the bush it entered Moses, and after him Joshua and other spiritual leaders until finally the Fire descended on Jesus in the Jordan, when, as the old Western text relates, a light shone around upon the waters. The oldest Epiphany hymns of the Eastern Churches make much of this episode.

Grass (p. 256) remarks that Russian students of the sect at first hand recognize as its tenet, everywhere and always, that Jesus of Nazareth was an ordinary man until he was thirty years of age, his birth from a virgin being interpreted to mean that he was brought up to the true faith by his mother. In the early days of Christianity we equally often meet with the idea that the holy virginal aeon, the Church, preceded Christ and was, spiritually of course, his mother. So Tertullian, the Montanist, recognized in the Church the *Mater Domini* and in his physical Mother Mary an image of the unbelieving Synagogue.

After a forty days' fast Christ came to baptism, and then the Spirit of God descended on him, whereby he was anointed the Christ. This ancient tenet was attributed by Justin Martyr (c. 140) to a large body of his fellow-believers. Such an adoptionist opinion underlay the old gnostic systems of the second century and was in the second century dominant among orthodox circles in Rome. The Khlysty may conceivably have

[1] Grass, p. 253.

inherited it from antiquity. On the other hand, as it is the apparent sense of the synoptic gospels [1] they may have merely inferred it from a study of those documents.

The Khlysty hold that Christ's body lay in the grave after his death, like any other man's body. The Resurrection really means that the Divine Spirit which had constituted him a Christ was bequeathed by him to successors worthy thereof.

Thus the incarnation, the man-becoming, or as the Fathers termed it, the *enanthrôpêsis* of God in Jesus of Nazareth, was a filling of Jesus with the Spirit of God, and was only the first of that series of such fillings which we witness in the Christian Church. The Khlysty, no more than the Shepherd of Hermas, know of any distinction between Christ the Son and the Holy Spirit. They are essentially a pre-Trinitarian sect, though in their hymns we meet with tags of Trinitarianism borrowed from the Orthodox Church.

The Khlysty *naves* or *ships* form a loose congeries united only by the cult of one Danila Philipov, whose legend I give below and whom they regard as their proximate founder and prophet. I use the word *proximate*, because Danila only lived in the second half of the XVIIth Century, whereas their hymns [2] recognize that the sect is as old as Dmitri Donskoi, prince or grand duke of Moscow from 1363 to 1389. For Dmitri crucified one of their Christs named Averzhan on the battlefield of Kulikov; another of their hymns also celebrates the memory of a Christ named Yemeljan who suffered under Ivan the Terrible (1533–1584). Danila was pre-eminent among their spiritual founders because he was not merely Christ, but God Sabaoth himself. He was 'godded,' to use a good old English word, by the descent of God himself upon him out of the seventh heaven in the shape of a bright falcon. As an incarnation of God himself, Danila precedes in dignity all the Christs and Mothers of God of the sect.

Such identification of a mere man with God himself is strange to our ears, but in fact Russian peasants are not far removed

---

[1] Except, of course, that the Gospels put the fast after the Baptism, not before it.

[2] Grass, p. 1.

intellectually from the oriental populations who were ready to accept an Augustus or a Tiberius as objects of divine cult. They style even their ikons *bogi* or "gods," as Grass remarks (p. 255). The men of Lystra were quite prepared to add Paul and Barnabas to their Pantheon, and we have seen a John of Kronstadt elevated in modern Russia into something higher than an ordinary saint of the calendar.

The question arises: what are the credentials of a Christ? How is he to be recognized? The answer is: By his sufferings. Danila the Founder was crucified at least twice over, and the Russian Government was certain to provide this test for many. The rack and the knout were ever handy. But mortification of the flesh by the candidate for Messiahship is no less essential. Thus Roman Likhachov late in the last century was believed by his followers in the Caucasus to have fasted for forty days on end. Some time before 1825 Avvakum Kopulov, a peasant of the Tambov Government, achieved the same feat. Early in the XVIIIth Century Ivan Pimenov, a peasant of Alatur in the Nijni Novgorod Government, attained the dignity by walking barefooted through the forests in summer and winter, feeding on roots and shrouding his thoughts in a perpetual mutism. He lived to be a hundred. The self-discipline of silence reminds us of Apollonius of Tyana and the Neo-Pythagoreans, and in general the exaggerated asceticism of the Khlysty reminds us of the Indian Fakhirs and of the monks of the Thebaid. The claims of rival pretenders to Christhood are settled by their followers who watch them for years to see which of them undergoes the worst sufferings. In such circumstances it is inevitable that the ascetic should sometimes trick his followers and even himself; and this was no doubt the case with Gregory Shevshchenko, who died and came to life again at Alexandropol in the Ekaterinoslav Government about the year 1889 to the surprise and delight of his adherents; parallels will occur to the reader of Hindoos buried alive and resuscitating themselves.

As Grass remarks (p. 260), all these exploits, together with the self-glorification which attends them, seem at first sight to be performed at the cost of Jesus of Nazareth, and Ivan

Gregoriev taught in Orlov Gai in 1858 that the Son of God was
not in the historical Jesus Christ alone.　Even before Christ
he was in the Righteous, and in the same way He has subsequently come down among us in many righteous and faithful
ones.　In such teaching, however, we have little more than a
protest against the Greek Churches which insist on the unique
Divinity of Jesus; the sectaries, if they were better read, could
adduce on their side the testimony of Justin Martyr (*dialogue
with Tryphon*, 268) that there were Christians in his day who
believed Jesus to have been born a man and to have been
anointed and become Messiah by way of election; or of Hege-
monius (Acta Archelai) who takes up the same standpoint, and
assumes that, as Jesus for his merits was chosen to be a vessel
of the Holy Spirit and became Christ by adoption, so were the
Apostles and the faithful in general.　In fact they do not yield
to ordinary Christians in their veneration for the Man of Nazareth.　This is evident from their hymns which address Jesus
as the Allmighty and heavenly Lord.　Not only the rank and
file, but their Christs equally, invoke him in prayer as God the
Father.　The Virgin Mary is equally an object of their cult,
none the less solemn and sincere because they venerate their
own mothers of God.

　Two of their hymns reproduced by Grass (p. 261) from
Barsov illustrate the above points.　The first is

"Our redeemer Christ hath consummated the task of his all
　　　　purest flesh,
Yet he still doth consummate it in other elect bodies of flesh.
He, ever the one and same Christ, God, Saviour,
Abideth inseparably with the Father in Heaven,
Sendeth his Holy Spirit, through whom he begetteth Christ.
We are the earth and the little world, but the Son is Son of
　　　　God.
He riseth in the hearts of those who love him, like the sun,
He riseth up, sets not again, but tarrieth always;
He transmutes his Word into flesh, whereby he redeemeth the
　　　　entire world;
The believing heart knoweth how the light streams forth.
Then doth God beget Christ, when all things die away.

When the Son of God shall appear, all things shall be changed,
The creature shall be reborn, shall be transformed into Christ,
When love, pure humility, faith and patience
In us, my friends, shall prevail, then will Christ come unto us.
Thou the only, the perfect, the word made flesh!
Thou, hypostatic Son of God, born before world and time
    began!
Where thou wilt, in whom thou restest — thou dost manifest
    thyself!"

The second is:—

"The Liberator, who is come into the world, sent from God,
He cometh forward, the fair sun; open ye your hearts!
Open them, welcome in the King of Glory,
And so well as ye may, my friends, cleanse your hearts!
In heartfelt penitence humble ye yourselves,
And with heartfelt tears wash yourselves clean!
Be ye pure, spotless, as the children of God.
Welcome ye the heavenly light, unfold the petals of the heart.
Praise ye in the flesh your little Father akin to you.
The Word of God was made flesh, revealed himself among us,
In his fulness it was revealed, appeared in the creature.
It dwelleth together with us and instructeth us.
For thee are temples made ready, O opened heart,
Come, eternal life, descend into our hearts!
Despise not, thou Son of God, our blackness."

But in this sect are many grades of holiness. Danila was
God of Sabaoth incarnate, and many are the Christs and
Mothers-of-God, presiding over the various ships. But the
vessel is also freighted, like the Church of St. Paul, with others
who in their measure have received the Gift of the Spirit, with
Apostles, Prophets, Prophetesses, People of God in general.
All are elect, all have the grace of God, but all are not in the
same measure endowed with the spirit. All initiates of whatever grade of sanctity, are admitted to the meetings which are
strictly secret. Then are chanted the hymns of which I have
given these two examples.

And these, be it remarked, for anything they contain, might

equally be Dukhobor compositions. They are composed in double rhymes, in stately rhythm and in pure well chosen language. Once I was in a Russian posthouse, a solitary place, perched high upon the lofty hills which confront Ararat across the plain of Erivan. It was a clear moonlight night, and a troop of Russian dissenters, whether Dukhobortsy or Molokanye or Khlysty I know not, came marching along the road, singing in parts such a hymn as the above. It was the most stirring devotional music I have ever listened to, transcending any elaborate Italianized chorus I ever heard in the Kazan Cathedral of Petersburg. St. Augustine describes in his inimitable way the impression which the devotional music of Milan made upon him: it must have resembled the singing of Russian dissenters, as I have heard it.

Among the Khlysty then the two chief sacraments, the essentials in order to salvation, are firstly mortification of the flesh, sufferings self-imposed or inflicted by a Russian Government ever ready to inflict them; and secondly, reception of the Holy Spirit, and the latter commonly shews itself, as it shewed itself in the early Church, in the form of trance, of ecstasy, of spiritual convulsions and contortions.

The Holy Spirit dwells in the seventh heaven and his sudden clutch of the devotee is likened in the hymns to the swoop of a falcon, or an eagle, seldom, as in our Gospels, to the gentle downward flight of a dove. The mere singing of hymns suffices to throw some of the faithful into an ecstasy, and a meeting commonly begins with a metrical paraphrase of the Lord's Prayer. The first lines of this in what Grass (p. 265) regards as its most primitive form runs thus:

"Give us, Lord,
    To us, Jesus Christ!
    Give us, Son of God,
    Light; have mercy upon us!
    Ruler, Holy Spirit,
    Have mercy upon us!
    Lady Ruler, our little Mother!
    Ask, Light, for us
    The Light, thy Son,

The Spirit of God, the Holy one!
Light, by thee are redeemed
Many sinners on the earth,
Unto the little Mother, unto our Lady Queen,
Light, unto her that cherishes us."

There are a hundred other hymns which contribute to the same effect; but the most potent means to produce union with the spirit is the religious dance known as *Radenie*, a word which implies zeal, labour, fervour. With Russians, emotion as naturally translates itself into dancing as among orientals; and it is possible that the Khlysty imitate in some degree the Mahommedan Dervishes of whose transports they were eye-witnesses during the long subjection of their country to the Tatars. Stephen Graham in his volume upon *Russia and the World* (London, 1915) has a graphic picture of Russian peasants dancing which reminds us of some of the *Radenie*.

The early Christians graced every festival of a Saint with "the customary dances"; [1] and if they were subsequently forbidden in the Spanish and other Churches, it was only because they were irreverently conducted and not because they were objectionable in themselves. Even in Spain I have myself witnessed the graceful dances of the Acolytes in the Great Church of Seville.

The following is an example of the hymns which among these people preludes the descent of the Spirit:

"Strings, his strings
The prophet David (smote)!
The prophet played upon the strings —
He burst into tears;
With the upper Powers
He prayed unto Sabaoth:
Have mercy on me, O God!
Pour out thy grace on me!
Mighty are the graces
Freely bestowed on thee, who prayest!
In thy sight have I sinned,

[1] *Acta* of S. Polyeuctes.

Before thee I bow myself down,
Give me faith, hope —
To thee I pray.
By thy grace
Am I for ever made strong,
Like a child
I am anew reborn.
By thy holy Spirit
Am I now swept away — in transport.
With us have they assembled,
In the assembling place the assemblage,
They have called the Spirit down,
They have shed tears,
They have dispersed their sins,
In themselves they have awaited
In fear the King of Glory.
And all with one accord
Lifted their voices to heaven:
Float down, Son of God,
Good Spirit, guide!
As in earlier days
A roar was heard from heaven,
Thou unto thine elect ones
In fiery tongues descendest,
Thus in thy speech to be heard by all
From that day unto this."

Picture the surroundings: it is the evening of one of the many feasts of the Russian Church, for a gathering of people on such a day is least likely to excite the attention of the police. The meeting is held in a long whitewashed chamber, with benches along the walls, and to one side there is a table on which is set loaves and a jug of water or of mild and unintoxicating kvas, the elements of the Khlysty Eucharist. Such is the scene of the rites to follow. The faithful enter; they have shed their heavy cloaks and foot-gear; for when you enter a Russian house you leave your over-boots at the door as a matter of course, and the floor here, like that of a mosque, is holy ground. Men and women alike are clad in a white flowing raiment, and, as in the sister sect of Skoptsy, each carries a white handkerchief to be waved aloft in the dance in imitation of an angel's wings. They approach in couples the presiding Christ or Mother of God, and prostrate themselves before them in token that God and Christ are in them made flesh. They probably listen to a little homily against the use of intoxicants and tobacco, against backsliding and on the duty of guarding in silence even on the rack and under the lash the mysteries of the sect. In the XVIIIth Century innumerable monks and nuns from orthodox convents frequented such meetings, and with them may have originated in the sect the practice which sporadically continues to-day of burning incense before the suspended ikons and of adoration paid to the Cross hung in a corner of the chamber.

The homily finished, the dance begins, at first an orderly circular dance in which men and women join hands; all are singing the Prayer of Jesus given above in alternation with other hymns. Faster and faster revolves the human circle, more animated become the vocal strains, and presently they burst into a chorus recalling that of the Bacchae in the ancient mysteries of Dionysus:—

> " Past us in paradise a bird is hovering,
>   It flies amain,
>   To yonder side it glances,
>   Where the trumpet's blast [1] is heard,
>   Where God himself is speaking:
>   O God, O God, O God,
>   O Spirit, O Spirit, O Spirit!
>   Float down, down, down!
>   Oi Yegá! Oi Yegá! Oi Yegá! [2]
>   It floated down, it floated down,
>   The Holy Spirit, the Holy Spirit!
>   'Twill blow where it will, where it listeth,
>   The Holy Spirit, the Holy Spirit.
>
>   O I burn, O I burn,
>   The Spirit burns, God burns!

---

[1] The trumpet means the Christ or prophet presiding over the scene.
[2] Perhaps the pronunciation is *yeha*, an abbreviation of the name Jesus.

Light is in me, Light is in me,
The Holy Ghost, the Holy Ghost!
O I burn, burn, burn,
Ghost! Oi Yegá! (four times)
Yevóye! Host Yevoí (thrice)

Soon isolated figures detach themselves from the throng and
spin round, like Dervishes, with incredible rapidity. Others
begin to stamp, kick, hop, leap, shriek; all are bathed in sweat,
all are foaming at the mouth, all are gesticulating wildly, all are
ejaculating such phrases as : Oi Duyh, Oi Dukh, Svkatoi
Duch, Okh, ŏkh, ŏkh![1]

It is a final token of the presence of the Spirit that they drop
exhausted and inanimate on the floor, insensible to external
impressions. On such occasions they have failed to notice
the entrance even of the hated police in their chamber; or, if
they have been warned in time, they have fled barefooted in
their scanty garments to their homes across fields of snow in
forty degrees of frost and suffered no harm thereby.

But some under the intoxication of the Spirit begin to speak
with tongues, which it is the task of others to interpret. Even
these uncouth utterances are often marked by rhythm and fall
into rhymed verses, but not always as the following inharmon-
ious specimen shews:[2]

Nasontos, Lesontos, phurtlis, natruphuntru, natrisinphur,
Kreserephire, Kresentrephert, tscheresantro, ulmiri, umilisintru,
geréson, drowolmire, tschésondro phorde, kornemila, koremira,
gśdrowolne, korlemire śdrowolde, kaniphute, jeschetschere
kondre, nasiphe nasophont, meresinti, pheretra.

Such is the tongue talked by the Holy Spirit in Russia, and it
especially affects a combination of consonants nt rare in the
normal speech. Harnack has conjectured that the gibberish
of the old Greek and Egyptian magic papyri was taken down
from the lips of devotees fallen into a religious trance, and these
utterances of the Khlysty go far to confirm his conjecture.

Khlysty of whom the Spirit has taken possession and who
have subsequently revealed their experiences to the profane, are

[1] "Ho Spirit, Spirit, Holy Spirit, Ho, Ho, Ho."
[2] Grass, p. 123 whose transliteration I follow.

agreed that in such moments its advent is marked by a feeling
of profound inward exaltation and joy. They are no more
themselves, the normal man or woman is dead in them, their
hearts flutter, their tongues are stirred by the new soul within
them, they are raised into the seventh heaven, are in paradise,
they even see God and the angels face to face. So the Bogomils
of the XIth and XII Centuries had ocular visions of the
Trinity. Occasionally, like the second century Montanist
prophetess Maximilla, they are conscious of being God and
cry out to that effect. Such 'enthusiasm' was almost normal
in Christians before A. D. 250 and sporadically continued,
especially among monks and nuns. Of such ecstasy many of
the Khlysty hymns are the fruit. They are the utterances of
the Holy Ghost speaking in the flesh; taken down in writing
or faithfully remembered, they form in their entirety the *Dove
Book* (*Kniga Golubina*), which like the hymns of the Dukhobortsi, takes precedence in the matter of inspiration even of
the New Testament; though no doubt the Bible, especially the
Book of Sirach and the Gospels, is held in high reverence.
The former was the only old Jewish scripture recognized by
the Manicheans and Cathars, no doubt because the Jews
rejected it, and these sects inherited the anti-Semitic bias of
Marcion. For those, however, who are recipients of the *Dove
Book* the Bible is really superfluous, save in so far as it serves
to confirm their faith, which by dint of allegory its most refrac-
tory passages may be made to do. For example they interpret
the veil of Moses as the holy estate of matrimony, which they
regard as did the Cathars, as being no better, perhaps worse
than adultery; 'the greater adultery' was the Cathar expression for it.

The Khlysty, male or female, so thoroughly repudiate worldly
marriage, that on initiation they take a spiritual wife or husband. Not that the wife of the unregenerate phase is wholly
discarded; for she often continues to sleep in chastity in her
husband's bed, in company with the spiritual wife; but her
children, born of sin, are denominated in the argot of the sect
'little sins, whelps, young cats,' and are not allowed to call their
parents father and mother. At initiation every Khlyst swears

to eschew orthodox marriage and not to attend a christening.
They teach that if God desires a virgin to conceive, he will
impregnate her with his Holy Spirit as he did Mary the Mother
of Christ.   In spite of such beliefs, however, they illogically
insisted on the line of their founder Danila Philippovich being
maintained for some generations in the ordinary manner until
his last female descendant was immured by the Russian
Government in a convent, where she was inaccessible.   After
that their devotion to his memory centred in his relics, his hat,
stick, the rags he wore and hairs of his head.

In their diet they are very abstemious.   They eschew meat,
like the Skoptsy (a branch of their sect), because flesh is the
product of copulation; at least this is their reason according to
Liprandi (*Raskolov Eres'*, 1853, Leipzig Ed. of 1883, p. 29).
The reason is probable enough, for the Cathars also gave it;
and it is perhaps the real basis of the Catholic rule of fasting.
But the Khlysty illogically forbid fish as well, which being
born in the water had not the same taint for the Cathars or for
the early Christians, who for that reason made it the symbol
of Jesus born again the Christ in the waters of Jordan,—
Piscis natus aquis as the old Latin Christian poet has it.   Like
the Molokanye and no doubt the Dukhobortsy, the Khlysty
abjure the onion and garlic, because they interfere with the
odour of sanctity which they detect in one another.   They
also avoid potatoes, a prejudice they have in common with
many Old believers, who believe it to be the identical fruit with
which Eve tempted Adam.   That the foreign-minded Catharine II introduced it from the West was enough to condemn it;
and for a like reason they abhor tobacco.   Both are 'western
poison.'

Khlysty girls enthusiastically uphold the Encratite rule of
spiritual wedlock, and regard a man's legal wife, assumed
before he entered the order, as a Gift of the Devil.   The ascetic
life they pursue gives to the members of the sect a peculiar
look by which they are easily recognized.   No one who has
encountered them will forget their deep-set intensely gleaming
eyes, their spare emaciated frames, their reposeful manner.
They seem to have dropped out of another world into this one.

They have been accused of ending their *radenia* or religious dances with wholesale debauchery, the lights being first put out. Grass examines the evidence very carefully and impartially, and rejects the story as calumny. The only thing that gives it colour is that often, when the ecstasies are over, the exhausted votaries drop down on the floor and sleep till dawn, the men on one side of the apartment, the women on the other. Their doing so, instead of going home at once, is a necessity dictated either by the climate or by fear of the Russian police, whose suspicions would be roused if they trooped home at a late hour.[1] Tertullian, after he became a Montanist, accused the Catholic deacons of deflowering the deaconesses at the close of their agapês; but no ecclesiastical historian wholly credits his story, although no doubt the then prevailing custom of *virgines subintroductae*, i. e., of nuns living for the sake of protection or human sympathy with monkish priests and laymen, occasionally gave rise to such abuses as Gibbon satirizes and Cyprian attests. That this may occur among the Khlysty also is undeniable, but those in a position to judge admit it to be rare. The same stories were current in Medieval Europe about the Cathars, and with equally little reason. Still more horrible stories are told of the Khlysty communicating in the blood of a baby boy born to one of their virgins and so forth. The ancient Jews accused the early Christians of such Thyestean banquets, and so did the pagan populace. All through the Middle Ages the Catholics accused the Jews of them, and rival monastic orders even charged one another with them. In Russia the same tradition of anti-Semitic calumny prevails to-day. Only just before the war, the orthodox were offering up prayers all over Russia, and especially in the Kazan Cathedral in their capital, for the conviction of a miserable Jew accused in Kiev of murdering a Christian child for ritual purposes. Such superstitions are hard to kill in Russia, which in many respects remains medieval. There every Jew is believed to bear the brand of Cain, not on his brow, where it could be seen, but under his clothes on his breast. Grass, then, examines this sort

---

[1] In a peasant's *izba* or hut it is usual for both sexes, old and young, to repose together on the top of the stove during the long winter.

of story about the Khlysty with his accustomed thoroughness, setting all the evidence in full before us, and no one will wade through it and not dismiss it with contempt. The extraordinary secrecy with which for two and a half centuries the sect has, under pain of being knouted, exiled and burnt alive, concealed its rites, often under the cloak of devout adherence to the Orthodox Church, sufficiently accounts for the genesis of such stories.

From their outward show of orthodoxy and perhaps from the circumstance that in the XVIIIth Century their cult flourished so vigorously inside convents and monasteries, certain orthodox observers agree that they regard the Greek Church as a sort of vestibule to their mysteries. They are the *perfecti*, the common church man is only an *auditor* or catechumen. But their affectation of orthodoxy is at best a screen. At the most, observes Grass (p. 348), the Khlysty would allow that the Orthodox Church witnesses even against its will to their own; but in reality they utterly reject it with all its sacraments.

They hold that if the Orthodox Church has any supernatural rôle, it is a purely satanic one. They are the only Apostolic Church, the true successors of the holy Martyrs whom the kings of the earth persecuted of old, as to-day the Orthodox "Jews and Pharisees" persecute the Khlysty.

Having, like the Dukhobortsy and the Cathars, a baptism of the spirit, they reject the water baptism of John as an institution that with the advent of Christ lost its significance. Like the Hydroparastatae and other followers of Tatian, numerous in the early church, they refuse to use wine in their communion, for wine renders the sacrament sinful and fleshly. Observers have recorded of them that when they go to church and partake of the village pope's cup of wine, as the law forces them to do at least once a year, they retain it in their mouths till they can quit the church and spit it out. What they signify by the simple meal of bread and water is not clear; we have seen that the Molokanye retain it, while disclaiming for it any sacramental significance; nor is it intelligible that alongside of the plenary inspiration of the *Radenie* it could possess any for the Khlysty.

Russian authorities (eunumerated by Grass, p. 278) declare that in one form of the *Radenie* the sectaries dance round and round a tub full of water, for which reason they are in some places popularly known as *Kadushniki* from *kadushka*, a small tub. As they dance round it, flagellating themselves, they sing a refrain:—

I scourge, scourge, I seek Christ.
Come down to us, Christ, from the seventh heaven,
Circle with us, Christ, in the holy ring,
Hover down from heaven, Lord, Holy Ghost!

There is no fire beneath the tub, yet presently it begins as their fervour waxes, to simmer and bubble. A vapour rises off it, and amid the vapour in a nimbus of golden light they discern a child, or a mother and a child. Some relate that not a child, but a dark bird, like a raven, is materialized in the steam. The votaries when they see the apparition fall prostrate in ecstasy and terror.

That they conduct some such dance round a tub, seems too well attested for us to doubt it. I believe, if it exists, it may be a relic of the Epiphany consecration of water in commemoration of the descent of the Spirit in Jordan upon Christ.[1] The raven variant is bred of their common comparison of the Spirit to a falcon or an eagle. In the Great Churches a stoop of water is consecrated for use in baptisms etc. on this festival. For the excited dancers to have such a vision is natural enough. Stranger miracles are worked every day among ourselves by mediums in spiritualist séances. It would be enough for one votary to cry out that he saw it, and all present would behold it too.

The prophecies indulged in by those of whom the Spirit takes possession on such occasions, are of the naïve and homely character we might expect among Russian peasants. The prophet foretells what the weather is going to be, whether the crops will fail or whether there will be a bumper harvest,— matters of

---

[1] Cp. the old Slavonic rite (translated from a lost Latin text) of exorcising the waters at Epiphany, published by Franz Radić from a Curzola MS. of c. 1400, in *Wissenschaftliche Mittheilungen aus Bosnien und der Herzegovina*, Wien 1894, p. 179 foll.

great concern in Russia. They also forecast the take of fish in
the rivers, conflagrations of individual cabins or entire villages,
which in Russia are mostly built of wood. They also predict
persecutions by the Government, a class of event which could
be safely predicted at any time and anywhere. Sometimes
the predictions relate to the death of members of the sect or to
their sins. All sorts of devices are employed by the prophet
to shadow forth the future, and there are rules for interpreting
his actions, no less than his utterances. For example, he swings
a lamp to and fro: if it remains alight all present are blameless;
if it goes out, someone has sinned. Or he takes, says Grass
(p. 287), all the handkerchiefs which they waved as they danced,
and lays them together in the form of a cross on the floor.
Then all step over them, but if anyone trips and touches the
pattern with his toe, he is a sinner and must do penance. Grass
enumerates other equally simple forms of old-world ordeal.
We must bear in mind that in the old Russian codes the ordeal
was much in evidence, and the peasantry still believe in it.
Among ourselves it has survived as an innocent method of
fortune-telling familiar to folk-lorists.

Auricular confession of sins to the Christ or Prophet or
Mother of God appears to be in vogue among all the groups of
Khlysty who exist under various popular names all over the
Russian empire. In some groups a simple form of spiritual
marriage exists; as also simple rites for the initiation of novices,
though, be it remarked, the *Radenie* is the only proper form
of reception of the spirit. We have also hints of a rite of
anointing for the sick and of funeral ceremonies.

The origin of the Khlysty is lost in antiquity, but Uzov and
Grass are clearly right in supposing it to be a form of Bogomilism at least as old in Russia as the prevalent orthodoxy.
Russian divines who regard Western Europe as the home of
rationalism derive it from that quarter; but it has nothing in
common with the Protestant Reformation; it has affinity with
the gospel of Madame de Guyon, and it resembles externally
the Avignon Brotherhood of the end of the XVIIIth Century,
the English Quakers, the Russian freemasons; but all these
points of contact are superficial. Still more ineffective is the
attempt of Russian anthropologists to derive it from the

Shamanism of the Finns, displaced by the Muscovite Slavs so far as the latter did not blend and become one race with them, only imposing on them their language and religion.

The determining factors to be borne in mind in any discussion of their origin are their Adoptionist Christology and their *disciplina arcani*. But neither of these necessarily implies, as Grass imagines, a gnostic origin, for the Great Church was largely adoptionist until the age of Paul of Samosata, as are the Synoptic Gospels themselves; and the *disciplina arcani* was maintained in the church long after it had lost its meaning and importance. The gnostic sects were Adoptionist because they grew up within an early Christianity that was dominantly such. As regards the *disciplina*, it is difficult to say just how far it is in the case of a Russian dissenting sect due to persecution and how far traditional.

We have seen that the Khlysty themselves recognize their sect to be older than their God Zebaoth, or Sabaoth, Danila, whose memory and relics are sacred to all its branches. He probably found the idea of divine incarnation current, put himself forward as a signal example of it and found devoted followers to accept his claims to godship. The descent of the Spirit on him took place at a fixed date and in a particular spot. He was a peasant of the Government of Kostroma, and lived during the reign of Alexis Michailovich (1645–1676). He had deserted from the Army, and is said to have been a Bezpopovets and a follower of Kapiton, after whom one of the Priestless groups was called. He could write and read, possessed Old-believer books and was recognized as a teacher. As he stood on the hill of Gorodina in the Volost of Starodub in the Government of Vladimir, the God Zebaoth descended on clouds of fire in a fiery car, with his cortège of angels, seraphim and cherubim, and took possession of his all-holy and pure person. Thus Danila became the living God. None of his successors have risen above the level of Christs, Prophets or Mothers of God. This second advent — the first was in Jordan — took place in 1645, a date which conflicts with the tradition that he was an Old-believer; perhaps the last year of Alexis's reign should have been assigned rather than the first.

Danila began his preaching in the Staraya village, 30 versts from Kostroma, and called his home the house of God, his followers the people of God. Presently he removed to Kostroma, the New Jerusalem of the sect, and to emphasize the fact that the *Dove Book* had superseded all Church books, he threw all he could find of the latter into the Volga. This, it is said, caused the Patriarch Nikon to imprison him in a dark cell in the Bogoyavlenski cloister. Escaping thence back to Kostroma, he delivered to his followers, like Jehovah on Sinai, his Twelve Commandments, as follows:—

1. I am God, foretold of the prophets, and am come down to earth a second time to save men's souls. There is no other God than I.

2. There is no other teaching but mine. Seek ye none other.

3. Whereunto ye are appointed, abide therein.

4. Keep God's commandments, be ye fishermen of the world.

5. Drink no intoxicant, commit no sins of the flesh.

6. Marry not. He that is married shall live with his wife as with his sister, as is declared in the old scripture. Let the unwedded wed not, the wedded separate.

7. Utter not foul words nor black speeches (i. e. invocations of the Devil).

8. Go not to weddings or baptisms, nor frequent drinking resorts.

9. Steal not. If a man steal but a single kopeck, it shall in the dread judgment be laid on his skull, and when the coin melts in fire on his head, and not before, shall he gain remission of his sin.

10. Keep these rules in secret, reveal them not even to father or mother, and even if men scourge thee with whip or burn thee with fire, bear it. So doing the true shall after the pattern of the old martyrs win heaven, and on earth spiritual satisfaction.

11. Visit one another, practise hospitality (*lit.* bread and salt), practise charity, keeping commandments, pray to God.

12. Have faith in the Holy Spirit.

Fifteen years after his Epiphany at Gorodina, Danila begot a spiritual son after the manner of St. Paul. This was Ivan Timofeyevich Suslov, the son of Timofe and Irina, respectable people of the neighbourhood. The legend is that Irina was a hundred when he was born, and that he was her firstborn. He was Jesus, incarnate over again, and in his thirty-first year received Godship at the hands of Danila, after being for three days translated with him to heaven. This incident took place at Staraya; returning to Michailizy on the River Oka, Suslov chose twelve apostles and a Mother of God. His brothers became his disciples, and began to spread the cult of Danila along the banks of the Oka and the Volga. When his fame as a thaumaturge spread abroad, the Tsar Alexis seized him and handed him too over to Nikon who sent him to the boyar Morisov; the latter recognizing that he was a divine being, excused himself from trying him on the ground of illness. The Tsar then set the boyar Odoyevski on to him, who racked him with irons and fire, but failed to extract from him any statement of his faith. In the end Suslov was crucified on a Friday, and rose from the dead the following Sunday. Then the Tsar seized him afresh and flaying him, crucified him afresh. A virgin had kept his skin which he donned afresh only to be crucified a third time. Apparently these crucifixions occupied a considerable space of time, and it was only Natalia Kirillovna, the wife of the Tsarevich Peter (the Great) who finally put an end to them. That is why the sect honours her pictures as those of a saint. In some of the hymns Suslov's rescue is set down to successful bribery by Danila or his followers.

Thus freed, Suslov continued to teach in Moscow for thirty years, living in a good house behind the Sukharev tower. Danila at Kostroma heard of his success and, though aged one hundred years, went to visit him. On January 1, 1700, at the conclusion of a long service of dancing, on the day of St. Basil, Danila in the presence of all the occupants of the New Jerusalem, as Suslov's house was called, went bodily up to heaven. But according to a rival legend his body was buried in the village Kriushino in the Government of Kostroma. Fresh persecutions, however, were in store for Suslov. He fled from Moscow, but returned, and after three years ascended into heaven, though he also left his body behind on earth. Peter the Great, according to the Khlysty, changed the beginning of the civil year to January 1, because Danila died on it! The limits of this work forbid me to follow Grass into his examination of the above legend, which I have given in outline, and as it is embodied in many hymns. After all its main interest lies in the glimpses it furnishes of the mentality of the sect. It is clearly designed to suggest a parallelism between Jesus Christ and the founders of the sect.

There can in the nature of things be no reliable statistics on the strength of the Khlysty and of the Skoptsy, their congeners. Pobedonostsev, with his customary effrontery estimated them together in his religious census of 1903 at 3,887 souls, although in the statistical tables of the Ministry of the Interior they were already as early as 1863 reckoned at 110,000. The two sects together may safely be to-day reckoned at 300,000. They are specially numerous in the Caucasus, where they are called Shaloputy.

Their increase, admitted by all authorities, depends on their preaching and teaching only, and in the Baltic provinces they convert not a few Lutherans. Their sobriety and mutual charity render the Khlysty sect attractive. They are careful of education, and in the Caucasus the converted send their 'little sins' to the orthodox schools. Their economic life resembles that of the peasants in general, and they adhere to the ancient four field system with common tillage. No one starves among them, they help one another in misfortune, and having rich merchants among their converts, they never want funds. A single rich convert has been known to rebuild an entire village which had been burned down, merely because there were a few Khlysty in it. Their charity is extended to the orthodox, partly to disarm the suspicions of the Holy Synod; but their industry, intelligence, purity of life, self-respect are acknowledged by the most hostile observers. They will not practise usury among themselves nor do they ever carry an internal dispute before any of the tribunals of the State. Their leaders settle it for them. They are clean in person and in dress, and the inns or rest-houses which they keep, especially in the Caucasus, are models of tidiness and sobriety.

The lines of the diffusion of Khlystism are difficult to determine. The legend of Danila establishes that in the last half of the XVIIth Century it already flourished both in Vladimir and Kostroma as well as in Moscow. The earliest inquisition began by discovering in Moscow in January, 1733, as many as 78 adherents; in July, 222 more. In all over 300 were condemned, 5 of them to death, the rest were knouted or had their tongues cut out, were sent to hard labour in Orenburg and Siberia, shut up in monasteries, etc. As many as 80 of them were monks or nuns, 50 merchants or craftsmen, 100 peasants. One of the ladies condemned belonged to the nobility.

In 1745–1752 followed a fresh inquisition also in Moscow, presided over by the notorious Grinkov. Victims were racked every day, searing with hot irons being the most approved method of torture. Five were burnt alive in public, 26 condemned to death, the rest to the knout, deprivation of their noses, exile, etc. In all 454 were punished, among them 70 monks and nuns and a few of the clergy, 50 merchants and craftsmen, over 300 peasants; of the victims only 164 were residents in Moscow, the rest mostly from the upper Volga. These data prove that about 1700 the sect was mostly confined to Moscow, where many converts harboured it. After the second persecution the members fled in numbers from Moscow and carried their tenets rapidly to all points of the compass. In 1746 we hear of it in Petersburg, and in Alatur to the East. By the year 1775, the history of the Skoptsy reveals it in some strength in the city of Tula.

CHAPTER II

THE SKOPTSY

It remains to describe the Skoptsy whose fame has spread outside Russia and is out of all proportion to their numerical importance; this being what one would expect of a sect whose history interests the criminologist at least as much as it does the analyst of religion. About 1770 there were some thousand Khlysty in Tula, divided into several 'ships' or congregations, all of them recognizing an aged woman Akulina Ivanovna as their Mother of God. Under her were ranged prophets and prophetesses, one Anna Romanovna being the chief of the latter Her prophecies, as usual, concerned fisheries and fields, and her fame in prediction extended even outside the sect. She had the merit, however, of discovering the religious value of one Selivanov. They seem to have lacked a Christ in Tula at the time, and we only hear of a chief prophet Philimon, who in spite of his own spiritual ambitions was constrained by the spirit to acclaim Selivanov, his rival, as his superior, just as St. John acclaimed Jesus. The congregations danced on ground measured off for them by the prophets, who prophesied in the name of God or of the Holy Ghost. Thus Anna Romanovna, like Priscilla, exclaimed in the spirit of the faithful, "Why have ye not found me, God, and seen where I dwell?"

These details come from Selivanov's autobiography, committed long afterwards to writing, and from it we also learn that marriage was rigorously forbidden in the Tula 'ships'; Selivanov alludes to the good old times, i. e., of Danila and Suslov, which were revived when he became the Christ.

Selivanov found matter for criticism in the behaviour of his co-sectaries. They were too lax in their morals; and this is his own account of why they quarrelled with him, delated him to the Government and slew his spiritual offspring Martin.

The name under which this obscene fanatic is venerated by the Skoptsy is Kondrati Selivanov. His real name was Andrei

Ivanov, and on one occasion he called himself Simeon, in order to evade pursuit. He also passed himself off as a Kiev monk. We have a contemporary picture of him in a writ for his arrest issued in August, 1775, when Catharine II was residing in Moscow. He is described as of middling height, of pale complexion, sharply cut nose, reddish-yellow hair, almost beardless, about fifty-three years of age, shorn in the peasant style and in the same style dressed, and withal a Skopets (emasculated). Some time before the year 1772 Kondrati, faithful to the text Mat. 19, xii, and convinced that baptism by spirit and by fire connoted no less, emasculated himself with a hot iron. He claimed in his later life to have done the deed when he was fourteen, i. e., about the year 1736; but his own followers believed he was a man of forty at the time. He was a peasant of Stolbov in the Oryol Government and a serf of Prince Kantemir. By his own testimony he was a Khlyst beforehand, having been converted to that sect by a woman, Akulina Ivanovna, who, after her convert became a "Christ," if not before, became herself, by the fact of having converted him, a Mother of God or *Theotokos*. His first converts were certainly members of the sect, and that he began his new gospel inside its pale is shewn by the fact that he himself initiated as a Khlyst one of his earliest adherents, Alexander Ivanovich Shilov. His original programme was merely to supplement the encratite rule of the Khlysty and raise a barrier against its infraction. From an ukase of Catharine II dated July 2, 1772, our earliest document respecting the new sect, we know that it had by that time gained many adherents. Catharine describes it as a new sort of heresy that had appeared among the peasants in Oryol, and instructs Prince Volkov that it is best to nip in the bud such rash follies and save innocent people from such chicanery. The author or authors of it are to be seized, knouted and sent to Nerchinsk in Siberia; the preachers are to be beaten with rods and sent to work on the fortifications of Riga; the mere dupes to be sent home to their masters, if they are private serfs, to the crown estates, if royal serfs.

At that date Kondrati had already mutilated or caused to be mutilated as many as thirteen peasants in Bogdanovka, and was conducting his propaganda in the provinces of Orlov and Tula. Presently he was arrested, tried with his chief associates at Sosnovsk in Tambov and exiled to Siberia, where he began to pass himself off as Peter III, who had been murdered by his own wife, Catharine II, on July 19, 1762. His assassination was shrouded in some mystery, as such deeds usually are; the episode of the False Dimitri's proves how easy it is in Russia for a pretender to a royal name to get himself accepted by the crowd. Nor was Kondrati the only claimant to the honour of being the murdered man. In 1773 a Don Cossack, Pugachev, was able to raise a peasant revolt by assuming his style and title. Five years before a Serbian adventurer, Stephen the Little, had posed as Peter III and in that guise grasped for himself the principality of Montenegro.

Such a pretension may naturally have been accepted in Siberia, but it is odd that they were accepted twenty years later in the best circles of Petersburg society, when the Emperor Paul (1796–1801) had brought him back to the capital. There he was at first interned in a home for lunatics, but later on the mild and enlightened despot Alexander I (1801–1825) released him, and at the request of rich Skoptsys and in particular of his chamberlain, Elianski, allowed him to live in a hostel and acquire the rank of a free citizen. As such he took the name Selivanov. He was now more at liberty than before to conduct his propaganda of baptism by fire and spirit, and with his own hand mutilated as many as 100 adults. His adherents now collected his reminiscences and miracles in a work known as *The Passion* which circulates widely among them and has been translated by Grass in its entirety. It is worth study, being full of autobiographic touches.

This lurid impostor now literally took Russia by storm. People, not by any means of the humblest rank, crowded from all over the country to visit and venerate him, and returned to their homes bearing relics of him in their bosoms; his nail parings, hairs, bath water, clothing, all was carried off and found to be endowed with magical powers: Every Skopets carried as an amulet a silver rouble of Peter III, burned tapers before the picture of the murdered Prince, prostrated himself and said his prayers. The same worship is still accorded all over Russia to his relics, and in the ecclesiastical archives are stored not a few of his portraits, seized at various dates by the police. Grass reproduces one of the most characteristic of them, made when he was already an old man. It is a convincing likeness, forcible but gruesome. The small mouth, the determined lips, the piercing eyes, are those of a fanatic who must have exercised a mesmeric power on all who approached him. His eyes and expression remind one of those of George Whitefield in the portrait hung in Mansfield College at Oxford. Whitefield in his letters was wont to describe himself as "this tottering tabernacle." His portrait barely gives us such an impression of him.

The crowds that flocked to see Selivanov and the number of his victims at last excited the suspicions of the Russian Government, and in 1810 he was forced to sign an undertaking to drop his peculiar propaganda. He continued it however, and his lodging was known as the House of Davidov (House of the Son of David), that of his prophetess Anna Safonovna as the monastery of the Virgin Mother of God. Officials of the Army, civil service, even the clergy succumbed to his dupery. In 1818 the Government again interfered and banished two of his intimates to the monastery of Solovets; but this only confirmed his own and their presumption. Finally the authorities in the hope of circumscribing the movement sent him in 1820 to the Spaso-Efimovski cloister in Suzdal, which at once became a holy place and resort of Skoptsy pilgrims. Pains were now taken to repress them and the leader died in 1830.

But the faithful discredit his death, and believe he will reappear alive in the neighbourhood of Irkutsk, to inaugurate the Millennium, as soon as the tale is complete of the 144,000 of the elect of the Apocalypse (14, iv) which "were not defiled with women, for they are virgins. These are they which follow the Lamb whithersoever he goeth...they are without blemish." Such texts the Skoptsy, as many other fanatics have done before and after them, interpret of their own nave or ship, as, following the Khlysty, they denominate their sect. He is believed, as many Skoptsy documents seized in the Inquisition of 1843 and on later occasions, reveal, to be still alive, to be indeed the living God. When at his second advent he reaches Moscow, he will sound the big bell of the Uspenski Cathedral. Regiment on regiment will then join him, to prevent the wolves from any more tearing of the sheep. Ships will arrive for his children freighted with gold and jewels.

The apocalyptic number of the elect is, according to Grass and other competent observers, not far short of completion. For the sect is reputed to number at least 100,000 and is extraordinarily active. How many of these are 'perfect' members and 'without blemish' is not known, but being great traders and usurers, they can be detected even by the eye of a foreigner in every bazaar in Russia, where, as Leroy-Beaulieu observes, everyone can see them, except as a rule the police whom they bribe to ignore their presence. Being knit together in mutual charity, being ascetics, thrifty and unencumbered with families, they have been able, like certain monastic orders, to accumulate great wealth; and the mere fact that they cannot waste money on mistresses recommends them in so corrupt a society as that of Russia. Financial magnates, who have important credit transactions to conduct, can trust them, just as a rich Turk trusts his harem with their Mahommedan analogues. Nevertheless they are often driven out of Russia by the police into neighbouring countries, especially Roumania, where many of the droshki drivers of Bucharest can be recognized as members of their sect, and where the Government seldom molests them, because for a Latin race their tenets have no attraction.

The Skoptsy rites are in general identical with those of the Khlysty; they meet and adore one another and sing their hymns, and dance until they fall into ecstasy and begin to prophesy. But the *Radenie* or ritual dance has not among them quite the same sacramental value as among the Khlysty. The rite of emasculation, baptism with *fire* and spirit, is their supreme sacrament. Their Christology is adoptionist like that of the Khlysty. Jesus was an ordinary man who was replenished with grace; and after his resurrection, his grace descended into Peter III who is head and defender of the faith. But Jesus was the first of the *White Doves*, as they call them-

selves, for he too emasculated himself. This rite is the sole
mode of redemption and means of grace. There is ground for
thinking (Grass, p. 655) that, like the Cathars, they do not
believe in the Crucifixion as an historical event, and wholly
reject the tenet that Jesus rose and ascended in the flesh into
heaven and sat down on the right hand of God. On the contrary, his body rotted in the tomb. In all this they agree with
the Khlysty, from whom they inherited their earliest hymns and
whose sacred poetry has supplied them with their models.

Wherever they spread, they formed *naves* or *Korablya*, presided over by Christs and prophets, male and female. Their
rigorous asceticism and simulation of orthodox piety often
leads the Russian clergy into the error of regarding them as
good Christians, and enables the officials and police whom they
perpetually bribe, to pretend, when the truth transpires, that
they thought they were orthodox. They never touch meat
and, like the Cathar elect ones, the men never go near or touch
women, if they can help it, even those of the sect. Meat they
religiously eschew, urging, as the Cathars did, that it is the
fruit of copulation. But they ignore the orthodox rules of
fasting and eat eggs, milk and cheese in Lent. Nevertheless,
as Leroy-Beaulieu remarks, their disgust for generation is no
more due to pessimism than was the same scruple in Origen
and in some early Christian circles that practised emasculation. That they are so singularly addicted to money-making
does not savour of an oriental pessimism.

There are other details of their origin or rather superstition
which are necessary to complete my account of them, but which
I would rather reproduce in the polished idiom of the accomplished French writer I have just named, than translate into
our own coarser tongue.

"Ce n'est point d'ordinaire sur les jeunes enfants que les
Skoptsy pratiquent leur rite fondamental; c'est le plus souvent
sur les hommes faits, alors que le sacrifice est le plus dur et
l'opération la plus dangereuse. Cette sanglante initiation a
parfois plusieurs degrès: la mutilation est complète ou incom-
plète; suivant l'un ou l'autre cas, elle porte, chez les sectaires,
le nom de *sceau royal* ou de seconde pureté. Les femmes